*f*P

Also by Jesse H. Wright

Cognitive Therapy with Inpatients

Also by Monica Ramirez Basco

Never Good Enough

*Cognitive-Behavioral Therapy
for Bipolar Disorder*

Getting
Your Life Back

THE COMPLETE GUIDE
TO RECOVERY FROM DEPRESSION

Jesse H. Wright, M.D.

Monica Ramirez Basco, Ph.D.

THE FREE PRESS

NEW YORK   LONDON   TORONTO   SYDNEY   SINGAPORE

THE FREE PRESS
A Division of Simon & Schuster, Inc.
1230 Avenue of the Americas
New York, NY 10020

10   9   8   7   6   5   4   3   2   1

Library of Congress Cataloging-in-Publication Data

Wright, Jesse H.
   Getting your life back : the complete guide to
recovery from depression / Jesse H. Wright,
Monica Ramirez Basco.
      p. cm.
Includes bibliographical references and index.
   1. Depression, Mental—Popular works.
2. Self-help techniques.   I. Basco, Monica Ramirez.
II. Title.
RC537.W744 2001
616.85'27—dc21
00-054361
ISBN 0-7432-0049-7

24866229 8/01

Contents

Authors' Note

Throughout this book we describe examples of people we have treated for depression. To protect the confidentiality of our patients, we have created composites of people we have known. Names, gender, backgrounds, and details of treatment have been altered so that none of our patients can be identified. No clinical example in this book corresponds to an actual person, living or dead.

Although we offer guidance for ways that you can help yourself to fight depression, this book should not be used as a substitute for treatment with a doctor or professional therapist. The depression screening test included in Chapter 2 is not intended as a method of diagnosing depression or assessing suicide risk. Readers who suffer from significant depression should consult a doctor or other mental health expert for diagnosis and treatment. Persons who have suicidal thoughts or intentions should seek help immediately.

Preface

When we were thinking of a title for this book, we asked our patients who had recovered from depression how they would describe what it feels like to defeat this problem. An answer we heard from many people was "It was like getting my life back." Before getting treatment, depression had robbed these people of the things that made life enjoyable and meaningful. All they could see ahead was darkness and misery. But, now they were back in gear. Life was good again. The future was full of possibilities.

Our goal in writing *Getting Your Life Back* was to bring together the most powerful ideas from modern, scientifically tested treatments in a complete and easy-to-use guide to recovery from depression. Because books on depression have often been slanted toward one approach or another, we thought it was time to offer an integrated program that would help people unite the best elements of biological, psychological, and spiritual treatment methods.

We organized this information into Five Keys to recovery. The Thinking Key teaches you ways of building healthy self-esteem, and gives you methods for controlling negative thinking, such as hopelessness and excessive worry. The Action Key helps you get moving again, solve problems, and stop self-defeating behaviors. The Biology Key guides you on using biological treatments such as antidepressant medications, and has suggestions for things you can do to improve your body chemistry. The Relationship Key helps you resolve conflicts with the important people in your world and get along better with others. The Spirituality Key helps you find direction in life, tap into the spiritual strength within you, and develop a sense of purpose. Each Key contains methods and techniques for overcoming the most common problems people face when they are depressed.

We've found in our clinical practices that there is no single best way to treat everyone who has depression. Each person is different. Each has his or her own unique blend of problems and resources to fight depression. One person may have low self-esteem. The next may be in the midst of a spiritual or existential crisis. Another person may have a troubled relationship that is keeping him or her depressed. And, each of them has a myriad of strengths to face his or her own personal challenges. This *Complete Guide to Recovery from Depression* was designed to provide you with the tools you need to develop a customized, personal plan for recovery that addresses your unique symptoms, problems, and strengths.

In the last part of the book, we'll help you fine-tune your recovery plan to improve your chances of success. Sometimes people can get stuck along the way to recovery by either hitting a plateau or getting distracted by other life problems. Because our hope is that you will put depression completely behind you, we've included a troubleshooting guide for breaking out of plateaus or coping with difficulties in making a recovery plan work. And, we offer suggestions for cutting the risk for return of depression after you are well.

Our hope is that this book contains methods that will help you fight off your symptoms of depression. If you feel like your troubles are too much to handle on your own, or if your symptoms won't easily go away, we recommend that you seek treatment from a mental health professional. If you are already in treatment, this book could help speed up your progress. In our own practices, we find that it is very helpful for people to bring written notes to sessions with their questions, topics to discuss, or self-help exercises from books that they are reading. We suggest you share your work in this book with your therapist.

Because we come to the writing of this book from the perspective of two different professions, Jesse is a psychiatrist and Monica is a clinical psychologist, we are able to offer you the best of both worlds as we integrate biological and psychological interventions. Although trained differently, we are both cognitive-behavior therapists who recognize the value of a combined approach to treatment. Our careers have been very gratifying because we have had the opportunity to help many patients recover. It's wonderful to see them feel good about themselves again, get back to their normal routines at work and home, and have enthusiasm for the path ahead. We are optimistic that if you follow the exercises we offer in this book, you too will find that the Five Keys can open the door to healing.

JESSE H. WRIGHT, M.D.
MONICA RAMIREZ BASCO, PH.D.

Acknowledgments

We want to thank Philip Rappaport, our Editor at The Free Press, for his helpful suggestions and guidance in the creation of this book. Many other people gave us ideas, inspiration, and support. We owe a particular debt of gratitude to our families for their patience as we spent time working on the book. Special thanks are due to Susanne Wright, who carefully reviewed each chapter and gave many excellent suggestions, and to Andrew Wright, M.D., who designed the data management system for our research on the Five Keys Depression Rating Scale.

Our colleagues and friends gave us a great deal of help. Michael Thase, M.D., and Randy Schrodt, M.D., psychiatrists, and Kris Small, a pastoral counselor, served as expert reviewers and provided many useful references for chapters from the Biology and Spirituality Keys. Jim Rives, one of Jesse's good friends, encouraged this project from the beginning and graciously provided a personal example of ways to face adversity.

We also want to thank the therapists and staff from the Norton Psychiatric Center and the University of Louisville who assisted with research on the Five Keys Depression Rating Scale. Jeff Hudgins, able research assistant at the Norton Psychiatric Center, helped manage this study. The statistical analysis for the research was performed by Dr. Jane Goldsmith. Colleen Newton was always there to solve problems in formatting the manuscript. Barbara Fingar, a pharmacist, supplied information on medication for depression. And, the creative energies of Steve Oldson from Presentation Graphics and Kyle Thatch and Ray Rieck from Digital Magic Studios were much appreciated in producing figures and diagrams.

Through our years of learning about cognitive-behavior therapy, biological psychiatry, spiritual approaches to healing, and the other treatment methods described in *Getting Your Life Back,* we have had many teachers, mentors, and associates who have shaped our thinking. Although these people are too numerous to mention here, we want to tell them that we will always remember their kindness and wisdom.

1

Getting Started

When you've been feeling down for a while, it's easy to get discouraged. You can begin to doubt that life will ever get easier, that the pain will cease, that the frustration will ever stop. You might think that if you can only figure out how you got this way, you could shake loose from it. So you blame it on your job, your spouse, your weight, your mother, or yourself; but those conclusions don't make you feel any better. In this book you will find answers to your questions about what makes you depressed and keeps you down, as well as specific instructions for how to find your way out of it. The fact that you are seeking a way to greater well-being is a sign that somewhere deep inside a bit of optimism remains. Hold on to that hope and use the Five Keys we present in this book to help unlock the door to your depression.

During our years of clinical practice, we have seen many people recover from depression. Each, with a unique story to tell, has taught us something new about how to overcome adversity. We have found time and time again, that even when all they were able to see were their weaknesses and flaws, our patients were able to learn how to call upon their unique strengths to fight off the symptoms and get their lives back. In some cases, they became even stronger after getting well than they were before their problems began. You'll meet some of these people in this first chapter and find out how they got started to overcome depression.

Michelle had thought her life was going well. She had two wonderful kids, a husband she thought loved her, a good job, close friends, and a home she took pride in. When her husband announced one day that he had fallen in love with someone else, Michelle felt her entire world come crashing down around her. Everything she believed in had failed her. She had failed herself. And now, as she watched herself become more and more withdrawn, losing her connection to all the things that mattered, she knew that she was beginning to fail her children.

> *I don't know what happened. It seemed that everything was going fine and then he dropped that bomb on me. At first, I thought I could handle it, but as the weeks have gone by, I've seen my life slipping away from me—my kids, my friends, my self-confidence, and my hope. I feel so ashamed.*

This is how Michelle described herself when she began treatment after several months of worsening depression. She had stopped sleeping well at night, had dropped some weight, was having trouble concentrating at work, and seemed to have lost her zest for life. Michelle was nothing like the woman she had been before her husband left. She had stopped singing in the church choir, quit exercising with her friends, couldn't concentrate well enough to read a book, and gave up altogether on the weeds that threatened to overtake her beautiful garden.

> *These kinds of things aren't supposed to happen to me. I'm not the kind of person who gets depressed. I'm supposed to be the strong one. It's so humiliating. Look at me. I look horrible. I know it's ridiculous to let a man bring me down like this. But I can't help it. It takes everything I've got just to make it through the day. I don't think I'll ever get over this.*

Michelle's hopelessness was a symptom of her depression. When her friends and family members looked at her they saw the strong woman who put her husband through school, raised two healthy and happy children, had a deep sense of spirituality, and brought joy into the lives of many people. But, Michelle saw herself as pathetic, weak, and unable to cope. Her friends knew that the real Michelle had only been knocked off her feet—she had not been defeated. When we see this type of situation in our clinical practices we try to help people look through the curtain of hurt and pain to find their real selves, and then to build on their strengths to defeat depression. The self-help exercises we offer in this book are based on cognitive-behavior therapy (CBT), a well-known, and scientifically proven, method of treatment. We'll show you how to use CBT methods when you learn the details of the *Five Keys to Recovery*. The goal of CBT is to help people gain a more realistic view of themselves and their world, and to take action to solve their problems. This is one of the ways we helped Michelle.

Medical breakthroughs, particularly over the past ten years, have led to newer and safer pharmacological treatments for the symptoms of depression. These medications can be extremely effective when used as prescribed. Since Michelle had both the physical and psychological symptoms of depression, she opted for a combined treatment approach using both antidepressant medications and psychotherapy. Throughout this book we will show you how to integrate effective psychological and biological interventions, along with those that help you develop healthier relationships and strengthen your spirituality, so that you can leave your distress behind.

Depression doesn't always cause as much pain and misery as Michelle experienced nor does it always require professional treatment. But, everyone who becomes depressed notices definite changes in his or her attitude, mood, and ability to function. Even if you have a mild depression, you'll not be your usual self. It will be harder to get things accomplished and to enjoy life. Your sleeping and eating habits may not be as regular as normal. You may be tense, irritable, or restless and you may tend to think very negatively about yourself and have pessimistic thoughts about the future.

When you are feeling down, your mind can be so preoccupied with worries that it's hard to remember the good times or to think of new ways to fix your problems. You might even miss out on opportunities to change your life for the better. In this book, we want to open your mind to new possibilities that will help you not only to feel better, but to grow in positive ways.

Jeff did this by overcoming a mild depression and making some positive life changes. "I just didn't feel right. I used to get a big kick out of teaching, but something changed and it became a real effort to act like I wanted to be there. I was still doing a decent job. But, I wasn't having any fun, and I started worrying about getting fired. My home life wasn't any better. It seemed like I was just going through the motions. My wife said that I was edgy and irritable with her and the kids. I'm sure she was right. I had to do something about it before it got worse and I turned out like my mother."

Jeff remembered his mother's struggle with depression and knew that these things often ran in families. He had always been a do-it-yourselfer, so he decided to read some self-help books and try to work his way out of his slump. As he read, it began to make sense to him that his problems had probably been there, to some extent, for several years. Although he'd been told that he was a good teacher, he'd always had his doubts. He realized that this recent downturn began after a job evaluation that didn't meet up to his usual standards. After reading about low self-esteem, Jeff concluded that he had probably always been his own worst enemy. He had been a good teacher for the last twenty years, but he kept telling himself that he wasn't as good as others, particularly the younger teachers coming out of school still perky and enthusiastic. Despite the self-criticism, he had always done well with his students, and had even received an award for being one of the top teachers in his school district. He decided that it was time to stop torturing himself. There was more to life than trying to be the perfect teacher.

Now I think I know what really counts for me and my family. I've tried to start enjoying all the good things I have in my life instead of always comparing myself with everyone else. I've noticed a big difference. I'm really enjoying going to work and being with my family again.

Your Plan for Overcoming Depression

Although depression can sometimes make you feel overwhelmed or helpless, there are many things you can do to cope with your problems. This book is full of exercises that can help you gain control over your emotions and your life. These are the same types of self-help exercises we give our patients in our clinical practices and the same exercises that have been used in research studies on depression. We also usually recommend professional help when there are symptoms of depression that are causing significant distress or don't go away. We'll talk later in the book about how to find a doctor or therapist to help you put your recovery plan into action.

As you work through the exercises in this book, we'll help you build a Personal Plan for Recovery. You'll be able to design a plan to address your own particular needs, take advantage of your strengths and opportunities for change, and help you resolve your problems. The core of your plan will be to learn to use the Five Keys to Recovery. We'll show you how to make best use of each Key and how to choose the Keys to use first.

Our patients usually find it helpful to have a notebook on hand to work through the exercises and to jot down ideas as they go along. We suggest you read this book with a notebook or diary nearby. Your notes will help you keep track of your progress and will serve as a written account of the path you've taken to a better life.

The Five Keys to Recovery from Depression

Although each person's personal story is unique, there are some common themes that thread their way through the lives of most people who become depressed. The Five Keys are directed at these common clusters of problems. We'll introduce you to the Five Keys in this chapter and give an example of how Michelle used each of them to fight depression. As you read along, you may find some similarities in your own life. At the end of the chapter we will ask you to begin to think about how each of the Keys might help you overcome your depression.

THE THINKING KEY

When you are feeling low, it is easy to slip into a negative style of thinking. Angry, upsetting, fearful or self-critical thoughts are some examples. They typically fuel your unhappiness and lead to actions that can make matters worse. If you find that you tend to get down on yourself, have excessive worry, or think pessimistically about the future, you can use the Thinking Key to learn methods to control your negative thoughts and solve problems more effectively. Research on the treatment of depression has shown that when your thought patterns become less negative and more accurate or rational, your mood brightens and your symptoms get better. If you can learn how to spot depressive thinking and change it in a healthy direction, you can take some very important steps toward getting your problems under control.

Did you notice that Michelle's thinking had a hopeless tone? The more she saw things this way, the worse she felt. To get back to a more balanced view of her self-worth and her prospects for the future, Michelle learned to spot her distorted thinking patterns and to correct her negativity when it was inaccurate. She also learned to take stock of the strengths and abilities she had forgotten that she possessed. As she mastered the methods offered in the Thinking Key, her natural optimism returned and she felt more hopeful about her future. You will learn to use these same techniques in Chapters 3 and 4.

THE ACTION KEY

When you feel depressed, you can't help but act differently at home, at work, or in your relationships with others. You can lose interest and be less involved in your usual activities, develop negative habits, procrastinate, or show too much irritability. Jobs that might have been routine or effortless can become so difficult or unpleasant that you have to push yourself to get them done. You might even avoid some of your responsibilities altogether. If your actions have changed in any of these ways, you can use the techniques from the Action Key to learn to take pleasure in life again, cope more effectively with problems, and become more energetic. When you begin to act in positive ways, you will feel better about yourself, and your depression could start to fade away.

Michelle had several good opportunities to use the Action Key. For example, when she avoided her friends and dropped out of social activities she felt more lonely and isolated. As a result, her mood worsened, and she became even more depressed. This was unlike the old Michelle who had always enjoyed being with people. She used the Action Key to figure out how to begin acting more like her old self. Michelle's recovery plan included use of several of the self-help methods described in Chapters 5 and 6, such as learning how to experience pleasure again, combating fatigue and lack of motivation, organizing her day to be happier and more productive, and getting back her sense of humor. She started with small goals for change. But as she began to improve, Michelle was able to tackle more challenging problems like being assertive in handling the legal side of her divorce.

THE BIOLOGY KEY

Scientific studies have provided convincing evidence that depression can be effectively relieved with biological treatments. In Chapters 7, 8, and 9 you'll find out how your brain chemistry is involved in producing depressive symptoms and how to promote recovery in two major ways: (1) modifying your life-style to stimulate healthy chemical processes in your body, and (2) using specific biological treatments such as antidepressants, herbal remedies, or light therapy. The Biology Key will help you decide whether or not to use medications or other biological interventions as part of your recovery plan. If you decide to take medication, you can learn how to limit the risk of side effects and get the most out of treatment.

The Biology Key was an important part of Michelle's recovery plan. She began taking an antidepressant medication early in her treatment. Both she and her doctor believed that the medication helped a great deal in relieving her symptoms. She also used techniques from the Biology Key to improve her sleeping and eating habits, and to get back into an exercise routine. As Michelle gradually got back into a healthy life style, she had more energy, and felt better about herself.

THE RELATIONSHIP KEY

Research studies have repeatedly proven what common sense tells us—relationship problems can be stressful and depressing. The Relationship Key focuses on teaching you how to identify problems in your relationships and take action toward making improvements. Even if your relationships are strong, you can use the methods in the Relationship Key to improve your communication, resolve conflict, eliminate resentments, and create more intimacy. Positive and caring relationships can be a tremendous help when you are trying to recover from depression. There are several things you can do to help create and nurture loving and supportive connections with others.

A crisis in her marriage was the main trigger for Michelle's depression. In Michelle's case it was too late to save her marriage. Instead, she needed to grieve the loss and find a way to strengthen the other important relationships in her life. Techniques from the Relationship Key (described in Chapters 10 and 11) helped her cope with her loss, focus on positive elements of her life independent of her marriage, and set positive goals for the future. One of her greatest assets was her close relationship with her children and friends. As Michelle succeeded at re-building these relationships, the feeling of emptiness that initially fed her depression disappeared.

THE SPIRITUALITY KEY

Lack of a sense of meaning in your life or feeling spiritually empty can be a breeding ground for despair. Drawing strength from having a purpose and being committed to your core values and beliefs can help you face depression and work on putting your life back together. The Spirituality Key will help you find meaning in your daily existence, and perhaps strengthen your faith, by teaching you ways to rediscover your lost spirituality, calm your mind, and open your heart. Elements of spirituality that cut across cultures and religious faiths and practices are discussed along with suggestions for defining your own sense of spirituality.

The Spirituality Key was a big help to Michelle in overcoming her depression. It helped her to regain hope for the future, brought her back to her faith community, and strengthened her sense of purpose. Michelle's divorce and subsequent depression, though seemingly life shattering, gave her an opportunity to redefine herself, reevaluate her beliefs, and rediscover the things outside her marriage that gave her life meaning. We hope that these same methods that are offered in Chapters 12 and 13 will help in fighting off your depression and in adding new dimensions to your life.

Are you getting some ideas about how the Five Keys to Recovery might apply to you? The following table summarizes the problems that can be addressed by each Key. Read through the list and think about which Keys you might want to learn how to use.

The Five Keys to Recovery from Depression

Keys to Recovery	Problems	Things You Can Do
The Thinking Key	Negativism, hopelessness guilt, low self-esteem	Learn to control negative thinking, develop effective problem-solving techniques, build self-esteem
The Action Key	Dropping out of usual activities, isolation from others, helplessness, procrastination	Organize and schedule your activities, set useful goals, break negative behavior patterns
The Biology Key	Symptoms of depression, poor sleep habits, change in appetite or weight, lack of exercise	Learn about biology of depression, improve sleep habits, start an exercise program, eat a healthy diet, take antidepressants
The Relationship Key	Difficulty communicating, strained or broken relationships, not able to get or use support	Build communication skills, learn how to resolve conflicts, strengthen support networks
The Spirituality Key	Lack of a sense of meaning, questions about values and commitment	Work on deepening your sense of meaning and purpose in life, take time to practice spiritual activities.

My Story—The Beginning

The exercises in this book are geared toward helping you develop a skill, sort out your feelings, set goals for recovery, and work toward making improvements. It can be easy to read through a book like this and think about how the various methods might be helpful to you. It is a different story altogether to put these ideas into action so that they begin to work. Therefore, we encourage you to not rush through reading the book, but to take time to complete those self-help exercises that might be applicable to the problems you are facing.

The first exercise will be to begin telling your own story. Take out your notebook and write out your answers to the following questions. Using Michelle's story as a guide, fill in as many details as you can.

Exercise 1.1
My Story—The Beginning

Open your notebook and title this exercise "My Story—The Beginning." The goal is to think about how your depression began, what has made it get worse or better, and how you might begin to change.
1. When did your depression begin?
2. What symptoms or problems bother you the most?
3. What seems to trigger your depression?
4. What usually seems to help?
5. How has your life changed since you have become depressed?
6. What have you started doing since you have been depressed?
7. What have you stopped doing since you have been depressed?
8. What ideas do you have now for changes that could be made to improve your situation?

Here's the next step. Go back over your story and circle all of the difficulties you are experiencing that could possibly be addressed with one of the Five Keys. You will find some clues in the table on page 8 called the "Five Keys to Recovery from Depression." On the next page of your notebook, summarize your observations by making a heading for each Key and listing the things you circled in your story. Try to match the problems with the Key. Title this exercise "My Problem List."

Michelle's Problem List

Biology Key

Tired, no energy
Not sleeping well

Action Key

Avoiding social activities
Spending too much time alone

Thinking Key

Self-criticism
Hopelessness about the future

Relationship Key

Grieving the loss of husband
Becoming distant from the kids

Spirituality Key

No purpose in life
Questioning basic beliefs

Problem Solving—Getting Started

How do you feel when you look at your problem list? Do you have a sense of accomplishment that you have made some progress in recognizing things that can be changed? Are you optimistic that something can be done to turn your situation around? Or do you feel a bit overwhelmed? It's a normal reaction to see a list of problems and to think that the road ahead will be difficult. But, one of the big pluses of accurately identifying problems is that you'll have a much better chance of finding solutions if you know exactly what is bothering you.

When we begin therapy with our patients, we usually ask them to pick one or two problems they can work on right away. Even before they have had a chance to learn everything they would like to know about the Five Keys, we want them to feel a sense of accomplishment. The program described in this book is similar to therapy in that it takes time to fully understand your problems, organize a plan for recovery, and implement the plan. However, there are some basic problem-solving techniques that you can use now to tackle some of your difficulties and begin to get some relief. Here's how to get started.

Review your problem list and rate each item for its degree of difficulty using the scale in the box below. A score of 1 suggests that it would be fairly easy to make some headway toward managing the problem. A score of 5 suggests that it would be extremely difficult for you to make any significant progress toward solving this problem at this time.

PROBLEM DIFFICULTY SCALE				
1	2	3	4	5
Easy to Accomplish		Moderately Difficult		Extremely Difficult

If all your items are rated a 4 or 5, you're probably only thinking about the big changes you have to make. Add to your list the smaller challenges, problems, and annoyances that need attention. Try to place them under the Key you think might be most helpful. Don't worry about matching the problem and the Key exactly. There will be plenty of guidance ahead on how to best approach your various problems. Of the problems you rated as 1, 2, or 3 in difficulty, choose one or two that you think you could make some progress on in the next few weeks. Circle these in your notebook. Next, make a list of ideas for managing the problems. These may be things you have thought about doing, but have not had the time or energy to try. Choose the solution that you think has the greatest chance of success and give it a try. You'll find that if you can make a small amount of progress, it can lighten the emotional burden you carry on your shoulders.

Michelle used this same problem solving exercise early in her therapy. When she was asked to rate her initial problem list for degree of difficulty, she gave them all a score of 4 except for "becoming distant from the kids," which she thought would be easier to change. She gave that problem a rating of 2. Because Michelle had some excellent ideas on positive changes that could be made and was ready to take some action to improve the situation with her children, we decided that this would be a good place to start.

Michelle's plan for beginning to do things differently with her children included the following: (1) Try to have an evening meal together with children at least four times a week, (2) After dinner, talk with kids about school or the other things that are going on in their lives, (3) Spend some time helping with homework or reading to children each weekday. In the past, Michelle had done many of these things routinely. So, when she spotted the problem and started to do something about it, she began to feel encouraged.

Try to follow Michelle's lead in using problem solving to get started toward recovery. If you can take at least one step in a positive direction now, it should boost your optimism and help prepare you to use the Five Keys to overcome depression.

A Plan for Recovery

This initial effort to solve a few problems is just the beginning of an overall plan for feeling better and getting your life back on track. In the next chapter you will start to build your Personal Plan for Recovery by measuring your symptoms, setting workable goals for improving your life, and figuring out what strengths you have to battle depression. As you read further you will learn about each of the Five Keys and will discover new ways to control your symptoms, solve your problems, and reach your goals.

Sometimes progress can be slow at first, but your efforts should pay off as you put in more time and effort. If you start to feel discouraged along the way, skip ahead to Chapter 6 and read about ways to increase your patience and persistence. Michelle was so upset when she began treatment that she had a hard time staying motivated. Her logical mind told her that she had the ability to make things better for herself, but her sad and anxious emotions kept undermining her confidence. To make herself hang in there even when she wanted to give up, Michelle learned to rely on two of her greatest strengths—her ability to dig in and work hard even when she dreaded the task, and the support of her friends. When she felt like throwing up her hands and giving in to her misery, Michelle called her two best friends to ask for help. They did their best to encourage Michelle by reminding her of her usual tenacious spirit and the successes she had in the past. If that didn't work, Michelle told herself, "I've just got to do it. I don't have the luxury of giving up on myself. My kids need me. I have to at least give it a try."

After she overcame depression, we asked Michelle to tell about how she got better. "If you keep working at it, you can find a way to conquer depression. For me, it was learning how to stop thinking so negatively and acting so lost and helpless—and using a medication that really helped. My family and friends were terrific. They stuck by me when I needed them. In the beginning I thought it would be impossible, but I did learn to solve my problems."

Michelle eventually realized that there could be many ways to lead a satisfying life without being married to her husband. Michelle's long-term goal was to get beyond the divorce to reach the point where her life had clear direction and purpose again. She was optimistic that better days would be ahead.

Hope for Getting Your Life Back

What do you think your chances are of getting better? Do you believe that there will be answers to your problems? Do you have a hopeful attitude about the future? Hopefulness can be one of the most significant influences on your progress toward recovery. People with a hopeful view about change are usually willing to try new things. But if you suffer from hopelessness, you may give up too easily or not give good ideas an opportunity to work.

Think for a moment about the effect of hope on your behavior. If you don't believe that any of your efforts are likely to make a difference, how hard will you try to change? On the other hand, would you act differently if you had faith in yourself to get beyond your difficulties, or even reach a higher plane in life? While a positive mental attitude is clearly helpful, it can be hard to come by when you are feeling down. There can be a "vicious cycle" in depression in which you lose your desire to take action. When you do less to get out of your rut, to spend time with those who love you, and to solve your problems, it is easy to become more discouraged about the future. Hopelessness feeds the depression, which slows you down even more.

The way out of depression is just the opposite. A "positive cycle" can develop when you find some reasons for hope, and either change your attitude or change your actions. After you take some positive steps, your mood lifts and your energy starts to return. You'll probably find that it's hard to make yourself feel more hopeful until you have a reason to feel that way. So you will have to take a few steps toward fixing your problems before your optimism returns.

For some people, this positive cycle keeps going even after the depression goes away because they have developed new skills, healthier habits, and better attitudes. These positive life changes help them to be stronger overall than they were before and to find greater meaning and purpose in their lives. Jeff, the teacher described earlier in this chapter, was able to lead a much more fulfilling life after he stopped comparing himself with others and began to pay full attention to family relationships and the other things that really counted for him.

We want to stop now to ask you these very important questions: What gives you hope? What keeps you going? Each of us has a unique response to these questions. But some of the common answers we have heard are: "My family, I would never want to leave them," "I know I can get better," "I really love life when I'm feeling well," "For me . . . I have lots of things I still want to do," "My faith keeps me going," and "I have a contribution to make in life."

Take some time now to write out answers to these two questions in your notebook. Try to think of as many reasons as you can. You can use the examples above to get you going with ideas. If you have trouble thinking of reasons for hope or what keeps you going, here are some things you can do:

Ways to Stimulate Hope for Recovery

1. Get started—do the problem-solving exercise outlined in this chapter.
2. Learn about the treatment of depression by reading this book or talking with a doctor or therapist—recognize that depression is a common illness that responds very well to therapy.
3. Ask someone you know well about your situation. If they are supportive and tell you that things will get better, try your best to believe them.
4. Remember that depression makes you focus on the negative and sometimes miss the positive. You can fight hopelessness by paying more attention to the positive things that happen in your life. These could be small things like seeing your children smile, finding a good parking space, or taking time to savor a special meal; or bigger things like completing a project, getting a raise, or making a new friend.

As you work through the exercises in the rest of the book, you should be able to identify more reasons to have hope for the future. For most people there are numerous possibilities for coping with difficulties and finding ways to get their lives back. After you write down your current reasons for hope, you can go on to find out more about how the Five Keys can be used to target your problems and find solutions.

2

Charting a Course for Recovery

I'm embarrassed to say this, Doc, but I feel like a loser. I have a job and everything, but my life isn't going anywhere. And I don't think it's ever going to change. My wife is doing great at work. She's climbing up the ladder, but she's got to be looking down at me saying, "Why did I marry this guy? He's going nowhere fast."

I see these guys at work who put in the hours just like I do and then have the time to go to business school. Or some of them even do volunteer work. I hate talking to them because I'm not doing anything with my life. Sometimes I just want to disappear so I don't have to face anyone anymore.

No disrespect intended, but I hate the fact that I have to come here and tell you all this. If the guys at work knew it, they'd probably lose what little respect they have for me. I haven't even told my wife yet. She knows something's wrong because she keeps asking if I'm all right. What's she going to think of me when she finds out I'm having so many problems? I'll be lucky if she doesn't walk out on me for good.

If I wasn't feeling so bad, I wouldn't have come. But I can't handle it anymore. Nothing I've tried seems to work.

Tony was a young man, not quite thirty years old. Even though he had faced tough challenges before, it was hard for him to come for therapy. Like many men, he believed that he should be "strong" at all times and be able to solve problems by himself. Being dependent on anyone else, especially a therapist, wasn't on his list of top things to do with his time. Yet, he was floundering and knew he was in trouble. Tony had been depressed once before when he was in college. He didn't take the college counselor up on her offer to start psychotherapy, but he did accept a prescription for Prozac from the doctor at the college infirmary. The Prozac seemed to help when Tony was twenty years old. However, the Prozac that his family doctor gave him this time hadn't budged his depression.

At the time Tony was referred by his primary care doctor for a psychiatric consultation and therapy, he had been on the Prozac for over two months. But, he had no organized plan for fighting his depression or making changes in his life. So early in therapy, we worked on putting a plan together that could rejuvenate his hope and give him a direction for change. Because Tony was skittish about being in therapy and had firm attitudes about the need for self-reliance, the plan emphasized the things he could begin to do to reverse the depression. Getting too dependent on a therapist, or always needing to be told what to do, doesn't breed the healthy self-esteem that helps you get well and stay well.

In this chapter, we will show you how to chart a course for recovery. First we'll describe the steps to building a Personal Plan for Recovery. The rest of the chapter will focus on helping you take the first three steps: (1) recognize the different types of depression and measure symptoms, (2) identify strengths, and (3) set goals. You will be able to see how Tony started to make real progress by following this system of planning the fight against depression. By the end of this chapter, you should have a good start for your own recovery plan.

How to Develop Your Personal Plan for Recovery

RECOGNIZE AND MEASURE SYMPTOMS

The first thing you need to do is to figure out if depression is the problem. There are many different levels and types of depression. Sometimes a sad or depressed mood is a normal response to grief, loss, or some other stressful situation. But severe or prolonged symptoms usually need to be treated. We'll show you how to measure your level of depressive symptoms now and at frequent intervals as you go along so you'll know if the recovery plan is working.

IDENTIFY STRENGTHS

One of the hardest things for people with depression to do is to fully recognize and use their strong points. The negative filter that clouds thinking in depression can make it seem like you are weak, inadequate, or powerless, when you actually have many positive features that you can use to help solve your problems. Your battle against depression can go much better if you take an accurate inventory of your resources and learn how to nurture your positive attributes.

SET GOALS

The next step is to set clear and realistic goals that will help you focus on what you will need to do to break out of depression. Generally, it's a good idea to have a range of goals—some that you can probably reach fairly quickly and that won't require an enormous effort, and others that will help you stretch to reach your potential. Because your goals will guide you on your way to recovery, you want to be sure that they are specific and measurable. That way you will know exactly what you are trying to achieve, and you will be able to accurately judge your progress. Hazy goals can undermine your efforts to get well. But, clear and specific goals can keep you on track toward recovery.

LEARN HOW TO USE THE FIVE KEYS TO RECOVERY

The most important step in building your recovery plan will be to learn the details of how to use each of the Five Keys. Beginning with the next chapter, you'll have the opportunity to develop your skills in using the Thinking, Action, Biology, Relationship, and Spirituality Keys to overcome depression. As you study the Five Keys, try to think about how each key fits with your strengths, your goals, and the opportunities you have to make changes in your life.

PUT YOUR PLAN INTO ACTION

Most of us have had the experience of making what seemed like a good plan for change, but for some reason we weren't able to complete the plan. New Year's resolutions or decisions to exercise regularly or stay on a diet are classic examples of plans that may go unfulfilled. Obviously if you expect meaningful change, you have to go beyond thinking about your plans or writing them down on paper. You need to get moving to follow the plan, and you must stay with the plan long enough to give it a real chance to work.

The program we describe in this book is designed to help you take action right away to fight depression and to sustain your efforts to follow your plan until your symptoms are resolved. These tips may increase your chances of success:

Putting Your Recovery Plan to Work

1. Try pieces of the recovery plan as they are developed, don't wait until you have the entire plan before you start to take action.
2. Recognize that difficulties in implementing plans are a normal part of the recovery process.
3. If you encounter roadblocks, try not to blame yourself or get discouraged—instead reassess the plan, make adjustments if necessary, and keep focused on reaching your goals.
4. Seek professional help if you need it.

USE METHODS FOR STAYING WELL

Part of the good news about depression is that there are many effective treatments that can relieve symptoms. The bad news is that depression has a tendency to return. Thus, your recovery plan should contain methods for decreasing the chances for relapse back into depression. The final part of this book will help you add a relapse prevention element to your recovery plan by recognizing ways you can use each of the Five Keys to stay well.

Key Point

The steps in building a Personal Plan for Recovery are:

- Recognize and measure depression
- Identify strengths
- Set goals
- Learn to use the Five Keys
- Put plan into action
- Focus on staying well

Recognizing and Measuring Depression

Now that we've outlined the steps to building your recovery plan, it's time to get started with the first step: recognize and measure symptoms. Do you think you are depressed? Are you trying to find out if a loved one or a friend is depressed? What type of depression do you have? Let's try to find the answers to these questions.

IS IT DEPRESSION?

If you suspect that you might have depression, you're not alone. Depression is one of the most common health problems in all age groups. A large research study by Ronald Kessler and his co-workers found that every year about 10 percent of adults in the United States have a major episode of depression. About 24 percent of women and 17 percent of men experience a significant episode of depression or manic depression at least once in their lives. Many more people have depressions with less extreme symptoms.

Depression often goes unrecognized by the person who is experiencing it, their family and friends, and even health care professionals. One of us (Jesse) performed a research study in family practice patients in which over 40 percent of the subjects had some symptoms of depression and 17 percent met criteria for diagnosis of major depression. Yet few of the patients were diagnosed as depressed by their family doctors.

Recent efforts to improve diagnostic skills of primary care doctors may be having a positive impact on recognition of depression. For example, researchers at the University of Colorado have shown that educating resident doctors with specific guidelines for diagnosing depression had positive effects on attitudes and knowledge. But, even if depression is recognized it often goes untreated. Darrel Regier and other scientific investigators have found that over 50 percent of persons with a major depression receive no treatment at all.

Researchers and experienced clinicians usually rely on a system endorsed by the American Psychiatric Association to make the diagnosis of the various types of depression. This system is published in a book by the American Psychiatric Association, the *Diagnostic and Statistical Manual of Mental Disorders—IV,* also called DSM-IV. Some of our patients like to refer to this manual to check out their symptoms, but most of them find the manual to be too technical for easy use. If you are interested in reading more about the diagnosis of depression, you can find the DSM-IV in most libraries and bookstores.

THE SPECTRUM OF DEPRESSION

Sometimes it can be a bit upsetting when people first hear the DSM-IV terms for clinical depression. Names like major depression, dysthymic disorder, or bipolar disorder may be unfamiliar and can sound rather serious. We'll try to fill you in here on what all these names mean. A thing to keep in mind as you learn about the different types of depression is that symptoms can run from very mild to severe, but people with all kinds of depression can benefit from treatment. Many people have low-grade symptoms, sometimes called "subclinical" depression, that don't reach the proportions of the diagnosable conditions we'll list below. As we'll discuss later in the book, even subclinical depression deserves treatment because it causes suffering and can limit potential for growth.

Major Depression. This is the most common form of clinical depression. When doctors make this diagnosis, they almost always believe that the depression deserves treatment with medications, psychotherapy, or both. Five out of nine core symptoms need to be present for at least two weeks to diagnose major depression. These nine symptoms are listed in Table 2.1. You can use this table to see if you might have major depression. We haven't included all the details in the DSM-IV in the table, so check with an experienced clinician if you want to be sure about a diagnosis.

Table 2.1: Diagnosis of Major Depression

A. Five symptoms on this list, including symptom 1 or 2, for at least 2 weeks:
   1. Depressed mood most of the day, nearly every day
   2. Marked lowering of interest or pleasure
   3. Significant weight loss when not dieting or weight gain, or decrease or increase in appetite
   4. Insomnia or sleeping too much nearly every day
   5. Marked agitation or being severely slowed down
   6. Fatigue or loss of energy nearly every day
   7. Feelings of worthlessness or excessive guilt
   8. Decreased ability to concentrate or make decisions
   9. Suicidal thoughts
B. The symptoms above are not due to:
   1. A drug of abuse or a prescription medication
   2. A medical condition
   3. Bereavement

Most of the DSM-IV diagnoses have a series of symptoms or features that must be present to make the diagnosis, and a list of exclusions, or reasons not to diagnose the condition. In the case of major depression, there are three primary exclusions. Sometimes depression can be due to substance abuse or to a prescription medication. Also on some occasions, medical illnesses, such as thyroid disease, can be the cause of depression. In these cases, a diagnosis of major depression wouldn't be accurate. But, the person is still suffering from depression and usually can benefit from treatment. You'll be able to find out more about the types of substances and medications that can trigger depression and the association between depressive symptoms and medical problems in Chapter 7 (The Biology Key).

Normal grief is another reason not to diagnose major depression. Often it is hard to distinguish bereavement from depression. If you are grieving a loss, and the symptoms in the table below persist for more than two months and are causing significant problems in daily functioning, you may be suffering from major depression. In this case, grief has evolved into depression and may require treatment to get it under control.

Occasionally, major depression can become so severe that the person develops psychotic symptoms such as delusions or hallucinations. The great majority of people with major depression do not have any psychotic symptoms. In situations where a person with major depression becomes paranoid, hears voices, or loses touch with reality, immediate treatment by an expert clinician is required. Usually major depression with psychotic features will not get better unless aggressive therapy with biological treatments is initiated.

Dysthymic Disorder. Some people who suffer from depression have a chronic low mood, but their symptoms do not reach the level of severity of major depression. The DSM-IV describes dysthymic disorder as a condition in which the person suffers from a depressed mood most of the day, more days than not, steadily for at least two years. Persons with this condition experience at least two symptoms of depression such as poor appetite or overeating, insomnia or sleeping too much, low energy, low self-esteem, difficulty concentrating, or feelings of hopelessness. However, they don't have the full cluster of symptoms listed above for major depression.

Dysthymic disorder used to be called a depressed personality and usually was not treated with medication. However, we now know that this milder, long-lasting form of depression can respond very well to biological therapies. All of the other treatment strategies described in this book can also play an important role in helping relieve the symptoms of chronic low-grade depression.

Bipolar Disorder (Manic-Depressive Disorder). The defining feature of this condition is the presence of manic symptoms. During the depressed phase of bipolar disorder, the person has the same symptoms as individuals with major depression. However, at least once during their lifetime they cycle into a state of inflated mood, hyperactivity, grandiose or expansive thinking, speaking more rapidly than normal, and other symptoms of mania. A milder form of upswing, termed "hypomania," is also diagnosed at times. Using the DSM-IV system, a person who has had a major depression and a hypomanic episode would be diagnosed as bipolar disorder, type II, while a person who has had a period of major depression plus a full blown mania would be diagnosed bipolar disorder, type I. Most people with bipolar disorder have many manic and depressed cycles during their lives. Fortunately, proper treatment with mood stabilizers, like lithium, Depakote, or Tegretol, can greatly reduce or even eliminate bipolar episodes.

This book focuses on treatment of depression, so we won't describe the diagnosis or treatment of the manic phase of bipolar illness in detail. There is an overview of the use of medications for bipolar depression in Chapter 9. The self-help methods described in this book can be used as supplements to the treatment of depression in people with bipolar disorder. However, we recommend that all persons with bipolar disorder receive professional treatment from clinicians who are experts in managing this condition. Bipolar disorder almost always requires life-long treatment with medication. Psychotherapies, such as cognitive-behavior therapy, can also help individuals cope with the illness.

Other Types of Depression. Research studies have typically found that a significant number of people have milder forms of depression that don't fit the categories developed by the American Psychiatric Association for the DSM-IV. Dr. Lewis Judd and his group from the University of California at San Diego discovered that depression with low levels of symptoms, which they called "subsyndromal" depression, was actually more common than major depression. We prefer the more frequently used term "subclinical" to describe this type of problem because people with milder symptoms are less likely than those with major depression, dysthymic disorder, or bipolar disorder to seek treatment with a clinician, take medication, or get involved in psychotherapy.

We agree with Dr. Judd that mild depression is an underrecognized and undertreated problem. Sometimes depressive symptoms are stimulated by a stressful life event such as the breakup of a relationship, a work situation, or a financial crisis, but do not reach the proportions of a major depression. Other times depressive symptoms just seem to simmer along at "a low boil." The criteria for diagnosis of dysthymic disorder aren't quite reached, but there is no question that something needs to be done to make the person's life happier or less troubled.

We've written this book for people with all forms of depressive symptoms. If you have a severe depression, you can use the self-help techniques in *Getting Your Life Back* along with professional help to fight your illness. If you have less intense symptoms, you may find that working with the ideas in this book will give you the tools you need to get back to feeling like your normal self.

Tony's Diagnosis. When Tony started treatment, part of his first session was spent outlining his symptoms and making a diagnosis. If you review the checklist of symptoms in Table 2.1, you'll see that Tony's problems fit the picture of major depression. He had one episode nine years before when he was in college, but had been feeling well until about six months ago when he didn't get a promotion he was expecting. At about the same time, his wife's career really seemed to take off. Although Tony was happy for her, he began to get down on himself.

Before long, he was having trouble sleeping and was losing weight without trying. Tony and his wife had always had a good sex life. Now he wasn't himself—he had lost virtually all interest in being intimate. In fact, he wasn't enjoying much of anything. It had been over two months since he had played his weekly golf game with his buddies. Tony was still going to work every day and was able to do his job, but he had to push himself to get going in the morning. He couldn't remember being as tired and slowed down as he had been the last few weeks. It was as if someone had poured molasses over all his joints and into his brain.

Fortunately, Tony had ruled out suicide as an option. Sometimes he thought that he would be better off dead. Yet, he knew that suicide would really hurt his wife and his parents. He also had hope that he could get over the depression. Even though he was feeling really low, he had always been a fighter, and he had gotten over depression once before.

Doctors make the diagnosis of major depression when a person has five or more of the nine core symptoms listed in Table 2.1 for at least two weeks. Tony had at least seven of these symptoms: depressed mood, decreased interest in life or ability to experience pleasure, poor appetite and weight loss, insomnia, feeling slowed down, poor energy, and feelings of worthlessness.

MEASURING DEPRESSION

We noted earlier that it is a good idea to check your progress as you move toward recovery. There are several well-known professional rating scales, such as the Beck Depression Inventory and the Zung Self Rating Scale, used by doctors and therapists in clinical practice. We've designed a unique rating method that evaluates depressive symptoms and measures degree of distress for all Five Keys to recovery. You can use this scale yourself, and you can show your ratings to your doctor.

The Five Keys Depression Rating Scale

Take time now to check your score on the Five Keys Depression Rating Scale. You can make copies of the scale so that you can fill in your own answers each time you take it, or you can download free copies of the rating scale from the gettingyourlifeback.com web site. Try to retake the Five Keys Depression Scale every week while you are working on your recovery plan. You can use your scores on this scale to help you see where you have been making gains and where you may need to direct your efforts toward recovery.

In a study we performed with the Five Keys Depression Rating Scale (FKDS) in patients with depression, we discovered that scores on the FKDS were very closely related to those from the most widely used depression scale, the Beck Depression Inventory. From this study, we concluded that a score of 41 or higher on the FKDS usually means that there are fairly severe symptoms of depression. Scores between 21 and 40 usually indicate mild to moderate symptoms. If the score is below 21 it probably means that there are minimal symptoms. Please remember that the FKDS was not designed to diagnose depression. You will need to see a doctor or another clinician for a definitive diagnosis.

Tony had significant problems in all five areas of the FKDS. When he took this scale for the first time, the scores were:

> Thinking Key 11
> Action Key 11
> Biology Key 12
> Relationship Key 7
> Spirituality Key 8
> Total Score 49

His score for the Biology Key was higher than any of the other Keys, but not by much. The Thinking Key and Action Key scores were also on the high side. Even though the Relationship and Spirituality Key scores were somewhat lower, Tony seemed to have enough problems in these areas to include them in his Personal Plan for Recovery. If you score 5 or higher on any Key, you should probably consider adding it to your recovery plan.

The Five Keys Depression Rating Scale

Instructions: Use this scale to rate symptoms or problems you have had over the past week. Each of the statements is scored from 0 to 4. The higher the number, the more severely you are affected by this symptom or problem. ***Circle a number for each question.*** Then add the numbers for individual questions to find your score for each key. To find your Total Score, add the scores for all five keys.

		NONE OF THE TIME	SOME OF THE TIME	MUCH OF THE TIME	MOST OF THE TIME	ALL OF THE TIME
Thinking Key	1. I think negatively about myself.	0	1	2	3	4
	2. I am more pessimistic than usual.	0	1	2	3	4
	3. I have trouble concentrating.	0	1	2	3	4
	4. I think about giving up.	0	1	2	3	4

Thinking Key Score _____
(Add scores for questions 1–4)

		NONE OF THE TIME	SOME OF THE TIME	MUCH OF THE TIME	MOST OF THE TIME	ALL OF THE TIME
Action Key	5. I can't seem to enjoy myself.	0	1	2	3	4
	6. I can't get things accomplished.	0	1	2	3	4
	7. I can't seem to cope with problems in my life.	0	1	2	3	4
	8. I'm less active than usual.	0	1	2	3	4

Action Key Score _____
(Add scores for questions 5–8)

(continued on next page)

Biology Key		NONE OF THE TIME	SOME OF THE TIME	MUCH OF THE TIME	MOST OF THE TIME	ALL OF THE TIME
	9. I feel sad.	0	1	2	3	4
	10. I sleep too little or too much.	0	1	2	3	4
	11. My energy is low, and I tire easily.	0	1	2	3	4
	12. My appetite is lower or higher than normal.	0	1	2	3	4

Biology Key Score _____
(Add scores for questions 9–12)

Relationship Key		NONE OF THE TIME	SOME OF THE TIME	MUCH OF THE TIME	MOST OF THE TIME	ALL OF THE TIME
	13. I get irritated easily with others.	0	1	2	3	4
	14. I'm more isolated from others than I should be.	0	1	2	3	4
	15. I feel lonely or rejected.	0	1	2	3	4
	16. My sex drive is low.	0	1	2	3	4

Relationship Key Score _____
(Add scores for questions 13–16)

Spirituality Key		NONE OF THE TIME	SOME OF THE TIME	MUCH OF THE TIME	MOST OF THE TIME	ALL OF THE TIME
	17. I feel empty.	0	1	2	3	4
	18. I'm not sure anymore about what I care about or believe.	0	1	2	3	4
	19. I feel disconnected from the important things around me.	0	1	2	3	4
	20. I have trouble finding a sense of meaning in life.	0	1	2	3	4

Spirituality Key Score _____
(Add scores for questions 17–20)

Total Score _____

Identifying Your Strengths

The Five Keys Depression Rating Scale can help you find out where your problems are and can give you ideas about where you will need to make changes. But what about your strengths? What resources do you have to fight depression? To get started on identifying your positive attributes, we'll give you some tips here on techniques you can use to pierce the gloom of depression and see the strong points you may have overlooked.

Tony certainly wasn't emphasizing his strengths when he first came for treatment. The negativity of depression was in full force. All he could think about was failure. "Everyone is passing me by. I should have known better than to think I could compete. Maybe I should just quit my job and do something that doesn't take any brains. Why do I feel so stupid all the time? I just don't measure up."

When people describe themselves this way, we consider at least three possibilities: (1) the negative self-statements are completely accurate (hardly ever the case), (2) the negative thoughts are a product of depression and are *not* accurate (a frequent explanation), and (3) there is a grain of truth to some of the negatives, but depression is exaggerating the problem (sometimes true). The only way to find out is to check the statements for their accuracy and to find out if strengths are being ignored. Tony's background suggested that depression was the biggest part of the problem. He actually had numerous strengths that seemed to escape him when he was depressed.

The questions that were used in therapy with Tony are the same ones you can ask yourself to recognize strengths. Because your ideas are narrowly fixed on problems and negatives when you are depressed, you will need to figure out a way to step outside the depression to get a different perspective on yourself and the positive assets you have to cope with difficulties. Let's listen in on a therapy session with Tony.

THERAPIST: Tony, You've been telling me all about how you get down on yourself and think that you are a failure. What about your positive features? What do you have going for you now?

TONY: I don't know. I don't feel like I have anything going for me right now.

THERAPIST: Maybe if we paid some attention to your strengths, it would give you some ideas on how to pull out of depression. Would it be OK if we started a list of your strengths?

TONY: Yeah, sure.

THERAPIST: Do you remember the first question I asked—What do you have going for you now? I'll bet if you concentrate on that question you can come up with some strengths to put down on the list.

We went on to ask the other questions in the next self-help exercise, "Recognizing My Strengths." Tony was able to come up with some good answers that improved his attitude about himself and helped him see the personal resources that he had to overcome depression.

Exercise 2.1
Recognizing My Strengths: Tony's Answers

1. What do you have going for you now?

   I love my wife, and we have a solid relationship. I have some close friends. I'm in pretty good physical shape.

2. If you asked someone who really knew you well and cared about you to describe your personal strengths, what would they say?

   I care about other people. I'm fairly intelligent, and I try to keep up to date on what is happening in the world. I like to have fun and have a good sense of humor. I don't give up easily.

3. Try to think back to the past, before you were feeling depressed. What were some of your strong points that you may be forgetting about now? How would you have described your strengths back then?

   I believed in myself—that I have what it takes to succeed. I got turned on by trying to figure out solutions to problems. I could fix almost anything around the house.

4. Now try to think into the future. What are your untapped strengths? What resources do you have that could be developed more fully? If you could build up your strengths and put them into action, how would things look different to you?

   I want to have children someday. I think I would be a good father. I think I could be much better at playing the guitar. I can figure out this job problem and get my career back on track.

Setting Goals

When Tony first came for therapy, he only could think of one goal—to "get better." Of course the aim of his therapy was to get better, but this goal was too broad to help him much in charting his course for recovery. Goals that work best to get you out of depression are specific and give you a clear picture of what you are trying to accomplish. If possible, your goals should be stated in a way that you will be able to measure progress or figure out if you are getting where you want to go.

Goals that work best are directly targeted at your problems and take advantage of opportunities you have to make changes in your situation. It's also important that your goals be reachable. Try to avoid setting unrealistic goals that will knock you down further if you have problems in accomplishing them. Effective goals lead to solutions. If a goal doesn't give you some ideas of what you might do differently, then you should probably rethink the goal.

One of the bonuses of setting clear and workable goals is that they can stimulate increased hope. If you have goals that give you a sense of direction and make you feel like change is possible, you'll probably start to have a better outlook on life. When Tony started therapy, he was feeling defeated by his problems and couldn't seem to get himself organized to do anything about the situation. By the time we finished writing out his initial list of goals, he was much more encouraged about being able to break out of depression. As you read about how Tony set his goals, try to think of how you might organize your own goal list.

Tips for Goal Setting

Goals work best if they:

- Are specific and give a clear picture of what you are trying to accomplish
- Are targeted at your problems
- Take advantage of opportunities for change
- Are reachable
- Lead to solutions

SETTING SPECIFIC GOALS

Tony's goal to "get better" wasn't very specific. We both knew that he wanted to pull out of depression. However, he needed some detailed goals to help him plan and implement a recovery strategy. The dialogue in one of the early therapy sessions went like this:

THERAPIST: Tony, you told me your goal was to get better. There's no question that we want you to feel like your old self again. But, could you think of some goals that are a bit more specific? I think you'll start to make progress quicker if you have goals that will keep us focused on ways to get out of this depression.

TONY: I'm not sure what you mean.

THERAPIST: Let me give you an example. If you had a goal to build up your skill level to a certain point so you could play in a golf tournament or use some new computer software, the goal would probably help you design a plan to reach it. You could increase your practice sessions, or read a computer manual or take a class. When a goal is vague or too general, it doesn't give you many of these sorts of ideas.

TONY: Well, I need to do something about my job. I'm real unhappy with it right now. Would a goal of making a decision about staying in my job be specific enough?

THERAPIST: That's more like it. Can you think of some things that would help you get to the point of making the decision?

TONY: Sure. I need to sort out my own thinking about what kind of job is best for me. I'd also need to take a good hard look at what the job market is really like. I'll have to figure out a way of getting my self-confidence back before I try to tackle anything new.

Learning how to be specific while still keeping focused on the most important issues or problems isn't always so easy. So, we'll give you another example of how to do this. Janet and her husband had been gradually drifting apart for some time. In the course of building their careers and family they seemed to have lost one another in the shuffle. It had been many years since it felt like they had anything in common. The only time they talked to each other was when they argued about the kids or the bills. Janet's sadness deepened when she thought about what they had lost. She wondered if they could ever go back to being best friends like they were when they were younger.

Janet wanted to improve her marriage and resolve her depression, but these goals didn't have the kind of detail that would give her ideas about what she would need to do. After reviewing her problems we were able to generate this goal list: (1) learn to communicate more effectively with husband; (2) spend at least fifteen minutes talking constructively with each other every day; (3) reestablish "best friends" relationship with husband including doing fun things together at least twice a week; (4) work together with husband as team in dealing with kids; (5) have plan for what to do with my life after kids leave home.

TARGETING YOUR PROBLEMS

In Chapter 1 we explained how to identify problems in each of the areas covered by the Five Keys. Tony's problem list helped him think of positive goals that would give him a direction for recovery. When you list your problems as Tony did, it can seem that you have a very large mountain to climb. At this point you are staring your negatives right in the face. To find a way over the mountain, it will help if you can move fairly quickly from the problem identification stage to setting goals that emphasize your strengths, opportunities, and possible solutions. The sample Personal Plan for Recovery at the end of this chapter illustrates how Tony was able to do this.

Tony's Problem List

Thinking Key

Lack of self-confidence
Comparing self to others
Want to give up

Action Key

Stopped many activities
Indecisive, feel paralyzed
Taking no action on job

Biology Key

Poor sleep, low energy
Sad all the time, can't laugh

Relationship Key

Can't handle wife's promotion
Don't want to see friends

Spirituality Key

Lack of direction or purpose
No sense of peace or calm

SPOTTING OPPORTUNITIES FOR CHANGE

When you set your goals, try to think of opportunities you have to make things different. There are three major ways to spot opportunities. First, you can review your problem list to identify which ones can be turned into opportunities. Next go over your list of strengths to see what positive resources you can emphasize in setting goals. The third way to recognize opportunities for change is to learn as much as possible about the Five Keys to Recovery. You can revise or add to your goal list as you learn more about the Five Keys later in the book.

Depression can make it difficult for you to see how a problem can be an opportunity. Sometimes all you can seem to see is the downside of your problems. Yet if you can turn the problem on its head, you may be able to find some excellent opportunities for change. Janet did this when she set specific goals to reverse problems in her marriage and in her personal life. Tony also was able to generate some effective goals by targeting his problems and looking for opportunities. As you can see from his list, Tony's goals emphasize positive directions that he might take to recover from depression.

SETTING REACHABLE GOALS

All of the examples of goals that we've given in this chapter have two important features in common—the goals were reachable and they led to solutions. Some of the goals were short-term and didn't require enormous effort to accomplish. Others were stretch goals that kept people working steadily to meet significant challenges. Although the goals didn't spell out exactly how to solve a problem, they did give them the

---

Tony's Goals

Short-term goals:

1. Resume healthy activities (exercise, intimacy with wife, doing things with friends)
2. Accept wife's promotion and support her success
3. Make effort to do fun things
4. Get a good night's sleep

Long-term goals:

1. Assess current job, make decision about whether to look for another job
2. Build self-esteem back to normal
3. Make sure I'm heading in the right direction in life, have a sense of purpose

sense that solutions were possible. Most of the goals gave them a feeling of hope that they were moving in the right direction.

In the midst of a depression, it may be difficult to make an accurate prediction about your ability to reach a goal. If your energy is sapped and you've lost your self-confidence, you may underestimate your chances of making progress to achieve goals. You don't want to set goals that are so difficult or impossible to reach that you won't have any realistic chance of success. But on the other hand, you may be more likely to break out of depression if you can think of goals that will inspire you to make significant changes.

These three suggestions can help you set reachable goals:

1. Discuss your ideas for goals with someone you trust and who will give you accurate feedback; or if you are in therapy, talk your goals over with your therapist.
2. Use one of the same techniques we described for identifying strengths. Think back to the time before you became depressed. If you didn't have the cloud of negativism over your thinking, what goals would seem realistic? Try to see through the negative filter of depression to what you actually can do to change your situation.
3. Develop a range of short and 5-term goals of varying degrees of difficulty. You can use a 1–5-point scale to rate the difficulty of reaching goals (a rating of 1 equals the easiest possible goal and 5 equals the hardest possible goal). If all of your goals are rated with higher numbers (4–5), you should probably think of some other goals that will be more realistic or less challenging.

Now let's work on setting your initial goals for your recovery plan. Remember that you'll be able to update or revise your goals as you learn more about the Five Keys.

Exercise 2.2
Setting Effective Goals

1. Review the exercise "My Personal Story" and your "Problem List" from Chapter 1. Try to identify specific goals that directly target your problems.
2. Check your scores from the Five Keys Rating Scale. Which Keys were scored the highest? Do you have goals that fit with any of the Keys?

3. Think of possible opportunities you might have to make changes. Review your list of strengths to get ideas on possible opportunities for change.

4. Ask yourself these questions. Will this goal help me find solutions? Will it give me some hope for getting better?

5. Do a reality check. Examine goals to see if you have a reasonable chance of reaching them. Follow our suggestions for setting reachable goals.

6. Try to focus primarily on reachable short-term goals that you can achieve in the near future or the next few months.

7. Now write out 3–6 short-term goals and 1–3 long-term goals.

Your *Personal Plan for Recovery*

If you have completed the exercises in Chapters 1 and 2, you have already taken the first three steps to building your recovery plan. In case you haven't been able to do the exercises yet, you can take time to do them now as you write out your plan. We've included an example here of how Tony took the first three steps: (1) recognize and measure symptoms, (2) identify strengths, and (3) set goals.

Blank worksheets for the Personal Plan for Recovery are provided in the Appendix. You can write your plan in the book or make copies for your notebook. If you make copies before you write on the plan, you'll have extra forms available if you want to revise the plan as you go along. Another option is to download copies of the worksheets from the gettingyourlifeback.com website. Try to write out the first portion of your recovery plan after you finish this chapter. You can add other sections to your plan after you read about each of the Five Keys.

The first part of Tony's plan records his ratings on the Five Keys Rating Scale when he first came for treatment and for the next three weeks. These ratings were used to assess the level of depression and to determine which keys offered the most potential for change. We suggest that you rate yourself on the scale every week to check on your progress. Space is provided for eight ratings. You can use extra worksheets to do ratings beyond eight weeks.

Some of our patients find that it works best to focus their efforts at first on the Keys with the highest scores. For example if you had Thinking Key and Biology Key scores that were much higher than the other Keys you might start by reading these sections and doing the self-help exercises for these Keys. If you had a doctor or therapist, you might want to emphasize these areas in your treatment sessions. However, keep in mind that you will want to use Keys that will give you a good chance of experiencing success in the near future. Also, you will want to work on things that are especially important to you or may need attention right away.

Tony decided to devote the first weeks of therapy to using the Thinking and Action Keys to reverse his negative thinking and break his pattern of withdrawal from activities. He also began a new medication that he hoped would help him with the symptoms of depression. His score on the Relationship Key wasn't as high as some of the others, but he set a short-term goal of accepting his wife's promotion and supporting her success. He thought he could learn to cope much better with this change and that he could do some things to strengthen his marriage.

Tony's scores fell more in some areas than others during the first four weeks of his therapy. There were big improvements in the Thinking Key and Biology Key scores. He also made a lot of progress with the Action Key. He still needed to keep using these Keys to reduce symptoms of depression, but the scores for the other two Keys hadn't changed as much after four weeks. Because he was feeling much better, he could now devote more energy to working on his relationships and meeting his goal of finding a sense of direction and purpose.

The second part of the plan lists Tony's strengths. These were taken directly from the exercise "Recognizing My Strengths" done earlier in this chapter. As you go further in the book, you'll be able to get a more detailed picture of your strengths for using each Key. The third part of the plan identifies the initial goals that Tony set for his recovery from depression. Tony refined these goals as he learned more about how to fight depression with the Five Keys.

After you review Tony's plan, it will be your turn to write out the first three parts of your Personal Plan for Recovery. Remember that you can always go back to revise or update this portion of the plan. We hope that you will check over your plan on a regular basis until you reach your goals and put depression behind you.

Exercise 2.3
Personal Plan for Recovery Worksheet—Parts I–III

Tony's Example

Part I. My Symptoms on the Five Keys Rating Scale are:

Rating	WEEK 1	WEEK 2	WEEK 3	WEEK 4	WEEK 5	WEEK 6	WEEK 7	WEEK 8
Thinking Key	11	9	5	2				
Action Key	11	8	6	4				
Biology Key	12	10	7	2				
Relationship Key	7	6	6	5				
Spirituality Key	8	8	8	6				
Total Score	49	41	32	19				

Part II. My Strengths are:

- Things I have going for me now:

  Solid relationship with wife, close friends, pretty good physical shape

- Strong points from the past that I may be forgetting:

  Believed in myself, liked challenges, can fix things

- Strengths that others would see:

  I care about others, intelligent, keep up to date, sense of humor, don't give up

- Strengths that could be developed further in the future:

  Desire to have children, would be a good father, musical talent, could have a better career

PART III. MY GOALS FOR MY RECOVERY PLAN ARE:

- Short-term goals (identify 3–6):
  1. *Resume healthy activities such as exercise, relations with wife, seeing friends*
  2. *Accept wife's promotion, give her support in doing new job*
  3. *Do fun things again*
  4. *Sleep at least 6–7 hours a night*

- Long-term goals (Identify 1–3):
  1. *Evaluate my job, decide on whether to look for new job*
  2. *Build self-esteem back to normal*
  3. *Have a sense of direction and purpose in my life*

The Thinking Key

3

Change Your Thinking—
Control Your Depression

Do you have worries that stream through your mind and make it hard for you to feel good or to relax? Are you the type of person who puts yourself down? Do you tend to dwell on the negatives in your life? Are you more pessimistic than you would like to be? If you answered yes to any of these questions, the Thinking Key could give you some solutions for your problems. In this chapter, we'll help you understand how your thoughts can make you feel depressed and how you can lift your mood by changing your thinking. The first thing we'll do is to explain how negative or dysfunctional thinking can set you up for depression. Then you'll learn about specific self-help methods from cognitive-behavior therapy that you can use to develop a healthier and more positive thinking style. There are lots of exercises in this chapter, so make sure to have pen and paper handy.

How Your Thoughts Control Your Feelings

If we asked you what controls your feelings—what makes you happy, or angry, or sad—you might think first of the events or situations in your life that seem to trigger emotions. Examples might be "My boss makes me nervous when he calls me into his office" or "I get sad when the holidays come around." On the surface it might appear that it is your boss that is making you nervous or the holiday season that is making you sad. But, it is the *thoughts* that you are having about these situations that are actually stimulating the emotions.

To explain how our thinking processes control emotions, let's take a look at different ways one might think about being called into a boss's office. In the first scenario, you get a call from your boss and start to think "I've really messed up . . . I won't know what to say or do . . . This is a total disaster." There's no question you would be nervous. In fact, you might be close to panic if you were having these types of thoughts as you opened the door to your boss's office. However, what would happen if you had these kinds of thoughts: "I know how to do this job . . . He might want me to make some changes, but everything will work out if I buckle down . . . Listen to him and show that you are on top of the situation." It's likely that your mood would be much better if you went to see your boss in this frame of mind.

The environmentalist Karsten Heuer told in *Smithsonian Magazine* about how he controlled his emotions by getting a grip on his thinking during a scary night he spent in the mountains of Montana. Karsten was on a long hike in very rugged territory. One midnight a horrendous storm blew up and flattened his tent and campsite. He spent the rest of the night outside his tent wrapped in a tarp as he tried to withstand a torrent of hail, icy rain, and blistering winds. "I was shivering uncontrollably. I thought I might die of exposure that night. But I got through it by saying, over and over again: 'This is only temporary, this is only temporary.' And the next day dawned beautiful."

If Karsten had allowed his thinking to spiral down into despair, he would have had a much harder time getting through the night. Can you imagine what kinds of emotions would have been raging through him if all he could think about was "I can't make it . . . This is too much for me . . . I'll never see daylight . . . How will it end?" Fortunately, he was able to focus on a positive thought that helped him push away his fears and gave him the strength to cope with a very tough situation.

When people become depressed they usually have trouble thinking in ways that calm their emotions and help them solve problems. In fact, their thinking style often intensifies their sadness and interferes with their ability to manage life stresses. Unlike Karsten Heuer, they tend to dwell on their worries and fears. The people with depression that you have met so far in this book all had problems with negative thinking. Michelle got down on herself after going through a divorce. Tony began to think that he was a loser after his wife got a big promotion at work. In this chapter we'll show you how Michelle, Tony, and others used the Thinking Key to control their depressions. You can use the same depression fighting techniques to overcome your own problems.

The Scientific Basis of the Thinking Key

There have been hundreds of research studies that have been directed at understanding cognitive, or thinking, disturbances in depression. The results of these studies have been distilled into a specific form of psychotherapy for depression called cognitive-behavior therapy (CBT). In this type of therapy, patients and therapists work together to reverse depressive thinking and the actions or behaviors that go along with a negative thinking style. Over the last twenty-five years, a great number of scientific investigations have shown that CBT is an effective treatment for depression. If you are interested in learning more about the research that has been conducted on this type of therapy, you can check the reviews listed in the references. The self-help methods we outline here for the Thinking Key are based on the proven techniques of CBT.

When patients ask us to tell them about CBT, we try to give them a shorthand version of how the therapy works. The basics of CBT for depression are learning how to: (1) *recognize* depressive thinking and behavior, (2) *change* the way you think and behave, and (3) *build* healthy attitudes. The Thinking Key will help you do each of these things as you work toward mastering your depression.

How to Recognize Depressive Thinking

One of the greatest pleasures in our clinical practices is to see "the light bulb go on" when our patients suddenly realize that their thinking is a big part of the problem *and* the solution in depression. People with depression typically are blind to the way their thinking has become twisted and distorted. Relatives or friends may be able to spot negative distortions, but sufferers usually assume that all their thoughts are completely true.

When Vic hadn't come home at his usual time, his wife, Sarah got worried. Vic was a creature of habit, always home about the same time each day or calling ahead when he was going to be late. When he didn't answer his office phone or cell phone, she called his sister, and then his best friend, but neither one had heard from him. Sarah remembered about how glum and withdrawn Vic had been lately, how frustrated he had been with work, and how much he had been criticizing himself lately. To soothe her own fears, she got in the car and went to his office, half expecting to find him engrossed in a big project. Instead, there he sat at this desk with his head in his hands surrounded by piles of paper, blueprints, phone messages, and files. Sarah asked what was wrong, but

Vic said little to help her understand what was happening to him. She used Vic's phone to call his doctor. While she was waiting for him to call back, Vic softly said, "I'm so sorry. I'm so sorry," and he began to cry.

At his doctor's suggestion, Sarah took Vic to the hospital emergency room. After a physical, some blood tests, and a long talk with the psychiatrist, it became clear that Vic was severely depressed. He repeatedly said to the doctor, "There's no way I can get my work done . . . I don't know what I'm doing. I've lost it . . . I'm trapped and there's no way out."

Vic didn't realize that depression was twisting his thoughts. He was convinced that he was a failure and that he had lost all ability to function. Although his wife and coworkers said that he actually was doing a good job at work and had only fallen a little behind since he had started to become depressed about a month ago, Vic saw his situation as desperate and hopeless.

When Vic met with his therapist for the first time, the most important task was to help him *recognize* that his thoughts had become distorted by depression.

THERAPIST: What were you feeling inside when you were sitting at your desk and couldn't move?

VIC: I was terrified. My heart was racing and I was shaking so hard that I couldn't even lift my hand to use the telephone.

THERAPIST: And what was going through your mind? What were you thinking about when you were so scared?

VIC: That there was no way I could ever get the project done and that I couldn't face anyone ever again. I had no idea of what to do. All I could think of was that I was a total fraud and that everybody would find out. So, I just sat there. I wasn't moving, but my mind was going a mile a minute.

THERAPIST: Did you stop to think about whether any of these thoughts could have been exaggerated? They sound pretty extreme to me.

VIC: No, it all seemed very real at the time.

THERAPIST: Vic, you've been depressed. And when people get depressed, their thinking turns extremely negative. You automatically think of all the negatives in your life and forget about all the pluses. How would you see the situation if you stopped putting yourself down so much?

VIC: I guess you're right. I think it's true that I've been slipping at work. But, I still know a lot about how to pull off this kind of project. My track record with big projects is actually pretty good. I panicked, and all I could see was a giant catastrophe.

THERAPIST: You look like you feel a bit better already. Would you like to learn some ways to get rid of the negativism and get your energies focused on solving your problems?

VIC: Sure.

THERAPIST: OK. We can start with trying to recognize your negative automatic thoughts. These kinds of thoughts go through your mind all day long and you don't realize how much they affect you. When you were frozen at your desk the other night, you had a whole lot of automatic thoughts.

AUTOMATIC THOUGHTS

When people are sad or anxious, thoughts often pop into their heads that they don't stop to check out. We call these types of cognitions "automatic thoughts" because they occur quickly while you are in the middle of a situation and you don't evaluate them carefully to see if they are logical or realistic. Automatic thoughts also can happen when you are remembering events from the past, daydreaming, or are wondering what might happen in the future.

Of all the thoughts we have every day, only a small portion are spoken out loud to others. We keep the great majority of our thoughts to ourselves. Automatic thoughts are part of this internal dialogue. Everybody has them. But if you are depressed, these types of thoughts are much more frequent and are likely to be negatively distorted.

Because automatic thoughts usually stimulate emotions, a surge of feelings can be a good indicator that automatic thoughts have just occurred. Patients who are in CBT learn to recognize their "mood shifts," which are sudden changes in feeling states, as markers for automatic thoughts. We recommend that you use the same technique to practice listening in to your automatic thoughts. If your feelings are good ones, you don't necessarily need to pause to check out your automatic thoughts. But if you are upset, sad, anxious, or mad, it may be a good idea for you to stop to see if automatic thoughts are part of the problem.

RECORDING YOUR AUTOMATIC THOUGHTS

You may have already been thinking of situations in your own life that have stirred up automatic thoughts. The next self-help exercise will help you identify and record some of these thoughts. Let your mind return to a recent time when a situation seemed to fire up your emotions. Put yourself back into the situation and remember it just as it happened. Try to remember details such as the characters in the scene, what you

Key Points

1. "Automatic thoughts" are the thoughts that just pop into your head when you are in the middle of situations or are thinking about events in your life.
2. Most people don't stop to check out the accuracy of automatic thoughts—especially if they are suffering from depression.
3. Automatic thoughts usually trigger emotions. A good way to recognize automatic thoughts is to tune in to your thinking when you have intense emotions.
4. If you can recognize your automatic thoughts, you will be taking a big step in the fight against depression.

were wearing, and what was said, so that you can accurately recall your automatic thoughts and emotions. Then take time to actually write out the thoughts.

Exercise 3.1
Recognizing Automatic Thoughts

1. Think of a recent situation or event, or a memory of an event, that seemed to trigger an emotional reaction.
2. Write down your automatic thoughts and emotions in a Thought Record in your notebook. (See examples.)
3. After you write down your automatic thoughts, step back from the situation to see if you could think about it in a more helpful way.

Here are some examples of using a Thought Record. In the first one, Michelle wrote down her automatic thoughts that occurred after being invited out to a movie. You might remember from Chapter 1 that Michelle began to isolate herself from her friends after she went through a divorce. Her Thought Record gives some important clues about why she was turning down invitations. After she began to reverse these types of automatic thoughts, she started to become more sociable again.

MICHELLE'S THOUGHT RECORD

Event	Automatic Thoughts	Emotions
Sally called to ask me to go to a movie.	She's calling me just because I'm lonely and miserable. What's the use in going? I'm no fun anymore.	Sad, More lonely

Vic and Tony also learned how to use Thought Recording to understand how their automatic thoughts were causing them so much trouble.

VIC'S THOUGHT RECORD

Event	Automatic Thoughts	Emotions
The new project deadline is approaching, and I'm behind.	I'll never get it done in time. This job is too much for me. I don't know what I'm doing. I'm the one to blame for all the problems.	Sadness, Intense Fear, Tension
Meeting with a client that I've worked for before.	I can't face him. He'll know I can't pull off this project. I'm a failure.	Anxiety, Sadness

Tony, the man from Chapter 2 who was having problems dealing with his wife's promotion, wrote out this Thought Record after he got upset about going to a party. His first reaction was to put himself down. But, his anger and sadness faded after he spotted the automatic thoughts and got back to a more realistic way of thinking.

TONY'S THOUGHT RECORD

Event	Automatic Thoughts	Emotions
I had to go to a party with all the people from my wife's office.	They'll look down on me. Everyone else seems so intelligent and has so much to say. Compared to them, I'm a real loser. I can't do anything right.	Sadness, anger

Thinking Errors

During World War II, resistance fighters often changed the road signs in occupied France to confuse the German soldiers and send them in the wrong direction. Depression does much the same thing to your thinking. It's as if the directions in your map of life have all been changed to send you traveling down a road toward despair. The worst part is that you do not know that you are basing your decisions on wrong information. In fact you probably have very little suspicion that you are being misled by your own thinking.

Research on thinking processes in depression has shown that depressed people typically make mistakes in the way that they perceive information about themselves and the world around them. Cognitive therapists use the terms "cognitive distortions" or "thinking errors" to describe these mistaken perceptions. When people are depressed, their automatic thoughts are usually loaded with cognitive distortions. If you can recognize these cognitive distortions, you can begin to modify your negative automatic thoughts and turn your life back in a more positive direction.

We'll describe the six most common thinking errors and then try to help you find them in your own automatic thoughts.

IGNORING THE EVIDENCE

The negative filter of depression can block out valuable information that would help you get an accurate picture of your strengths, your possibilities, or the support others might be able to give you. Vic was ignoring the evidence when he was having automatic thoughts such as "This job is too much for me. . . . I don't know what I'm doing." Vic was a very well-trained and accomplished architect who had managed many projects successfully. But, depression had clouded his thinking so much that he was completely ignoring these obvious assets.

The relationship between thinking and emotion is a two-way street. If you ignore evidence about your good points or about ways you could solve problems, you are more likely to become sad or anxious. Then if your mood gets worse, you are even more likely to ignore the evidence or have additional cognitive errors. This interrelationship between thinking and emotion is part of the vicious cycle of depression described in Chapter 1. You can start to reverse the vicious cycle by recognizing your thinking errors.

JUMPING TO CONCLUSIONS

Michelle was "jumping to conclusions" when she had the automatic thought "She's calling me just because I'm lonely and miserable." It was quite possible that Michelle's friend invited her because she was looking forward to going to the movie with Michelle. It even was possible that her friend was the one who was lonely and would appreciate having Michelle join her for an evening out. Yet, Michelle jumped to the conclusion that her friend was asking her to go to the movie because of a sense of pity. As a result, her mood dropped, and she turned down the invitation.

When depressed people jump to conclusions, they usually think of the worst possible interpretations of situations. Then they become certain that bad things will happen. Vic did this when he began to worry about the deadline for his project. One of his automatic thoughts was "I'll never get it done in time." After he jumped to this conclusion, he had a cascade of other negative automatic thoughts such as "I'll never get another commission if I mess this up . . . I'll lose my job . . . I'll lose everything." He was jumping to conclusions with all of these thoughts.

Have you started to think of how to stop thinking errors like jumping to conclusions? The first step is to recognize that you are having thinking errors. If Vic had realized that he was jumping to conclusions, he might have been able to interrupt the vicious cycle before he became frozen with fear and indecision.

OVERGENERALIZING

Try to imagine mixing a single drop of red color in a gallon of white paint. If you mixed the paint well, you might expect to see a very slight tinge of pink in the gallon of paint. But, what would you think if the paint turned completely red? Would this seem improbable? People with depression don't see the improbability of their thinking when they allow one small problem or perceived flaw to define everything about them. This type of thinking error is called "overgeneralizing."

When Tony was invited to go a party with his wife's co-workers, he had a flood of negative automatic thoughts ending with one of the most damaging of all: "I can't do anything right." This thought was a classic example of "overgeneralizing." Michelle got into the same pattern of thinking when she had to take her car into the garage for repairs: "Nothing seems to work right anymore . . . Everything is going wrong in my life!"

One of the problems with overgeneralizing is that it makes you conclude that your situation is much worse than it really is. When this happens, you'll probably feel more sad and anxious and will have more trouble figuring out solutions to your difficulties. On the other hand, if you can isolate your trouble spots and keep them in perspective, you will be in much better position to fight depression.

MAGNIFYING AND MINIMIZING

One of our colleagues gave us a cartoon from a magazine to use in our workshops in cognitive-behavior therapy because he thought it was a great example of "magnifying" and "minimizing." The cartoon shows a statue of an apparently successful businessman in a public park. The plaque under the statue reads: "Edward T. Jones—colossal failure." This cartoon always gets lots of laughs—probably because it strikes a chord for most people.

How many of us have fallen into the trap of magnifying our faults and minimizing our strengths? Tony was magnifying the attributes of others and minimizing his abilities when he thought: "Everyone else seems so intelligent and has so much to say . . . Compared to them, I'm a real loser." These types of comparisons don't do us any good. They knock down our self-esteem and get in the way of using our strengths to the greatest advantage. It would have been much better for Tony to see the situation this way: "Most of these people have more important jobs than I do, but they aren't perfect. Everybody has their own problems. I have a good education, and I read a lot. I can be just as interesting as anybody else. Keep your head up and try to enjoy the party."

PERSONALIZING

People with depression often get caught up in taking personal blame for everything that seems to go wrong. They take full responsibility for a troubling situation or problem even when the facts don't support this conclusion. "Personalizing" can deflate your self-esteem and make you more depressed.

When Vic thought about the deadline for his project, he took complete responsibility for any difficulties they were having ("I'm the one to blame for all the problems"). The facts were that there were numerous problems that had delayed their work. The customer had added a set of complex new requirements after the project had been started. There were five other architects and draftsmen working on the plans—some of which were behind on their schedules. And they had run into unexpected problems with the stability of the site where they planned to build.

"Personalizing" is an extremely common thinking error when relationships are in deep trouble or when they end. After her divorce, Michelle often felt that she was the reason the marriage didn't work out.

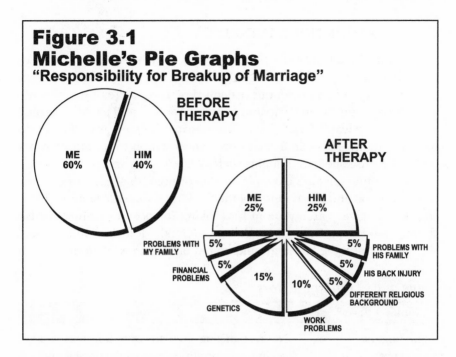

Figure 3.1
Michelle's Pie Graphs
"Responsibility for Breakup of Marriage"

BEFORE THERAPY

ME 60%

HIM 40%

AFTER THERAPY

ME 25%

HIM 25%

PROBLEMS WITH MY FAMILY 5%

FINANCIAL PROBLEMS 5%

15%

10%

GENETICS

WORK PROBLEMS

PROBLEMS WITH HIS FAMILY 5%

HIS BACK INJURY 5%

5%

DIFFERENT RELIGIOUS BACKGROUND

She incessantly criticized herself with automatic thoughts such as: "I really blew it . . . It was my fault the marriage fell apart . . . Where did I go wrong?" Usually when relationships break up, there are a multitude of factors involved. But, when you are depressed it is very hard to recognize anything but your part of the problem.

In therapy sessions, we sometimes ask patients to use a pie graph to diagram the responsibility or blame they take for themselves in comparison to other possible influences. Early in therapy, the pie graph typically shows the lion's share of the blame is accepted by the patient. Usually there are only two categories displayed in the graph (for example, Me-Him, or Me-Her). If the therapy is successful, the pie graph changes in two major ways: (1) the patient accepts a more reasonable share of responsibility for the problems and (2) a much higher number of influences are noted on the pie graph (for example, job pressures, health problems, genetics, conflicts with other family members, finances, "midlife crisis," etc.).

We aren't suggesting that you "sweep your problems under the carpet." You need to own up to your problems and accept responsibility when you have made mistakes. Taking an honest look at your problems can help you start to turn things around. However, if you let "personalizing" go on unchecked, you will take excessive blame for situations, put yourself down unnecessarily, and miss out on a great opportunity to fight depression.

ALL-OR-NONE THINKING

If you would be able to listen, as we have, to the stories of many depressed patients, you would be struck with the black-and-white nature of their thinking. When one of our patients described the reason for his depression, he said, "I am incapable of love." Another told us that "nothing ever goes my way." One of Tony's automatic thoughts was "I can't do anything right." Michelle turned down an invitation to go out with her friend, because she had thoughts such as "I'm no fun anymore."

These thoughts are examples of "all-or-none thinking," one of the most common and most hurtful of the thinking errors. All-or-none thinking doesn't give you any room for looking for positive features or for finding good options for doing things differently. It locks you in to seeing yourself and the world around you in black-and-white terms. When

Table 3.1 Thinking Errors

Thinking Error	Examples
Ignoring the Evidence	Not recognizing strengths or opportunities; not seeing your positives. You view yourself and the world with "tunnel vision."
Jumping to Conclusions	Concluding prematurely that a negative event will happen or that you are bound to fail. You act like a "fortune teller."
Overgeneralizing	Allowing a small problem or perceived flaw to affect how you think about everything.
Magnifying and Minimizing	Blowing up the seriousness of your difficulties; playing down your assets or resources. You magnify the positive features of others, and you minimize your good points, such as ability to make friends, sense of humor, or intelligence.
Personalizing	Believing that you are mostly or completely to blame for negative events such as a breakup of a relationship, a job loss, or a financial downturn when there are many other factors involved.
All-or-None Thinking	Thinking in absolutes. You conclude that you are completely wrong, can do nothing right, or have no future.

you only think in extremes, you miss the myriad of explanations between all good or all bad, completely competent or incompetent, or a total success or failure.

Most of our experiences and our accomplishments in life fall somewhere in the gray area between all or none. How many of us have a perfect marriage or have achieved complete success in our work—or are total losses or abject failures? Even our problems or failures often can have redeeming qualities or can help us grow stronger. We have had innumerable patients in our practices who have sustained major losses or personal crises but have learned to avoid the negative pull of all-or-none thinking. Instead of concluding that all is lost or that they are incapable of managing the situation, they have been able to identify their strengths and put their coping skills to work. You can do the same thing by recognizing and changing your all-or-none thinking.

Tips for Spotting Thinking Errors

Identifying thinking errors is one of the most helpful CBT techniques. However, be careful to avoid getting hung up with trying to always find the exact type of distortion that is occurring. You can get a great deal of benefit from simply recognizing that any thinking errors are happening. There is a good deal of overlap between the thinking errors, and often there will be more than one type of thinking error involved in a single automatic thought. Take for example, Tony's automatic thought "I can't do anything right." This is a great example of all-or-none thinking. But, he is also *ignoring the evidence* (he was doing many things well), *magnifying* the extent of his problems, and *overgeneralizing* his difficulties to the point that he was condemning himself through and through.

Exercise 3.2
Recognizing Thinking Errors

1. First write down your automatic thoughts for a specific situation or a memory of an event.
2. Next, go through the list of six thinking errors described here. Write down as many of the thinking errors that you think might be happening for each of the automatic thoughts.
3. Write out a brief description of why you believe your thinking may be distorted.

Vic's exercise looked like this.

Event: The project deadline is approaching, and I'm behind.

Automatic Thoughts	Thinking Errors
I'll never get it done on time.	Jumping to conclusions, All-or-none thinking: There's a reasonable chance we can get the project done if everybody gets down to work. We've had plenty of projects that have been delayed a bit and still have been a success.
This job is too much for me.	Ignoring the evidence, Magnifying and minimizing, Overgeneralizing: I know how to pull off this kind of project. I'm exaggerating the difficulties and downplaying my capabilities.
I'm the one to blame for all the problems.	Personalizing, All-or-none thinking: I'm the lead person in charge, but lots of others are involved. The customer has changed his mind so many times that it has thrown us behind. If everyone pulls together as a team, we can get this done.

How to Change Depressive Thinking

If you have grasped the principles of *recognizing* depressive thinking you will already be well on your way to *changing* the way you think. The simple process of tuning in to your automatic thoughts can help you start questioning the accuracy of your thinking. For example, Vic first started to identify some of the reasons why his thinking was distorted. Then he listed some alternative ways of looking at the situation that were more logical or realistic than his automatic thoughts. Finding *logical alternatives* to negatively distorted automatic thoughts is one of the essential skills in using the Thinking Key in your recovery plan.

Breaking out of the rut of depressive thinking can be easier said than done. Your family or friends may mean well when they say things like "You get down on yourself too much . . . You've got everything going for you . . . Don't mope so much . . . Come on, just snap out of it." Unfortunately, their cheerleading can make you feel worse because it may seem that they don't really understand; or your guilt can deepen because you can't *"just snap out of it."*

What you need is a systematic method to examine your thinking and make changes that you can accept and believe. A Thought Change Record is an excellent way to develop a more rational or realistic style of thinking.

THE THOUGHT CHANGE RECORD

The Thought Change Record is one of the most helpful techniques from cognitive-behavior therapy. It will help you pull together the techniques you have already learned for spotting dysfunctional cognitions, plus give you an effective method for modifying your thinking. The first three columns in the Thought Change Record (Event, Automatic Thoughts, and Emotions) have already been described when we discussed ways to *recognize* depressive thinking. The fourth and fifth columns (Logical Thoughts and Outcome) are used to *change* depressive thinking and to note the effects of these changes.

Are you ready to try to fill out a Thought Change Record? First we'll go over the instructions for completing your own record and then we'll show you an example. We suggest that you make lots of copies of this form, because often it is the most frequently used self-help exercise in the Thinking Key. Thought Record worksheets are also available on the gettingyourlifeback.com web site.

Instructions for Completing a Thought Change Record

1. In the first column, write down an event, or a memory of an event, that seemed to trigger automatic thoughts and an emotional reaction.
2. Next write down any automatic thoughts that occurred in response to the event. Indicate how strongly you believed the automatic thoughts *at the time they occurred* by putting a percentage of belief rating after each thought. A rating of 0 percent would mean that you didn't believe the thought at all; a rating of 100 percent would mean you believed the thought completely. Use any number between 0 and 100 to describe your degree of belief in the thought *before* you stopped to check it out.
3. In the third column, note the emotions that you had in response to the automatic thoughts. Rate the degree of emotion on a 0–100 percent scale (0 = lowest possible level of this emotion, 50 = a moderate degree of the emotion, and 100 = the most intense degree of this emotion that you could experience). Remember that emotions are feeling states such

THOUGHT CHANGE RECORD

	Event	Automatic Thoughts	Emotions	Logical Thoughts	Outcome
Date	a. Describe actual event preceding emotion(s), or b. stream of thoughts or memories of events preceding emotion(s).	a. Write automatic thought(s) that led to emotion(s). b. Rate belief in automatic thought(s), 0–100%.	a. Specify sad, anxious, angry, tense, etc. b. Rate degree of emotion(s), 0–100%.	a. Identify thinking errors. b. Write logical or realistic response to automatic thought(s). c. Rate belief in logical response, 0–100%.	a. Rate degree of emotion(s), 0–100%. b. Describe changes in how you could handle the situation.

as sadness, happiness, anger, or anxiety. You also can note physical reactions such as tension, rapid heartbeat, or fast breathing.

4. The fourth column is used to evaluate the automatic thoughts and to develop logical thoughts. Note any thinking errors in your automatic thoughts. Then write down some rational alternatives to the automatic thoughts. Rate your degree of belief in the logical thoughts on a 0–100 percent scale.

5. In the last column, you can make observations on the outcome of revising your thinking. Were you able to reduce unpleasant emotions by developing logical thoughts? Did you think of better ways to handle the situation? Use the 0–100 percent scale to rate changes in your emotions. Also note how your behavior has changed or will change.

Exercise 3.3
The Thought Change Record

1. Think of a recent situation that stirred up strong feelings such as sadness, anger, or anxiety.
2. Use a Thought Change Record to identify and change the automatic thoughts that occurred in this situation.
3. Repeat this exercise as many times as necessary until you get control over your automatic thoughts.

It usually takes some practice to be able to use the Thought Change Record to make effective changes in your thinking style. Negative thinking can be as deeply ingrained as a bad habit. We strongly recommend that you: (1) take time to work with Thought Change Records, (2) write them out in your notebook, and (3) make them a fundamental part of your Personal Plan for Recovery. Even after you have finished this book, you may want to refer back to your records to keep depression in check.

A peek at Michelle's notebook should give you some ideas on how you can use thought recording to control depression. When Michelle started treatment, she had been refusing invitations to do things with her friends and was even having trouble getting out of the house. Her self-esteem had been at rock bottom. After she began to make some progress, Michelle decided to make the effort to go out to dinner with

THOUGHT CHANGE RECORD: Michelle's Example

	Event	Automatic Thoughts	Emotions	Logical Thoughts	Outcome
Date	a. Describe actual event preceding emotion(s), or b. stream of thoughts or memories of events preceding emotion(s).	a. Write automatic thought(s) that led to emotion(s). b. Rate belief in automatic thought(s), 0–100%.	a. Specify sad, anxious, angry, tense, etc. b. Rate degree of emotion(s) 0–100.	a. Identify thinking errors. b. Write logical or realistic response to automatic thought(s). c. Rate belief in logical response, 0–100%.	a. Rate degree of emotion(s), 0–100. b. Describe changes in how you could handle the situation.
Jan 25th	I went out to dinner with two of my friends. We ran into a group of couples that I used to socialize with when I was married.	We look like real losers. 95%	Sad—90 Anxious—85	*Jumping to conclusions, magnifying, ignoring the evidence.* How do I know what they are thinking? We are single women out for dinner, but that doesn't make us losers. (95%) I'm divorced, but I'm still a good person. (90%)	Sad—25 Anxious—20 I could talk in a friendly way with the couples. These changes in thinking will help my self-esteem.
		After you're divorced, nobody wants to have anything to do with you. 90%	Angry—75	*All or none thinking, magnifying, ignoring the evidence, overgeneralizing.* It's true that people treat you differently after a divorce, but most of my friends have been a big support. (100%) I'm letting the reactions of a few people govern what I think about the whole world. (90%)	Angry—15 If I adjusted my attitude, I could start socializing more and have some fun.
		I should never have gone out to dinner. I'm not ready for this. 85%	Anxious—85	*Jumping to conclusions, ignoring the evidence, minimizing.* Wait a minute, this evening could still work out OK. (70%) I can handle seeing these people. (80%) It's time for me to get out of my shell. (95%)	Anxious—20 Facing these kinds of situations is just what I need to start getting over the divorce. I'll plan more nights out.

two of her women friends. They were having a good time until they ran into some couples that Michelle socialized with before her divorce. She wrote down her reactions in this Thought Change Record.

LOGICAL THOUGHTS: A WAY OUT OF DEPRESSION

Logical thoughts are accurate and reasonable, but they aren't always positive. One of the misunderstandings about CBT is that this treatment approach is based in part on Norman Vincent Peale's *The Power of Positive Thinking*. Peale made a great contribution by drawing our attention to the strength of thinking in a positive way. However, the reality of life is that sometimes our negative thoughts are true.

If you had a serious medical illness, a financial crisis, or were in an abusive relationship, some of your automatic thoughts about these situations could be on target. It's generally not a good idea to try to think unrealistic positive thoughts when you are facing actual problems like the ones noted above. If you started to have abdominal pain and a change in bowel habits, and kept saying to yourself "It's nothing . . . I eat right and exercise every day," you could be ignoring a problem that needs attention. A woman that was being abused by her spouse could get in deeper trouble by thinking "He's just upset because he works too hard . . . This is bound to stop soon."

In both of these examples, the persons had positively distorted thoughts. They were ignoring the evidence and were minimizing their problems. Depressed people need to think accurately and to face their problems—not to cover over difficulties with false positive thoughts. The Action Key will give you detailed methods for developing strategies to handle problems or difficulties more effectively. Our goal for now is to help you stop depressive thinking and move toward a more realistic perspective in which you can take a valid inventory of your strengths and opportunities. Try out these methods to develop logical thoughts.

How to Find Logical Alternatives to Negative Automatic Thoughts

1. Open your mind to possibilities
2. Think like your old self
3. Brainstorm
4. Examine the evidence
5. Learn from others
6. Use the other Keys to recovery

OPEN YOUR MIND TO POSSIBILITIES

In order to spot alternatives to depressive thinking, you can try to free yourself up to think about a full range of options. A good way to do this is to practice thinking like a scientist or a detective. For these professionals, a closed mind is a plague that should be avoided at all costs. Instead of looking at a problem from one angle, they open up their thinking by exploring as many angles as possible. You can do the same thing when you evaluate your negative automatic thoughts.

Try to imagine what objective outsiders might say if they looked at your situation. One of the observers might be a scientist, a detective, or a consultant that you hired to point out alternative ways of seeing things. This person would be on your side, but would be objective and *tell it like it is*. You also could imagine that you have a great coach working with you who is building your psychological strength by pointing out all the positive, but accurate, alternatives you have been ignoring. What would your coach be telling you? Some other vantage points from which you could get a different perspective on your thinking might be to put yourself in the position of someone who knows you very well such as a close friend, a trusted family member, or a supportive coworker.

Breaking out of the closed thinking style of depression usually requires some time and effort. You will need to work at opening up your mind to logical alternatives. So, take time each day to think about your thinking. And, don't allow your mind to speed along on automatic pilot. Regularly monitor your automatic thoughts by writing them down on a thought record. Remember that your goal is to open your mind so that your logical thoughts will come through.

THINK LIKE YOUR OLD SELF

When the cloud of depression settles over your thinking, it's almost like you have amnesia for the times when you felt OK. To break through this amnesia and get back to a more rational style of thinking, you can use this "memory booster" technique.

We can usually remember things better if they are associated with specific images in our minds—especially images of important or emotionally charged events. For example, most people can remember what they thought and felt when they graduated from school, got married, were promoted, or their children were born. Sometimes we call these types of memories "flashbulb memories" because you can see an actual picture in your mind of yourself in the scene.

If you are having trouble thinking of logical alternatives to negative automatic thoughts, you can imagine yourself back in times and places when you felt well and were enjoying success. Think of specific, positive, highly memorable situations. Let the thoughts and feelings from those times flow through you again. Now from that perspective, review the automatic thoughts you are having in the present. How would your old, more positive self view the situation? What alternatives would your old self be able to see that your depressed self has ignored? What advice would your old self give you?

BRAINSTORM

Writers, artists, business people, and many other creative individuals use brainstorming to come up with new ideas that they might have missed if they just kept thinking in their normal, routine way. When you brainstorm, you step out of the rut of everyday thinking by temporarily throwing out the rulebook on what you believe may work or not work. You tap into your creativity and put any idea, no matter how far out there, on your list for consideration. Generating all these ideas helps you find the ones that are the most accurate or have the greatest potential.

In Sarah's job she was known as an expert at brainstorming business solutions. She hadn't put this skill to work, however, in trying to come up with ways to overcome her negative thinking about her daughter.

SARAH: I've really been getting down about my daughter not wanting to come home from college for Thanksgiving. It upset me so much, I wrote down my automatic thoughts on one of those Thought Change Records.

THERAPIST: What kind of thoughts did you have?

SARAH: She doesn't want to come home. She doesn't need me any longer.

THERAPIST: What did you write in the Logical Thoughts column?

SARAH: I couldn't think of much except that maybe she has better things to do.

THERAPIST: How about doing some brainstorming to see if we can come up with some other possibilities? What possibilities pop into your head?

SARAH: (Thinks for a moment then says:) OK, I'll never see her again . . . She must hate me . . . She's desperately homesick and afraid to admit it . . . Maybe she'll see the light and come home after all. Is this what you want me to do?

THERAPIST: You're off to a good start. But, you probably have lots of other ideas that we haven't heard about yet. When I brainstorm, I try to hold off on checking out my thoughts until I get them all down on paper. That way, I don't get stuck on just one idea.

SARAH: OK. Here are some others. I've taught her to be independent, and she's learned the lesson . . . It will be good for her to spend time with another family and to see their traditions . . . Maybe she is trying to save us some money, all these plane trips back and forth to college have been adding up . . . If I were in the same position, I'd probably want to do some different things on school breaks—to travel, be with friends, and see new things . . . We have a great relationship, her not coming home doesn't mean anything . . . I won't be able to stand not seeing her . . . I'll see her again in just another month, don't make such a big deal over this thing.

THERAPIST: Now you're rolling! I'll bet you could think of a lot more options if we took the time. Knowing your daughter, what do you think is the most logical conclusion so far?

SARAH: I think she's like a lot of kids who want to explore things on their own. Thanksgiving break is one of the few times a student can travel and relax. I'm sure it's not personal. We've always been close. I'll miss seeing her, but I need to respect her independence.

EXAMINE THE EVIDENCE

Another good way to develop logical alternatives is to act like a judge and weigh the evidence for and against your automatic thoughts. This technique usually works best if you write out the evidence you collect on a balance sheet. You place all the pros you can think of in one column and all the cons in a second column.

Vic used this method to help with his reactions to a problem at home. His wife had started to complain about his spending too much time worrying about work and not having fun with the family any more. His first response was a series of automatic thoughts that seemed to make him more depressed and withdrawn. "She's right, you're messing up at home too . . . You're a real slug . . . You're not good for much of anything." When Vic examined the evidence, he found some excellent ideas for changing his thinking and his behavior.

In the accompanying example, Vic used "examining the evidence" to revise his automatic thoughts and plan new ways of behaving. If you can start to find more logical thoughts, it often will stimulate you to take actions to cope with your problems or to do things differently. We suggest that you try this self-help exercise now.

Examining the Evidence
Vic's Example

Automatic Thought: "You're not good for much of anything."	
Evidence For	**Evidence Against**
I've been having trouble with a deadline at work.	I'm still working and supporting my family.
I'm not my usual self at home.	I'm getting into a better frame of mind to manage the problems at work.
I don't laugh anymore.	
I've been staying to myself at home and stewing about work.	I've been a good husband and father through the years.
I haven't done much of anything with my wife or kids for the last two months.	I know things I can enjoy doing with the kids (reading, shooting basketball, movies, etc.).
	They love you and just want you to get back to your old self.

Conclusion: "I'm good for many things. I'm just down on myself because I've been depressed. I need to put my work completely aside for at least seventy-five percent of the time I'm at home. I can make an effort to do things with my family and to lighten up. We all need to start enjoying life."

Exercise 3.4
Examining the Evidence

1. Pick an automatic thought that is particularly troublesome to you or is causing strong feelings.
2. Be a good judge. Collect and weigh all of the evidence, pro and con, that you can find. Be fair and objective.
3. Write down the evidence in two columns.
4. Now come up with a conclusion. Which thoughts are the most logical or realistic? How could you act differently if you believed the logical thoughts?

LEARN FROM OTHERS

The techniques for recognizing logical thoughts discussed so far have all involved searching your own mind for alternatives. You also can check out your thinking by getting the opinions of others. Instead of imagining what others might say, you can ask them directly for feedback. In some instances, this method can be riskier than asking yourself to be more objective. You have to carefully gauge the potential reactions of others before you take the plunge and ask them what they think.

As a general rule, we have found that people with depression overestimate the downside to talking directly with family members, friends, coworkers, or supervisors. Because they fear criticism or rejection, they tend to not ask for or get accurate feedback. This in turn, makes them assume that their negative predictions are true. They are like ostriches hiding their heads in the sand. Of course, it is possible that asking for feedback could backfire. Maybe your spouse or boss will unload on you and tell you that things are even worse than you thought. However, getting accurate feedback could help you recognize and own up to problems, if any. And if you are negatively distorting the facts, you may hear that others see positives or opportunities that you are ignoring. If you decide to ask someone for feedback, you can follow these tips to increase the chances of success.

First, pick someone you trust who you think will be honest but supportive. Then test the water first. Think of something to talk about that is not overly revealing. Tell them you want to get an objective opinion about the way you have been seeing things.

Remember this person isn't your therapist. Even if it's a good friend or someone else who is close to you, you probably shouldn't dump all of your problems on them. At this point, just try to see if they are willing and able to give you accurate feedback on how you are viewing yourself or a situation you are facing.

If you are trying to get feedback from a boss or another person who may not be entirely on your side, phrase the questions in a way that will protect your interests. For example, instead of saying: "I've been so depressed, I think I've screwed everything up," you could say: "I'd like to get your opinions on how I've been doing with this project . . . Could you let me know what you like about my plans and tell me if there are things you want me to change?"

A good way to get accurate feedback is to be in therapy with a professional who will help you sort out fact from fiction. A therapist can help you recognize your true strengths and take advantage of your assets, but also should be a reliable sounding board. When you have real problems or flaws, an effective therapist will work with you to find ways to cope or begin to act differently. Spiritual leaders like pastors, priests, and rabbis also can help point your way through the negative filter of depression to a more accurate and uplifting view of your life.

The Thinking Key isn't the only way to revise negative automatic thoughts. As you will see in the other chapters, all the keys can play a role in developing a more positive thinking style. For example, if you use the Action Key to change your behavior, your self-esteem will probably get a boost. Vic recognized that he needed to make an effort to do enjoyable activities with his family. After he changed his behavior, he had a much more favorable view of himself as a husband and father. Tony realized that he would like himself more if he got to work on a plan to go back to school so that he could get a new job. These examples point out the importance of taking action to make changes in your life. Try to avoid being an "armchair philosopher" who sits and thinks about changes but never does anything about it.

Antidepressants and other biological therapies described in the Biology Key also can be effective ways of reversing the negatively distorted perspective of depression. When these treatments are successful, they almost always help clear away the fog of depressive thinking. If you use the Relationship Key to promote better social interactions with the important people in your life, you are likely to think more positively about yourself and your loved ones. Michelle thought that she was a stronger person after she reestablished good relationships with her friends. The Spirituality Key can be another effective tool for revising the negative thinking of depression. If you can focus on finding meaning and having a sense of spiritual identity, you should have more strength to fight off negativity, hopelessness, and defeat.

Building Healthy Attitudes

So far you've learned about some of the methods for recognizing and changing depressive thinking. But, have you been able to rid your mind of all distortions or self-defeating tendencies? Is your self-esteem solid as a rock? Are your attitudes as healthy as they could be? If you have achieved all these things at this point, you are a rarity. Almost everyone who uses the self-help techniques of CBT will have the best success if they *practice* the methods over and over until they are almost like second nature. We'll ask you to update your Personal Plan for Recovery at the end of the next chapter when you complete your reading of the Thinking Key. Try to keep in mind that you will probably get more benefit from using cognitive therapy techniques if you build regular practice into your recovery plan.

The next chapter is all about building a healthy thinking style, one that will help you feel genuinely good about yourself and look forward to the future with real enthusiasm. We'll show you how to uncover the underlying rules of your thinking and work toward developing attitudes that can make you a happier and more effective person. The first stage in building this healthy thinking style is using the self-help methods you've learned in this chapter to recognize and change the negatively distorted thoughts of depression. After getting control of the negativity of depression, you can focus your efforts on developing a healthier thinking style that will increase your chances of staying well.

What Strengths Do You Have for Using the Thinking Key?

In Chapter 2, you made a list of personal strengths as part of your recovery plan. Now that you have learned some of the fundamentals of using the Thinking Key, you might be able to identify some additional strengths that could help you reach your goals. To get you started, we've put together a list of strengths that people commonly have for using the Thinking Key. This is only a partial list of numerous strengths that you may have for changing your thinking to help solve problems. Read over the list to see which of the statements apply to you.

The Thinking Key: Personal Strengths Checklist

Instructions:
Although you may feel weakened by depression, you probably have strengths that can help you to solve problems and to feel better. Use this rating system to identify possible strengths for using the Thinking Key.

> ++ = *I'm reasonably sure I have this strength.*
> + = *I may not have this strength right now, but I think I have the ability to build it.*

___ I have the ability to stand back from a situation and think through my reactions.
___ I am curious to learn about how my thinking could be involved in depression.
___ I like the idea of using my thinking to get better control over my emotions.
___ I have the capacity to learn how to use Thinking Key methods.

__ I have some positive attitudes about myself that could be strengthened.

__ I can see how my life could improve in the future.

__ I can recognize automatic thoughts that could be changed.

__ I can recognize thinking errors that could be changed.

__ I have support from others in trying to develop a healthier thinking style.

__ I want to change my thinking to help control depression.

Putting the Thinking Key into Action

Before going on to the next stage of the Thinking Key—learning how to change the basic rules of your thinking—we want to pause to give you some strategies for building the skills outlined in this chapter. There are two general strategies for putting these skills into action.

In both methods you first use the techniques described in this chapter to develop logical, realistic alternatives to depressive thinking and behavior. Then you either: (1) go right ahead—try out the changes and learn from the experience, or (2) rehearse the changes carefully in advance—then do what you planned. In the first method, you immediately put your new or revised thinking into effect and then check it out to see what happens. In some respects you are doing an experiment. Like a scientist you want to know if your theory (in this case a different way of thinking) is true.

If everything works out OK, then keep practicing so that the changes take hold. The self-help methods of the Thinking Key are designed to help you have success. But, you need to be open to the possibility that changes in your thinking may be off target. It could be that you have overestimated your ability to manage a situation or haven't anticipated certain problems. If this happens, you will need to go back to the drawing board. Take a problem-solving approach. Try not to get down on yourself. Rethink the situation and come up with some other alternatives.

The second method involves taking time to rehearse different scenarios in your mind. Therapists call this technique cognitive rehearsal because it involves practicing changes in both thinking and behavior. You forecast how you might respond to a specific situation if you let automatic thinking go unchanged. Then you plan out and rehearse one or more different approaches. The rehearsal can just be in your mind, or you can get someone you trust to help out. One of the advantages of being in therapy is that you have a pro to coach you on better ways of handling situations.

Tony used cognitive rehearsal when he was preparing to go to his wife's office party. He knew that if he fell back into his old style of automatic thinking he would put himself down and be miserable. So he did a Thought Record before he went to the party. He imagined how he might think and feel if he didn't make any changes. Next, he wrote out a plan for how he could think in a logical, self-affirming way. After he rehearsed the new thoughts and how he might act, the next step was to do what he planned.

Part of Tony's plan was to counter negative automatic thinking with thoughts such as: "The other people at the party won't be perfect . . . Everybody has problems . . . Don't fall into the trap of comparing yourself with them . . . Just because I don't have a high powered job, it doesn't mean that they're better than I am . . . I have a bunch of things going for me . . . I'm an interesting person and have lots to say . . . You can ask them questions about their own lives . . . That will get the ball rolling." Without these changes he probably would have stayed mostly to himself and tried to leave as early as possible. But, after rehearsing a healthy way of thinking, he was able to hold his own at the party.

You probably will not need to use cognitive rehearsal before you put most of your revised thoughts into action. Often just checking out your negative thinking will be enough to help you begin thinking and acting in a more adaptive way. However, if there is a situation that is especially important to you, the rehearsal technique may give you a better chance of doing well. Examples might include preparing for a job interview, discussing a significant problem with a loved one, or trying to resolve a conflict with a friend.

No matter which methods you use to put logical thoughts into action, it's a good idea to remember that you are *testing* a different way of seeing things. In a way, this is like trying a key in a lock. If it fits, use it. If it doesn't, try another one. You will be able to tell when it fits if you start to feel better and you realize that you are finding solutions to your problems.

4

Rules of Depression—
Rules of Wellness

D.r. Anne Marie Elliott was a dedicated and successful family physician. She had always believed that if she chose to do something, whether it was starting a practice or being married, she had to succeed, no matter what the cost. In fact, Anne Marie had been working so hard for so long to prove that she could make it both personally and professionally that she hadn't even noticed when it had stopped being fun and when depression had set in. It all hit her one dreary afternoon when she caught herself looking at the medications in her cabinet at work and thinking how easy it would be to take a bottle or two and quietly die. She went to her office and closed the door behind her, shutting out a world that had become full of demands and disappointments. She realized that her drive to be successful at all costs had been effective, but gave her no real pleasure. Her life felt empty. There was no passion in her marriage, no children in her home, no close friends, no sense of purpose. All she had time for was a practice full of financial burdens and fears. She had created her own misery just to prove that she could make it, that she was good enough to succeed.

Luckily, Anne Marie's office manager Manesha was very perceptive and noticed the change in her boss's demeanor that day. When she got no response to her knock on the doctor's door, Manesha used her master key to let herself in. Anne Marie looked up, tears streaming down her face. "I'll be out in a minute. Just taking a little break." Manesha noticed the bottles of medicine on the desk and took a seat across from the doctor. "What can I do to help?" she gently inquired.

After some time, Anne Marie began to open up about how empty her life seemed. She and her husband had grown so far apart that it seemed unlikely they could ever find their way back to one another. "I realize now that when I married him it was partially out of fear of never finding anyone better. I thought I could learn to love him the way you are supposed to love a man. I really wanted our marriage to be successful just like I wanted my career to be successful, but somewhere among the long workdays and finding excuses to avoid one another on the weekends, the distance grew. I've failed us both."

Anne Marie wept and confided further in Manesha that although she had always believed she had to succeed at whatever she chose to take on, it wasn't worth it any more. "It would be so much easier on everyone if I could just disappear."

Manesha excused herself from the office and called Dr. Bell, a psychiatrist whose office was on the same floor of their professional building. He agreed to stop by and have a talk with Anne Marie. Although she pretended to be angry with Manesha for overreacting, Anne Marie trusted Dr. Bell as a colleague and thought that she should give him at least one try before giving up altogether.

Anne Marie told Dr. Bell how she had been feeling. He listened and thoughtfully replied, "It sounds like you have been telling yourself for years that you had to succeed at work no matter what the cost. Now that you have made it, you are realizing how much wear and tear it's had on you, on your marriage, and on the quality of your life. You are falling into the mindset that many driven people have when they are depressed; you feel like a failure at life because your success has not led to the rewards you expected. Having the attitude that you must succeed at whatever you choose to do no matter what the personal costs has helped to motivate you to work hard all these years. But that single-minded drive has also kept you from looking around at what you were losing in the meantime. Now that all or nothing view is making you think that just because your life is not as perfect as you had planned, it has no value at all."

"That's exactly how I feel. Am I a hopeless case?" Anne Marie inquired.

"No you're not hopeless," Dr. Bell reassured her, "but you do need some help to find your way out of depression and to develop a new attitude toward life. I want you to see a therapist I know. She can help you figure out what you need to do to have a healthier and more balanced view."

Attitudes play a big role in depression. Your attitudes are your rules of thinking—they tell you who you are, how to behave, how you expect others to react to you, and how you expect things to go in the future. These basic attitudes are sometimes called "schemas." The thinking rule about success that got Anne Marie into trouble is an example of a schema. Some other examples are "To be accepted, I must always please others" and "I must always be in control."

One of the central principles of cognitive-behavior therapy (CBT) is that underlying, dysfunctional, or hurtful schemas become intensified in depression, while healthier schemas tend to lose their force or be forgotten. When these changes occur, your rules of thinking shift so far to the negative side that it becomes difficult to think clearly or to figure out solutions to your problems. You are operating primarily with self-defeating rules that drag you down and make you feel like a failure. An important goal of this chapter is to show you ways to spot unhealthy schemas and turn them around.

While there was no question that Anne Marie was having actual problems in her relationship with her husband and in her work, it was her rigid rules of thinking that were driving her to the verge of suicide. She revealed later that she had come to believe that suicide would be easier than admitting "failure" to her parents, friends, colleagues, and her husband.

Can the Rules Be Changed?

Cognitive-behavior therapists devote a great deal of energy and effort to uncovering and changing basic rules of thinking. It can be a bit more challenging than uncovering automatic thoughts that you learned about in Chapter 3. Schemas are the core beliefs, attitudes, or basic rules of thinking that are deeply embedded in your thought processes. Your schemas have been developing since you were a small child and have been shaped by all of your life experiences. Some of these rules may be very useful to you; others may be holding you back or even driving you into depression.

Often these basic rules operate under the surface of our thinking without our being fully aware of their presence. For example, Anne Marie was totally unaware of the powerful effects of her schema "If I choose to do something, I must succeed no matter what the cost" until she started therapy. People who are involved in CBT work together with their therapists to uncover these basic rules of thinking. The self-help exercises in this chapter can help you do the same thing.

Often stressful life events, such as relationship disputes or breakups, job problems, health issues, or financial difficulties, can trigger the emergence of negative schemas that have been dormant or suppressed. When this happens, the dysfunctional rules of thinking cloud perception and

Key Points

1. Underlying rules of thinking are called schemas.
2. One of the primary goals of cognitive-behavior therapy is to change unhealthy or dysfunctional schemas.
3. The self-help exercises of this chapter are designed to help you find your schemas and to work toward changing the ones that are giving you trouble.

make you have depressing automatic thoughts. The next example shows how this can happen.

Vic had several schemas that came to the surface after he was stressed with the demands of an important building project. Like many successful people, Vic had an underlying negative attitude that he was a fake and didn't know what he was doing. Despite years of experience as an architect, lots of positive feedback from customers and partners, and awards for many of his designs, Vic still had this damaging schema: "If people really knew me, they would realize I'm a fraud." When things were going well, this rule didn't affect Vic very much. It faded into the background. But when he ran into trouble at work, this negative belief reemerged and played a big role in the downward spiral of his depression.

In the course of Vic's therapy, he discovered that he had a number of other dysfunctional schemas such as: "I must be perfect to be accepted," "No matter what I do, I won't succeed," and "I must always be in control." Can you see how these types of basic rules would set Vic up for problems when things didn't go perfectly at work? Fortunately, all of us have also developed positive or adaptive schemas that help us manage the challenges of life. Vic had healthy ones too, but they had been submerged in a sea of depressive thinking. He needed to use techniques from the Thinking Key to counter the negative schemas and promote or build up his positive or adaptive thinking rules.

In Chapter 3, you learned about the three steps of using the self-help methods of CBT: (1) *recognize* depressive thinking and behavior, (2) *change* the way you think and behave, and (3) *build* healthy attitudes and coping styles. You will use the same three steps here to make your schemas work as friends instead of foes. You *can* change your basic attitudes. We'll show you examples of how schemas can be changed and give you self-help techniques that you can use to rewrite some of your own rules of thinking. First you will need to find the schemas that may be setting you up for depression.

Be a Detective: Discover Your Basic Rules

Because schemas are deeply embedded in your thinking, it may be hard to spot them at first glance. Like automatic thoughts, they can operate without your being aware of what is going on. My (Jesse) personal example will show you how a rule that is operating just below the radar screen can be difficult to detect.

For the past two generations on both sides of my family, a disaster that led to financial troubles occurred to most of my close relatives between the ages of forty and sixty. My grandfather and father had a family business that ran into difficulties and then failed. All three of my uncles lost their jobs at one point. And, my mother's father died suddenly of appendicitis when she was thirteen and my grandmother was forty years old. This was at the height of the depression of the last century. Although I didn't realize it until I was in my forties myself, I had developed a schema that had an enormous influence on my life: "No matter how hard you try, the same thing (a loss leading to a financial disaster) will happen to you."

Many of our thinking rules have both advantages and disadvantages. In my case, the schema probably influenced my decision to become a physician. In retrospect, I think that I piled more and more degrees after my name in an effort to insulate me from the troubles that befell my family members. I probably believed that the medical profession was safer than going into business. The schema may have had some positive benefits in stimulating me to study to become a doctor and to be careful about how I managed money, but it also had its downside.

Several years ago, a patient who was in the hospital where I am Chief of Psychiatry attempted suicide and injured herself. I was really upset about the suicide attempt, and was even more upset when she sued all of the doctors who had seen her or were in an administrative position at the hospital. I felt sorry for the patient, but didn't think I had done anything wrong. One part of my brain was telling me that I would get through this OK. But, my schema about financial disaster was making the situation a lot worse than it needed to be. At times my automatic thoughts were spinning out of control.

"You'll lose everything . . . You'll be out in the street . . . Your reputation is ruined . . . No one will ever refer you another patient . . . It's only a matter of time before things will fall apart." Of course when I started thinking this way, my emotional state was a sorry sight. I was tense, on edge, and full of dread. As a practicing cognitive-behavior therapist, it was time for me to take my own medicine. I needed to use the techniques from Chapter 3 to recognize and change automatic thoughts. But more importantly, I had to discover the underlying schema that was driving me to have these types of automatic thoughts.

RECOGNIZING THINKING PATTERNS

One of the methods used in CBT to discover schemas is to look for recurring patterns or themes. If you keep having the same types of automatic thoughts, it may mean that a basic rule is operating below the surface. Exercise 4.1 can help sharpen your skills for finding underlying rules of thinking. Try to pick the schema that fits best as a controlling rule for these thought patterns. Match one number to each of the letters in the exercise.

=====

Exercise 4.1
Finding Schemas in Patterns of Automatic Thoughts

Automatic Thoughts	Dysfunctional Schemas
1. "You'll lose everything . . . You'll be out in the street . . . It's only a matter of time before things will fall apart." (Jesse)	__ A. I'm a fake.
2. "This job is too much for me . . . I don't know what I'm doing . . . Everyone is bound to find out soon." (Vic)	__ B. Without a man, I'm nothing.
3. "She's calling me just because I'm lonely and miserable . . . My husband didn't want me . . . Why would anyone want to be around me?" (Michelle)	__ C. I'm not as good as other people.
4. "Everyone else seems so intelligent and has so much to say. Compared to them, I'm a real loser." (Tony)	__ D. No matter how hard you try, the same thing (financial disaster) will happen to you.

Answers: A.2, B.3, C.4, D.1.

We included this exercise to show you that you can spot negative schemas by looking for patterns of automatic thoughts. You can use the same technique to find your healthy schemas. An excellent way to uncover both negative and positive rules of thinking is to go back over the Thought Change Records that you completed in Chapter 3. Look at several different thought records. What themes or patterns start to emerge? If you can't see any patterns at this point, keep writing out thought records until you begin to recognize the underlying rules that control your thinking.

USE A SCHEMA INVENTORY

If you read over a list of common schemas, you will probably be able to recognize some of your own rules or beliefs. Read over the list of schemas in Exercise 4.2 and check the ones that you think might apply to you. You might find that they apply to some situations, but not all; for example they apply at work, but not at home.

Later in the chapter, you'll learn methods of changing schemas. It might help now for you to review the inventory and mark the dysfunctional attitudes that you are relatively certain you want to rewrite. Changing these beliefs will be an important part of your Personal Plan for Recovery. You could also mark healthy schemas that you might not believe very strongly right now, but could build up in the future. Some of these could be excellent opportunities for improving your self-esteem through positive rules of thinking.

REVIEW YOUR LIFE EXPERIENCES

Dr. Benjamin Carson is a world-renowned neurosurgeon who has performed some of the most complex neurosurgical operations in history. One of his triumphs was a twenty-eight-hour procedure to separate Siamese twins who were joined at the head. Both twins survived and were neurologically normal. This success is remarkable in itself, but is even more remarkable when you hear about Dr. Carson's early life. He grew up as a fatherless, African-American boy in Detroit. In an interview in the *New York Times*, Dr. Carson described how a change in attitude opened up a world of opportunity.

Q. "You were an underachiever as a child?
A. "Yes. I had a low opinion of myself—like so many young people today. When I thought I was stupid, I acted like a stupid person. And when I thought I was smart, I acted like a smart person and achieved like a smart person. . . . Even as late as my

Exercise 4.2
Take an Inventory of Your Schemas

Instructions: Use this checklist to search for possible underlying rules of thinking. Place a check mark beside each schema that you think you may have.

Healthy Schemas

___ No matter what happens, I can manage somehow.

___ If I work hard at something, I can master it.

___ I'm a survivor.

___ Others trust me.

___ I'm a solid person.

___ People respect me.

___ They can knock me down, but they can't knock me out.

___ I care about other people.

___ If I prepare in advance, I usually do better.

___ I deserve to be respected.

___ I like to be challenged.

___ There's not much that can scare me.

___ I'm intelligent.

___ I can figure things out.

___ I'm friendly.

___ I can handle stress.

___ The tougher the problem, the tougher I become.

___ I can learn from my mistakes and be a better person.

___ I'm a good spouse (and/or parent, child, friend, lover).

___ Everything will work out all right.

Dysfunctional Schemas

___ I must be perfect to be accepted.

___ If I choose to do something, I must succeed.

___ I'm stupid.

___ Without a woman (man), I'm nothing.

___ I'm a fake.

___ Never show weakness.

___ I'm unlovable.

___ If I make one mistake, I'll lose everything.

___ I'll never be comfortable around others.

___ I can never finish anything.

___ No matter what I do, I won't succeed.

___ The world is too frightening.

___ Others can't be trusted.

___ I must always be in control.

___ I'm unattractive.

___ Never show your emotions.

___ Other people will take advantage of me.

___ I'm lazy.

___ If people really knew me, they wouldn't like me.

___ To be accepted, I must always please others.

first year in medical school, my faculty advisor advised me to drop out. He said I wasn't medical school material. Interestingly, I told that story last June when I was the commencement speaker at my medical school."

This inspirational story emphasizes the tremendous importance of attitudes in determining the outcome of our lives. Dr. Carson gives credit to his mother, who he said always believed in him and "kept telling me I was smart." Of course Dr. Carson must have had the basic intelligence and personality strengths to serve as building blocks for his education and experience as a neurosurgeon. Yet without this attitude change it is unlikely that his life would have taken such a positive course.

Our attitudes or rules of thinking can be shaped to a large extent by the important people and events in our lives. Dr. Carson's mother kept telling him he was smart. When this message finally got through, Dr. Carson was able to eliminate his self-defeating attitudes and become a successful neurosurgeon.

In contrast, Anne Marie's parents were very loving and supportive, but they were also perfectionistic and demanding. Her father was a successful businessman who was very self-determined and seemed to be an expert at everything. After she started therapy, Anne Marie began to realize that growing up in a perfectionistic environment had played a large part in coming to believe that "if I choose to do something, I must succeed no matter what the cost."

Exercise 4.3 asks you to take the role of a detective in thinking back over the significant influences in your life. Use your notebook to write out the answers to these questions.

Exercise 4.3
How Life Experiences Have Shaped My Rules of Thinking

1. Who are the most influential people in your life? These people might be parents, other family members, friends, classmates, teachers, bosses, heroes, mentors, or even inspirational persons you have read about. Which people do you believe have made a real difference in the way you think about yourself or the world around you?

2. How did each of these people shape your way of thinking in a positive direction? Which affirmative or adaptive messages got across? What rules of thinking did they teach you that you want to retain and nourish?

(continued on next page)

3. What negative schemas do you think may have been stimulated by your relationships with any of these people?
4. To boost your memory, try to think of important or emotionally charged interactions with these people. Imagine yourself back in these situations and concentrate on what rules of thinking may have been communicated.
5. Next we want you to think back over any especially significant events in your life that could have affected your rules of thinking. Write down some happy events or times of accomplishment or success. Also note some of the more upsetting or traumatic events in your life. What basic attitudes do you think may have been stimulated or influenced by these events?
6. Now consider your spiritual, religious, or philosophical beliefs. Do you have personal schemas that have been affected by these beliefs?

Changing Your Schemas

In the last chapter we emphasized that just recognizing your automatic thoughts can get you to the point of making changes in your thinking. The same thing is true for schemas. The difference is, your schemas have been with you a long time, and it may take you a while to modify or revise them. We've included some exercises here that you can use to rewrite your dysfunctional schemas and build healthier attitudes. At the end of the chapter, we'll make suggestions for how you can incorporate these methods in your Personal Plan for Recovery.

KEEP A PERSONAL SCHEMA LIST

One of the easiest and most helpful things you can do is to keep a comprehensive written list of all the rules of thinking that you have been able to uncover. A written list will help keep schema change at the top of your mind. In our therapy practices, we have been confounded many times by alert and intelligent patients who seem to forget the schemas that we spent so much time unearthing in previous therapy sessions. There is a natural tendency for schemas to slip into the background of our thinking where they continue to exert their effects without us recognizing what is going on.

Exercise 4.4 will help you get started. Don't forget to refer to the list frequently as you focus on changing your basic rules of thinking.

Exercise 4.4
My Personal Schema List

1. Allow enough room in your notebook to make a list of all the schemas you've identified. Save some space for schemas you may think of later or revisions that you will make.
2. Write out two columns and label them "Healthy Schemas" and "Dysfunctional Schemas."
3. Review Exercises 4.1–4.3. Record all of the schemas that you have spotted so far.
4. Some rules of thinking may have both positive and negative features. Place the schema in the column that you think describes its strongest or most potent effects.

EXAMINING THE EVIDENCE FOR SCHEMAS

You learned how to *examine the evidence* for automatic thoughts in Chapter 3. We'll use a version of this method now to check out the validity of your underlying rules of thinking. You probably will be able to find at least a small amount of evidence that supports some of your negative or dysfunctional schemas. After all there must have been some reason you have hung on to these beliefs for such a long time. Spotting the evidence that supports these schemas can give you good ideas on what you might need to change. Maybe you will need to make some adjustments in the rule to make it work better for you. Or, it might be that you will need to set some goals to change your behavior.

Before getting started with this exercise we want to warn you about one potential pitfall. Sometimes people with depression record evidence for their negative schemas that is actually *false* evidence. They are so locked into their negatively distorted way of seeing things that they magnify or exaggerate evidence that backs up their dysfunctional schemas. Sometimes they cook up evidence where none exists. Sally fell into this trap as she was trying to overcome the negative schemas that fueled her eating disorder and her depression.

One of Sally's beliefs was "I have to be perfect to be accepted." When she did the examining-the-evidence exercise, she wrote these things in the "evidence for" column: "I'll never find the right man unless I look my best . . . Only thin people get what they want in this world . . . People always treat me better when I try to be perfect . . . Everybody likes people who are a success." Most of these statements are loaded with the thinking errors that you learned in Chapter 3. Sally was using all-or-none thinking, ignoring the evidence, magnifiying and minimizing, and other cognitive distortions to support her belief in this rule. When you examine the evidence for your schemas, keep your mind on finding the truth. To do this, you will need to shed your cognitive distortions.

Jeb had the same negative schema ("I'm stupid") that Dr. Benjamin Carson fought successfully. But, Jeb wasn't quite in the same league of intelligence and talent as Dr. Carson. He had scraped through high school without studying at all and had then gone into the Army because he didn't think he was college material. Even though Jeb had done well during his eight-year stint in the military, he was scared that he couldn't make it in the civilian world. He had signed up for a two-year associate-degree program in electronics and computers because he had studied these things in the Army. Now he was depressed and was thinking of dropping out of the course before he even got started.

The following example shows how Jeb was able to use the examining the evidence technique to change a negative schema. The steps used here were: (1) identify a schema, (2) list evidence for and against the rule, (3) look over the "evidence for" to see if there are any cognitive distortions that are leading to false conclusions, (4) write down some ideas for changing the rule.

Examining the Evidence for Schemas
Jeb's Example

Step 1:

Schema I Want to Change:	Degree of Belief in Schema:
I'm stupid.	*90%*

Step 2:

Evidence for Schema:	Evidence Against Schema:
1. I got bad grades in high school.	1. When I buckled down in the Army, I got some of the best marks in the class.
2. I always think that other people are smarter than I am.	2. I got regular promotions in the Army.
3. I don't have a college degree.	

(continued on next page)

4. I feel stupid around people that have made it (officers, people with good jobs, guys that didn't go into the Army who are way ahead of me in life).

3. I know a lot about computers.
4. I never studied in high school. I could have done much better.
5. I'm more mature now, and I can study hard.
6. I know how to do things that some "smart" people can't do (fix cars, build fishing rods, do electrical wiring).

Step 3:

Cognitive Errors in Evidence For Column:

1. All-or-none thinking—I need to stop this black and white thinking. It's not true that everybody else is smart and I am dumb. I'm not the most brilliant guy in the world, but I can hold my own.
2. Overgeneralizing—Because I messed up in high school, it doesn't mean that I'm totally stupid or that I'll always get bad grades.
3. Ignoring the evidence—I'm smart enough to get a degree.

Step 4:

After examining the evidence, my degree of belief (0–100%) in this schema is now: *15%*

Ideas I have now for changing this schema are:

1. I haven't always used it, but I have enough intelligence to succeed.
2. I need to use my intelligence well.
3. I'm smart in some ways.
4. I can build my knowledge through study and hard work.

Jeb's example of examining the evidence shows how thinking through both sides of the argument can give you ideas on how you might rewrite your schemas and begin to act differently. Anne Marie used the same method to attack her schema "If I choose to do something, I must succeed no matter what the cost." When she examined the evidence, she found plenty of reasons to drop this belief and find new ways to live her life. Her "evidence against" this schema included these observations: "This rule is too demanding—no one can be a success at everything they do . . . My parents never really told me I had to be a success at everything I did—I just assumed that they required this of me . . . There have been many times in the past that I've coped well with decisions that haven't worked out (such as the time I bought a car that was a 'lemon') . . . I can make a mistake, like all the rest of the people in the world, and still be a good person."

Now that you've seen some examples of how to examine the evidence for maladaptive schemas, we want you to try out this method for reworking some of your own rules of thinking.

Exercise 4.5
Examining the Evidence for Schemas

1. Check over your Personal Schema List and put a mark beside some of the rules that you would like to change. If you haven't written out a Personal Schema List yet, you can review the other exercises in this chapter to identify an attitude or belief that you want to examine.
2. Choose a schema that is causing problems—one that you believe could be revised into a healthier rule of thinking. Use a 0–100% scale to rate how strongly you believe the schema now.
3. Write down the evidence for and against this schema in two columns. Remember to be a detective—look for as much evidence as you can collect.
4. Next look over the evidence to see if there are any cognitive distortions in your thinking. Record the distortions and write down comments you have on ways to think more clearly or logically.
5. Now rate your belief in the schema again on a 0–100% scale.
6. Try to think of any possible changes you could make in this rule so that it would work better for you. Write your ideas in your notebook.

WEIGHING THE ADVANTAGES
AND DISADVANTAGES

Anne Marie's schema, "If I choose to do something, I must succeed no matter what the cost," had caused a great deal of pain, but it also had been a positive force in many areas of her life. She had been a top student and now was a hard-working doctor who always tried to do her best. Because the rule had both advantages and disadvantages, she couldn't just throw it out without considering how to retain some of its good features. In revising these types of schemas, it's usually best to modify them so that you don't give up all of their benefits. One thing that we have seen over and over in our therapy practices is that people do not give up schemas easily if they have had a positive payoff for them in life—even when their negative effects are very harmful. The trick here is to rewrite the schema in a way that continues the positive or adaptive behavior, but removes the downside to the rule of thinking. Anne Marie used the "Weighing Advantages and Disadvantages" technique to help her do this.

Weighing Advantages and Disadvantages
Anne Marie's Example

Schema I want to change:
"If I choose to do something, I must succeed no matter what the cost."

ADVANTAGES	DISADVANTAGES
1. I have always worked hard.	1. If things don't work out, I'm devastated. I feel like a failure.
2. I've had many successes (school awards, grades, scholarships, medical practice is very busy).	2. I don't know how to handle situations where I can't solve the problem.
3. I don't quit easily.	3. I'm so driven, I can never relax.
	4. There are some things I don't even try because I don't want to be second rate. I have to be an expert at everything I do.
	5. I can't admit any of my problems to others. I have to look like I'm strong and in control at all times.

(continued on next page)

Ideas I have now for changing this schema are:

1. If I choose to do something, I would *like* to succeed. But, I don't have to succeed at everything I do.
2. I can learn to handle situations where I don't have total success. Imperfections or problems don't mean that I'm a failure.
3. It will be good for me to do things where I'm not an expert. I can learn to enjoy myself and relax if I'm not always striving for success.
4. Sometimes the costs of success are so great that they make it not worth the effort. You need to keep your eye on the big picture while you are working to achieve.

Changing this schema made an enormous difference in how Anne Marie coped with her marital and work problems. Her old, rigid attitudes had boxed her into a corner. The new schema was much more flexible. She was able to revise the rules so that she had room to "fail," or to be less than a total success, while she still maintained high standards of performance.

Anne Marie realized that her old schema had limited her ability to enjoy her medical practice, develop a better relationship with her husband, and relax and have fun. The adjustments in her schema didn't take anything away from her skills as a physician. But, she noticed that her attitudes about work were shifting toward a much healthier perspective. Instead of worrying incessantly about making a mistake or continually focusing on problems with the business side of her practice, Anne Marie was getting back in touch with why she went into medicine in the first place—to help people. One of the signs that she had changed at work was that she had started to use her sense of humor again. Instead of walking around all day looking tense and unhappy, Anne Marie could sometimes joke with her patients to get their minds off their problems.

The schema revisions also had a positive effect on Anne Marie's life outside work. The biggest difference was in her relationship with her husband. She had been close to giving up on the marriage because it didn't seem to match up to her ideal of a loving and romantic relationship. And, she had been continually berating herself for not being able to make the marriage work. With therapy she was able to be more accepting of the mistakes that both she and her husband had made, and was more realistic about her expectations for the relationship. More importantly, Anne Marie started to take some constructive actions to improve the situation. Her new schemas helped her make good use of some of the specific techniques for improving communication described in the Relationship Key section of this book.

Another area of Anne Marie's life that needed to be changed was her use (or lack of use) of leisure time. Her driven, perfectionistic schemas had taken a toll in this area too. For example, Anne Marie had always wanted to learn how to play tennis and had been invited many times to join a doubles league for beginners. But, she couldn't handle looking like a beginner. Playing tennis for fun, and possibly making new friends along the way, was just one example of the many opportunities she had avoided because of her old schema: "If I choose to do something, I must succeed no matter what the cost."

As part of her therapy, Anne Marie agreed to join the tennis league and to follow these guidelines: (1) focus on enjoying the experience and meeting new people, (2) try to learn basic skills, but don't strive to be the top player at the club—save the quest for total excellence for areas where it really counts, such as being a great doctor, (3) realize it's OK to make mistakes when you are a beginner—lighten up and laugh at the situation instead of putting yourself down or getting frustrated. The tennis league experience helped Anne Marie learn that in many situations she was actually more successful and got along better with others if she didn't pursue perfection.

TIPS FOR CHANGING SCHEMAS

We hope you will be like Anne Marie and be successful in reworking the schemas that make you depressed or hold you down from reaching your potential. Some of these tips may help you change your basic rules of thinking.

LOOK FOR THE ABSOLUTES

Words such as "always," "never," and "must" in a schema usually mean that you are falling victim to all-or-none thinking. Try substituting others that are more reasonable. Changing just one word ("I would *like* to succeed," instead of "I *must* succeed") made a big difference to Anne Marie in how she coped with her marital problems and the other difficulties she was facing.

WATCH FOR "IF-THEN STATEMENTS"

Schemas can be constructed so that *if* the first part of the rule is applied or the first part of the condition exists, *then* you are locked into responding in a certain way. Examples might be "If I choose to do something, I must succeed no matter what the cost," "If I make one mistake, I'll lose everything," "Without a woman (man), I'm nothing," and "If people really knew me, they wouldn't like me." Use the Thinking Key to break the lock of "if-then statements." Go over your Personal Schema List to look for these types of rules, and modify them so that they are more reasonable and give you more room for personal growth.

BRAINSTORM

In the previous chapter, we gave an example of using brainstorming to come up with alternatives to automatic thoughts. This technique also works well in generating ideas for changing schemas. Instead of sticking to a rigid or narrow way of thinking about the possibilities, write down all your ideas—even if they may seem to be on the wild side. Think of the most extreme change you could make in a thinking rule and then think of the smallest or most subtle ways you could rewrite it.

Michelle had a very common schema that has caused trouble for many people when they go through a separation or divorce. Somehow, she had come to believe that "without a man, I'm nothing." When Michelle was trying to modify this belief she did some brainstorming and came up with several different ideas. Some of the possible modifications were minor ones that wouldn't help her very much: "Without a man, I won't be accepted by others . . . Without a man, I'll always be lonely . . . Without a man . . . I'll have trouble fitting into society." She also was able to think of some more extreme changes: "Men are worthless, I don't care what they say or do . . . I'm immune to men, they don't mean anything to me . . . I have no need for a close relationship with a man." It made her feel better temporarily to fantasize that men were worthless or meant nothing to her, but Michelle knew that these changes were too extreme to be realistic.

Her list contained some other possibilities that held more promise: "I can believe in myself, no matter how men react to me . . . I'm a good person and deserve to be happy, even if a man is not in my life . . . I won't let a man be the judge of my self-worth . . . I would like to have a relationship with a man again, but my worth will never be dependent on any man." After doing the brainstorming exercise, she decided to adopt all of these helpful attitudes. Michelle recognized that she needed to sever the link between her self-esteem and having a relationship with a man. But, when she was honest with herself, she admitted that she would still like to have another man in her life sometime in the future.

IMAGINE HOW YOU WOULD ACT DIFFERENTLY
IF YOU ADOPTED A NEW SCHEMA

Changing your rules of thinking can pay big dividends in making you act in more effective or self-affirming ways. Take a few minutes to write down the ways you might act differently if you developed a new schema. Try to imagine how your behavior would change. Do you like the picture you see? Could you make any additional revisions in the rule that would make it work even better for you?

One of Tony's negative schemas was "I'm not as good as other people." When he believed this rule, he had poor self-esteem and had trouble feeling comfortable in social situations. Part of his therapy was to imagine how he would change if a new one were put into effect. He decided that the best alternative was "I have many strengths and can hold my own around others."

Some of the changes that he predicted for how he would act around his wife's coworkers were: (1) I will initiate conversations instead of just hanging on the fringes of the group; (2) I will stand taller and exude more self-confidence; (3) I won't be afraid to talk about things in my own life (my job, movies I've seen, books I've read, my hobbies, etc.); (4) I will show a genuine interest in other people instead of being so defensive and self-absorbed; (5) My wife will be happier because I'll be more relaxed when I'm socializing with other people.

USE YOUR SENSE OF HUMOR

If you listen closely to comedians, you'll hear many of them use self-deprecation as a major part of their act. They put themselves down, look silly, have a bumbling attitude, or even fall to the ground to get laughs. When Chevy Chase was interviewed for a *New York Times* article after release of his movie *Snow Day,* he talked about having to wear Jack Frost and Hawaiian get-ups: "No, I've never stooped quite this low in any film." Then the reporter reminded him of *Oh Heavenly Dog* with Benji. "Yeah, I stooped pretty low in that one—I'll give you that."

Did you ever stop to think about why comedians can make us laugh when they criticize themselves, but people with depression are deadly serious about all of their perceived weaknesses? Depression makes most people become so negatively self-absorbed that they lose their sense of humor. Unlike Chevy Chase, Steve Martin, or a host of other comics, they see absolutely no humor in their plight. Depression certainly isn't any fun. You can't laugh your way out of it. But, you can try to relax a bit and look for a vein of humor in your situation. Who knows? A laugh here and there might give you some new ideas for changing your rules of depression to rules of wellness.

Try Asking Yourself These Questions About Your Sense of Humor:

1. Is there a way that you could find some humor in your maladaptive schemas? Are some of them so extreme that you could gently laugh with yourself at having them?
2. Can you experiment with being more playful or lighthearted in thinking of changes in your schemas? When you brainstorm, are there some ideas that are so outrageous that you can begin to chuckle?
3. If you imagine different ways of acting with a new schema, are there some funny situations that might occur? Could you handle these funny situations? Would they help you fight depression?
4. Can opportunities to use your sense of humor be built into your new schemas?

Rules of Wellness—Building a Healthy Thinking Style

Rules of wellness are the adaptive, healthy schemas that make you think clearly and use your assets to their best advantage. So far in this chapter we've focused primarily on spotting and changing dysfunctional schemas—the rules of depression. Building your rules of wellness can also be an important feature of your Personal Plan for Recovery.

When people try to change, it almost always helps to log the efforts. Whether it's an exercise program, a diet, or something more complex like changing attitudes, a written record can help you stay on course to meet your goals. We've used this technique many times in our own lives—even to keep on track to complete this book! A good log should help you organize your efforts to change, stimulate you to monitor your progress, and reinforce you for making gains.

Exercise 4.6 will give you some ideas for a Schema Change Log. You can use this system, or devise your own method for setting up a log. We've often seen our patients skip over this step of logging schema change because they think they can do all of their attitude adjustments in their heads. This is usually a mistake. A Schema Change Log will help you stay focused on strengthening your rules of wellness until you forge a new style of thinking.

Exercise 4.6
Schema Change Log

1. Use your notebook to log your efforts to develop healthier rules of thinking.
2. On separate pages, write down each schema that you are trying to change.
3. Then note at least one new or revised schema to substitute for each of the ones that are giving you trouble. These new attitudes will be part of your rules of wellness.
4. Write down your plans for putting the rules of wellness into action. Think of specific situations where you can apply them.
5. Do the things you planned.
6. Record your progress on the Schema Change Log.
7. If you run into difficulties in implementing the rules of wellness, note your ideas for further changes in your schemas or in your plans to put them into action.

PRACTICING RULES OF WELLNESS

When you develop new schemas, make sure to try them out in real life situations. In order to make the new rules stick, you will need to use them over and over until they replace your old ones. Take time every day to think about how you are building your rules of wellness, use the Schema Change Log to keep a record of your progress, and try to keep using the new rules until they become second nature. The three most important words to remember to strengthen healthy attitudes are "practice, practice, practice."

If you are not sure you can actually follow a new rule or are having trouble seeing how you could put it into action, use the rehearsal techniques we described in the last chapter to try out new ways of thinking and behaving. Cognitive rehearsal involves imagining and practicing in advance how you would act in a specific situation if you adopted a revised schema. If you can think through a situation before you actually are in it, you may have a better chance for success.

Anne Marie used cognitive rehearsal to help her prepare to use new schemas when she joined the tennis league. Some of her ideas for rules of wellness were: "Imperfections or problems don't mean that I'm a failure. It will be good for me to do things where I'm not an expert. I can learn to enjoy myself and relax if I'm not always striving for success." Before getting started with league play, Anne Marie had to go to a tennis clinic where she would get rated on her skill level. When she used cognitive rehearsal, she first tried to imagine how she would react if she followed her old schema, "If I choose to do something, I must succeed no matter what the cost." The outcome wasn't very pretty. Anne Marie concluded that she would be tense and driven, would be focused entirely on herself instead of getting to know the others who were joining the league, and wouldn't enjoy the experience at all.

Practicing how she would act with the new schemas led to a happier conclusion. She was able to see lots of opportunities for breaking away from her old rules of depression. However, as Anne Marie rehearsed the scene in her mind, she could identify several trouble points. One of these was having to wear a tennis outfit that would show that she wasn't in terrific shape any longer. Over the past few years, she had gained a few pounds. Now she was faced with the dilemma of whether she could handle looking less than perfect in order to get involved in a sport that could help her relax, enjoy herself, and shape up. Another potential trouble point was getting a rating from the instructor on her skill level. What would happen if she got the worst rating? How would she react? How could she use her new schemas if she had to start at the lowest rung of the beginner's league?

Many successful people use rehearsal techniques to prepare themselves for doing well in upcoming events. Championship athletes visualize how they could react to challenging situations in the game ahead. Downhill skiers imagine themselves on the slope and have a plan in advance for how they will handle a treacherous part of the course or sudden changes such as a gust of wind or an icy patch. Business executives think through how they will answer difficult questions in an important meeting. Top performers and lecturers envision the possible reactions of the audience, and are well prepared to make adjustments if the audience isn't responding.

Anne Marie certainly wasn't a championship athlete, and her goal in using cognitive rehearsal wasn't to be the best tennis player in the league. In her case, the rehearsal was geared toward sticking with her new rules of wellness in situations where she wasn't a total success. She worked out these plans for managing the two potential trouble spots.

1. Appearing in tennis shorts in front of others: "I'll write the new rules on the palm of my hand and look at them if I start to feel like quitting. I won't lose sight of why I'm doing this in the first place—to have fun doing something where I'm not the top dog! It actually will be good for me to show up looking less than perfect. I'll buy a new tennis outfit that I feel comfortable wearing. Then I'll just start playing and forget about how I look."

2. Getting rated by the tennis instructor: "I'll think to myself—this is just a tennis game, it isn't an ultimate test. Even if I get placed in the lowest class, I can still enjoy this sport. There would be some pluses to getting a lower rating—there wouldn't be so much pressure to perform, and there would be more room to move up in the rankings as I practice more. I'll just try to be myself when I play, and not try to impress the instructor. She'll know which league will be best for me."

Have you been thinking of ways you could rehearse your rules of wellness? Exercise 4.7 can help you build your skills in using healthy schemas to recover from depression.

Exercise 4.7
REHEARSING RULES OF WELLNESS

1. Think of a specific situation(s) where you would like to try to apply a rule of wellness.
2. Now imagine yourself in this situation. Forecast how you would think and act if you followed this rule.
3. Identify any potential trouble spots or problems in implementing the rule.
4. Work out a solution for the trouble spots by using methods from the Thinking Key or other Keys to recovery.
5. Put your plan into action.

COPING CARDS

This simple, but effective, technique can help you take an action-oriented approach to using your rules of wellness. The front side of a small index card is used to write down a problem or situation you want to tackle. The flip side of the card contains a succinct action plan. When we work with our patients to develop coping cards, we usually ask them to think of "bullet points" that they can put on the card. Bullet points will work best if they remind you to use your rules of wellness and give you specific instructions to cope in a positive way. Jeb wrote out this coping card to help him with getting back into school.

Jeb's Coping Card

Side 1.

Getting discouraged about being able to make it in Tech School.

Side 2.

- Keep my mind on the positives: I have enough intelligence to succeed . . . I can stick it out when the going gets tough . . . I can build my knowledge if I study and work hard.
- Take school one step at a time.
- Don't worry about taking the tests at the end of the course now. Just go to class, put in the time studying, get any help you need, and it will work out in the end.

Getting New Ideas for Rules of Wellness

Earlier in the chapter, you did two self-help exercises, the "Schema Inventory" and "How Life Experiences Shaped My Rules of Thinking," which helped you identify some of your adaptive or positive schemas. But, there may be other healthy attitudes that you haven't considered before that could make a big difference in your happiness and satisfaction in life. Usually we pick up our adaptive schemas as we grow up from our parents, teachers, friends, and spiritual leaders. But, there is still plenty of room to develop new rules of wellness as an adult. One of the most gratifying experiences in our clinical practices has been seeing people transform their lives by finding new rules that open the door for personal growth.

LEARN FROM OTHERS

If you are fortunate enough to have a good marriage or a long-standing relationship, you may be able to learn some new ways of thinking from this person. Or perhaps your children can teach you to see the world differently. Do you have any current heroes or heroines—models for how you would like to live your life? What lessons can you learn from them? How are your friends influencing your thinking? Stop for a moment to think about new rules of wellness that you have learned, or are learning from others, and write these down in your notebook.

STUDY AND SELF-REFLECTION

One of the time-tested ways of learning something new is to study the subject. If your goal is to learn more positive or growth-oriented rules of thinking, you might consider embarking on a self-study program in which you read books with ideas on healthy attitudes and try to incorporate some of these ideas into your thinking style. There are so many differences between individuals that it is hard to recommend a single book that will best fit each reader's needs. Some people respond best to books with a deep spiritual message or a philosophical orientation. Others prefer something lighter or more humorous.

We've listed some books in the Appendix that we think you might enjoy reading. There should be at least one book on this list that can give you some inspiration for building your rules of wellness.

PROFESSIONAL COUNSELING

Working with a professional counselor can give you a big boost toward developing healthier rules of thinking. If you are not currently in therapy and are considering starting professional counseling, you may be wondering how to choose a therapist who can give you the help you need.

Psychotherapy is a very personal encounter. Because you will be talking with a therapist about your inner fears and your most troubling problems, you want to be sure that you find a therapist whom you can trust. This person should be kind and understanding, but very professional in how he or she conducts the therapy. And of course, you will want a therapist who is very knowledgeable—someone who has the necessary training and skills to help you overcome your depression.

Probably the most valuable strategy for finding a therapist is to ask your family doctor, a pastor or rabbi, or someone else you know who is familiar with the professional therapists in your community. Family doctors and clergy usually have experience referring people for therapy and know at least one or two therapists whom they can recommend. Another option is to contact your local or state medical association or psychological association for suggestions. There also are several national and international professional organizations that may be able to help. We've listed some of these associations in the Appendix.

An important thing to be aware of when you are looking for a therapist is that there are many different types or "schools" of psychotherapy. The form of psychotherapy that has been tested most extensively for depression and proven to be effective is cognitive-behavior therapy (CBT). The methods we described for the Thinking Key, the Action Key, and many of the other self-help interventions in this book are based on CBT. This type of psychotherapy is very practical and problem oriented. Typically, a course of CBT for depression ranges from 5 to 20 sessions.

Another widely available form of therapy is psychodynamic treatment. This therapy has been derived from the theories of Freud and other psychoanalysts. Psychodynamic therapy has much more of a "here-and-now" orientation than classic psychoanalysis. If you receive this type of treatment, the therapist will help you deal with issues such as facing loss and gaining trust in yourself and others. Psychodynamic therapy for depression has not received much attention in research studies. So, the efficacy of this type of psychotherapy is still unclear.

Interpersonal therapy (IPT) is a newer form of treatment that is based on the idea that depression may be aggravated by or controlled by the relationships that you have with other people. Although there aren't a large number of clinicians that have been trained in this approach yet, there is good research evidence that IPT works for depression. Like CBT, interpersonal therapy is practical and action oriented. Therapists help people learn how to cope better with issues such as role transitions, grief, and disputes or conflicts with others.

Inquire about the clinician's theoretical orientation when you are attempting to select a therapist. This information can help you choose someone who does the type of treatment that you think will work best for you. You also may want to consider special qualifications of a therapist. For example, if you want to emphasize a combination of CBT and medication, good choices would be a psychiatrist who is an expert at both treatments, or a team of two clinicians who work closely together (a doctor who prescribes the medication and a psychologist or social worker who does CBT.

Because some psychotherapists are beginning to use computer tools to help with the process of psychotherapy, it is possible that you will be asked to spend time working with a specialized computer program as part of your treatment plan. Most of the research on computer-assisted therapy for depression has focused on ways to improve the efficiency of CBT and to offer depressed people new ways to learn CBT skills.

Jesse and his research team have developed a multimedia form of computer-assisted CBT for depression. Research on this program has shown that the amount of time that you need to see a therapist can be reduced almost in half if the computer software is used as part of treatment. One part of this program helps people change their schemas and develop healthier attitudes. A professional version of the computer program is used by therapists in their offices to augment CBT, medications, or other therapies for depression. An electronic self-help book version of the software is also available for people who want to work on the computer program at home. Web sites that contain information on this software and other types of computer-assisted therapy are listed in the Appendix.

The Thinking Key in Your Personal Plan for Recovery

In Chapter 2, you worked on the first three parts of your recovery plan. Now that you have learned about the Thinking Key, we can add some important details. First, let's update the plan by reviewing your symptoms, strengths, and goals. If you need to refresh your memory on how to organize your Personal Plan for Recovery, you can go back to Chapter 2 for more information. Part I of the plan is a measurement of your symptoms with the Five Keys Rating Scale. Take this test again to see if there have been any changes since you started to use the Thinking Key. Part II is a list of your strengths. Read over this list and add any other strengths that you have been able to recognize. The self-help exercise in Chapter 3, "Identifying Thinking Key Strengths," and your rules of wellness from this chapter should be good places to look for additional assets. Part III is the goals for your recovery plan. Take another look at your goals. Are there any goals that should be modified or added to fit with your plans to use the Thinking Key?

The next part of the Personal Plan for Recovery is a summary of your ideas for changing your thinking. You can find a worksheet for this part of your plan in the Appendix. Try to answer the questions on the worksheet and then follow your plan. Vic, the architect who froze at his desk one night, developed this plan for using the Thinking Key.

Exercise 4.8
Personal Plan for Recovery Worksheet—Part IV
'My Plan for Using the Thinking Key':

VIC'S EXAMPLE

1. What are some common automatic thoughts that can make me depressed?
   I don't know what I'm doing, and everyone will find out. I'm the one to blame if things don't work out. I'll never get it done in time.

(continued on next page)

2. Which kinds of thinking errors cause me the most trouble?
   Ignoring the evidence, jumping to conclusions, personalizing, all-or-none thinking.

3. What do I plan to do to reduce my negative automatic thoughts and thinking errors?
   Keep a thought record and try to use it every day. Examine the evidence for automatic thoughts. Find logical thoughts to substitute for automatic thoughts. Take a thought record to work and put it in my locked desk drawer. Take a break once a day to make some notes on the record.

4. Which schemas are causing me the most trouble?
   I'm a fake. I must be perfect to be accepted. No matter what I do, I won't succeed. I must always be in control.

5. What do I plan to do to modify my negative schemas?
   Remember my strengths. Accept positive feedback as genuine. Check out my negative attitudes by examining the evidence. Convert disadvantages into advantages by changing the schema. Instead of worrying all the time about being a fake, adopt a new belief—"You know what you are doing, but you can always learn more." Recognize that everyone has some doubts about their competence. Practice new schemas that reduce my emphasis on perfectionism and control. Realize that it will take time to make these changes. Be patient and keep trying.

6. What are my most useful positive schemas or rules of wellness?
   I'm intelligent. I can figure things out. If I keep working on something, I can usually succeed. I'm a good husband and father. If I prepare in advance, I usually do better.

7. What do I plan to do to build up these positive schemas?
   Keep a list of these schemas and review it at least once a week. Reinforce positive schemas by acting them out. Spend more time doing things with my family. For my work projects I'll keep my overall goals in mind, but take it a day at a time and just try to accomplish a part of the project each day. Give myself credit for my positives.

8. What ideas do I have for finding new rules of wellness?
   Schedule some talks with my pastor. Ask pastor for ideas on good books to read. Get to know my friend Owen better. He has been

through a whole lot and always seems to have a good attitude. Listen to my kids.

As you go on to learn about the Action Key and other methods of fighting depression, we hope you will continue to practice Thinking Key methods until you replace the rules of depression with rules of wellness. You heard the stories of Dr. Benjamin Carson and our patients who found that their thinking style controlled the way they faced the challenges of life. Your story is still being written. We hope that the Thinking Key will help give your story some of the same kinds of success.

The Action Key

5

Taking Action

Shannon had always had a busy life with her three young children. She worked out of her home selling cosmetics so that she could spend more time with her family. Her youngest child had medical problems since birth. So, Shannon needed to be close to home to give him the help he needed. She had a good relationship with her husband and was deeply connected to her spiritual faith.

> *I have everything going for me. I'm truly blessed. But I can't make myself get my work done, and it makes me feel guilty and depressed. I'm so useless. My house is a wreck all the time, and to be completely honest, I really don't care. I know that I need to tend to my cosmetics business so that I can make some money and help us get out of debt, but I'm not doing what my mind says I should. When I finally start making phone calls to customers, the kids make noise and interrupt me. I hear myself screaming at them. I know it's wrong. The words just seem to sneak out of my mouth before I can stop and think. I'm usually a very good mom, but I feel like I'm being held by this giant octopus that makes me feel bad, holds me back from my responsibilities, ties me to my bed so that all I want to do is sleep, and squeezes ugly words out of me. I can't seem to move, can't get a foothold. And you know what the worst thing is? I know that I am the octopus. I know what I should be doing to get out of this, but I can't make myself do it.*

Shannon's story is a common one for people who get depressed. There seem to be two parts of them doing battle with one another. The logical, rational part of them knows what they need to do and feels bad for not doing it. Unfortunately, this part is not strong enough to overcome the more powerful emotional part that keeps them stuck, making them feel as if they are in the grips of a powerful octopus, of *20,000 Leagues under the Sea* proportions.

Shannon saw her doctor about her sleepiness and fatigue, but he could find no physical explanation for her symptoms. After hearing her negative self-talk and recognizing her other physical symptoms of depression, difficulty sleeping, and a poor appetite, Shannon's doctor referred her for therapy. Once Shannon had an explanation for her symptoms, it was easy for her to see how her depression was making her tired and disinterested in her work and household chores. Her inactivity was making the depression worse because it made her feel bad about herself and because it created financial problems when she was unable to work. Sleeping off and on throughout the day made it hard for her to tend to her children the way she liked and left her with little time to pick up after the kids or cook healthy meals.

Shannon's score on the Five Keys Rating Scale was highest for the Action Key items. And since these problems were bothering her the most, she decided to start by working with the Action Key. She knew that if she could take better care of her household and children she would feel better about herself. Whenever she was able to accomplish even a small task, Shannon felt energized by the success. This broke the cycle of lethargy, inactivity, increased problems, and guilt. Seeing herself take care of things seemed to improve her self-esteem and gave her confidence that she could overcome depression. As she began to work on taking action, Shannon noticed that she was feeling hopeful for the first time in months. She started her days with a curiosity about what new feats she could accomplish rather than dreading the daylight. Her energy and her motivation slowly returned. This was the key to turning around her depression.

Tips for Using the Action Key

Are you having trouble getting things done? Do you feel stuck? Does it seem that even though you are actively trying to cope with your problems they keep getting worse? If you answered "yes" to any of these questions, you can use the Action Key to learn new ways to get moving, solve problems, and enjoy life more. Take a moment and try to remember times when you felt like you were more in control of your life. How did you get things accomplished? How did you make yourself do difficult or unpleasant tasks? What did you used to do for fun? What positive actions are you taking now to cope with your depression? In *Exercise 5.1* "Identifying Action Key Strengths" we pose some questions to help you to identify the skills and abilities you currently possess or have made use of in the past. Jot down your answers in your notebook. These are the skills you will put to use in the Action Key.

In this chapter and the next we try to remind you how to take control of your life and be happy. Most of the interventions we offer are common sense; nothing fancy, just simple methods for overcoming inertia, for coping more effectively, and for solving problems. In fact, you probably already know how to do most of the exercises we suggest. But, our experience in treating people with depression is that even though they may know the right thing to do, they still may not do it because depression takes away their drive and their patience.

We know that most of the methods for overcoming depression are more easily said than done. Because of this, we emphasize throughout this chapter and the next how to start taking action when you are stuck, how to persist when you want to give up, and how to change gears and try new approaches when progress is too slow.

Exercise 5.1
Identifying Action Key Strengths

In your notebook under the heading "Action Key Strengths" try to answer the following questions.

1. How have I made myself do difficult or unpleasant tasks in the past?
2. What positive actions am I taking now to cope with my depression?
3. What advice would I give others to help them increase their motivation or to solve problems?
4. What kinds of things have I enjoyed in the past?
5. What are some ways that I could add pleasure back into my life?

Feeling Stuck and Going Nowhere

Masako is like many people who suffer from severe forms of depression. She is so tired and depressed that she has to struggle each day just to make herself get out of bed. Her depression feels like a heavy blanket that covers her, blocking out the world. In fact, all she really wants to do is hide in her bed with the blankets over her head. Although she was once an active and capable woman, she now feels powerless. Here is an example of Masako's struggle with inactivity and depression that she tries to overcome in therapy.

MASAKO: "I can't do it. I've tried. I just can't do it."

THERAPIST: "When you tell yourself that you can't do it, what kinds of feelings does it stir up inside of you?"

MASAKO: "I feel sad and frightened. What if I stay like this forever? I'll just stop existing. My husband will leave me. I'll be alone. I'll have nowhere to turn."

THERAPIST: "When you think these scary thoughts what does it do to your self-confidence?"

MASAKO: "I have none."

THERAPIST: "When you tell yourself that you can't do it and you feel scared and sad, what happens to your motivation and your energy?"

MASAKO: "I feel so bad, all I want to do is go to bed, pull the covers over my head, and disappear."

THERAPIST: "And when you do that, does it make you feel better about yourself when you wake up?"

MASAKO: "No. It just passes the time."

THERAPIST: "What would you have to do to regain your confidence? What would convince you that you will not stay like this forever?"

Masako sat and thought about this for several minutes. By the end of the session, she had decided that to be convinced that her life could be better she would have to see herself doing something that helped to solve problems, and she would have to spend much less time in bed. She agreed to do an experiment before she came back for therapy the next week. Masako picked three small tasks that she would try to accomplish each day. If she could do any of them it would prove that she was not completely helpless. Her list included making her bed first thing in the morning and changing out of her pajamas so she would be less tempted to crawl back into bed when she felt bad. The third thing was to talk to at least one person each day.

Of course, the experiment was a success. Masako saw that she was not completely helpless. By changing her actions, her self-confidence started to return. This helped to break the cycle of depression and she lived happily ever after. Well, not immediately, but Masako did pull herself out of the depths of depression by taking action. It improved her outlook and even made her husband feel more hopeful about their future together. As Masako increased her activity and reduced the amount of time she spent in bed, her energy level began to improve. Without naps, she was able to sleep better at night and felt more rested in the morning.

Masako had a very common problem. Like many depressed people, she lacked motivation. Most of the time when you feel depressed you are inclined to wait for your motivation to pick you up off of the couch and carry you out the door, hoping that this will make you feel better. But, sometimes this is a long wait. It is far better to take some action first. Your motivation and energy will catch up with you.

ACTIVITY SCHEDULING

If your depression keeps you from taking action you may find it helpful to plan your daily activities on a schedule. Activity Scheduling is a commonly used exercise that helps people get going when they are having trouble making themselves move. In your notebook take a page to make yourself a daily schedule. Write hour or half-hour blocks of time on the first column just like in the example. Plan ahead for what you would like to do in each block. If you are having trouble getting out of bed, you can make a plan for when you will make yourself get out of bed. In the example, Masako wants to be up by 9:00 A.M. This might seem late, but if you are regularly sleeping until noon, 9:00 A.M. is a reasonable starting place. Fill in the activities you would like to do each day. If you have a plan for the day, you do not need to debate with yourself each morning about when it would be best to get out of bed.

As you go through your day, check off the activities you were able to accomplish and add new ones that you did spontaneously. Seeing your progress will help motivate you to go further. If the schedule does not seem practical, change it to fit your needs. Once you get back into a regular schedule of activity you will not need this exercise to get you going.

Masako found that she needed to have a plan or purpose for her day or she would, most likely, do nothing. She thought that once she was back into a normal routine she would not have to think or plan so much. She was right. She trained herself back into a normal routine by setting new goals each week that challenged her to work harder and accomplish more. Before she got depressed, she had always liked a challenge. If there were some days when she could not make herself get out of bed as planned, she challenged herself to be more consistent the next week.

MASAKO'S ACTIVITY SCHEDULE

Time	Monday	Tuesday	Wednesday	Thursday	Friday	Saturday	Sunday
8:00 A.M.							
9:00 A.M.	Wake up, make bed	Wake up, make bed	Wake up, make bed	Wake up, make bed	Wake up, make bed	Wake up	Wake up, make bed
10:00 A.M.	Eat breakfast	Eat breakfast	Eat breakfast	Eat breakfast	Eat breakfast	Eat breakfast	Eat breakfast
11:00 A.M.	Change clothes	Change clothes	Change clothes	Change clothes	Change clothes	Make bed	Change clothes
Noon	Laundry	Chores		Laundry		Change clothes	Go to church
1:00 P.M.		Chores	Run errands	Laundry		Clean house	
2:00 P.M.	Exercise & shower		Exercise & shower		Exercise & shower		Visit mom
3:00 P.M.				Go to therapy			
4:00 P.M.	Visit or make calls	Visit or make calls	Visit or make calls		Visit or make calls	Visit or make calls	
5:00 P.M.							
6:00 P.M.	Watch TV	Watch TV	Watch TV	Watch TV	Watch TV		

UP AND AT 'EM

There are a few other things you can try when your brain says "Get up!" and your body doesn't move. One is to set a smaller goal for yourself. For example, on those rough days, Masako would say to herself, "Just get up! You do not have to do anything else today if you don't want to, but you must get out of the bed." After she got out of bed she would set the next small goal, "Eat something." Masako found that keeping it simple made the day seem less overwhelming. Once she got up and ate, she was able to follow the rest of her Activity Schedule. She didn't always want to, but if she made the effort she would not feel like a failure at the end of the day.

Another thing you can do when you have no motivation is to follow the Nike slogan and "Just Do It!" Do not overthink it, analyze it, bargain with yourself, or criticize yourself. Just do it and see how you feel when you are done. One of our patients calls this Nike Therapy. Take action even when you don't want to. You can complain about it while you are doing it, you can curse your therapist for suggesting the activity, you can even feel sorry for yourself while you are doing it, but just do it anyway.

MASAKO: "That's it? After all your years of training all you can come up with is Just Do It?"

THERAPIST: "Yep. That's it. I can give you a much more psychologically sophisticated instruction, tell you about brain function, what this might have to do with your feelings about your mother, and throw around a lot of psychological jargon. But, the answer to making yourself get up and get moving often comes down to making yourself do it even when you do not want to."

MASAKO: "Just do it, huh?"

THERAPIST: "Just try it and see what happens."

Key Point

Most of the time when you feel depressed you are inclined to wait for your motivation to pick you up off of the couch and carry you out the door, hoping that this will make you feel better. Sometimes this is a long wait. It is far better to take some action first. Your motivation and energy will catch up with you.

DISQUALIFYING YOUR POSITIVES

When you take action you can't help but watch yourself do it, "Hey, look at me I'm finally doing it." This thought can stimulate a feeling of relief or a sense of self-confidence. Positive thoughts have the opposite effect of negative automatic thoughts. The positive ones actually improve your mood and your motivation to do more.

It is also possible that you can "undo" your new found sense of accomplishment with negative thoughts like "I should have done that long ago," "So what! I should be doing more," or "Big deal! My four-year-old can make his own bed and change his clothes." Be aware of these negative and punishing thoughts. If they come to mind, try telling yourself to "Stop it," "Shut up," or "Lighten up." Don't let negative thinking take away your moment of pleasure.

"I Can't Get No Satisfaction": Unlocking the Door to Pleasure

Being depressed obviously isn't any fun, but having fun can be a way out of the misery. Pleasure, laughter, and fun can brighten your mood and remind you that life is worth living. You may be thinking, "I don't want to have fun. I don't have the desire or the energy." Those are symptoms of depression. To fight them off you have to ignore your instinct to avoid people and fun. Instead schedule time to play. If your depression is severe, it will take some practice before you can have a good time. You may find that you are only going through the motions and not feeling much of anything. Be patient. Even if you are not having a great time to start with, keep trying until you feel some pleasure.

Start by making a list of activities that give you pleasure. If you hear yourself say, "Nothing gives me pleasure," list the activities that used to give you pleasure before you got depressed. These do not have to be big activities like going on vacation. They should be small things like visiting a friend, reading the Sunday comics, walking in the park, taking a bubble bath, or playing with your children. Choose one or two pleasurable activities to do each day and put them on your Activity Schedule. You might remember from Michelle's story in Chapter 1 that she once enjoyed music, exercising, gardening, and taking long walks in the woods with her children. She stopped doing these things when her depression began, and she had no real interest in picking them up again. As part of her recovery plan, she decided to do something enjoyable each day. Acting like her old self helped her to start feeling like her old self.

It's OK to plan ahead for fun. It does not have to be spontaneous to be enjoyable. Once you get back into the swing of things, fun will come more naturally and will not have to be as structured. Michelle forced herself to go to church and sing in the choir again. It was hard for her at first, but paid off very quickly as she began to feel her mood lifting and her energy returning.

"THAT'S NOT FUNNY"

When our patients get depressed they seem to be drawn to entertainment that matches their negative mood. They watch sad or violent movies, read stories about loss, death, or hardship, listen to songs about heartache, and then walk away feeling worse. Watching other people be tormented or betrayed will not brighten up your mood. One of Vic's goals was to have more fun with his wife. He had been battling depression for several months and was trying to follow his therapist's advice to increase his positive activities. He and his wife began their evening out with a good meal at their favorite restaurant. Dinner was fun and relaxing, but they chose a sad love story to watch, the kind where the hero does not get the girl. In fact, she died and he was left alone wondering if he would ever love again. During the movie, Vic thought about his life, his losses, how his marriage might never have the passion and excitement he wanted. By the end of the movie, he had retreated to a faraway place in his mind and was acting distant from his wife. She got annoyed because he had "ruined" their only night out in months. Soon they were into an argument that started with her saying, "I told you we shouldn't have gone to see that movie." Although Vic started to defend himself, he knew she was right. He was to blame, he was a terrible husband, and his life was going nowhere.

Here are some suggestions for making entertainment choices. (1) Do not watch movies about someone whose mood is worse than yours. (2) Avoid "real life" stories of human tragedy. (3) Read reviews or ask your friends about them before you make your choice. (4) If you realize part of the way through a movie or book that you have made a bad choice, walk away or close the book. (5) Choose activities that you used to enjoy when you were less depressed, knowing, of course, that you will probably enjoy it less for the time being because of your mood. (6) Take someone fun with you.

Look back at Exercise 5.1. Perhaps one of your previous strengths was that you used to have a pretty good sense of humor. Think for a moment about what your sense of humor used to be like. Was it silly? Sarcastic? Did you like to tell jokes or play jokes on people? Did you like making fun of family members or other people? Did you enjoy a good play-on-words? What would make you laugh? Who would make you laugh? Take out your notebook and jot down a few things about your sense of humor. It is hard to have a sense of humor when you are depressed, but it is possible that the following suggestions can help.

Getting Back Your Sense of Humor

1. Try to act as if you had a sense of humor.
   (Tell a joke. Laugh at yourself.)
2. Choose things to do that used to be fun.
   (Go to a flea market or a yard sale. Laugh at the unusual or funny things you see.)
3. Watch a funny movie or read a funny book.
   (Videos of stand-up comics, classic comedies)
4. Look for humor in daily life.
   (Watch for funny expressions on people's faces.)
5. Be around light-hearted people.
   (Call a friend who makes you laugh.)
6. Read the jokes in your favorite magazine.
   (*Reader's Digest, Newsweek, New Yorker*)
7. Play with children.
   (Play catch, throw a Frisbee, play a game.)

Any of these activities can be added to your Activity Schedule. When you have put pleasure back into your life, think about how it affects your mood. Does it lighten your sadness, decrease your irritability, or put a smile on your face, if even for a little while? If so, this is good. Keep going.

How does having fun make you feel about your world? Does it make you more optimistic about recovering from depression? Does it give you hope? Remember that negative thinking can ruin a good time. So if you are not as happy as you think you *should be,* try again another time. Try to keep from getting upset because you are not having fun yet. Continue to do things to bring some light-heartedness into your life.

Overwhelmed and Overwrought

When Adriana started thinking about all that she needed to do, she immediately became overwhelmed. In an instant she saw in her mind's eye all the things she should do, all the things she wanted to do, and all the things others wanted her to do. They flew past her eyes, down to her stomach, and landed, "plop," like a stone in the pit of her stomach. She felt her brain shutting down as she rolled over and pulled the blankets over her head.

When you are depressed, the sheer volume of problems you face can overwhelm you and keep you from taking any action and making progress. You shut down before you have a chance to sort out all of the "shoulds," "ought to's," "have to's," and "want to's." Everything seems like a high priority, and since you can't do everything, you end up doing nothing. It wouldn't be so bad if you could do nothing and be happy about it. But if you are like most people, as you sit overwhelmed and immobilized, your mind flips through your fears of what will happen to you if you don't get up and get moving.

"I'm going to lose my apartment," Adriana worried, "not because I don't have the money for rent, but because I haven't paid my bills. I can't do that until I balance my checkbook, and I can't do that until I figure out what checks I have written, and I can't do that until I find my receipts, and I can't do that until I clean up around here. It's too much for me to handle."

Adriana's fear of being kicked out of her apartment only intensified her depression. Her self-criticism, the lectures she gave herself about responsibility, even the nudging from her landlord did not motivate her to take action. Adriana saw her problems as one big unsolvable mess. She did not have the energy to climb the mountain so she avoided her landlord's calls, made promises she never kept, and prayed that tomorrow would be a better day.

Since Adriana could not solve her financial problems all at once, she needed to break them down into smaller and more manageable steps. We often recommend a simple exercise called Graded Task Assignment, or GTA, in such a situation. Adriana already gave us some clues that her financial problems actually involved a series of steps, progressing in a logical sequence. Exercise 5.2 lists the steps to complete a GTA. In the box, we include an example of how Adriana worked through the steps as a way of solving her immediate financial dilemma.

Once Adriana got started she had her rent paid in one week. It turned out that she was not as far behind as she had thought. She had forgotten that she had balanced her checkbook at the end of last month when she paid her bills. Since she had been too depressed to go anywhere, she had not written many checks since then. Her only deposit was her paycheck. When she was finished she could not believe how she had made the task so overwhelming in her head when it could have been solved weeks ago and saved her a lot of self-torture.

Exercise 5.2
Graded Task Assignment Instructions

1. Choose a problem to solve.

   Adriana: Pay rent.

2. Make a list of all the steps required to accomplish the task.

   Adriana: Pay rent, balance checkbook to make sure I have enough money.

3. Break the larger steps down into smaller steps.

   Adriana: Balancing checkbook—

   a. Stop the self-criticism long enough to get the job done.
   b. Find the information needed to balance checkbook.
   c. Gather receipts and call bank to get the amounts of recent deposits.
   d. Write the transactions in ledger.
   e. Add in the deposits and subtract the checks until reaching final balance.

4. Put the steps in order of priority or in a logical sequence.

   Adriana: Balance checkbook before paying rent.

5. Assign yourself the first step. Include a deadline for completion.

   Adriana: Gather information to balance checkbook by end of week.

6. Do it!

7. Check your progress and assign yourself the next step.

8. Praise yourself or give yourself a reward for completing the task.

KEEP IT SIMPLE

Some people find it helpful to make it a habit of assigning themselves tasks each day. This seems to keep them from falling too far behind. A simple exercise for doing so is to organize your day by making a note to yourself, mentally or on paper, of things you want to accomplish that day. Pick two or three things that you have to do. This will become your "A List." Add one or two things you would like to do if you have the time. This will become your "B List." You can make your lists first thing in the morning or before you go to bed at night. Whatever you are unable to accomplish on one day can be put on your "A" and "B" lists for the next day. If you are limited in time and energy, keep the lists short and realistic. Try to avoid setting unreasonable expectations for yourself. Forget about what you "should" be able to do and plan for what you might reasonably be able to do given all of your other responsibilities and your limited energy.

NOTHING LIKE A GOOD NIGHT'S SLEEP

One of the most common reasons that people feel overwhelmed and overwrought is that they are exhausted. When depression disturbs your sleep it lowers your energy, interferes with your concentration, and reduces your frustration tolerance. There are some guidelines you can follow to increase the chance that you'll get a good night's sleep. Doctors call this good "sleep hygiene." One suggestion is to limit your use of stimulants like caffeine and nicotine before you go to bed. Depending on how sensitive you are to these substances, you may want to stop using caffeine altogether or at least have none in the afternoon and evening. Remember that coffee, tea, soda, and chocolate all contain caffeine.

Another rule of good sleep hygiene is to reduce stimulation at night. Start quieting your mind long before bedtime. For example, avoid watching highly stimulating or action-packed movies, and try not to engage in highly emotional conversations just before bedtime. Exercise or surfing the Internet at night helps some people to fall asleep. Others get too wound-up. Know yourself and make the needed adjustments in your routine.

As a rule of thumb it is best to use your bed for sleep and sex and not for any other activities such as paying the bills or watching television. If you are lying in bed and cannot sleep for a long time, most sleep experts recommend that you get out of bed and go to another room. If you are worried about something, take a moment to make a plan for addressing the problem the next day. If your mind is too alert, try reading a book or magazine. Don't read something that will be so exciting that it is hard to put down.

It is generally a good idea to go to sleep and to wake up at about the same times each day. Consistency in routine and schedule can help you to sleep more soundly. It is best to sleep only at night, so try not to take naps during the day. Naps can make it harder for you to fall asleep at night.

Another solution for insomnia may be to take a medication that helps you to sleep. Look ahead to Chapter 7 for information on natural substances and medications that might help to improve your sleep. Even if you do not like the idea of taking medications, it may be worth a try for a few nights so that you can catch up on your sleep and regain your energy.

Key Point

One of the most common reasons that people feel overwhelmed and over-wrought is that they are exhausted. Take action to improve your sleep and you will have more energy and better concentration.

RUMINATION

If you have trouble falling asleep at night because you cannot stop thinking, mental distraction techniques may help to divert your attention to other things so that you can relax enough to fall asleep. Distraction can be as simple as counting backwards from 100 or as complicated as you need it to be. Mantras or prayers said repeatedly can serve the same function. Read ahead to the section on "Thought Stopping" in Chapter 6. There, you will find steps for shutting off distressing thoughts by switching to more positive and relaxing images.

HYPERSOMNIA

When some people get depressed they have the opposite problem. They sleep too much. This is called hypersomnia. Despite having ten or more hours of sleep each day, they may still feel tired when they awake. Low energy, in this case, can be mistaken for the need for more sleep. Unfortunately, the additional sleep usually makes them feel worse rather than better.

Low energy and sleepiness are symptoms of depression. Giving in to the urge to sleep too much can slow recovery because you are depriving your mind and body of needed stimulation and activity. Although it may be difficult at first, increasing activity rather than resting will help you recover faster.

The ACTION Plan for Solving Problems

When you are depressed it may seem easier to avoid dealing with problems than to tackle them. You might even hear yourself wishing that they would just disappear. Unfortunately, as much as you might like it, most difficulties do not go away by themselves.

Facing your problems is tough. It requires energy, concentration, and some degree of confidence and optimism, all of which are generally lacking during depression. So what can you do until you are feeling better? First, you have to be convinced that it would be worth the effort to take action toward solving your problems. What do you stand to gain? Is the long-term benefit of dealing with them worth the short-term discomfort? If so, we think we can help you.

Under normal circumstances you can probably work your way through problems on your own. When you're depressed you may have trouble figuring out how to get started. The step-by-step procedures we describe below may help you figure out a course of action and reach resolution on the things that are bothering you most.

Self-confidence is a characteristic of good problem solvers. However, it is hard to build self-confidence or optimism without having some success first. Until your optimism returns we would like to offer you a bit of ours. The reason we can afford to be optimistic about teaching you how to solve problems is that we have successfully taught many people to do so over the years. We had faith in their abilities just as we have faith in yours.

Problem solving usually involves six steps proceeding in a specified order. Here they are:

1. **A**ssess the problem.
2. **C**ome up with solutions.
3. **T**ake the best option.
4. **I**mplement the solution.
5. **O**utcome OK? Evaluate your results.
6. **N**ow what? Repeat steps if needed.

ACTION: ASSESS THE PROBLEM

To solve a problem, you first have to define it. A useful definition should be specific enough to lead you to a solution and allow you to

know if the solution has worked. Here are some examples of poorly defined problems and well-defined problems.

Poorly defined problem	What's wrong with it?	Well-defined problem
I can't handle the kids.	Not specific enough. What can't I handle?	I'm getting too upset when the kids make a lot of noise.
No one cares about me.	Probably an overgeneralization. How would I know if they cared?	I'm not getting the support I need from my partner. I need to ask for help, but I'm not certain if I will get it.
If I don't get busy my husband is going to leave me.	Fortune telling. I could be right, but I don't really know for sure.	The house is cluttered and dirty. I need to spend time cleaning. I need to know if my husband is thinking of leaving me over it.
If I mess up this next project, I'm going to be fired.	Doesn't tell me what I must do to solve the problem or avoid the consequences.	It is important to do well on this project so I need to put in more time this week and ask for help if I get stuck.
He's so irresponsible.	Too vague. In what way is he irresponsible? What do I want from him?	He does not call me when he is going to be late. Waiting for him causes tension and then conflict when he gets home.
My car won't work.	Not specific enough.	My car will not start, and I do not know why.

If you have difficulty defining your problems, you can use the following questions as a guide. A clearly defined problem will give you
some direction for change.

Questions to Help You Define the Problem

Who?
Who has the problem?
Who needs to make changes?

What?
What is the problem?
What part of the problem is most troublesome?
Could there actually be several problems that affect each other? What are they?

Where?
In what situations is the problem most noticeable?
Is it more bothersome in some situations (like work) than in others (like home)?

When?
When is this problem most likely to stress you?
Does it bother you more when you are tired, busy, hungry, or irritable?

How?
If you could fix the problem how would things be different for you?
How could you tell that the problem was solved?

A common pitfall is trying to solve too many problems at one time. Sylvia, a bank teller who had been feeling depressed and nervous for the previous six months, was faced with this kind of dilemma.

I don't know where to start. The main problem this week is that my boyfriend wants to go out to clubs, and the last time I went to one I had a panic attack. I don't want to hurt his feelings and say no. He likes to go out with friends. He'll go out without me if I'm not in the mood, but I don't like that either. He drinks too much sometimes and I'm afraid of what he might do. I don't really want to talk to him about this, so I don't know what to do. I'm running out of excuses for not wanting to go out drinking in those places. My sisters and my mom are on my back about it because they think I should tell him the truth or dump him. They know that I'm thirty-three years old and my biological clock is ticking. I want to settle down and have a family. What if my boyfriend is 'the one'? I think I love him and I can make compromises to get along better, but I don't want to take a chance at losing him. What can I do?

There is no single solution to Sylvia's dilemma because she is actually having several distinct, but overlapping problems. The main ones seem to be (1) she has panic attacks in crowds, (2) she does not like her boyfriend's drinking, (3) she has difficulty being honest with him, (4) she is worried about losing him although she is not certain if he is the right one for her, (5) she wants to settle down and have children, and (6) she is being pressured by her family. To solve these various problems we have to put them in some order of priority. Start with the issue that is most pressing, most important, or the most annoying. If they are all about equal, choose one problem that, if solved, might make the other problems better. In Sylvia's case, it would seem at first glance that if she could talk with her boyfriend about her concerns, several problems could be solved. If she agreed to start with communication as the problem, we would need to know why she finds it difficult to communicate, under what circumstances or on which topics, and how she would like their communication to be better. Remember that defining a problem can be a difficult step, but once accomplished you'll have a roadmap to follow that will lead to solutions for your difficulties.

Key Point

Try to solve one problem at a time. If in defining the problem you come up with several different ones, make a list of them, but choose only one as a starting place. It is tempting to try to find one big solution that addresses several problems at one time. Resist this temptation. It frequently makes the task more complicated.

ACTION: COME UP WITH SOLUTIONS

For most problems there are a number of possible solutions. Some will be more effective or more practical than others. In this second problem-solving step, all you have to do is come up with some possible solutions. Do not worry about whether or not they will work. Just make the list without stopping to evaluate their feasibility as you go along. Try to come up with at least a dozen possible solutions before you stop to evaluate and choose an option. Throw in a few silly solutions as well. Include solutions that involve getting help from other people. Add doing nothing as a solution.

Kelly hadn't finished her income taxes and the deadline was nearing. She seemed to be stalled because there was some information she needed that she couldn't find. Each day she told herself that she needed to call her old employer to ask for another copy of her W-2 form. Because Kelly left that job when she got too depressed, she was embarrassed to call back to tell them that she had gone to work for someone else. She told herself, "Kelly, this is stupid. Just make the call." The new job kept her busy, so it was easy to forget about the taxes until the end of the workday, when it seemed too late to call. She didn't call first thing in the morning because she started work at 8:00 A.M., and the person she needed would not be available that early. Kelly promised herself that she would call at noon, but she got caught up at work or imagined the embarrassment of having to tell her old boss that she lost her W-2, so she didn't make the call. When Kelly described this dilemma in therapy, it seemed as if she was stuck on one solution, calling for a duplicate copy during office hours, and could think of no others. After some discussion of alternatives, Kelly came up with the following possible solutions to her dilemma.

Kelly's List of Possible Solutions

1. Write a letter to my employer asking for the W-2.
2. Call the personnel office instead of my boss.
3. Ask my husband to call for me.
4. Ask my accountant to make the call.
5. Ask for an extension on my taxes to give me more time to get the form.
6. E-mail a note to the office making the request.
7. Call at 8:00 a.m. when I'm thinking about it and leave a message.
8. Make the call instead of eating lunch.
9. Call my old boss, but pretend to be the accountant making the request.
10. Call the boss's office and accuse him of never sending the W-2.
11. Get a friend at work to call pretending to be me.
12. Fax a note to the office with the request.

ACTION: TAKE THE BEST OPTION

Now that you have your list of solutions, eliminate the ones that you do not like or that do not seem reasonable. Of the ones that are remaining, put them in order according to how effective you think they will be in solving your problem. Kelly eliminated all the options except for numbers 1, 2, 3, 6, and 12. She decided that they would all be equally effective, but that 6 and 12 would allow her to solve the problem without having to deal with her ex-boss. Lots of people see faxes that come in before they reach the boss's desk, so she chose number 6.

ACTION: IMPLEMENT THE SOLUTION

The next step is obvious. Put your solution into action. Decide where and when you will implement your plan. Since it has been hard to solve your problem up to this point, there may be some unexpected obstacles that could keep you from taking action now. Before you try to implement your solution, take a moment and think of all the things that could keep you from following through with your plan. What kinds of things have held you back in the past? For Kelly, it has been anticipating embarrassment if she would speak with her ex-boss. Getting busy at work and forgetting to call had kept her from taking action before. Her plan to send an e-mail avoided this problem because she could use her computer any time. It is possible that even if she sent an e-mail message requesting what she needed, he could decide to call her before mailing the W-2. Thinking about this prospect made her anxious, so this was one of the obstacles she would have to overcome to send her e-mail.

If you identify things that can keep you from implementing your solution, take time to figure out how to avoid these obstacles (have someone screen all your calls) or how to cope with them if they do occur (think about what to say when he calls). Kelly decided to figure out how to deal with his questions if he made contact. This was planned out in a therapy session and rehearsed until she felt confident in her ability to handle the situation.

Once you have figured out your plan, it is time to take action. Kelly e-mailed her old boss with a note requesting a duplicate copy of her last W-2.

ACTION: OUTCOME OK? EVALUATE YOUR RESULTS

Because even well-thought-out and perfectly executed solutions sometimes do not work, you should take time to review your efforts to determine whether the final outcome is OK. The day after Kelly e-mailed her boss, he responded with a simple message: "Kelly, hope you are doing well. I'm happy to get the W-2 for you. Sincerely, Bill." A few days later she received the form she needed in the mail. Kelly was mad at herself for wasting so much time and energy worrying about her boss's response.

ACTION: NOW WHAT? REPEAT STEPS IF NEEDED

Although Kelly's solution worked out for her, it could have turned out differently. Her ex-boss could have failed to respond at all. In this case, Kelly's solution would have been ineffective, and she would have had to go back two steps and select another solution from the list. It is always a good idea to have a back-up plan. Kelly had planned to make herself call the personnel office if the e-mail request had been unanswered.

Key Point

Just because a solution does not work the first time, it does not mean it was a bad solution. Rethink your execution of the plan. Was it your timing? Or your attitude? Is there something you could change that might make it work the second time?

Troubleshooting the ACTION Plan

If the ACTION steps do not seem to work, it may be that you need some help from one of the other Keys to solve the problem. For example, if you cannot concentrate well enough to work through this book or work through the ACTION steps, you might find a solution in the Biology Key. Perhaps you might benefit from taking an antidepressant medication to improve your concentration. If you could think more clearly, the answers might seem more obvious.

Often the most bewildering problems in our lives involve our relationships with other people. In this case, trying to solve the problem on your own may not be enough. You can control your own actions, but you usually cannot change the actions of others. Read ahead to the Relationship Key chapters for some ideas on how to resolve problems with others in your life. You can solve relationship problems using the ACTION method if you get the other person to work through the steps with you. This means that you must be able to listen to one another and compromise on the solution. If this creates more conflict, you may need a referee such as a psychotherapist, a social worker, or a member of the clergy. You need someone who will stay neutral and not take sides, so do not try to use friends or family members. Not all mental health professionals are trained in counseling couples, so be sure to ask before you make the appointment.

In working through the ACTION steps, people sometimes get stuck at the point of defining the problem because they are looking at it incorrectly. Remember the thinking errors described in Chapter 3 of the Thinking Key? If your definition of the problem is distorted by a thinking error then it will lead you in the wrong direction. A common mistake in defining a problem is to assume there is a problem where there really is none. This can happen if you make the cognitive error of jumping to conclusions about something before you have all the facts, such as assuming you know how another person is feeling or what he or she is thinking before you ask.

Another way that thinking errors can interfere with defining and solving problems is if you ignore some of the available evidence. This happens when you are so upset you only see one side of a problem and do not stop to look at the big picture. For example, you might see how someone else has wronged you, but miss what you might have done to contribute to the problem. Perhaps someone hurt you with critical words. If you did not catch what you might have said first to instigate the argument, you would be ignoring the evidence.

If you are having trouble working through the ACTION steps, examine your definition of the problem to see if you might be making some thinking errors. Use the exercises in Chapter 3 to get things straight and then come back and try to work out the problem again using the ACTION plan.

You may remember from Chapter 4 in the Thinking Key that schemas you have about yourself, about others, or about the world in general govern your actions. Therefore, if the ACTION plan is not working, it may be that your schemas are getting in the way. Negative schemas, such as "It doesn't matter how hard I try I'll never be good enough," "I'm not very strong," or "No one wants me," might lower your motivation to act. When you get in a slump you need a way to bring your positive beliefs back to the surface to challenge your negative beliefs. The exercises in Chapter 4 of the Thinking Key will help you keep your negative schemas from interfering with problem solving.

The inward focus of depression will make you think more about the meaning of your life, but these thoughts may not motivate you to take action toward making your life better. Some of the common questions people ask themselves when they are depressed are: "Why is this happening to me?" "What have I done to deserve this?" and "What if this is just who I am and who I am destined to be?" "What purpose do I serve in this world?" Many people think that if they can find the answers to these questions it will resolve their depression. Unfortunately, it's not usually that simple.

Rather than lie in bed searching your mind for answers, take a look at the Spirituality Key in Chapters 12 and 13. Take action to get the answers you seek rather than waiting for them to find you. A word of caution, understanding and insight do not necessarily lead to behavior change. Therefore, when you have worked through the Spirituality Key come back to this chapter and use the activating techniques to help you turn your life in the right direction.

This chapter has focused on helping you learn ways to solve problems, enjoy yourself more, and start to have fun again. Coping actively with your world can reverse the negative cycle of depression because positive activity leads to a better outlook and improved mood. The next chapter will help you to refine your coping strategies and further develop your Personal Plan for Recovery. Our goal will be to get you back into full gear as you take action to overcome depression.

6

Developing Positive Coping Strategies

Martha recently lost her best friend to cancer. She was at the hospital during Ethel's last days. Although the emotional strain was great, she felt she owed it to Ethel to stay by her side. Ethel would have done the same for her. Martha sat and stroked her friend's hand and helped her to recall the fun times they had during their thirty-five years together. There was nothing Martha could have done to save Ethel, but she resisted the urge to run from the unpleasantness of it all. Instead, she fought her fear and sadness and stood by Ethel until her last hour.

When Martha went home at the end of her long days standing vigil she indulged herself in a vodka tonic. She had lost her appetite for real food, but felt better after a little snack. Chocolate was her favorite, especially chocolate cookies. Martha's husband, Ralph, wished she would talk to him about it so he could do something to ease his wife's pain. He wanted to forbid her to return to the hospital when he saw how emotionally spent she was at the end of the day. But, he knew that would only strengthen her resolve. So he did the next best thing and brought Martha her favorite cookies home from the bakery near his work. No matter how bad Martha felt, these chocolate delights always seemed to relieve her tension, at least for a while.

Martha buried Ethel—just after Christmas. Although the painful trips to the hospital stopped, Martha never seemed to regain her joy for life. She smiled when people looked, but Ralph could see that it was only a façade. She laughed at his jokes, though she obviously failed to see any real humor in the world. She tried not to think of Ethel. In fact, she tried not to think of anything. She went through the motions of life, attended to her family, but avoided friends. She felt that having fun without Ethel was a betrayal of their friendship. The only treat she allowed herself was those chocolate delights. She "refused" to become an alcoholic like her uncle, so she quickly gave up the vodka tonics when she realized they were becoming too important to her. Twelve months and thirty pounds heavier after losing her best friend, Martha looked for help. She knew she had been putting Band-Aids on her pain with food and was running from the overwhelming sorrow that threatened to swallow her. She was doing what her instincts told her to do to avoid the emotional pain. However, using these coping strategies actually prevented Martha from recovering from her grief.

Some of the ways we respond to stress give temporary relief, but do not really resolve problems. In fact, they can easily cause new problems. Sometimes to cope we run away from a problem or pretend that it does not exist. Sometimes we fight back or attack others as a way of defending ourselves in times of stress. Sometimes in response to overwhelming stress we simply shut down, tune out the world, and go numb. Although these coping behaviors temporarily dull the pain, we ultimately have to deal with the problems life presents us or suffer the consequences of ignoring them. The last chapter focused on helping you to take action when depression was making it hard for you to get moving. In this chapter you will learn to recognize when your natural coping actions are actually making things worse and how to find more effective and lasting solutions.

Coping strategies that give temporary relief are not always the wrong choice. For example, when Ethel was in the hospital, Martha talked about pleasant memories to distract Ethel from her discomfort and make her feel that her life had meaning. In this case, temporarily distracting Ethel served a purpose. It gave Ethel some short-term relief, and helped her focus on some of the positive things in her life.

So how can you tell when your coping strategy is good or bad? In this example, coping with food and masking her own pain gave Martha only temporary relief and left her with weight gain, a negative self-view,

Key Point

Coping strategies can be a problem when:

1. They do not really resolve the problem.
2. They create new problems along the way.

and depression. This is one of the signs of a faulty coping strategy; short-term relief is traded for longer-term misery. Another sign that your coping strategy is faulty is that it creates a new problem of its own along the way. For example, a drink to calm your nerves can turn into a drinking problem, snacking to relieve tension can lead to weight gain, shopping sprees give temporary satisfaction, but create new tensions if the debts can't be easily managed.

Coping Errors

There are some common coping behaviors that can be problematic or faulty. We call them "Coping Errors." Table 6.1 provides a summary of fourteen common reactions to stress that, although giving some temporary relief, either do not really solve problems or create new problems. Coping Errors fall roughly into five categories. In the first category, "Avoidance," the pattern is to escape stressful situations rather than address them directly. This can include avoiding chores, avoiding unpleasant people, or avoiding facing your problems. Some people try to avoid unpleasant feelings by ignoring them or by refusing to talk about them.

The second category, "Self-Defeating Behaviors," includes actions that might seem helpful or pleasurable, but taken too far or done too often take on a life of their own. These include self-indulgence through food, alcohol, or shopping. Another self-defeating behavior is self-injury. "Impulsive Acts," the third category, are actions that are driven by emotion rather than by logic. Impulsive acts include striking out at others or making hasty changes that you regret after the fact.

The fourth group of Coping Errors is called "Going in Circles." Crying spells, ruminating about problems, and feeling overwhelmed all leave you feeling like you are going in circles, making no progress toward resolution.

The final category, "Giving Up," includes quitting easily out of frustration and running out of steam before finishing a task. In either case, the person finds that he or she cannot persist in trying to accomplish a goal or solve a problem. The rest of this chapter is devoted to a description of each coping error and suggestions for alternate ways to respond. If you recognize your own behaviors as you read about the coping strategies of our patients, make a few notes in your notebook. You will have a chance to add your plans for developing new coping strategies to your Personal Plan for Recovery at the end of the chapter.

Table 6.1 Coping Errors

Category	Coping Error	Definition	Example
Avoidance	Procrastination	Putting things off that need attention	Wait until the last minute to finish a job
	Dodging the issue	Avoiding a stressful person, thought, or situation	Not returning a phone call you dread
	All-or-nothing actions	You cannot do it all, so you do nothing	Feeling overwhelmed by a big task
	Running away	Escape from an unpleasant situation or person	Getting lost in the computer, leaving town
Self-Defeating Actions	Miseating and overeating	Eating excessively or eating the wrong things	Snack when you are not hungry
	Alcohol use and abuse	Relying on alcohol to sleep or change your mood	Drink alcohol to fall asleep at night
	Mall therapy	Shopping to make yourself feel better	Spend money on things you don't need
	Self-injury	Any act of intentional self-injury	Cut, burn, or hit yourself when upset
Impulsivity	Emotional acts	Taking action before thinking things through	Vengeful acts, breaking things
	Hasty changes	Making sudden changes in work or relationships to try to make things better	Change jobs just to get away from someone unpleasant
Going in Circles	Ruminating	Obsessing or worrying excessively	Replaying conversations in your mind
	Crying jags	Crying frequently or for long periods of time	Crying yourself to sleep
Giving Up	Too quick to quit	Giving up if the first attempt fails	"I tried and it didn't work, so forget it"
	Running out of steam	Unable to sustain effort long enough to achieve a goal	Giving up on a diet or other effort that will take time to achieve

---

Exercise 6.1
Coping Errors

Take a minute to look over the list of Coping Errors. Mark the ones you use commonly and jot them down in your notebook. Call the list "Exercise 6.1— Coping Errors." As you read through the chapter focus on those sections that cover the Coping Errors that give you problems.

AVOIDANCE BEHAVIORS

PROCRASTINATION

Putting things off for another day, doing nonproductive activities when you could be working on real problems, and starting new projects before you finish the old ones are all common forms of procrastination. They are ways to avoid stressful activities such as paying bills, calling your mother-in-law, or confronting a co-worker. When you put things off, you give yourself temporary relief from the stress you think you are going to feel when you have to face it. But, the relief you feel by procrastinating makes it more likely that you will avoid things again. The bad part of procrastination is that you do not have a chance to learn that if you confront problems rather than avoid them, things can turn out OK. You miss out on learning that you can cope with problems despite your fear. Procrastination is not a good coping strategy because when problems are ignored they often grow and get more complicated, more intense, or more difficult to stop or solve.

Do you remember Michelle from Chapter 1? Michelle was procrastinating about cleaning out the rec room in her basement. Even though she knew that her kids couldn't use the room any longer because it was so jammed with stuff, she kept putting off doing anything about it. It seemed like there was some kind of magnet that kept pulling things down into the basement and was keeping them there with no hope of return. There were boxes of books from her old classes in college, bags and bags of clothes the children had grown out of, piles of newspapers and magazines, and mounds of toys that her kids didn't play with any longer. But the worst part was all the old sporting gear, electronic equipment, tires, and auto parts that her ex-husband refused to do anything about. When he left her, he said he would be back to pick up these things. But, he kept asking her to hold on to these things for a little bit longer until he had more room to store them.

Fighting Procrastination. When you procrastinate, you can buy some time away from your anxiety and avoid something you don't want to do. But it can stir up guilt, another unpleasant feeling, and knock down your self-esteem. So here is a way to beat procrastination. First you have to define what you are supposed to do. If you are procrastinating you usually know what it is that you are avoiding. Second, you need to ask yourself what you are afraid of or what is interfering with your taking on this task. Could anything bad happen if you took action and stopped procrastinating? Could it be unpleasant or difficult? Are you having any negative automatic thoughts like the ones we described in Chapter 3?

Michelle had a mixture of automatic thoughts. Some of these were about the task itself ("It's just too much for me to handle. . . . It would take forever . . . What could I do with all of that stuff?"). The thoughts that were giving her the most trouble centered on her relationship with her husband ("If I tell him he has to get his things out of the house, I'll lose my last chance for us to get back together . . . He'll get so mad that everybody will be upset . . . I can't put up with any more of his anger"). As you can probably see, Michelle needed to work on spotting her thinking errors and developing some more logical thoughts before tackling this project.

Third, estimate how likely it is that if you take action it will be unpleasant in some way. Is it 100 percent likely or only 10 percent likely? When Michelle really thought about it, she knew it was very likely to be unpleasant, but not terribly so. She rated it about 60 percent. If after thinking about it, you realize that it is probably not likely to be unpleasant, skip the next step and take action right away.

If you think taking action is likely to be unpleasant, the fourth step is to plan ahead by thinking of ways to make it less stressful or more enjoyable. If you can come up with ideas that could help, take those precautions and see what happens. Michelle could not think of a way to make cleaning out her rec room enjoyable, but she did think of ways to make it less unpleasant. She made a deal with herself to work for twenty minutes each night just before her favorite television show aired and then to relax in front of the TV. She also decided to buy some new CDs so she could listen to some upbeat and interesting music while she worked.

Another way to plan for an unpleasant experience is to think of ways to cope if taking action does cause a lot of stress or upset. What can you do to handle the situation? Can you make a plan for coping with any new problems that might arise? Michelle did not look forward to the sorting, cleaning and boxing of all that mess, but most of all she was not looking forward to the reaction of her ex-husband. She used what she had learned from the Thinking Key to calm her fears and plan how to deal with his response. Some of the logical thoughts she developed were: "This marriage is over, stop your fantasies and deal with reality . . . It's his responsibility to take this stuff out of here . . . I'm jumping to conclusions that he would get angry, and so what? His anger doesn't mean that much to me anymore . . . I'll just call him and ask him to move his things."

Here is another example of how to fight procrastination. Remember Adriana from the last chapter? She had the habit of putting off doing her laundry. It did not make her nervous to think about doing it, it was just a lot of work, and it wasn't any fun. What was the likelihood that it would be unpleasant? Adriana said 99.5 percent likely. Was there anything she could do to make it less unpleasant? If she had to do the work herself, there was no way around it being a pain. She could not afford to have someone else do it for her, and she was too old to ask her mother to do it. So if it was going to be unpleasant what could she have done about it? Tough it out? Continue to avoid it? Adriana searched her memory for a time when doing laundry wasn't quite so bad. She recalled times when she and a friend did laundry together at the local laundromat. She had her own washing machine now so it made sense to do the laundry at home. The key seemed to be able to do something fun while she did something unpleasant. She made a plan for doing laundry that included watching videos of some comedies, and she also asked her sister to keep her company. Adriana decided that there was no way to make the task entirely pleasant so she would just deal with the misery of it. It wasn't going to kill her to do laundry, and she knew she would feel better once it was done.

In the last chapter, Masako used Activity Scheduling to help herself get out of a slump of inactivity. She wrote out a day-by-day plan for how she would use her time. Making a plan helped her cope with her indecisiveness as well as her low motivation. Activity scheduling can also be used to overcome procrastination. You can use the Graded Task Assignment (GTA) approach you learned in Chapter 5 if the activity you are avoiding is large or overwhelming. You might remember that Adriana used GTA to deal with her financial problems by breaking down the task into smaller steps.

To give yourself some added incentive to stop procrastinating, plan to reward yourself with an outing, some relaxation time, or an ice cream cone for finishing a chore. Take a leisurely stroll through a mall or go to a bookstore after you have made the phone calls you have dreaded or run the errands you've been putting off. For this method to be most effective you should do the pleasurable activity only *after* you have stopped procrastinating.

DODGING THE ISSUE

When Tony thought about his problems it just made him feel worse. His wife, Jill, tried to get him to talk about the situation, but he couldn't see the point. "Why dwell on it if you can't do anything about it? There is nothing I can do about it. It makes me sick to think about my problems. Nothing is going to change. Just leave me alone." Jill's intentions were good. However, she mistakenly thought that getting things off his chest would make Tony feel better. She wanted to "talk it out" with him, "share feelings," "get it all out on the table." Tony just wanted to be left alone. "I'll deal with it, Jill, just give me some time." Tony, like many people, prided himself on being able to solve problems himself. He didn't really need to talk about it, let out his feelings, or share anything. He just needed time. Sometimes the solutions came to him when he changed the oil in his car or when he mowed the lawn. In the past, Tony's best solutions came to him during the half-time report of the Cowboys game on Sunday afternoons. Under normal circumstances, they came to him without effort. Since his depression began, no matter how hard he thought about it there did not seem to be any solutions, so he dealt with it by *not* dealing with it.

Are you like Tony, dealing with a problem by *not* dealing with it? Have you noticed that even when you are not thinking about a problem it is still there? Are you secretly wishing that you will wake up tomorrow and your problems will have disappeared? That is a wonderful fantasy, but unless you live in a Walt Disney movie, it's not likely to happen.

Solving Problems. In the last chapter we talked about the ACTION plan for solving problems. Rather than putting it off with procrastination or trying to put it out of your mind, choose an annoying problem and try to solve it using those steps. If you are having difficulty working through the steps, get some help from a friend, a family member, or a therapist. Take action and pay attention to how much better it feels when it is done. You may find in trying to solve the problem that things do not turn out exactly as you would have hoped. Sometimes this occurs if your original goal was unrealistic or because you encountered unexpected obstacles or complexities along the way.

When you are depressed, you may mistakenly believe that you have lost your ability to solve problems. The confusion, slowed thinking, and overall negative outlook that accompany depression can block your brain's ability to be logical and rational. The negative self-talk we covered in the Thinking Key can be like a dark cloud over your mind. It can convince you that your problems are too big to be solved or that you are incapable of handling them. Although depression can make it difficult to concentrate, you do not lose your intelligence when you get depressed. Your abilities are still there. Do not let the negative self-talk of depression try to convince you otherwise. The only real way to know whether you can solve a problem is to give it a try. If your solution does not work, try another one. If you were not depressed, that is exactly what you would do. If at first you don't succeed, give it another shot.

ALL-OR-NONE ACTIONS

When you have a lot to do or when you have a big task ahead of you, it is not uncommon to feel overwhelmed. Feeling overwhelmed can keep you from getting up, moving, taking action, and solving problems. You might say to yourself, "I can't do it" or "I can't handle it." Remember that your thoughts ("I can't handle it") and feelings (overwhelmed) directly affect your actions (taking no action). You can break the cycle with the thought-recording exercises in Chapters 3 and 4 or with the behavior activation exercises from Chapter 5. Here are a few other suggestions.

Getting Unstuck. Michelle usually felt less depressed when she was able to accomplish something. It didn't always matter what task it was. She followed her doctor's advice and spent thirty uninterrupted minutes twice each week all by herself. Sometimes she paid bills. Sometimes she rearranged her pantry. Sometimes she sent thank you notes. Sometimes she gave herself a manicure. Once she made some progress, she felt the burden begin to lift. Getting unstuck gave her hope and made her believe that she had some power to overcome her depression.

Finding the Middle Ground. Rather than looking at a problem as being either manageable or totally overwhelming, try to get a more accurate appraisal. If a task seems too big and your energy too limited, you will probably avoid it altogether. In the depths of her depression, Michelle saw her household as completely unmanageable, so she stopped trying to handle it. She thought of taking care of her physical appearance as a useless task since she believed that no one would ever want her. She slacked off on that as well. She was looking at housekeeping and personal grooming in an all-or-none way. Finding the middle ground means viewing the problem in less extreme terms. You can use the exercises in Chapter 3 to help you stop thinking and acting in an all-or-none style.

Another way to find the middle ground is to set smaller and more manageable goals. Perfect appearance or a perfectly clean home may not be possible to attain when you are low on energy and motivation. Set a goal for what would be "good enough for now" and get yourself to that level of performance. Michelle decided that if her living room and kitchen were clean, her house would be in good enough condition to satisfy her for now. She thought she looked better with makeup on and when her hair was styled. Because her hair was too much of a hassle to fix each day, she decided to keep it in a pony tail, but put on enough makeup to hide the splotches and dark circles and to give her cheeks and lips a little color. That would be good enough for now. When she looked better and her house was in order, she felt less depressed.

Exercise 6.2
Make It Happen Today—Get Unstuck

Pick one problem that needs your attention and take a step toward solving it today. Schedule thirty minutes of problem solving time and make something happen.

RUNNING AWAY

Bob had a nice piece of land in West Texas where he would go to commune with nature, hunt, fish, and relax. He believed that weekends in the country did him a lot of good. He usually came back feeling refreshed. Unfortunately, that peace of mind didn't last long. The reality of his problems always seemed to hit him like a ton of bricks as soon as he drove into the city limits. He wanted to turn around and drive back, but he knew that he had to go to work the next day and do his best to take care of his family. Inevitably, Bob returned from the country to complaints from his wife, Brenda, chores to do, or problems to solve. When he couldn't run away he tuned out his wife by turning on his computer to play a game or surf the web. Brenda prodded him to join her in the living room, which he usually promised to do after he finished one more task. Before he knew it, it was past midnight, and Brenda had gone to bed.

Running from his problems had become a habit for Bob. He had opted for temporary reprieves from his difficulties rather than taking them on and overcoming them once and for all because he believed that his efforts would be futile or would only make things worse. He hated arguing with anyone, and talking over his concerns inevitably seemed to end in an argument. Running away was not making things better for Bob; instead it seemed to make things worse.

How to Stop Running. The strategies described above for controlling procrastination and for getting unstuck also can work for making yourself stop running from your problems. Another solution is to try to think of how you used to cope with problems before the depression began. Think of the times in your life when you had to deal with problems straight on. Try to image what you were like during those times. Were you more confident? What would you have done differently at those times to cope with the problems you are facing today? Try to think like the old you. Make a plan that would have worked back then and put your plan into action. Try acting like your old self for a while and you may start feeling like your old self again.

SELF-DEFEATING ACTIONS

MISEATING AND OVEREATING

"This chocolate fudge nut brownie may not solve my problems, but I deserve it. I have worked hard all day, no one cut me any slack, and it took everything I had just to get out of bed this morning. I'll just run an extra mile tomorrow or I'll skip lunch." Isabella paused to stare at her chocolate fudge brownie wondering whether or not she should have ice cream with it. While at the same time she was thinking, "Who am I fooling? I have no self-control. That's why my life is so messed up." Sound familiar? Other common errors in coping include denying that eating the wrong things is a problem, bargaining with yourself to do better next time, and criticizing yourself after the last bite is swallowed.

Why is eating such a common problem? The answer is because food tastes good, you can have it any time you want, it's legal, and it never talks back or makes demands of you. Some would say it is the perfect companion. Eating gives you immediate gratification in a world where rewards are usually hard to come by. Comfort foods that are sweet, or soft, or remind us of our childhoods are the ones that beckon us. They promise us that sense of serenity we long for. And they often deliver on that promise, if only for a short while. We also are surrounded by images of happy people eating sweet or fattening foods. The displays at restaurants are intended to tantalize, lure you, tempt you. They are very effective. Not to mention the fact that Halloween candy starts hitting the stores by the truckload early in September and is quickly replaced by Christmas sweets and New Year celebration foods. Then comes Valentine chocolates, marshmallow bunnies, jelly beans, and chocolate-filled Easter yummies. These are followed by Memorial Day barbeque fixings, Fourth of July picnic makings, and Labor Day cookouts. Then the whole thing just repeats itself. It is no wonder that over 50 percent of the people in the United States have a weight control problem.

We all struggle with temptations. There is the logical side of us that says no, sets limits, tells us not hide behind food but to face the problems that stress us. Then there is the emotional side of us that just wants to feel better quickly and is willing to do anything to make that happen. You are stuck in the middle, feel lousy anyway, can't make decisions about food, and are hopeless about your chances of gaining self-control. So you give in and eat. For a while the world does seem like a better place. Then you come back to reality and it starts all over again. Many people deal with eating problems by telling themselves that they will swear off high-carbohydrate foods, desserts, or fast food. Total abstinence from these foods is hard to accomplish. In the next section we will suggest some other coping strategies.

Keep a Lean Household. Stock your pantry and refrigerator with healthy things to eat that are not overloaded with fat, sugar, and calories. Keep reasonably healthy snack foods around for those times when you have the munchies. Beware of fat-free foods that are high in sugar. Read the labels.

Check Your Basket. While you are waiting your turn in the checkout line, look over your basket and take inventory of the number of junk foods or high-fat foods you are about to purchase. For each one think about whether or not you really need it, whether there might be a health-ier alternative, and whether or not you could put a few items back. Do not let yourself be fooled into thinking that these items are just for the kids or for your partner. Be honest with yourself. If you do not want to go back and put them away, tell the checkout clerk that you have changed your mind and do not want the items any more. They will have them reshelved.

Ease into It. If you are a serious junk food eater you may have a hard time changing your eating habits all at once. Try these suggestions for getting started. If you eat junk food everyday, try to limit your intake to one item each day or limit yourself to indulging every other day. The idea is to move toward better eating habits by making smaller changes at first. This way you will not feel completely deprived.

Just Say No. Some people do not have the willpower to limit the amount of junk foods they eat. They find it easier to just give up these items altogether. When you are trying to gain control over your eating habits you may want to give up one troublesome food product at a time. For Isabella, the biggest problem was eating sandwiches. She liked the bread more than the things she put inside it, so she decided to give up sandwich bread altogether. It was much easier for her than trying to eat it every other day, especially when the loaf was in her house all the time just begging to be eaten. For Isabella, this was a new way of dealing with overeating. She knew that her eating was partly driven by stress and partly just a series of bad habits she had developed over time. In the past, when she had tried to diet she approached it as an all-or-nothing task. She was either on the diet totally or she "blew it" and forgot about it. It was hard for her to stick with it 100 percent of the time, so diets usually failed. This new approach of fixing one habit at a time allowed her to make permanent changes without dieting being so painful.

Food Is Fuel. Some people overeat or eat the wrong things when they are stressed or depressed. Others get so busy that they forget to eat or they lose their desire to eat. Food is fuel that your body needs regularly. It is important to make time to eat regularly even if you have lost your appetite. Eating regularly does not mean that you have to eat three large meals each day, but it does mean that you have to eat something at least three times each day. Ask your doctor for some suggestions on a diet plan if you are uncertain what to eat.

Exercise 6.3
Take Action Today with Food

Make a change in your eating habits today. Do something different. Add something you should be eating or skip something that you really should not be eating. Don't wait for the motivation to come to you. Just start something positive right now and the motivation will follow. Keep track of your successes in your notebook.

ALCOHOL USE AND ABUSE

Alcohol is so socially acceptable that it is easy to become dependent upon it without realizing it. "How much is too much alcohol?" Vic inquired almost defensively. "What harm is it, it's not like I'm driving drunk, getting sloppy, or dancing naked in public. No one gets hurt. The kids are asleep, my wife could care less, and I still make it to work." Vic defended his drinking habits to his therapist, but he didn't really believe his own argument. He had heard that alcohol was a depressant that could worsen his mood. And he knew that a few drinks helped him drift off to sleep, but made his sleep restless and disturbed. His wife complained that he spent more time at night with Jack Daniels than with her. Even before Vic finished his argument for drinking "to calm his nerves," he stopped and said, "I know I need to stop." His therapist knew how hard it was to stop, so she encouraged Vic to get some support from the people at Alcoholics Anonymous and helped him to make a plan for how to control the alcohol.

Do you think that you might have a drinking problem? Here are some questions to ask yourself about your drinking habits.

1. Have you ever felt that you should cut down or discontinue your alcohol use?
2. Have you ever been annoyed by someone criticizing your alcohol use?
3. Have you ever felt bad or guilty about your alcohol use?
4. Have you ever had to drink first thing in the morning to steady your nerves or get rid of a hangover?

If you answered "yes" to any of these questions, then there is a good chance that you have a drinking problem that needs treatment. It may not be easy to admit this, but it is important that you take steps to control your alcohol or drug use.

Stopping Alcohol Dependence. There is not enough space in this book to fully discuss how to stop drinking alcohol to excess. It's not a small task. You will need all the help you can get. Alcohol use has been studied extensively as clinicians have searched for answers on how to help people quit. The findings of this research have shown that getting involved in Alcoholics Anonymous is a very effective way to get sober and stay sober. Many of our patients have found that AA is the only thing that has worked for them. The trick is to make yourself go to the meetings and stick with it until you get the right results.

A very helpful part of being in AA is having a sponsor who can work with you. This is usually a more senior member of the group who serves as a mentor or coach or just a friend when you need one. An AA sponsor has been through the program and can answer your questions, give you advice, and help you make sense of the hard times.

Other alcohol treatments exist, including cognitive-behavior therapy. Hospital-based programs can be helpful for people who tend to get severe physical symptoms of withdrawal from alcohol. Psychiatric medications can help with underlying emotional problems such as anxiety or depression. There are many day treatment programs and outpatient therapies that help people to quit. AA is often a component of these programs.

When your alcohol use has stopped, you may find that many of your symptoms of depression, such as insomnia, low energy, and irritability, also go away. These changes are generally noticeable within several weeks of sobriety. While you are waiting for the symptoms caused by alcohol use to subside, you can use methods from any of the Five Keys to help you feel better.

Exercise 6.4
Take Action Today with Drinking

Take stock of your drinking habits. If you answered "yes" to any of the four questions about alcohol use, write out a plan for change. Set a specific goal and commit to a method of changing your habits. Look up the number of Alcoholics Anonymous in the phone book. Ask for help from others if you need it. Most important, stop trying to convince yourself that it's not really a problem.

Exercise. A wonderful example of how changing your actions can really change your mood and your self-view is exercise. The research on exercise and depression has proven that it can be a powerful tool for improving your symptoms. There are many direct physical benefits such as helping to control your weight, keeping you healthy and fit, and increasing your energy. When you use up physical energy to exercise you are also burning emotional energy and freeing yourself of anger or anxiety. An improved self-image is one of the indirect benefits of exercise. Seeing yourself take action in a positive way and watching the improvements in your health and appearance can boost confidence and make you want to keep going. Exercise also can give you a break from the stresses in your life. Time away to think can help you gain a new and better perspective on your problems. With a clearer perspective, more energy, and a brighter mood, you will be ready to make improvements in other aspects of your life.

Before getting started, you should check with your doctor to make certain that you are healthy enough to begin an exercise program. The American Heart Association recommends walking as a way to begin your exercise program. Set a weekly exercise goal for yourself, for example to walk three times each week for at least fifteen to twenty minutes each time. Although you may have to start out slowly, the goal is to walk at a pace that raises your heart rate. Try walking as if you are late for an appointment. As you become more physically fit, you can increase the length of time you spend walking, the distance you walk, or the speed at which you walk. Treadmills that track these features are helpful in measuring your accomplishments. The nice thing about walking is that it is a very convenient form of exercise. It does not require any special equipment and you do not usually have to go to any special locations.

There are, of course, many other options for exercise. You just need to find something that you like to do. Perhaps variety in exercise is appealing to you. Many enjoy a combination of aerobic exercise and weight training. For others, playing a sport or attending exercise classes with others is fun. Even heavy chores such as gardening, scrubbing floors, or cleaning out your garage can be a way to begin to get more physical. An exercise program should be something that you can look forward to. It's often hard to get started, but once you make that commitment to yourself, exercise can become a healthy part of your usual routine.

One of the most common reasons given for not exercising is not having the time. Job and family demands can take up most of your waking day. If you wait until the end of the day, you might not have the energy. Before you give up on the idea altogether, consider getting up a little earlier in the morning to exercise. If it is too early to go outside for a walk, invest in an exercise video that you can use at home or get a book from the library on exercise and create a short exercise plan that you can follow at home. If you have early morning family duties, ask your partner or an older child to help out at home so that you can exercise. Exercising first thing in the morning eliminates the problem of having to find time or energy at the end of the day. Of course, if you are not a morning person, you might prefer to find time after work or at the end of the day to exercise.

Remember what we said in Chapter 5 about the ACTION steps to solving problems? You can usually come up with at least a dozen different solutions for every problem including finding time to exercise. Be creative. Make sure you are not just making excuses to avoid exercise. Give some thought to how you want to increase your physical activity and add it to your Personal Plan for Recovery at the end of the chapter.

Remember in the last chapter when we talked about Nike therapy? This method is useful for getting into an exercise routine as well. Some people wait for motivation to pick them up, carry them off the couch, slide on their sneakers, and push them out the door. If that is what you are waiting for, you are likely to have a long wait. Make a decision about exercise. If you want to give it a try, schedule the time. Make an appointment with yourself and keep the appointment. It also can be very helpful to take a friend along with you. Being with a friend can make the exercise more fun, and the time will probably go by more quickly.

Exercise 6.5
Take Action Today with Exercise

Make a plan for starting to exercise or improve your current exercise program. Write the plan down in your notebook. Do this now before you forget or change your mind. Keep an exercise log in which you record the type and length of each exercise period. Logging your exercise can help you recognize your achievements and stay with the program.

MALL THERAPY

"There is nothing like a day at the mall to lift my spirits," Geneva confessed. "I call it Mall Therapy. Rather than spending the hundred dollars for therapy, I spend it on myself."

"Does it work?" her therapist asked.

"Yes, for a while anyway. Actually after a few hours at the Mall my mind seems to clear, and I can see things more clearly. It's not like I'm going from store to store shopping for an answer to my problems. But it does put me in a better frame of mind. It makes me feel more hopeful," Geneva explained.

"Is there a downside to doing this?"

"Everything has a downside if you're not careful, especially using credit cards. I've let the spending get away from me in the past. It took me a long time to get out of debt," Geneva admitted. "That was depressing in and of itself."

"You said that Mall Therapy helps you see things more clearly. Why do you suppose that happens?" the therapist inquired, although she suspected she already knew the answer.

"It's because I get to do something for myself for a change and get away from the drudgery of my life. I can act like a normal person just like everyone else who is walking through the Mall, carefree and happy. No one knows the real me, the depressed me, the hopeless me. I'm just Miss Normal."

"It seems to be that when you are depressed you think so negatively and hopelessly that it interferes with creative problem solving," the therapist offered. "When you are in a better mood, your mind is clearer and freer to think, to be hopeful, and to come up with ways to address your problems. Shopping may be only one of the many activities that lift your spirits. Rather than giving it up altogether, maybe there are some things

you can do to keep yourself out of trouble. Or maybe we can work together to think of other things that can lift your spirits and make you feel
normal."

Mall Therapy can work, but it usually gives only temporary relief.
When you are depressed, you need bigger interventions that solve problems more permanently, not just distract you from them. Use some of the
other methods from this chapter and from Chapter 5 to help you take action in ways that give you the results you need. In the meantime, here is
an idea for enjoying Mall Therapy without creating new problems along
the way.

Hide the Credit Cards. One of the most creative strategies we have
heard for controlling overspending came from a story told by a woman in
a self-help group for depression. She said that she would put her credit
cards in a glass of water and freeze them. When she had the urge to shop
she had to take the time to thaw out her credit cards before she could use
them. This gave her enough time to regain her self-control and decide
not to shop when she was feeling weak. It was a little more hassle, but
"saved her from herself" in those stressful moments when she just "had
to" shop.

Many people think they feel better when they buy something for
themselves. It is not always the actual item that brings pleasure but the
process of hitting the mall or just taking time out to do something nice for
yourself. A new purse is nice, but it can hardly cure a depression. A new
toy is fun to play with, but the thrill wears off. Bigger items can be enjoyable until the credit card statement comes or until you come up short
at the end of the month and can't pay your bills.

Perhaps you can have some of the benefits of shopping without the
problems associated with the purchase. Take time to do something else
nice for yourself. Go to a movie, sit in a comfortable chair at your favorite
bookstore, or spend a quiet hour at home before everyone comes home
from school or work. The important thing is that you are taking time for
yourself.

If the hunt for a bargain is what you like, then hunt away, but leave
your money and credit cards at home. If you find something you really
like, you will have to put it on lay-away or go back home to get your
money. Either way you have bought some time to think through your
plan before spending the money. These delaying techniques can help
you avoid impulsive spending.

HURTING YOURSELF

"The first time I did it, it was just an urge. I knew it wasn't logical or
rational. I just felt the urge to put the curling iron closer to my skin

and burn myself. It hurt, but in a strange way, I felt better. I can't explain it."

THERAPIST: What do you think about what you did to yourself?

ADRIANA: Oh, it was really stupid. I can't believe I did that. It makes no sense at all.

THERAPIST: Have you done this more than once?

ADRIANA: I'm embarrassed to admit it, but yes. It happened twice in the same week. And there have been other times when I had the urge, but I stopped myself from doing it.

THERAPIST: What did you do to keep from hurting yourself?

ADRIANA: I went for a walk to calm down until I felt like I had more self-control.

THERAPIST: You hit on the answer. Intense emotion can be what stirs up the urge to hurt yourself. To gain control you have to reduce the emotion in some way. Taking a walk is one way to do it.

Some people feel an overwhelming urge to hurt themselves when they are feeling down. At these times, they are often lonely and sad or feel empty inside. The urge starts as a thought and continues to build into an impulse.

Getting in the Safety Zone. A good way to fight the urge to hurt yourself is to get support from other people. Try talking with a friend or visiting someone until you feel more self-control. People are not usually comfortable in telling others about these urges. It might be easier to tell a friend that you are upset and you don't want to be alone. Loneliness is a key factor in self-injury. So do what you can to be with others.

If the urge to hurt yourself came after a bad experience with another person, especially one that made you feel rejected, take some time to do the thought-recording exercises from Chapters 3 and 4 to try to sort out your feelings. It can be helpful to talk about your feelings with a friend or family member. You can also call the suicide and crisis center in your community. Usually there will be someone who can help you regain your perspective and your self-control.

If you know that you are prone to self-destructive acts, prevention is important. Plan ahead by removing those objects from your home that you are likely to use in harming yourself. If you remove the temptation, the urge is more likely to pass.

IMPULSIVITY

EMOTIONAL ACTS

Sometimes Michelle gets so upset that she feels her whole world is crashing down on her. She gets overloaded with demands, worries, and aggravations and runs out of patience to cope with them. During those times she feels so overwrought she thinks she will explode. If something or someone upsets her, she has the urge to strike back in some way. "I get so overwhelmed, I feel like grabbing something and pitching it right through my front window. I mean it. I feel like I'm going to explode or go running out of the house screaming. I don't have any strength left to fight the world or to give myself a pep talk. I can get so completely overwhelmed that I cannot imagine feeling any better."

Michelle is describing times when she is too stressed out to think through her problems, to be creative in solving them, or even to slow down and reason with herself. She feels compelled to release the pain through some act that shows just how bad she feels, like breaking something or throwing something out the window. Before she does any of these emotional acts that she will later regret, she has to find a way to calm herself and to gather her senses.

Relaxation Exercises. You have probably heard people say "just relax," or "take it easy," or "chill out." These are good ideas, but often they are easier said than done. Rather than rely on sheer will alone to calm down, many people find relaxation exercises beneficial in helping them to reduce muscular tension associated with stress. When your body is physically more relaxed, the intensity of your emotions will decrease.

There are numerous relaxation exercises you can try. The most common type is called progressive muscle relaxation. You relax your muscles one by one from head to toe starting with the muscles in your face and ending with your feet. To do this exercise, start with imagining your muscles loosening, letting go of any tension you might feel. For example, as you are reading this, relax the tension in your forehead. Smooth out your forehead. Don't furrow your brow. Now turn your attention to your jaw. Loosen your jaw, letting your teeth separate slightly. Can you feel yourself relaxing? It is very common for people to hold their tension in their faces. Even if you only tighten your jaw slightly or bring your eyebrows together just a little, you can create enough tension in your face muscles to give yourself a headache. Learning to recognize the sensation of tension in those muscles will cue you to relax and let the tension go. Try it and see what happens.

You can buy relaxation tapes at the bookstore or you might consider learning to do yoga. Take a class or rent an instructional video. Some businesses offer relaxation training to their employees, and some hospitals offer courses as well. Whichever method you choose, it will take practice to learn to relax. It is a skill that you can acquire. At first it may take a great deal of effort to relax your whole body. But once you learn how to feel relaxed, you can put yourself in a relaxed state in a matter of minutes.

Self-Care. Self-care can be a good coping strategy when you feel so uptight that you are about to burst. One of the simplest self-care activities is to spend some time alone away from the noises, demands, and stresses of your life. Be sure to set a time limit for yourself so that your self-care time does not turn into avoidance of the problem. The goal of that quiet time is to calm down, clear your mind of worries, and rest. If you have not eaten in a while, this is a good time for a meal or at least a snack. Slow down and rest your mind and your body. While you are having your quiet time, do not try to figure things out or solve problems. You can do that after you rest.

Some people, like Bethany, prefer to get out of the house to clear their minds. The wind blowing in their faces feels refreshing. Getting away from phones or television, listening to the sounds of nature, and getting physically away from the things that stress you, if only for a short while, can revitalize you. If you have kids, play outside with them or take them to the park. Take the dog for a walk.

Other kinds of self-care activities involve doing things that make you feel good. Here is where it gets tricky. Remember that eating or drinking alcohol to make yourself feel good can create new problems. So choose your activities wisely. Indulge yourself in something that you will not later regret. Michelle takes a bubble bath. Tony takes his car to the car wash. Geneva gets a massage. Vic goes fishing alone at the stream near his house.

Response Prevention. Response prevention is a method for keeping yourself from engaging in an emotional act that you will later regret by doing an alternative and safer behavior. For example, if you feel the urge to throw something, grab a pillow instead of something breakable. Squeeze the pillow until the urge passes. If you tend to say mean things when you are feeling upset, walk away until you feel more self-control or write down your angry words rather than speak them aloud. If you can keep yourself from engaging in an emotional act, you will feel much better in the long run.

HASTY CHANGES

There are times when a situation is so bothersome that you want to escape, but out of fear of the consequences you try to hang in. A new opportunity may come along that appears to be the answer to your prayers.

It seems to provide a reasonable means to escape an unpleasant situation. Perhaps a new job opportunity comes your way. Or if the problem is a relationship, you meet a new potential partner who promises to take you away from it all. This is where the problem begins. When you are in emotional or psychological pain, any alternative might seem better than your current situation. The urge to escape can make you see only the "bright side" of making this change and ignore the downside. Just because the grass looks greener on the other side, it doesn't mean you aren't jumping into quicksand.

Adriana dated Terry on and off for about six months. He was a nice guy, but he drank a little too much and could be obnoxious when he was drunk. Despite knowing that Terry was wrong for her, Adriana hesitated to break it off because she knew it would hurt his feelings.

Rick, Adriana's old boyfriend, came back into town and looked her up. Adriana remembered the history of conflict that led to the end of that relationship, but still found herself accepting Rick's invitations. With Rick in her life, Adriana felt she had the courage to break it off with Terry. She thought about Rick's good points and the fun they used to have together. Although she tried to convince herself that she and Rick were a better match than she and Terry, a little voice in her head told her that she was jumping out of the frying pan and into the fire.

It took only two weeks for the old Rick to reemerge. Adriana caught him taking money out of her purse. And she saw him flirting with a girl at the bar, though he claimed they were just old friends. She had allowed him to "semi-move in" with her, and his stuff was everywhere. He had already made several long-distance phone calls from her phone, had eaten all her food, and had used her number for potential employers to call. Now she was faced with another dilemma. If she kicked Rick out before he had a job, she would be out all the money he owed her. Adriana wished that she had listened to that little voice in her had that said, "Don't make any hasty changes. Think this through before you act."

Think before You Act. The obvious way to avoid making hasty decisions is to take more time to think things over before you act. Make yourself be objective about a situation by considering the advantages and the disadvantages of making a change to an unpleasant situation. Also consider the advantages and disadvantages of *not* making that change. Look at it from all sides and then use that logical part of your thinking to make the decision. If you have that little voice in your ear telling you to stop and think, listen to it. Consider other ways of solving your problems. The easy way out may not be the best way out.

GOING IN CIRCLES

RUMINATING

When you are troubled by an event or by a conflict with another person, it is hard to stop thinking about it. Thinking about your difficulties is not a problem unless you find that you are overthinking, overanalyzing, and getting nowhere. Rumination is nonproductive thinking or nonproductive worry. You think about something over and over, getting more and more upset with each repetition. Rumination can start with replaying an incident in your mind's eye. Your imagination can take it from there, filling in the missing pieces about how the event could have turned out or how it might turn out. Ruminating uses a lot of mental and emotional energy. In fact, in a *USA TODAY* Snapshot poll, 67 percent of adults surveyed said that they regretted wasting time on worry.

To cope with obsessing or ruminating, you have to change gears, go down a different path, and let go of the upsetting event. You need to quiet your mind and disengage from the bad feelings long enough to relax, regroup, and go forward in a positive way. One of the best methods for doing this is called thought stopping.

Thought Stopping. This exercise can help you control obsessional and ruminative thoughts and excessive worry. It usually involves three steps. The first step is to recognize that you are obsessing over something. If you can't seem to let go of an issue or an event, then you are probably ruminating. Once you recognize that you are ruminating you have to tell yourself, "There I go again."

The second step is to imagine a large stop sign popping up before your eyes. This is your way of telling yourself to interrupt the ruminating. You might prefer the image of a hand, like that of a traffic cop, telling you to halt. It can be helpful to say "Stop" loudly and forcefully to yourself. If you are in public, you can give yourself the stop command in your mind without actually verbalizing the word. Some people find it helpful to use self-talk in which they tell themselves to stop thinking about the upsetting event, that rehashing it serves no real purpose, and that they must get beyond this.

The third step in thought stopping is to divert your mental image or thoughts to something new and more pleasant. You can choose an image of a peaceful place you have been or have wanted to visit. The image can be like a photograph or video of a location or can be a scene in which you imagine yourself doing something pleasant like taking a walk through a park or watching waves crash on the beach. If you find that you ruminate when you are lying in bed at night, the image visualized should be one that ends with seeing yourself somewhere safe and comfortable where it is easy to fall asleep.

Thought Stopping

Step 1: Recognize that you are ruminating.
Step 2: Imagine a big stop sign and tell yourself to *"Stop!"*
Step 3: Switch the image to something pleasant and relaxing.
You can repeat the steps as needed until the negative thoughts dissipate.

CRYING JAGS

One of the common symptoms of depression is tearfulness. Sometimes the tears flow when you are overcome by sadness, touched by a positive event, or have reached your limits of frustration. Some people find that a "good cry" is cleansing, leaving them emotionally and physically spent, but calmer and ready to move forward. Others find crying jags emotionally draining and annoying.

"I cry for no reason," Julie complained. "It doesn't matter where I am, at work, at home. It's so embarrassing and irritating. I'm not usually a crybaby. But once I get started I can't seem to make myself stop."

Crying is not a character flaw and it cannot hurt you. However, if you are not used to crying it can feel very uncomfortable. You can mistakenly assume that it means that you are "falling apart" or "coming unglued." If you are crying too often or for long periods of time, here are a few ideas that might help.

Setting Limits. Keep in mind that there is nothing wrong with crying when you are upset. It is a normal human response to distress. Rather than try to not cry at all, it may be easier to set a time limit on it. When you start to cry, look at the clock and tell yourself that you can cry for ten minutes. When your time is up, do all that you can to calm yourself and put your mind on other things. You can even use the thought-stopping exercise we described previously.

Distraction Techniques. To cut down on crying spells, try to distract yourself temporarily from your tears. This may sound a bit like procrastination. But, it is briefer and comes with an agreement you make with yourself to go back to the problem that upset you after you have calmed down. Distraction techniques are activities that temporarily take your mind off your troubles. Distraction is intended to stop the flow of negative thoughts so that you calm down and feel more capable of dealing with problems. Some good distractions include cooking, gardening, reading, playing games, exercising, watching a good movie, talking to friends, and doing puzzles.

GIVING UP

TOO QUICK TO QUIT

It was clear in talking with Clayton that he was feeling frustrated with his inability to control his depression. Any suggestion his doctor made was quickly rejected with "Tried that. It didn't work." In fact, Clayton had tried several different strategies for fixing his depression on his own. But, when he did not see the results that he expected, he gave up and tried something else. He felt as if he had tried everything. That's why he finally decided to ask his doctor for some help. Clayton is not the kind of person who asks for help very often. He is a do-it-yourselfer and has always taken pride in that.

As Clayton described his efforts at controlling his depression, a distinct pattern emerged. Although most of his ideas sounded like reasonable approaches, Clayton gave up too quickly when the results he expected did not occur as quickly as he would have hoped. He described his frustration and irritation when he took medicine, exercised, tried to think more positively, took a vacation, talked to a friend, and still found himself depressed.

If you have a clinical depression and not just momentary sadness over a bad event, then it will take some time and effort to get over your symptoms. Clayton was impatient because he expected quick results. Rather than trying the same intervention a second time, he switched too soon to something new. He did not give any intervention enough time to work.

Persistence and Patience. It is tough to have patience when you are feeling badly. If you tend to be impatient by nature, depression will probably make it worse. The suggestions for building persistence and patience can help you when your recovery from depression is progressing slowly.

1. Don't set yourself up for disappointment by expecting a quick cure. Understand ahead of time that a sustained effort will be required.
2. If you are trying a biological treatment, realize that medications and other biological interventions take several weeks and consis-

tent use to begin working. Plan to use additional strategies to help you feel better the first three to four weeks.

3. If a solution to a problem does not work, go back and evaluate what went wrong. Use the ACTION steps from Chapter 5 to help you better define the problem and select another solution that might be more effective.

4. Anger and frustration can rob you of patience. Know this and take steps toward curbing them by using the exercises in this chapter.

5. Remember that in depression your emotions color your thinking and affect your actions. Do not let your frustration control your behavior by making you give up too easily. Use your logical side to help you hang in.

6. All-or-none thinking can lead you down the wrong path. If you think a treatment strategy should work either all at once or not at all, you probably will be wrong. Recovery often happens in small steps. Day-to-day improvement may not always be easy to recognize.

7. Know yourself. If it is your nature to be impatient, recognize this as one explanation for giving up too quickly.

RUNNING OUT OF STEAM

"It is just so hard. I'm tired of trying. I'm tired of feeling bad. I don't want to have to work this hard." When you have struggled with depression for a long time you may occasionally run out of steam. It takes a great deal of effort to cope with the demands of your life while you are trying to overcome depression. Some people can reach "burnout" and want to stop trying. When this occurs, the idea of suicide may start to sound like a reasonable solution. If our patients feel burned out from trying and want to give up, we try to help them hang in long enough to give the treatment a chance to work. These techniques often help them get back on track.

Take a Break from Trying. Rather than giving up altogether, we sometimes suggest that patients take a brief vacation from trying. During a short break of a few days up to a week or two, they simply try to do the best they can while doing only the bare minimum that is required of them. They do not make great efforts to change, to control their habits, or to change their outlooks. They simply try not to think about their depression, read about it, or even talk to their therapists about it. The only exception is that if they are currently on medications, they continue their medications without interruption. We help patients set a limit on this vacation by agreeing to see them or call them after a specified time interval to reevaluate their options and get back to work. Just like you sometimes need a break from your work or your family, there are times when you may benefit from a break in treatment.

Set Smaller Goals. Another way to cope with burnout is to set small goals for recovery. Instead of trying to fix a major problem in your life, fix a series of smaller things. Add some pleasure as well, not big Disneyland-size pleasure, but smaller "walk in the park"-size pleasure.

Ask for Assistance. You do not have to overcome your problems all by yourself. There are people in the community and probably in your family and social network who would gladly help you through the rough spots. Reread the earlier section on how to ask for help and reach out to someone you trust.

Look for Inspiration. Sometimes we need an inspirational boost to make it through times when we have given up hope or have run out of energy. Go back to a person, a reading, or a place where you have felt inspired in the past. If you are a member of a support group, ask others how they got through these difficult times. If you know someone who has struggled with adversity that was not easy to overcome, ask him how he dealt with wanting to give up. Some people find spiritual guidance to be the key to sustaining their effort. If you have a spiritual guide or leader, ask him or her for advice. Pray about it if that has been helpful in the past.

Key Point

When you take action, you begin to break the cycle of depression.

When you use the Action Key to solve problems, a number of other changes can occur. For example, when you actively cope with and solve problems you begin to feel better about yourself. Your self-confidence will begin to return as you prove you can make changes and overcome difficulties. Even small successes can improve your motivation and give you hope that you will get your life back to normal.

Look Ahead

When it seems like everyday life throws you another problem, it is easy to become so focused on survival that you forget about making plans for the future. It is the hope of positive things to come that helps motivate us to work hard, to resolve our troubles, and to feel optimistic. We need to be able to look forward to better days.

You have already begun to set goals for overcoming your depression in your Personal Plan for Recovery. Look beyond this and begin to set some goals for what you would like your life to be like in two years, or five years. Think ahead and write down some of your ideas in your Personal Plan for Recovery under the heading "Goals for the Future." You may find that along the way your goals change as your life circumstances change. That's OK. What's most important is that you continue to look ahead to better days. Assume that your depression will pass. Let yourself dream and turn it into a plan for the future.

The Action Key in Your Personal Plan for Recovery

It's time to update your Personal Plan for Recovery. You've already measured your symptoms, identified your strengths, and set some preliminary goals for change. You may have already added ideas from the Thinking Key to your Personal Plan for Recovery. Now you have a chance to write down your thoughts about changes you would like to make in the ways in which you cope with difficulties. There are blank worksheets for this exercise in the Appendix. Here is an example of how Martha updated her plan to improve her coping skills. Martha lost her friend Ethel to cancer and was having difficulty coping with her feelings. The coping strategies that she was used to relying on were not doing the trick. Martha made new plans for overcoming her depression using the Action Key.

Exercise 6.6
Personal Plan for Recovery Worksheet—Part V
'My Plan for Using the Action Key':

   MARTHA'S EXAMPLE

1. What are my strengths that can help me to take action in solving problems?

   I used to know how to have fun, how to solve problems, and how to motivate myself. I have always been the type of person that takes action when it's needed.

2. Is there anything that I am doing in response to stress that is either not really helpful or is causing new problems for me?

Yes. Eating too much food and drinking alcohol is making me feel worse. Keeping my feelings to myself isn't working. I try to ignore them, but they don't go away.

3. Am I using avoidance as a way to cope? If so, what do I want to do about it?

   I guess that I'm avoiding talking about the loss of my friend Ethel. I don't really like talking about her, but everyone tells me that it's the best thing for me. I guess I'll start with talking to my husband more and then talk it over with a therapist.

4. Are there any self-defeating actions that I need to change? What other coping strategies do I want to use instead of those that can be self-defeating?

   I stopped drinking already, but I've also got to stop eating sweets. I'm going to try not buying sweets anymore. If they are not in the house, I won't have to try to resist them. I'll get my husband to stop bringing them home. I need to get back on an exercise program to help me lose this weight. I used to walk with a friend every evening. I'll make a commitment to start walking again tomorrow.

5. Are there times when I am impulsive in my words or in my actions? Which ones do I want to start learning to control?

   I don't have a problem with being impulsive.

6. Am I going in circles instead of solving problems? Which strategy do I want to try to overcome this cycle?

   I don't ruminate or cry a lot.

7. Do I give up too easily? What encouragement can I give myself to keep trying?

   I give up on exercise and dieting too easily. I've tried several weight loss programs, but they work too slowly. I need to make up my mind to keep trying even when the results come slowly. In the past, I would tell myself "don't give up." I need to get back into that habit.

8. Goals for the Future. After I start to feel better, what goal would I like to achieve over the next year? The next 5 years?

   1-year Goals: *Lose 15 pounds; get closer to my other friends*
   5-Year Goals: *Travel more with my husband when he retires; stay as healthy as I can; teach my granddaughter to play the piano.*

The Biology Key

7

The Biology of Depression

Antidepressants and other biological therapies have been one of the great breakthroughs of recent medical history. Over the past few decades there has been an explosion of research on understanding changes that occur in the body when a person becomes depressed. As a result, doctors now know a great deal about the biology of depression and have a host of options that they can use to help relieve symptoms. The good news about effective biological treatments isn't limited to just the antidepressant medications. Scientists have discovered that there are many other things, such as light therapy, exercise, and herbal remedies, that may help reverse the chemical changes of depression.

We want to empower you to get the most out of biological therapies by learning some of the same things doctors know about the physical side of depression. If you understand the basics of the biology of depression and antidepressant therapy, you will be able to team up with your doctor to maximize the benefits of treatment. And, you will be in a better position to cope with side effects or other problems that may come up along the way.

This first chapter from the Biology Key will help you learn about chemical imbalances that may cause depression and about how antidepressants can correct these imbalances. You'll also find out about research on the genetics of mood disorders that may lead to new treatments in the future. Because physical illnesses like hormone abnormalities, heart disease, or other common medical problems can play a role in triggering depression, we'll help you understand the link between your mood and physical health. If you are taking medicines for a medical illness, you'll want to check out our tips on how to spot possible depressive reactions to prescription drugs.

Part of the Biology Key will be to discover ways to help yourself by modifying sleep, exercise, and diet patterns to lead a healthy life-style. We'll also discuss methods for treating mood problems that have a seasonal pattern. After getting versed on the biology of depression in this chapter, you'll be able to explore the details of antidepressant therapy in Chapters 8 and 9. So, let's start our journey through the biological realm of depression.

How Can Brain Chemistry Make You Depressed?

Many scientists believe that changes in the chemistry of transmitting nerve impulses from one brain cell to another can cause depression. Each human being has billions of brain cells, and each of these cells has thousands of connections with other brain cells. Even though the possibilities for combinations of connecting pathways between these cells seems almost endless, researchers have been able to identify specific areas of the brain that regulate thought, emotion, sleep, appetite, and the ability to experience pleasure—functions that are altered in depression.

In order to understand the biology of depression, you will need to know some of the basics of how brain cells function and what changes occur when people become depressed. We'll begin with a few definitions:

1. *NEURON*—a general term for brain cells. There are many types of neurons in the brain.
2. *NEUROTRANSMITTER*—a chemical substance that transmits messages between neurons. The brain has a number of different neurotransmitters. The three neurotransmitters that have been most commonly associated with depression are *serotonin, norepinephrine,* and *dopamine.*
3. *SYNAPSE*—the space between neurons. In order for a message to be transmitted from one neuron to another, a neurotransmitter must be released into the synapse and travel to the next neuron.
4. *PRESYNAPTIC AND POSTSYNAPTIC NEURONS*—the neuron that is sending a message is called a presynaptic neuron, and the neuron receiving the message is called the postsynaptic neuron.
5. *RECEPTOR*—a specialized chemical structure located on the surface of the postsynaptic neuron that receives messages sent between neurons. The receptor must be activated for

the message to get through. Neurotransmitters fit into the receptor almost like a key fits into a lock.

6. *NERVE IMPULSE*—the event that occurs in an activated neuron to send the message through one neuron and onto another. After the neurotransmitter attaches to the receptor, the postsynaptic neuron is fired (activated), and this nerve impulse carries the message down that neuron to the next synapse. When the nerve impulse reaches the next synapse, neurotransmitters are released, and the chain of events in sending messages between brain cells continues.

7. *REUPTAKE*—the process of recycling neurotransmitters back into the presynaptic neuron so that they can be used again. There is a chemical pump (called a reuptake pump) located on the presynaptic neuron that is responsible for this recycling process. The reuptake pump brings the neurotransmitter back into the presynaptic neuron after the neurotransmitter is finished sending the message.

Figure 7.1 gives a simplified, general picture of how messages are transmitted between brain cells. If you want to learn more details about neurotransmitters and the biochemistry of depression, a good book to read is *Psychopharmacology of Antidepressants* by Dr. Stephen Stahl.

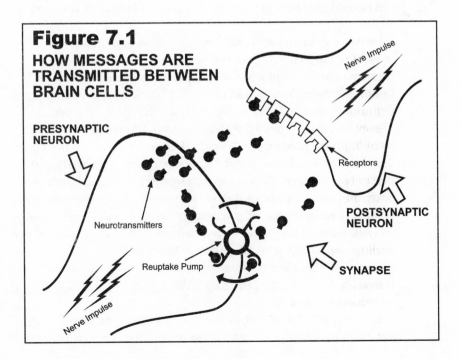

Figure 7.1
HOW MESSAGES ARE TRANSMITTED BETWEEN BRAIN CELLS

Nerve Impulse

PRESYNAPTIC NEURON

Receptors

Neurotransmitters

POSTSYNAPTIC NEURON

Reuptake Pump

SYNAPSE

Nerve Impulse

In depression, there can be abnormalities in the activity of neurons that are controlled by any one of three different types of neurotransmitters—serotonin, norepinephrine, and dopamine. Doctors often describe depression to their patients as being caused by a chemical imbalance. What they mean by this is that there is a lowering of the activity of serotonin, norepinephrine, or dopamine in the brain, or a disturbance in the function of these neurotransmitters. Antidepressants are prescribed with the goal of restoring normal functioning of the neurotransmitters and neurons involved in depression.

How Do Antidepressants Work?

The neurotransmitter most frequently linked with depression is serotonin, and the antidepressants that affect serotonin neurons are called serotonin selective reuptake inhibitors (SSRIs). You may already be familiar with some of these medications. Probably the best-known antidepressant is Prozac, an SSRI. Some other SSRIs are Zoloft, Paxil, and Celexa. Other antidepressants, such as Effexor and Wellbutrin, have effects on multiple neurotransmitters including norepinephrine and dopamine. We'll use the example of a serotonin neuron to explain how antidepressants work.

The SSRIs, like most other antidepressants, have at least three actions that can increase the activity of neurons that are involved in depression.

1. *Blocking the reuptake pump.* The first and most immediate action is to block the recycling of the serotonin neurotransmitter. This point is usually confusing to people who aren't familiar with brain chemistry. You would think that blocking something having to do with serotonin would decrease the levels of this neurotransmitter. But, actually the amount of serotonin goes *up*. Here is what happens. Because SSRIs are selective "reuptake inhibitors," they turn down the activity of a chemical pump located on the presynaptic neuron. This pump is designed to bring the serotonin back into the neuron so it can be reused. When the pump is blocked, more serotonin stays in the synapse and there is increased firing of the postsynaptic neuron. The overall effect is to turn up the activity level of serotonin brain cells.
2. *Stimulating the release of serotonin.* SSRIs promote the release of serotonin into the synapse. This is the second step in activating the serotonin neuron.
3. *Correcting abnormalities in the postsynaptic neuron.* Because there is a deficiency of serotonin in depression, the postsynaptic

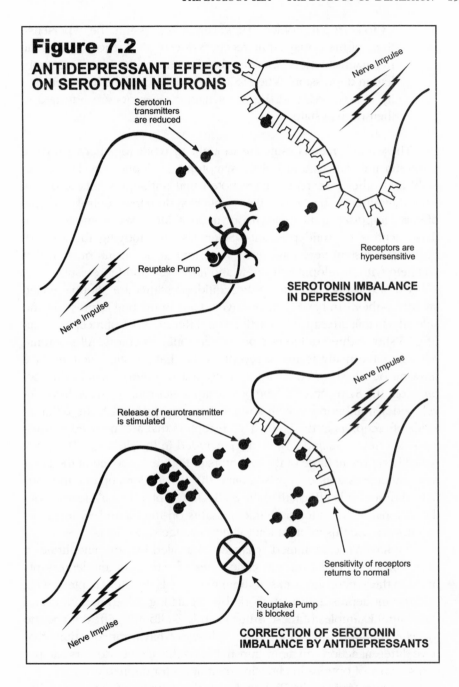

Figure 7.2

ANTIDEPRESSANT EFFECTS ON SEROTONIN NEURONS

Serotonin transmitters are reduced

Nerve Impulse

Reuptake Pump

Receptors are hypersensitive

Nerve Impulse

SEROTONIN IMBALANCE IN DEPRESSION

Release of neurotransmitter is stimulated

Nerve Impulse

Sensitivity of receptors returns to normal

Reuptake Pump is blocked

Nerve Impulse

CORRECTION OF SEROTONIN IMBALANCE BY ANTIDEPRESSANTS

receptors become hypersensitive. These receptors try to compensate for lowered levels of serotonin by becoming more active. In a way, this reaction is like the increase in white blood cells that usually occurs when you get an infection. The body is working to try to correct a problem. However, in depression, the hypersensi-tivity of the postsynaptic receptor doesn't do the job. In fact, the hypersensitivity is considered to be part of the biological prob-lem in depression. When SSRIs are prescribed, the hypersensitiv-ity is reversed, and the postsynaptic receptors are returned to their normal state.

These three mechanisms are thought to work together to reverse serotonin imbalances and relieve symptoms of depression. Dr. Steven Stahl and other researchers have noted that antidepressants also may exert their effects on a "second messenger" system that controls the flow of nerve impulses in the postsynaptic neuron. Much less is known about these actions of antidepressants. Scientists are studying the second-messenger system very intensively and hope to learn information that will help with development of new and improved antidepressants.

Unfortunately SSRIs and other antidepressants are "double-edged swords"—they can have both positive effects in treating depression and side effects that are caused by actions on different types of receptors. Fig-ure 7.3 shows three different types of serotonin receptors. All serotonin neurons have many forms of receptors that have distinct actions. The drawing below shows one of the important receptors for relieving de-pression, the S1 receptor on the postsynaptic neuron. Scientists have de-veloped a numbering system so that they can distinguish the different kinds of receptors in the brain. Two receptors that are involved in caus-ing side effects (S2 and S3) are also included in the drawing. The SSRIs typically act on all three of the receptors in Figure 7.3. Some of the other new antidepressants do not stimulate the S2 or S3 receptors and thus have different side effects than the SSRIs. In Chapter 9, you'll learn about the actions of the different antidepressants on the S2 and S3 receptors and how to use this information to help manage side effects.

We haven't diagrammed synapses controlled by norepinephrine or dopamine here. However, the same types of actions of antidepressants occur in these neurons as in serotonin nerve cells. In later chapters, we'll discuss antidepressants that work by regulating norepinephrine and dopamine. Examples of these drugs include Wellbutrin, Effexor, and the tricyclic antidepressants. One of the pluses of having medications that have different actions on neurotransmitters is that it gives doctors and pa-tients plenty of options in choosing treatments for depression.

Our next topic in the Biology Key is the genetics of depression. Re-search studies have still not determined exactly how genes can increase the risk for depression. But, one of the possible mechanisms is that your genetic makeup can make you prone to develop an imbalance in sero-tonin, norepinephrine, or dopamine. Because many people with depres-

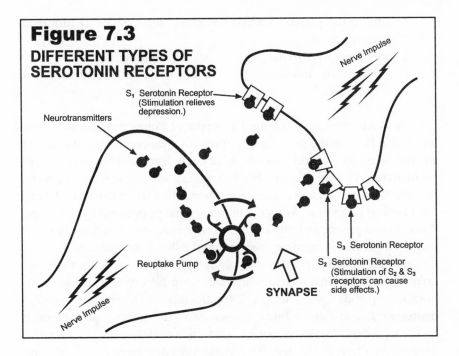

Figure 7.3

DIFFERENT TYPES OF SEROTONIN RECEPTORS

S₁ Serotonin Receptor (Stimulation relieves depression.)

Neurotransmitters

Nerve Impulse

Reuptake Pump

Nerve Impulse

SYNAPSE

S₃ Serotonin Receptor

S₂ Serotonin Receptor (Stimulation of S₂ & S₃ receptors can cause side effects.)

sion, or those who have family members with this problem, are curious about the chances of inheriting the condition, we'll explore the influences of genetics on depression.

Is It in Your Genes?

There are some medical disorders, such as cystic fibrosis and Huntington's disease, that are completely due to a genetic defect. However, the linkage between genes and illness is much less clear for depression. Most experts currently think that the onset of depression can be influenced by many factors including environmental stress, personality makeup, physical health, and/or genetic background. For a number of years, research on the genetics of depression focused on determining whether mood disorders run in families. More recently, newer methods for discovering the exact chemical sequences of genes have been used to study mood disorders.

If you have depression or a family history of this disorder, there are several important questions to ask:

1. What is my risk for becoming depressed if I have a parent with this problem?

2. What is the risk of my child becoming depressed if I suffer from this condition?
3. Are there any specific genetic tests for depression?
4. Are there any treatments that will correct genetic disturbances in depression?

Dr. Wade Berritini from the University of Pennsylvania, one of the top researchers on the genetics of depression, has concluded that having a parent with major depression doubles your chances of having the same problem during your lifetime. For example, studies of the severe, recurrent forms of major depression have shown that the chances of having this problem jump from 8 percent in the general population to 16 percent if you have a parent with the condition. The exact contributions of genes and environment in creating this increased risk are still unknown.

Bipolar disorder is more heavily influenced by genetics than unipolar depression (major depression without a history of a manic or hypomanic episode—see Chapter 2 for definitions of different types of depression). The rate of bipolar disorder in the general population is about 1 percent. Having a parent with this condition leads to about a ninefold increase in the risk for bipolar disorder. Because of this pronounced elevation in risk, most doctors believe that bipolar disorder has a stronger genetic background than the unipolar form of depression.

Researchers are actively studying human genes and are searching for possible culprits in causing an increased vulnerability to mood disorders. As yet there is no genetic test that your doctor can order to tell you whether you have a heightened risk for unipolar major depression or bipolar illness. And, there are no specific medications or other treatments for mood disorders that can reverse suspected abnormalities in genes. However, many scientists predict that new medications will eventually be developed that will repair genetic defects and give new hope to people who suffer from depression.

Could It Be a Thyroid or Adrenal Gland Imbalance?

Sometimes hormone imbalances, such as abnormalities in the function of the thyroid or adrenal glands, can play a role in causing depression. If this is part of your problem, it is very important to make an accurate diagnosis so that you can get the treatment you need. The value of looking for dysfunction of the thyroid gland or other medical problems was particularly evident for Amanda, who consulted her doctor for a variety of troubling symptoms.

Although she was only thirty-five years old, Amanda felt tired and weak all the time. No matter how hard she pushed herself at work, there never seemed to be enough energy to get through the day. To make things worse, she was steadily gaining weight despite being on a diet and trying to exercise regularly. When she looked at herself in the mirror, she saw a puffy face that didn't look like it belonged to her. One day, Amanda's hairdresser told her that her hair was getting coarse and was starting to fall out.

Amanda had always been an upbeat person even when times were tough. She had weathered the death of her mother three years earlier and had handled chronic back problems without letting it get her down. But, now she was feeling depressed. The physical changes she was noticing made her feel like she was getting old too fast. In the last couple of weeks, she had been getting scared for the first time about whether she could manage her job.

When Amanda went to her doctor to ask for help for depression, the first things he did were to take a careful history and perform a physical exam. Her doctor was on the ball—he looked for other possible explanations of her symptoms before assuming that the only problem was depression. He knew that weakness, weight gain, changes in hair thickness, and depression could be indicators of a hormone imbalance. The physical exam confirmed his suspicions. Amanda was very sluggish, had slow reflexes, and was showing signs of fluid retention. The most likely diagnosis was a thyroid deficiency. But, he also wanted to check for the possibility of an adrenal hormone (cortisol) insufficiency, anemia, or other medical problems.

The next step was to get lab tests including thyroid and adrenal hormone levels, a blood count, and tests for liver and kidney functioning to find out if a physical illness could explain her symptoms. As her doctor expected, all of the tests came back normal except the thyroid levels. Amanda had a classic case of hypothyroidism—a condition that is easily correctable with a daily thyroid supplement. After he ran a few additional tests to check for causes of the hypothyroidism, her doctor reassured Amanda that she didn't have any serious medical problems. But, she was suffering from depression and would need to take thyroid pills to correct the physical problem and get her normal mood back.

Hormone imbalances are an uncommon cause of depression. But, Amanda's case illustrates the importance of being on the lookout for physical illnesses that can make people depressed. The two glands that have been linked most closely with depression are the thyroid and the adrenal. Having either too little or too much of the hormones (thyroid hormone and cortisol) produced by these glands can lead to numerous emotional changes such as depression, anxiety, irritability, and mood swings. Ordinarily doctors do not order lab tests to check for hormone

Table 7.1
Possible Signs of a Thyroid or Adrenal Hormone Imbalance

Thyroid Deficiency *(Hypothyroidism)*	**Adrenal Hormone Deficiency** *(Lowered cortisol levels)*
Weakness, lethargy, depression, weight gain, poor appetite, thinning hair, slowed heartbeat and reflexes	Weakness, weight loss, depression, loss of muscle strength, skin pigment becomes darker or mottled
Thyroid Hormone Excess *(Hyperthyroidism)*	**Adrenal Hormone Excess** *(Elevated cortisol levels)*
Feeling jittery or agitated, increased appetite, weight loss, fast heartbeat and very quick reflexes, bulging eyes, irritability, depression	Weight gain, fatty "hump" on back, stretch marks not associated with childbirth, depression, anxiety, mood swings

imbalances in the evaluation of depression unless there are telltale signs of a possible hormone imbalance or the individual has been treated for depression and hasn't responded to a full course of an antidepressant.

The great majority of people with depression do not suffer from a thyroid or adrenal gland disease. However, scientists have been exploring the possibility that thyroid and adrenal hormones can play a role in depression, even in the absence of a diagnosable glandular problem. The most intensive research has been conducted on the adrenal gland hormone, cortisol. (See References for a good article on this topic by Drs. Plotsky, Owens, and Nemeroff.) This hormone has been shown to be very sensitive to stress. When humans are stressed, a hormone system called the hypothalamic-pituitary-adrenal (or HPA) axis is stimulated to help them respond to the threat. The hypothalamus and the pituitary glands are located at the base of the brain and secrete hormones into the bloodstream that control output of cortisol from the adrenal gland (located just above the kidneys).

Studies of the HPA axis in depression have found evidence for increased secretion of the hypothalamic hormone corticotropin-releasing factor (CRF) and elevations in cortisol levels. These changes are not observed in all persons with depression. But, studies of severely depressed patients have often discovered increases in the average levels of CRF and/or cortisol. Scientists still haven't determined the exact significance of these changes and thus do not recommend routine testing for CRF and cortisol in the diagnostic evaluation of depression.

Dr. Michael Thase and co-workers at the University of Pittsburgh have conducted studies that suggest that people with abnormalities in CRF or cortisol may have a "biological marker" for depression. Presumably, these individuals have a heavier genetic component to their depression and may be somewhat less responsive to psychotherapy than persons who do not have these biological changes. Further research will be needed to determine whether measurements of cortisol, CRF, or related hormones could help in selecting the most useful treatment approach.

The most productive studies of thyroid function in depression have focused on the possibility that giving thyroid supplements could improve the chances of recovery, even when thyroid functioning is normal. In a comprehensive review of research on thyroid metabolism in depression that appeared in the *Psychiatric Clinics of North America,* Drs. Victoria Hendrick, Lori Altshuler, and Peter Wybrow concluded that there is good evidence that thyroid hormones can augment or accelerate the response to antidepressant medication. Interestingly, this effect is much stronger in women than men. The exact reasons for this gender difference are still unknown. Generally, the use of thyroid hormones in the biological treatment of depression is reserved for persons who do not respond to standard therapy with antidepressants. Chapter 9 contains additional information on using augmenting strategies to improve the chances of responding to antidepressant medication.

Estrogen and Depression

For many years, doctors have suspected that estrogen imbalance could be a possible cause of depression. The most obvious reason is that depression is much more common in women than men. About twice as many women suffer from depression than men. Also, mood fluctuations are commonly associated with the menstrual cycle, pregnancy, the postpartum period, and menopause. Despite these connections, research studies typically have *not* discovered estrogen deficiencies in depressed women and have not found differences in estrogen and other female hormones in women who have premenstrual syndrome (PMS) compared to those that do not have these symptoms.

Many of our female patients tell us that their depressive symptoms vary with their menstrual cycles. Mood cycling can be more extreme in those with PMS. We generally recommend that women with PMS consult with their gynecologist or family physician about available options. Although there is no universal solution, many women are helped by antidepressants (such as the SSRI Prozac), pain relievers, or other medications.

Research on menopause has disproved the common belief that having gone through the "change of life" increases the risk for depression. According to Dr. Steven Stahl from the University of California at San Diego, women who have gone through menopause do *not* have more depressive illness than younger women. In fact, the rate of depression in women actually falls after menopause. Men and women have the same amount of depression before puberty and after menopause. But, there is dramatic rise in the frequency of depression in women during the child-bearing years.

The decision to use hormone replacement therapy during or after menopause is a complex one and should be made only after considering all the potential benefits and risks and discussing the situation thoroughly with a physician. Dr. Stahl has suggested that estrogen replacement could be a useful addition to other treatments for depression during and after menopause because the hormones can decrease troublesome physical symptoms such as "hot flashes," problems with vaginal lubrication, and osteoporosis.

The Link between Physical Illness and Depression

Several years ago, a medical student named Beth Rush came to Jesse with a good idea for a summer research project. She had heard that patients with medical problems might have a high risk for depression and wanted to find out if this was true. We were able to work out a plan to give a depression rating scale (the Zung Scale) to patients who were attending a large family medicine clinic and to do clinical interviews with the people who scored in the range of possible depression on this rating scale.

We thought that we would see a significant amount of depression in these patients. But, both of us were surprised to find that the rate was so high. Forty-one percent of the patients had evidence of possible depression on the Zung Scale. Because this scale is designed to pick up mild or suspected cases of depression, in addition to the more severe forms of the disorder, it doesn't allow a doctor to make a definitive diagnosis. So, the study included a follow-up examination with an experienced psychiatrist to determine how many of these patients had major depression. The follow-up evaluation revealed that 17 percent of the family medicine patients met the criteria for diagnosis of major depression, and many others had enough depressive symptoms to cause distress. Other studies of medical patients in many different settings also have found elevated levels of depression.

Earlier in this chapter, we told you about Amanda's hypothyroidism, which appeared to play a direct role in causing depression. In some cases, like this one, there is a known biochemical explanation for an increased risk for depression. But, in most instances there is no clear physical reason for why certain medical illnesses are associated with depression. Having virtually any serious physical illness can predispose you to becoming depressed, probably because medical problems can be highly significant stressors.

Alan was a hard-working, fifty-two-year-old small business owner whose life changed dramatically from one day to the next. On a sunny Saturday afternoon in May he was in good spirits as he was tearing down an old fence in his backyard. But then he began to experience severe chest pain. His wife quickly drove him to the nearest emergency room where he was evaluated and immediately scheduled for coronary artery bypass surgery. It was a frightening experience for everyone. However, he pulled through the surgery well and within two weeks he was back at home, though not ready for gardening duty. The whole event left Alan severely shaken. He was still very weak from the surgery, but he also felt scared and depressed.

If we could have heard Alan's thoughts we might have heard something like this: "How can I possibly get back in charge of my business? . . . Everything hinges on me . . . I'll never be the same . . . I could lose everything . . . I won't be able to make it." These thoughts fueled his emotions and became reinforced by the slowness of his recovery. In this case, the heart disease itself was not making Alan depressed. His emotional reaction to this traumatic event and what he feared it might mean for his future were getting him down.

These types of scenes are played over and over in the millions of people who have to confront illnesses such as heart disease, cancer, stroke, bone and joint disease, kidney problems, chronic pain, and numerous other medical conditions. The types of reactions will vary depending on the form and severity of the medical illness, the personality of the sufferer, family support, age, and many other influences. However, there are several common themes in the thought processes of people who have to face severe or lasting physical problems. (See Table 7.2.)

Of course physical illnesses can and do cause some of the problems listed in Table 7.2. But, you may remember from the Thinking Key that people with depression often put an excessively negative spin on stressful events. One of the ways to cope with having a medical illness is to use methods from the Thinking Key to check out the accuracy of your thoughts about having a physical problem. Try to develop a rational or logical view of your health problems and think of healthy attitudes that will help you fight the illness. The Spirituality Key, which we will learn about in Chapters 12 and 13, also can be a very important part of coping

Table 7.2
Common Reactions to Physical Illnesses

General Themes	Examples
Loss of Health/Fitness	I'll never be the same.
	I won't be able to do the things I did before I got sick.
	I could die.
Loss of Control	I've lost control of my life.
	The illness will control me.
Fear of Dependency	I won't be able to take care of myself.
	I don't want to have to depend on others.
Anger	It isn't fair.
	Why me?
	How could God allow this to happen?
Fear of Pain	I won't be able to stand it.
	My life will be nothing but pain.
Loss of Love or Acceptance	Others will give up on me.
	He/she could leave me.
Financial Loss	I'll lose my job/business.
	We'll go broke.
Unmet Goals	I'll never accomplish my goals.
	I won't get to see my child/grandchild get married.

with medical diseases. Some people may be able to use their spiritual orientation to help them face severe or life-threatening illnesses without slipping into depression.

If you have a depression that seems to be associated with a medical problem, there are two things you should do. First you should be sure to see your doctor for a checkup. Treatment for a medical condition may possibly be an answer to your depression. Second, you should get treatment for the depression. Your Personal Plan for Recovery would be a good place to write down your ideas about physical illnesses and depression and to record your efforts to get help for medical conditions.

In some situations, the presence of depression may aggravate the physical illness or even increase your chances for a premature death.

This is particularly true for heart disease. According to a review by Dr. Dominique Mussleman and her associates from Emory University and the University of Pennsylvania, numerous research studies have shown that depression is a major risk factor for death after a heart attack. They concluded that depression could cause heart problems by overactivation of pituitary and adrenal hormones or other chemicals that are known to be involved in the physical reaction to stress.

Dr. Mussleman suggests that people who have heart disease and become depressed should receive treatment with antidepressant drugs. There are two reasons for doing this: relief of depressive symptoms *and* positive benefits on physical health from resolution of depression. The SSRIs and other newer antidepressants are considered to be safer than the tricyclic antidepressants (described in Chapters 8 and 9) for people with heart disease. Psychotherapies such as cognitive-behavior therapy (CBT) also have been found to be useful for people who have medical illnesses. Because of the association between depression and an increased death rate in heart disease, we strongly recommend professional evaluation and treatment for anyone who has this combination of significant problems. Table 7.3 lists some of the more common medical problems that are associated with depression. Aggressive treatment of both the medical illness and the depression is indicated for any of the problems listed here.

Table 7.3
Medical Problems Commonly Associated with Depression

Cancer	Hypo- or Hypercortisolism
Chronic Pain	(Adrenal Hormone Imbalance)
Chronic Fatigue Syndrome	Infections
Dementia	(AIDS, Hepatitis, TB, and others)
(Memory Loss Disorders)	Kidney Failure
Diabetes	Multiple Sclerosis
Epilepsy	Parkinson's Disease
Fibromyalgia	Rheumatoid Arthritis
Heart Disease	Sleep Apnea
Hypo- or Hyperthyroidism	Stroke
(Thyroid Imbalance)	Vitamin Deficiencies

Is Medication Part of the Problem?

Imogene was a middle-aged woman who had never experienced depression until she started taking medication for some stomach problems. She had developed a burning sensation in her stomach, so her doctor suggested she try Reglan, a medication that is used to treat conditions such as reflux of acid from the stomach into the esophagus. Reglan helped the burning in her stomach, but after about two weeks she began to feel so tired that she could hardly get through a day at work. Before long, she was having trouble sleeping at night and was noticing that food didn't taste good any more. Within a month, she had lost her usual self-confidence and was feeling depressed all the time.

When Imogene called to schedule a psychiatric evaluation, her assumption was that she would be told that she needed to take antidepressants or start psychotherapy. But, her story had some clues in it that suggested that she might have a drug-induced depression. For example, before becoming depressed, she had excellent self-esteem and a positive attitude about life. There hadn't been any stressful life events that could have triggered depression, and she reported having good relationships with her family. In short, Imogene didn't have the typical background that sets people up for depression. Instead of starting psychotherapy, we talked with her family doctor about switching medications for her stomach problems. After discussing the alternatives with Imogene and her doctor, we also started her on an antidepressant, Zoloft, at least on a temporary basis, because she was having difficulty functioning at work and she wanted to get some relief as soon as possible. Just because the Reglan was probably producing the symptoms of depression didn't mean that an antidepressant would not be helpful to her. Another strategy that was offered Imogene was to simply stop the Reglan to see if this action alone would lead to recovery. Imogene's immediate discomfort and difficulty on the job were the deciding factors in starting Zoloft.

She had a complete return to normal about ten days after stopping Reglan. The Zoloft was tapered and discontinued after about four months. It has been almost five years since Imogene had this episode, and there has been no return of depression. In retrospect, it appears that Imogene's symptoms were probably due to a side effect of Reglan. This type of case, where there is a clear association with a single medication and there are no other factors that seem to be involved in causing a depression, is less common than situations where there are many possible contributing problems, such as negative thinking, stressful life events, troubled relationships, and so forth.

As shown in Table 7.4, there are a number of prescription medications that may possibly trigger depression. A few of these, beta blockers (high blood pressure and heart medicines such as Inderal), cortisone (and other steroids such as prednisone), and amphetamine (especially during withdrawal from this stimulant) are fairly commonly associated with depressive symptoms. A multitude of other drugs have been reported to cause depression in at least a few cases.

It is very important to remember that most of these medications *do not* trigger depression in the great majority of people who take them. For example, we have seen many patients who have used Reglan without having it cause or worsen depression. Imogene was one of the few patients in our practices who have seemed to become depressed when taking this drug.

Key Point

When you have concerns about possible side effects of prescription medications, you should always discuss the situation with your doctor before making any changes.

If you are depressed and are taking a medication on this list, *do not* stop the drug without consulting with your doctor. Because many of the medications listed in Table 7.4 are infrequent causes of depression, your doctor will need to study the entire picture before recommending changes. In situations where it is fairly certain that a prescription drug is part of the problem, the positive benefits of the medication will need to be balanced against the possibility that it could be playing a role in causing depression. If you need to continue a medication with a reported association with depression, antidepressants and/or other therapies could help counteract the possible depressive effects of your prescription drugs. A good resource for further reading on possible links between medications and depression is the book *Psychiatric Side Effects of Prescription and Over-the-Counter Medications* by Drs. Thomas Brown and Alan Stoudemire.

Sleep Biology in Depression

Research on the biology of sleep has helped unravel the mysteries of what is happening in our bodies during the time we are sleeping and dreaming. The most important studies have focused on measuring electrical brain waves, muscle tone, heart rate, and other physical functions during different stages of sleep. These studies are usually done in special

Table 7.4
Prescription Medications That May Cause Depression

Category A: Medications Commonly Associated with Depression

Beta blockers—Inderal (propranalol) and others used for high blood pressure and heart problems

Cortisone—prednisone, Decadron (dexamethasone), and others

Amphetamine—Dexedrine (dextroamphetamine) and others, especially when withdrawing from these medications

Category B: Medications Associated with Depression in Some Cases

Accutane—used for acne

Aldomet (methyldopa)—a drug for high blood pressure

Anabolic steroids—Oxandrin, Winstrol, nandrolone, and other "male" steroids used by bodybuilders

Lioresal (baclofen)—used for muscle spasms and neurological conditions

Parkinson's disease medications
　　　　—Sinemet (carbidopa and levodopa)
　　　　—Parlodel (bromocriptine)

Cholesterol and lipid-lowering drugs
　　　　—Lipitor
　　　　—Zocor

Norplant—used for birth control

Stomach and gastrointestinal medications
　　　　—Reglan (metoclopramide)
　　　　—Tagamet (cimetidine)
　　　　—Zantac (ranitidine)

Novaldex (tamoxifen)—used for breast cancer

Tranquilizers—antianxiety drugs such as Xanax (alprazolam), Ativan (lorazepam), and Valium (diazepam), especially when withdrawing from these medications

NOTE: Trade names of medications are given where possible. Generic versions, if available, are listed in parentheses.

laboratories where monitoring devices are used to help doctors diagnose specific problems such as sleep apnea and to investigate sleep in depression and other emotional disorders

Healthy, normal sleep usually lasts from about seven to nine hours. Any more or any less on a regular basis may have negative effects on your health. Problems with sleep can interfere with concentration, lower your energy, and make you irritable. And, of course, sleep impairment is one of the hallmarks of depression.

Researchers have found that there are four stages of normal sleep, plus another phase called "Rapid Eye Movement," or REM sleep. Stage 1 is the lightest form of sleep. Stage 4 is the deepest. It is good to get as much of the deep stages as possible because these parts of sleep are the most restful. REM sleep is when we do the majority of our dreaming. Typically, there are several periods of REM sleep during the night. The first episode of REM starts about ninety minutes after you go to sleep.

Depression often causes profound changes in sleep patterns. Insomnia, hypersomnia (sleeping too much), or both are some of the most common symptoms of depression. Sleep laboratory studies have shown that depressed people often have difficulty falling asleep, frequent awakenings through the night, and reduced amounts of deep sleep. Also, in some cases, individuals with the most severe forms of depression have abnormal REM sleep. One of these changes is a quicker-than-normal onset of REM after falling asleep.

We described nondrug methods of getting a good night's sleep in Chapter 5. These techniques can be very useful for depressed people who are having sleep problems and for all others who have insomnia. However if nondrug methods aren't effective, your doctor will be able to recommend several other options. Sometimes over-the-counter medicines can help. Melatonin is probably the most frequently used nonprescription drug. Valerian is another "natural" remedy that can promote sleep.

Among the prescription drugs for sleep, usually the best choices are newer medications, such as Sonata or Ambien, that are less likely than older types of sleeping pills to cause dependence, and have minimal or no effects in disrupting sleep stages. A number of medicines in the benzodiazepine group, including Dalmane (flurazepam), Restoril (temazepam), and Prosom (estazolam), also are widely prescribed. These drugs can be very useful in treating insomnia, and they have the advantage of being less expensive because they come in generic forms. However, the benzodiazepines can suppress REM and the deeper stages of sleep, and they can cause dependency. These medications are not like drugs of abuse that are highly likely to cause intense physical dependency. But, if you have been on a benzodiazepine for longer than a few weeks, you may notice increased insomnia and/or anxiety when you try to stop the drug.

Benzodiazepines can also cause a "hangover" effect, such as sedation and trouble concentrating, the morning after you take them. This is especially true for longer-acting drugs like Dalmane. Our best advice is to use nondrug methods or the newer medications, Sonata or Ambien, if possible. Your doctor also might recommend that you try Desyrel (trazadone), a medication described in Chapter 9. This antidepressant is especially good for sleep and is a safe alternative to other prescription drugs. Although Desyrel is usually not prescribed alone as an antidepressant because there are many other medications that may be more effective for mood symptoms, it often is used in combination with other antidepressants to treat insomnia.

Is Exercise an Effective Treatment for Depression?

Of all the potential physical remedies for depression, exercise has a special appeal of leading to other health benefits. It has been well established that regular exercise can improve physical fitness, reduce weight, help prevent heart disease, and improve quality of life. And, according to major reviews by Lynette Craft and Daniel Landers, and Kathleen Moore and James Blumenthal, results of research on exercise and depression have been very positive as well.

One of the best studies on the effects of physical activity was performed by a group of researchers headed by Dr. James Blumenthal at Duke University, the University of Colorado, and the University of California at San Diego. They compared the benefits of a program of aerobic exercise (walking or jogging) three times a week, to antidepressant medication (Zoloft) without exercise, or a combination of both treatments. The people who exercised improved as much as those who received Zoloft, a medication with proven effectiveness.

No one is certain how exercise relieves depression, although the best guess is that people who are physically fit have improved mental health. This means that if you work out regularly and stay in shape, and like the way you look and feel, you are likely to stay in a better mood. It's still not clear what type of exercise works best. Most research has been done on aerobic exercise (walking, jogging, riding an exercise bike, using a treadmill, etc.) that raises heart rate but doesn't push you to the point you are out of breath. But, some studies have shown that strength training, such as using exercise machines to build muscle strength and tone, also can help relieve depression.

Some experts now believe that exercise may play a role in changing brain chemistry. One intriguing idea is that physical exercise might raise the level of beta endorphins, naturally occurring body chemicals that may be involved in soothing pain or allowing us to feel pleasure. Exercise also could work by altering the levels of neurotransmitters or hormones involved in depression.

Our only caution is to have a checkup with your doctor before starting an exercise program, especially if you have significant medical problems or are over forty. If you decide to use exercise as part of your plan for recovery, methods from the Action Key can help you begin and stick with a workout routine.

Diet and Depression

Many claims have been made for the value of altering diet to control mood, but there is little solid research evidence that depression can be treated successfully by changing what you eat. In her book *Food and Mood,* Elizabeth Somer discusses possible dietary influences on depression including sugar, carbohydrates, vitamins, and omega-3 fatty acids. Some dietary experts have speculated that sweets could trigger a release of endorphins and give a temporary "high" followed by a crash into depression. Others have suggested that a diet rich in carbohydrates could raise levels of a chemical called tryptophan that is a building block for serotonin. However, most authorities, including Drs. David Benton and Rachael Donohoe from the University of Wales, have concluded that eating a high-carbohydrate diet is unlikely to have a significant effect on the level of brain serotonin. Drs. Benton and Donohoe also noted that most edible foods can release endorphins and may improve mood. This may partly explain why people often feel better after they eat.

We don't believe that there is enough scientific evidence to recommend special high carbohydrate or low-sugar diets as specific treatments for depression. Nevertheless, we generally suggest that our depressed patients try to eat regularly and follow a balanced diet with a good representation of all the major food groups. There is a natural tendency in depression either to lose your appetite and eat too little, or to have an increased appetite and eat too much. Part of the recovery process is getting back to a more normal pattern of food intake.

Several different research studies have found that B vitamins, including B_2 (riboflavin), B_6 (thiamine), and B_{12} (cobalamine), and folic acid may be deficient in some individuals with depression. However, the results of investigations on B vitamins and folic acid have been inconsistent and inconclusive. For example, a large study by Dr. Maurizio Fava and a group of researchers from the Massachusetts General Hospital and Baylor University found no association between vitamin B_{12} levels and depression, but people who had lower folic acid levels had a reduced response to therapy with Prozac. Another study by Dr. Iris Bell and co-workers discovered just the opposite. None of the subjects in her study had folic acid deficiencies. A small percentage of the older patients had low vitamin B_{12} levels, and a few other patients had subnormal vitamin B_2 or vitamin B_6 levels.

At this point, there is no systematic evidence that the B vitamins or folic acid are effective treatments for major depression. Yet, there are some situations where tests for B vitamin and folic acid levels may be useful. The first and most important is when there is a suggestion that a vitamin deficiency might be causing a significant physical problem such as decreased memory, anemia, or loss of sensation or balance. Sometimes depression can be associated with states of severe vitamin deficiency that lead to these types of physical symptoms. Proper diagnosis and treatment can help relieve the medical problems and can have the bonus of improving depressed mood.

Another possible reason to test levels of B vitamins and folic acid is failure to respond to standard treatments for depression. If a deficiency is found, it would be reasonable to add a vitamin supplement to other therapies. Although we usually don't prescribe B vitamins or folic acid as a routine part of the treatment of depression for people who have a good nutritional status, many of our patients take vitamin supplements every day. If you are taking B vitamins or folic acid, be sure to follow the recommended dosage guidelines. As long as you don't exceed the maximum daily dose there is little risk that vitamin supplements could cause problems, and there is the chance that you could be reversing an underlying deficiency.

One of the most fascinating lines of research on nutrition and depression has focused on the influence of omega-3 fatty acids on mood. In an article in the medical journal *Lancet,* Dr. Joseph Hibbeln noted that the rate of depression is lower in countries where there is high consumption of fish. Fatty fish such as salmon, halibut, bluefish, mackerel, and herring are excellent sources of omega-3 fatty acids.

It would be great to be able to sit down to a tasty fish dinner with the assurance that it would cure or prevent depression. But, Dr. Alan Gelenberg, one of the world's top experts in biological psychiatry, has urged caution in recommending omega-3 fatty acids as a treatment for depressive symptoms. While Gelenberg acknowledges that some studies have found lowered levels of these fatty acids in depressed patients, he believes that there is no convincing research evidence that omega-3 fatty acids can relieve depression. He also observed that it would be very difficult to consume enough of the fatty acids to reach the suggested dose of five to ten grams a day. For those who want to try a diet high in omega-3 fatty acids, foods that should be emphasized are the fatty fishes listed above plus green leafy vegetables, nuts, flaxseed oil, and canola oil. Also, capsules of flaxseed oil and fish oil are available in health food stores and pharmacies.

Seasonal Affective Disorder (SAD) and Light Therapy

Are you one of those people who tend to get depressed in the months of the year with short days and low light? Do you tend to perk up when the days get longer and you are out in the sunshine? If so, you may suffer from a special type of depression called seasonal affective disorder, or SAD. The Canadian Consensus Guidelines for the Treatment of SAD, available on the web (see Web Resources in the Appendix), give a very useful and readable overview of therapy for this condition. According to these guidelines, SAD occurs in about 2–3 percent of the population in Canada and less than 1 percent of residents of the United States. In order to make the diagnosis of SAD, the following features must be present.

Diagnosis of Seasonal Affective Disorder (SAD)

1. Depressive episodes start around the same time each year (usually in the fall or winter in the northern hemisphere).
2. The depression goes away during other periods of the year.
3. SAD occurs in people who have recurrent major depression or bipolar disorder.
4. Seasonal episodes of depression are more frequent than non-seasonal episodes.
5. Seasonal episodes occur in two or more consecutive years.

Most experts believe that SAD is a disturbance of biological rhythms—the tendency of humans to have cyclical variations in behavior and the metabolism of body chemicals. Examples of biological rhythms are the sleep-wake cycle, the menstrual cycle, and seasonal shifts in responding to the amount of light during the day. Research studies have found that serotonin may cycle with the seasons and thus be involved in the development of SAD. Serotonin levels are typically lowest in the winter and spring and highest in the summer and fall. Two other areas of research point to a serotonin theory for SAD: (1) light therapy, a proven treatment for SAD, may act through serotonin mechanisms, and (2) antidepressants that stimulate serotonin have been shown to relieve SAD.

Researchers also have been studying the possible influence of other neurotransmitters, hormones such as cortisol and thyroid, and psychological factors on seasonal affective disorder. Some of the early studies of the biology of SAD centered on the brain chemical melatonin because this substance plays a role in controlling patterns of seasonal change in animals. But, research studies didn't find consistent changes in melatonin levels in people with SAD. The Canadian Consensus Guidelines concluded that variations in melatonin are probably not a direct cause of seasonal depression.

Although the biology of SAD hasn't been clearly defined yet, there is a large amount of research evidence that light therapy works for this condition. The Canadian Consensus Guidelines reviewed over sixty studies of light therapy conducted around the world and concluded that response rates were usually about 65 percent. They give the following recommendations for light therapy:

Guidelines for Light Therapy*

1. A fluorescent light box, with an intensity of greater than 2,500-lux, is the preferred device for light therapy.
2. A 10,000-lux fluorescent light box, used for thirty minutes each day, is the recommended starting dose.
3. A 2,500-lux fluorescent light box may be used for two hours each day as an alternative.
4. Light boxes should use white, fluorescent light. Ultraviolet light should be filtered out.
5. Light therapy should be done in the early morning to get the best response.

*Adapted from the Canadian Consensus Guidelines for Treatment of SAD.

Because the antidepressant actions of light therapy are thought to be due to exposure to the retina and not the skin, it is important that you keep your eyes open during the treatment and that you sit close enough to the light box that the illumination reaches your eyes. You can read or do other routine activities to make the time go by quickly while you are having light therapy.

Generally, side effects of light therapy are mild and disappear with time or by cutting back on the dose of light. Some of the most common side effects are eye strain, headache, feeling restless or "wired," nausea, sweating, and drowsiness. Light therapy hasn't been shown to cause eye damage. But, an examination with an eye doctor is recommended before starting therapy if you are elderly, have eye diseases (such as cataracts, detached retina, or glaucoma), have illnesses that are known to affect the retina (such as diabetes), or are taking medications that may make your eyes more sensitive to light (such as lithium, certain antipsychotic drugs, melatonin, or St. John's Wort).

Light therapy is recommended only for individuals who have a seasonal pattern to their depression. If you have this type of depression and decide to try light therapy, you should give it at least two to four weeks to see if it works for you. The light box is usually needed only during the fall and winter months. When spring comes around, you will probably be able to put away your light box because there is enough natural light to stop the seasonal blues. Light boxes have become widely available through medical supply stores, mail order, and the Internet.

Using the Biology Key to Fight Depression

In this introductory chapter to the Biology Key, we've tried to help you understand how brain chemistry, genetics, hormones, and other parts of your physical health can be involved in depression. The antidepressant medications that will be described in detail in the next two chapters are the most widely used, scientifically proven biological treatments for depression. Unless you rely on over-the-counter preparations such as St. John's Wort or SAMe (see Chapter 9), you will need to work together with your doctor to use antidepressants. Learning about the biology of depression should prepare you to ask your doctor good questions and to play an active role in your treatment.

Before going on to learn about antidepressants and other biological therapies, it could help to try to spot some strengths you may already have for using the Biology Key. After you do Exercise 7.1, you can add some of these strengths to the list you developed earlier for your Personal Plan for Recovery.

Even though most of the Biology Key methods are prescribed by doctors, self-help strategies also can play an important role in your recovery plan. You might consider some of these options. Begin an exercise program or increase the amount of exercise you are getting now. Change your habits to encourage a better night's sleep. Use self-help methods from the Action Key or other parts of this book to reduce the amount of stress on your body. And, if you have a seasonal pattern to your depression, give light therapy a try. Any of these options could become a part of your recovery plan. As you read about antidepressants in the next two chapters, try to think about the things you can do to help these medications do their job.

Exercise 7.1
The Biology Key: Personal Strengths Checklist

Instructions:

Although you may feel weakened by depression, you probably have strengths that can help you to solve problems and to feel better. Use this rating system to identify possible strengths for using the Biology Key.

++ = "I'm reasonably sure I have this strength."
+ = "I may not have this strength right now, but I think I have the ability to build it."

___ I have some basic knowledge of antidepressants.
___ I feel comfortable with a doctor who can treat my depression.
___ I'm involved in an exercise program.
___ I am physically fit.
___ I don't have any major medical problems.
___ My medical problems are under control.
___ I know what to do to improve my medical problems.
___ I have responded to an antidepressant in the past or have a family member who has done so.
___ I have a positive attitude about using biological treatments for depression.
___ I usually take medications as prescribed or discuss adjustments with my doctor.
___ I know healthy things to do to help me get a good night's sleep.
___ I limit my use of alcohol.
___ I eat a healthy diet.

8

An Insider's Guide to Medications for Depression

When Jan first sought help for her depression, she had mixed feelings about taking medication. Her mother had taken tranquilizers for many years before the new antidepressants were developed, and Jan had always been kind of embarrassed about it. On the other hand, she had seen her mother suffer through severe bouts of depression until she started taking Prozac in the early 1990s, and Jan did not want to end up like that. Before she agreed to take medication she had a few questions that needed to be answered. If Prozac worked for her mother would it work for her? What were the risks of taking medication? What options did she have? Would an herbal remedy provide a more "natural" solution?

If you are like Jan, you probably have lots of questions about taking medication to treat depression. Having questions about antidepressant therapy is a good sign. It means that you are curious and that you would like to know some basic facts about medications that you might put into your body. This chapter should help you understand how these drugs work and how to increase your chances of a good outcome.

What Are the Choices?

Until the last several years there were only two classes of antidepressants, and both types caused many troublesome side effects. Now it's a whole new ballgame. The list of available antidepressants has grown to include over twenty different medications. Even more choices are avail-

Table 8.1
Medications for Depression

Serotonin Selective Reuptake Inhibitors (SSRIs)	Tricyclic Antidepressants (TCAs)
Celexa (citalopram)	Elavil (amitriptyline)
Luvox (fluvoxamine)*	Norpramin (desipramine)
Paxil (paroxetine)	Pamelor (nortriptyline)
Prozac (fluoxetine)	Sinequan (doxepin)
Zoloft (sertraline)	
	Monoamine Oxidase Inhibitors (MAOIs)
Other New Antidepressants	Nardil (phenelzine)
Effexor (venlafaxine)	Parnate (tranylcypromine)
Remeron (mirtazapine)	
Serzone (nefazodone)	Over-the-Counter Remedies
Wellbutrin (buproprion)	St. John's Wort and SAMe*

*Luvox, St. John's Wort, and SAMe are not approved by the U.S. FDA for depression but are used throughout the world for this purpose. Trade names for medications are capitalized. Generic names are listed in parentheses for each of the prescription drugs.

able when you consider herbal remedies and other groups of drugs, such as mood stabilizers and hormones, that can be used in the treatment of depression. Table 8.1, "Medications for Depression" lists some of the most commonly used medications for depression.

With so many options you may be wondering how you and your doctor will choose the best antidepressant for you. A good first step is to learn about the four major groups of antidepressants. Knowing more about your choices will better prepare you to talk with your doctor about selecting a treatment strategy.

The two oldest groups of medications are the tricyclic antidepressants (TCAs) and the monoamine oxidase inhibitors (MAOIs). Because they are useful in relieving depression, these medications are still prescribed in some cases. Unfortunately, TCAs are not easy to take. They cause a number of bothersome side effects, such as sleepiness, dry mouth, and constipation. The MAOIs are prescribed infrequently because their safe use requires a restrictive diet and avoidance of a number of other medications.

The two newest groups of medication for depression are the serotonin selective reuptake inhibitors (SSRIs such as Prozac, Zoloft, Paxil, and Celexa) and the other new antidepressants (such as Effexor, Wellbutrin, Serzone, and Remeron). These newer drugs produce fewer seri-

Key Point

The serotonin selective reuptake inhibitors (SSRIs) and other new antidepressants have fewer side effects and are much easier to take than older medications for depression. However, there is no scientific evidence that any single one of the commonly used antidepressants is more effective than the others.

ous side effects and eliminate the need for special diets. Although there are many differences between the older drugs (TCAs, and MAOIs) and the newer ones, all of the antidepressants have been found to have about the same degree of effectiveness and work in about the same amount of time. About 55 to 75 percent of depressed persons who take any single one of these medications have a good treatment response. Researchers are still searching for the drug that will work 100 percent of the time.

SSRIs and other new antidepressants were developed to alter specific chemicals in the brain. In Chapter 7 we described how these chemicals, called neurotransmitters, act like messengers to send and receive information. When a person becomes depressed, there may be a decrease in the amount of the neurotransmitter available in the brain, or the chemical messages may have a harder time getting through. SSRIs help the serotonin brain pathways process messages more efficiently. Several of the other new antidepressants affect norepinephrine and dopamine.

The good news about the newer antidepressants is that because doctors know how they are likely to affect your brain, they can make better decisions in selecting or changing medications so that you have fewer side effects and better overall results. However, despite all the scientific advances in understanding the actions of antidepressants, there is still no reliable laboratory test that can help doctors find out which neurotransmitters may be involved in your depression. Thus to some extent, antidepressant medications are still chosen, at least initially, on a trial-and-error basis. Later in our description of the Biology Key we'll suggest some strategies for making good choices for antidepressant therapy.

Doctor and Patient as a Treatment Team

One of the themes throughout this book is that you can promote recovery from depression by being an active participant in your therapy. Most people know that psychotherapy requires the patient to share in the

Key Point

There are numerous medication choices for the effective treatment of depression, but unfortunately there are no specific laboratory tests that will help your doctor pick exactly the right one for you. It may take a bit of trial and error and some patience to find the antidepressant that will give you the best results.

work of treatment. But when people see a doctor about taking medication, they can make the mistake of assuming that the responsibility is completely in the doctor's hands. You can miss many opportunities for helping the recovery process if you don't get fully involved in your therapy. After briefly discussing your doctor's role in medication treatment, we will tell you what you can do to help yourself by using the Biology Key.

YOUR DOCTOR'S ROLE

Before prescribing an antidepressant, your doctor will likely take a detailed medical history. Some of the most important questions that you could expect your doctor to ask are: (1) What is your main problem? (2) What symptoms have you been having? (3) Have you thought about suicide? (4) What types of stresses have you been experiencing? (5) Have you ever been depressed in the past? (6) Do you have a family history of depression or of other illnesses? (7) Do you have a history of medical illnesses? (8) Do you have problems with drinking too much alcohol or using street drugs? (9) What medications or other treatments have been tried in the past? (10) How did these treatments work?

Primary-care doctors will usually perform a physical examination unless one has been done in the recent past. Most psychiatrists will not do a full physical exam, but may take your blood pressure and pulse. If there is any significant concern about a medical illness that could be part of your problem or could affect the actions of an antidepressant, the psychiatrist will usually suggest that you see your primary-care doctor for an examination. There is no specific laboratory test or brain scan for diagnosis of depression. But as we learned in Chapter 7, in some cases a doctor may order thyroid hormone levels, blood counts, or other laboratory tests to see if you have a physical illness that is causing depression or making it worse. By the end of the medical evaluation, your doctor should have enough information to prescribe a course of treatment that will help you pull out of depression.

What you can do to help

1. Be prepared and organized with your medical history
2. Give your doctor the facts
3. Learn about treatment options
4. Voice your opinion
5. Keep the doctor informed of your progress
6. Don't act on your own
7. Check your attitudes about taking antidepressants

YOUR ROLE

You are the one who will make the ultimate decision on whether or not to take a medication for your depression. There are some things that you can do to help your doctor make the best recommendation for you. You should give your doctor as much information as possible about your symptoms and your background. You can prepare for your meeting with the doctor by writing out a list of your symptoms or sharing with him or her your responses to the Five Keys Depression Rating Scale from Chapter 2.

It can really help if you are prepared to give your doctor an accurate account of medications that you have taken in the past for depression, major illnesses or injuries you have experienced, your current medications, and any ongoing health problems. If you have family members who have been depressed, ask if there have been any medications that have worked especially well for them. When a medication has been helpful to a family member, there is a good chance that the same drug will work for you. As practicing clinicians, we can tell you that we are delighted when patients arrive for their first appointment with a detailed record of their medical history. It saves time and helps us understand them better.

You might be wondering how much you need to know about antidepressants to help your treatment go smoothly. In general, we suggest that patients who take antidepressants should know at least these four things: (1) the usual recommended dose and length of treatment for their medication, (2) possible side effects, (3) what to do if side effects appear, and (4) options for treatment if the first drug doesn't give adequate relief. Although you can get much of this information from reading this book, make sure your doctor gives you specific instructions.

Your role in treatment also includes communicating regularly with your doctor about the progress of your therapy. Your doctor needs to know if the medicine is working or not and if it is causing side effects. We frequently see patients who decide on their own to change doses or stop their medications. Doing this often leads to problems because many of the antidepressants will produce uncomfortable physical symptoms, such as headache or nausea, if stopped suddenly. More importantly, some medicines work slowly; so if you stop taking them too soon, you may miss the opportunity to find out if the medication can really work for you.

Get in touch with your doctor if you experience any discomfort from your medication. He or she may be able to suggest ways to reduce side effects so you can stay on the antidepressant long enough to give it a chance to work. If you experience severe or troubling side effects, be sure that your doctor gives you advice on alternative treatments or other interventions that will make you feel better. In situations where your doctor can't help, ask for a second opinion. If you are seeing a family doctor who is not familiar with all the new medications and their side effects, a psychiatrist who specializes in treatment with antidepressants may be able to find a solution.

Steve, a forty-two-year-old truck driver, was a great team player in managing antidepressant therapy. Steve had been depressed twice before and recovered quickly after his family doctor prescribed Paxil. This time, however, the Paxil hadn't helped, even after eight full weeks of treatment at a reasonable dose of forty milligrams per day. Steve had been tempted to stop the Paxil altogether, but instead asked his doctor for a referral to a specialist. Although he was feeling badly, Steve did the right thing in not stopping his medications on his own.

Both of us frequently receive referrals of patients who have not fully responded to first efforts at treating depression. Because one of us is a psychiatrist (an M.D. who prescribes drugs) and one is a psychologist, we may get different types of referral requests. In this case, Steve was referred to Jesse, a psychiatrist, for a consultation that would include a review of antidepressant therapy in addition to any other treatment options that could get the depression under control.

At our first visit, I took a complete medical history and reviewed records of a recent physical exam completed by Steve's family doctor. Steve helped by knowing the dates of his prior episodes of depression and dose and length of his past treatments. He was familiar with the symptoms of depression so he was able to tell me all that I needed to know to make a diagnosis of major depression. I explained to Steve that his family doctor could find no medical factors that were contributing to the depression. From what he described, it appeared that part of the problem was that he was getting no exercise and had poor sleep habits. He also had chronic low self-esteem and was having difficulty managing stress in all areas of his life.

We discussed options for treatment including medication changes, working on improving his exercise and sleep, and possible psychotherapy. Steve had done his homework. He knew the names of a few new antidepressants that he was interested in trying and had started to read a pamphlet about depression. After some discussion, Steve decided to follow my advice to pursue a combined treatment approach of medication and psychotherapy.

We then sorted through several alternatives for antidepressant therapy. One possible strategy was to increase the dose of Paxil to sixty milligrams per day. Psychiatrists usually recommend increasing the dose of a medication before considering a switch to a new drug. However, there were two reasons why Steve and I decided not to increase the Paxil. First, he was discouraged with the results of Paxil on this occasion and had little hope that more of the same drug would help. He clearly wanted to try something new.

Over the years, I've found that if a patient has a negative view of a particular treatment, it has a reduced chance of working. One of my cardinal rules is *"listen to the patient."* Because there were so many other good options, I decided to follow Steve's lead and move to another medication for depression. However, if I had believed that staying with the Paxil was clearly the superior choice, I would have tried to work with Steve to help him understand that this strategy offered him his best chance of recovery.

Steve had also reported a problem with low sex drive on Paxil. Although there are several possible antidotes to this side effect, which we will look at in the next chapter, the sexual problem added more weight to our decision to choose another medication. We finally decided to use Serzone, one of the other newer antidepressants that usually helps with sleep and has a very low rate of sexual side effects. After discussing the side effects of Serzone, I gave Steve instructions on how to begin his new medication and on how to gradually taper the dose of Paxil before stopping it. Steve agreed to call me before the next appointment if he had any problems.

Seven days later, I got an urgent call from Steve. The Serzone had helped him sleep, but it had worked too well! He was feeling very sleepy in the morning and was having problems with drowsiness at work. I explained that the sedation from this drug often subsides with time. But, his problem at work needed immediate attention. We decided to temporarily cut the morning dose in half. If he didn't start to feel more alert in the next two days, we agreed that he would call back to discuss other op-

Key Point

Take an active role in your medication treatment. Even if your doctor seems busy, voice your opinions, ask questions when you have them, and get the doctor to repeat any instructions that are not clear.

tions, including finding another antidepressant. Fortunately, Steve began to feel much better. He eventually was able to take a full dose of Serzone without any difficulty. Within three weeks of starting Serzone, Steve's depressive symptoms were much less severe, his sex drive was improving, and he was starting to use psychotherapy to improve his habits and attack his problem with low self-esteem.

A trusting partnership between patient and doctor usually makes the treatment process flow more smoothly and leads to better outcomes. Steve took an active role in providing information and making decisions. This made him more comfortable with the medication plan and contributed to the excellent outcome of treatment.

Is Taking an Antidepressant a Good Idea for Me?

Steve certainly believed that antidepressant therapy was an important part of his recovery. What about you? Do you think an antidepressant could help you overcome depression? What are your attitudes about taking medicines for depression? The last question may be the most important because your attitudes will influence whether or not you take the drug and what you expect it to do for you.

HOW YOUR ATTITUDES CAN MAKE A DIFFERENCE IN THERAPY WITH ANTIDEPRESSANTS

Most people have very strong feelings about taking medicines that affect their mood, how they think, or how they act. Yet, few of us have any qualms about taking medicines for other illnesses that are clearly "physical." For example, would you have any second thoughts about taking an antibiotic if you had pneumonia? But when it comes to medicines for our minds, we may hesitate before we commit to treatment.

If you have beliefs such as "I should be able to do it on my own" or "taking an antidepressant means I'm weak," you may have limited interest in trying an antidepressant drug. However if you believe, as most doctors do, that depression is like any other physical illness and deserves to be treated with effective medication, you may be very likely to accept antidepressants and to follow all treatment recommendations.

The attitudes of your family members, friends, and co-workers also can influence your decision to take medications for your depression. Strong support and encouragement from your family can be an important factor in getting proper treatment. But, we've seen some families who do not believe in medications go out of their way to interfere with treatment. You'll learn about techniques for communicating with your family, friends, and others in the Relationship Key section of this book.

Do you know what attitudes you have about taking antidepressants? Let's take a moment to check them out. The following Medication Attitude Survey contains a list of common beliefs about taking medications for depression. If your score is seven or below on this survey, we'd recommend that you look at ways to improve your attitudes about medication. You can do this by reading about the basics of treatment with antidepressants and by using the techniques for changing attitudes that are explained in the Thinking Key.

DISPELLING MYTHS ABOUT ANTIDEPRESSANTS

Some of the negative beliefs in the Medication Attitude Survey are commonly held myths about antidepressants. For example, people often fear that they will become dependent on antidepressants. The facts are that you can't become physically addicted to medications for depression. We have never seen antidepressants used like drugs of abuse to get a person high or to alter his or her sensations. It's a good idea to gradually reduce the dose of antidepressants when you decide to stop, but you won't go through the kind of withdrawal that can be seen with addicting drugs.

Another myth about antidepressants is that if your depression stems from a stressful event, medicines won't help. You might think that a drug couldn't be of any benefit when all of your problems seem to be due to a breakup of a relationship or some other major stress. Research has shown repeatedly that people can get significant relief from the symptoms of depression when they take medications, regardless of how the depression began.

Some people think that if you take antidepressants you will not be in control of yourself. Medications for depression are not the kind of mind-altering substances that make you lose touch with reality, get you high, or make you act like someone you are not. Actually, when you decide to

Medication Attitude Survey

Instructions. Read each of the statements and note whether you agree or disagree with the attitude. If you find that you are somewhere in the middle between agreeing and disagreeing with the statement, try to pick the answer that is closest to the way you think.

Attitudes about Using Medication for Depression	Agree	Disagree
1. I should be able to get better on my own without antidepressants.		
2. If I take an antidepressant, I could become dependent on the medication.		
3. If I take antidepressants, I may not be able to feel my normal emotions.		
4. I won't be in control if I take medication for depression.		
5. If I have a real life problem, antidepressants won't help.		
6. Emotional problems are real illnesses like ulcers and high blood pressure.		
7. Many other people have been helped by antidepressants.		
8. Antidepressants could help me think more clearly.		
9. I want to learn about medications for depression.		
10. I believe medication could help me recover from depression.		

How to score the Medication Attitude Survey. Score one point for disagreeing with each of the negative attitudes (questions 1 to 5). Score one point for agreeing with each of the positive attitudes (questions 6 to 10). Add up the total points. The maximum score is 10, and the minimum score is 0. The higher your score, the more positive your attitude about taking medication for depression.

take medication for your depression, you are taking control. These medications can help you gain better control over your life because they reduce symptoms and return your energy and motivation.

Do you agree with the statement "If I take antidepressants, I may not be able to feel my normal emotions?" Some people believe the myth that antidepressants can make you turn into a "Zombie" or interfere with your feeling the normal emotions of everyday life. From our experience in treating many depressed patients, we can reassure you that you will be able to feel your full range of emotions if you take these medications. When something sad happens, you'll feel sad. When good things happen, you'll feel happy. The feelings that antidepressants do take away are the abnormal and dysfunctional symptoms of clinical depression.

If you have some of the negative beliefs from the Medication Attitude Survey, it could help to write these attitudes in your notebook and then try to use the procedures in the Thinking Key such as "examining the evidence" to generate some alternatives. We recommend you make having a positive attitude about medication a part of your recovery plan. Let's go on now to discuss some of the other considerations in deciding whether or not to take medication for depression.

Are There Types of Depression That Require Antidepressants for Recovery?

Some research studies have suggested that people who have severe, recurrent, or long-lasting forms of depression may be in special need of antidepressant therapy. These include depressions that are severe enough to require hospitalization, those that have been present for two or more years without any relief from symptoms, or those that return two or more times. Other researchers have shown that psychotherapies such as cognitive therapy and interpersonal therapy work as well as medication for symptom relief for people with less extreme forms of major depression. These studies have helped us understand that in many instances you can get over an episode of depression without using medication at all.

A large and influential research investigation by Drs. Keller, McCullough, and co-workers from twelve major universities showed that a form of CBT developed for severe, long-lasting depressive symptoms worked as well as an antidepressant (Serzone) in treating chronic depression. However, patients who received both psychotherapy *and* Serzone had a much higher response rate than those who were treated with either psychotherapy alone or Serzone alone. Findings of this important study suggest that if you have a severe, chronic depression, you will probably get better results if you can arrange a combined treatment approach that includes both medication and psychotherapy.

There are two conditions for which most clinicians agree that medications are required. People who have experienced episodes of mania or hypomania in the past almost always must be treated with medications to get their depressive symptoms under control. This form of depression is part of manic-depressive or bipolar disorder—a condition that has an especially strong biochemical basis. Depression with psychotic features is another situation where medication is mandatory for recovery. This is a relatively rare type of severe depression in which the person hears voices, sees visions, or develops paranoia or other totally irrational thoughts such as being convinced that he or she has a fatal illness although a complete medical exam has been negative. When psychotic symptoms are present, biological treatments must be used in order to have a successful outcome. Doctors usually treat psychotic depression with a combination of an antidepressant and an antipsychotic medication or electroconvulsive therapy (ECT).

If you think you might have one of the types of depression that requires medication, review the information about diagnoses in Chapter 2 and consult with your doctor. We strongly recommend that patients who have severe or chronic depression, bipolar disorder, or depression with psychotic features use medication as a cornerstone of their recovery program. When the disabling symptoms of depression begin to lift, you will have more energy and a better ability to concentrate so you can learn and make use of the therapeutic strategies covered in the other four Keys.

We also recommend medications be used most or all of the time when a full course of psychotherapy has been tried and there has been little sign of improvement. Similarly, if medication alone has been given a good trial and symptoms are still present, treatment with psychotherapy would be in order. In fact, several recent studies by Giovanni Fava and his associates from the State University of New York at Buffalo and the University of Bologna in Italy have shown excellent results when CBT is used to treat depressive symptoms that remain after pharmacotherapy has been tried.

Most people do not have bipolar disorder or any of the other severe forms of depression. Therefore, it is usually the case that there are a wide variety of treatment options. Medication could be part of your treatment program. To help you decide, learn more about the use of medication to treat depression and about how the other Keys to recovery fit with your unique set of problems.

Situations where Medication May Be Required

1. Depression that is severe enough to keep you from your responsibilities at home or work
2. Depression lasting two years or more
3. Depression that has recurred two or more times
4. Bipolar depression
5. Depression with psychotic features
6. When therapy hasn't helped

Can Antidepressant Medications Do More than Treat Depression?

In his best selling book *Listening to Prozac*, Peter Kramer, M.D., describes changes in personality in some of his patients treated with this SSRI. What do you really hear when you *"listen to Prozac?"* Can SSRIs actually change your personality? If you have chronic problems such as excessive temper outbursts or crippling obsessive-compulsive symptoms, you might welcome some relief. But, if you like your basic personality or don't want to change, should you be afraid of SSRIs?

The simple answer to these questions is that you have little to fear from Prozac or other new antidepressants. These drugs can't change your fundamental personality. If you have always been outgoing and fun loving, Prozac won't make you a hermit. If you are interested in music, an SSRI won't take it away. However, the SSRIs and other new antidepressants can reverse a wide variety of symptoms and make it easier for the positive parts of your personality to shine through.

Chad was a hard-working restaurant owner who loved his family deeply and had great respect for his employees. He considered himself lucky to have top-notch cooks and waiters who had helped him build a very successful business. But, Chad couldn't figure out why he continued to drive himself and others so hard. He had a short temper, and often blew up over the smallest concerns. Chad admitted that he just couldn't relax at work. He was on edge all the time.

His tendency to have excessive irritability and anger had been present many years and had predated the recent onset of depression. When Chad sought treatment for his depression, he made it clear he did not want to start psychotherapy. Although counseling probably could have helped him with both the depression and the anger problem, Chad decided to try antidepressants alone. Chad said that one of his cousins had taken Prozac and had responded nicely. Since what works for one family member can often work for others, prescribing Prozac seemed like a reasonable idea.

Even though there was a good chance that Prozac could help with Chad's symptoms, he appeared to need talk therapy to work on his anger and on another issue—his impending retirement. In fact, it was possible that Chad's depression and anger were related in part to his difficulty in coping with this important life change. He seemed to be ignoring his feelings about selling his restaurant and leaving a job that meant so much to him. Also, his workaholic life-style hadn't prepared him for living a meaningful life in retirement.

When Chad appeared for his next appointment in about three weeks, he looked like a changed man. The deep worry lines in his face were gone, and he was cheerful and upbeat. Much of his depression had lifted. The most surprising development was that his long–standing irritability and temper outbursts had almost completely gone away. Chad said that his wife and his co-workers had all noticed a big improvement in his anger. Despite his negative statements about psychotherapy in the first session, Chad now showed interest in coming in with his wife to talk about his adjustment to retirement.

What had happened to Chad? Did Prozac relieve his depression and stop his problem with anger? Did the medication make it possible for him to start making the adjustments that would be required for a happy and healthy retirement? Would his lifelong pattern of tense and driven behavior melt away under the spell of Prozac? His wife was able to help with some of the answers. She described a remarkable change in Chad's behavior after starting on Prozac. He used to come home from work with an extremely short fuse. Because he was so easily annoyed, she had learned to keep her distance. Now at the end of the day he appeared relaxed and comfortable and was much more interested in hearing about her experiences.

Over the course of the next year, Chad worked in therapy to fully resolve the depression and prepare for retirement. He built on his initial improvement by continuing to make many positive changes. Many of these required use of the other four Keys to recovery. As expected, Chad's basic personality remained intact. He continued to be rather perfectionistic and demanding of himself and others. But, Prozac helped him in many ways. Most of the time he was able to respond to others without anger and to relax enough to find a sense of true well-being.

It's hard to know whether the SSRI was fully responsible for Chad's behavior change or if feeling relief from his depression opened the doors to other changes. In general, SSRIs and other antidepressants relieve depressive symptoms but do not modify long-standing personality traits. However antidepressants can have a variety of positive effects that go beyond the relief of depression. They can help with problems such as anger, anxiety, impulsiveness, social withdrawal, and eating disturbances.

Research studies have consistently shown that SSRIs and many of the other antidepressants are effective treatments for panic, obsessive-compulsive disorder, social phobias (avoiding social situations), and bulimia. Antidepressants can also be very useful for treatment of chronic pain. Likewise, TCAs have been found to be helpful in reducing symptoms of chronic pain, certain types of headache, and severe anxiety symptoms such as panic attacks.

I don't think it's working. What should I do?

1. Am I certain that it is not working?
2. Have I taken the medication long enough?
3. Have I been missing doses?

When Your Medicine Doesn't Seem to Work

There are some important questions you should ask yourself if your antidepressant medication does not seem to be working. These questions can help you determine whether you are doing your part to make the Biology Key work for you.

ARE YOU SURE IT'S NOT WORKING?

It is not uncommon to get better, but not notice it. This is because the symptoms of depression often improve slowly at first. You don't notice the small changes that occur day to day. When they add up, the change becomes more obvious. Sometimes changes that are subtle are more noticeable to others than to you.

Another reason that small changes in depression can be hard to detect is that the physical symptoms may improve before the mood or negative attitude changes. If you are still sad and thinking badly of yourself, the small changes may seem unimportant or not good enough to recognize as significant changes. To be certain, it is helpful to use some objective way of measuring change. The Five Keys Depression Rating Scale in Chapter 2 can be used to check your progress. Without looking over your last set of answers, rerate the twenty questions and then compare your score.

HAVE I TAKEN THE ANTIDEPRESSANT LONG ENOUGH? HAVE I BEEN MISSING DOSES?

If you don't think your antidepressant is working, the most important thing to consider is whether you have taken the medication for an adequate amount of time and at a sufficient dose to give it a real test. Usually at least six weeks at a therapeutic dose (see Chapter 9 for guidelines) should be allowed before changing medications. Have you been taking your medication regularly? If you have been missing doses on a regular basis, for example, one to two times a week, it is the same thing as taking too small of a dose. In either case, you haven't been giving the medication a fair chance because you haven't gotten enough of it to be helpful. In Chapter 14, "Making Your Plan Work," we'll give you tips on how to remember to take your medication regularly.

Are There Nondrug Therapies that Could Help?

This section of *Getting Your Life Back* is focused on biological treatments. However, there are lots of other effective strategies for combating depression. In our clinical practices we have been asked to see many patients for second opinions when a wide variety of antidepressants have been tried without success. We almost always find that methods from the other Keys to recovery can benefit these patients. The next chapter will help you learn the details of treatment with antidepressants. As you check out the options for antidepressant therapy, remember that the other parts of this book can give you ideas for alternative ways to relieve symptoms and work toward recovery.

9

Antidepressants and Other Biological Treatments

Antidepressants are one of the most frequently prescribed groups of medications in the world—and for good reason. These drugs have been proven to be effective in relieving suffering and helping people get back to feeling like themselves again. In this chapter, we will help you learn how to get the most out of treatment with antidepressants and how to make biological treatments an important part of your Personal Plan for Recovery. The first type of medications we will describe are the serotonin selective reuptake inhibitors (SSRIs), the most widely used drugs for depression. You'll also be able to learn about a broad selection of other useful medicines and biological remedies. In case you don't want to or can't take a prescription medication, St. John's Wort, an herbal preparation, or SAMe, an over-the-counter drug, might be part of your answer to depression. If you are interested in using the Biology Key, this chapter will give you the information you need to chart a path toward recovery.

The Serotonin Selective Reuptake Inhibitors (SSRIs)

THE PROZAC STORY

The first SSRI, Prozac, was introduced in 1988 and almost immediately became a sensation. Even today Prozac remains one of the best-selling antidepressants in the United States. Prozac is prescribed by so many doctors and taken by so many patients because it has distinct advantages over the older tricyclic antidepressants (TCAs) and monoamine oxidase inhibitors (MAOIs). It has fewer side effects and is much safer. But, there isn't any real evidence that Prozac is better than any of the other SSRIs or the other newer antidepressants. One reason that Prozac is prescribed so frequently is that as the first new antidepressant, it was heralded as a breakthrough drug and was advertised very heavily. Now when most people think of antidepressants, Prozac is the first name that comes to mind.

There is no question that Prozac is a fine medication that has helped millions of people fight depression. But, like other antidepressants it isn't a perfect medication. It has its own group of side effects, and it doesn't work for everyone. One of the least understood facts about Prozac among the public is that there are few differences between Prozac and all the other drugs in the SSRI class. If you are prescribed Zoloft, Paxil, or Celexa, you will be receiving a medication that is very similar to Prozac in the way it affects your brain chemistry.

HOW DO THE SSRIs RELIEVE DEPRESSION?

All of these drugs work by increasing serotonin, a chemical in your brain. Serotonin is one of the special chemicals, called neurotransmitters, that affect our thinking, moods, and energy. We talked about the different types of neurotransmitters earlier in the Biology Key. Chapter 7 contains a detailed description of serotonin neurons and how medications increase the flow of nerve impulses in brain areas involved in depression.

It can be a bit confusing to try to understand the actions of SSRIs on the brain. But if you keep in mind a few basic facts, you'll have a better understanding of why SSRIs relieve symptoms of depression and produce certain types of side effects. SSRI's exert their positive effects by stimulating the serotonin type 1 (S1) receptor, a portion of the brain cell that receives and sends messages. It usually takes about two weeks for SSRIs to start to relieve depression, because the actions on the S1 receptor take place through a complicated series of chemical processes that do not occur immediately. The side effects of SSRIs are a result of their actions on a different set of brain receptors.

WHAT ARE THE SIDE EFFECTS OF SSRIs?

Unfortunately, SSRIs also act on two other types of serotonin receptors (S2 and S3). Stimulation of these receptors can cause unwanted side effects. When the S2 receptor is stimulated, side effects such as anxiety,

Table 9.1
Common Side Effects of SSRIs

Anxiety	Insomnia
Decreased sexual functioning	Nausea
Diarrhea	Restlessness or agitation
Drowsiness	Tremor

insomnia, and decreased sexual functioning can occur. Stimulation of the S3 receptor can sometimes cause nausea and diarrhea. Later in this chapter, you'll find out how some of the other new antidepressants can reverse the side effects caused by SSRI stimulation of the S2 and S3 receptors.

One of the best features of SSRIs is that their side effects are usually mild and do not cause nearly as much distress as the illness itself. Although gastrointestinal side effects such as nausea and diarrhea can occur, most people experience little difficulty in tolerating SSRIs. Many of the side effects decrease with time, so people are often able to outlast these problems. Changes in sexual functioning, including decreased sex drive and difficulty reaching orgasm, are some of the most common roadblocks to the use of SSRIs.

There are a number of useful strategies to reduce sexual side effects and other bothersome problems associated with SSRIs. Your first step should be to tell your doctor about your side effects and ask for advice on how to manage the situation. Two frequently used techniques are to reduce the dose or to switch to another medication. Don't give up on an SSRI too soon because it seems to be causing difficulty. Often there is a simple solution that can eliminate the problem or make you feel much more comfortable. SSRIs share many side effects in common with the other new antidepressants. After all the new antidepressants have been described, we'll give you a series of helpful tips on how to manage side effects.

Key Point

It usually takes several weeks for SSRIs or other antidepressants to work, so give them a chance to do their job. Your doctor will have recommendations for reducing or eliminating bothersome side effects.

DOSAGE GUIDELINES FOR SSRIs

Usually SSRIs are taken once a day in the morning because these drugs can sometimes interfere with falling asleep. But, SSRIs also can have the side effect of making you feel a little drowsy. If this happens, it may work out better for you to take this medicine at bedtime. Often the starting dose is enough to relieve symptoms, so your doctor may never have to recommend an increase. However, if you don't start to feel better in a few weeks, a larger dose may be needed.

Table 9.2
Dose Ranges of SSRIs

SSRI	Dose Range (mg/day)
Prozac (fluoxetine)	20–80
Zoloft (sertraline)	50–200
Paxil (paroxetine)	20–60
Celexa (citalopram)	20–60
Luvox (fluvoxamine)	50–300

HOW LONG SHOULD YOU TAKE AN SSRI?

The American Psychiatric Association's *Practice Guidelines for Treatment of Patients with Major Depressive Disorder* state that at least sixteen to twenty weeks of treatment are required *after* remission from a single episode of depression. This means that the total length of treatment for most people who have had one period of depression should usually be in the range of six to twelve months. Research studies have shown that the chances of depression coming back are much higher for persons who stop taking antidepressants too quickly. If there is a history of recurrent depression (two or more episodes), the usual recommendation is to stay on antidepressants for a much longer period of time. People who have experienced many recurrences may require indefinite maintenance therapy with medication to stop the depression from returning. We will discuss strategies for long-term treatment and relapse prevention in the final section of the book.

Key Point

Keep taking SSRIs or other antidepressants until both you and your doctor decide it is safe to stop. If you go off an antidepressant prematurely, you will increase the chances that depression will return.

ARE THERE ANY DIFFERENCES BETWEEN THE SSRIs?

Antidepressants in the SSRI class are more alike than different. They all act primarily by promoting the action of serotonin neurons and have limited or no effect on increasing the activity of norepinephrine or dopamine neurotransmitters. One characteristic of the SSRIs that can make a difference is variability in the time it takes for them to leave the body. Except for Prozac, all of the SSRIs have a half-life of about one day. This means that if a person stops taking any of the SSRIs, other than Prozac, the level of medication in the bloodstream will drop by one-half in approximately one day. By the next day, the level will drop by half again so it will only be one-quarter of today's amount. You can see that drugs with relatively short half-lives of about twenty-four hours can be eliminated from your system rather quickly.

Prozac stands out from the other drugs because it has a very long half-life of four to sixteen days. Thus, one to two weeks after stopping Prozac, it will be decreased in your body by only about 50 percent. Because of Prozac's long half-life, it can take weeks or even months to get this drug completely out of your bloodstream. The long half-life can be both a disadvantage and an advantage. If you have a problem with Prozac or want to stop it for any other reason, you won't be able to get rid of the drug for a long time. But on the positive side, if you miss a dose of Prozac you will still have a fair amount of medication in your bloodstream to help you with depression. Even more important, your doctor can advise you to stop Prozac abruptly without worrying about tapering (gradually reducing) the dose.

Because the other SSRIs like Zoloft or Paxil leave your body more rapidly, you may experience some physical symptoms as your body gets used to not having the antidepressant. This does *not* mean that you have become dependent on SSRIs like drugs of abuse. The physical discomforts are indications that your system is adapting to not having the SSRI.

If you stop taking an SSRI too abruptly, you may experience dizziness, nausea and vomiting, fatigue, muscle aches and pains, headache, insomnia, anxiety, and irritability. You can also begin to feel more depressed again.

It is a good idea to taper the dose of all SSRIs, except Prozac, if a decision is made to go off the medication. This strategy is especially important for Paxil. A typical tapering program for Paxil would be to reduce the dose by ten milligrams a week until the medication is completely discontinued. If you go off SSRIs slowly, you usually won't experience significant physical symptoms.

Key Point

If you stop an antidepressant too abruptly it can cause some uncomfortable physical symptoms and put you at risk for relapse.

Paxil has a mild tendency to cause dry mouth and constipation, side effects that are rare with other SSRIs. Usually this isn't a major problem. But, if you are having significant difficulty with these symptoms, you could ask your doctor to consider another antidepressant. One of the SSRIs, Luvox, is not approved by the FDA for treatment of depression in the United States. However, it has been certified for treatment of obsessive-compulsive disorder and is widely used for depression in many other countries. Luvox is generally considered to be an effective and safe treatment for depression and is prescribed by many doctors in the United States despite lack of FDA approval for this purpose.

Another significant difference between antidepressants in the SSRI class is their variability in interactions with other medications. You should *always* tell your doctor and your pharmacist about all the medications you are taking so they can check for possible drug interactions. Although most of the newer antidepressants can be taken safely with most other drugs, there are certain interactions that can cause problems. For example, later in this chapter, we will describe a group of drugs, the MAOIs, that can have a dangerous interaction with SSRIs. So, don't forget to have your doctor or pharmacist review your medications to look for potential interactions. Be sure to ask your doctor about interactions with alcohol. Generally, it is recommended that alcohol be avoided or minimized when taking antidepressants.

Other Newer Antidepressants

In addition to the SSRIs, several other newer antidepressants like Wellbutrin, Effexor, Serzone, and Remeron have been proven to be effective for depression. Each of these medications has unique effects on brain receptors that produce different patterns of antidepressant activity and side effects. Because these drugs have such distinctive actions, doctors can now choose specific medications to stimulate specific receptors. The positive effects on depression of the other newer antidepressants can be explained by their ability to stimulate one or more of three receptors—serotonin type 1 (S1), norepinephrine, or dopamine.

Table 9.3
Neurotransmitter Effects of New Antidepressants

Transmitter	SSRI	Wellbutrin	Effexor*	Serzone	Remeron
Serotonin	X		X	X	X
Norepinephrine		X	X	X	X
Dopamine		X	X		

Key: X = The medicine stimulates this receptor in the brain.

*Effexor has the unusual property of stimulating serotonin at low doses, norepinephrine at medium doses, and dopamine at high doses. It is the broadest-spectrum new antidepressant if prescribed at the higher end of the dose range.

You might think that the best strategy would be to pick a drug that stimulates the most receptors. However, research studies have shown that the chances of responding to treatment are about the same for all of the antidepressants. The great value of having medications with different receptor effects is that if one drug doesn't work, there are other options to consider. Another thing to keep in mind is that people can react differently to the same medication. That is why some people have side effects from a drug and others do not, just as some people respond well to a drug while others do not. If you want to read more about the different antidepressants, a good resource is the Agency for Health Care Policy and Research publication *Treatment of Depression—Newer Pharmacotherapies*. This publication is available on the Internet (see Web Resources). Also, a detailed explanation of the neurotransmitter effects of medication for depression can be found in the excellent book *Psychopharmacology of Antidepressants* by Steven Stahl, M.D.

THE DOUBLE-BARRELED ACTIONS OF SOME ANTIDEPRESSANTS ON SIDE EFFECTS

Some of the newer antidepressants (Wellbutrin, Serzone, and Remeron) have the ability to both cause and reverse side effects. SSRIs and Effexor do *not* have this double-barreled effect. While antidepressants act on the receptors in your brain that help your depression, they also can act on neighboring receptors. When this happens, side effects such as insomnia, anxiety, nausea, and decreased sexual function can result. Because the SSRIs and other antidepressants affect different receptors, sometimes a second drug can be given as an antidote for the side effect caused by the first drug. The tricky part of understanding the double-barreled actions of certain antidepressants is that each of the medications has a different pattern of positive and negative influences on side effects.

Table 9.4
Understanding the Side Effects of Antidepressants

Side Effects	SSRIs	Wellbutrin	Effexor	Serzone	Remeron
Anxiety Insomnia	↑	↑	↑	↑↓	↓
Sexual Dysfunction	↑	↓	↑	↑↓	↓
Nausea Diarrhea	↑		↑	↑	↓

Key: ↑ = Stimulates receptors that cause this side effect
↓ = Can reverse this side effect

Table 9.4, "Understanding the Side Effects of Antidepressants," summarizes the activity of the different medications in either producing or protecting against three main types of side effects. Although antidepressants can have other side effects, these three groups of problems are some of the most commonly experienced difficulties in using the newer medications for depression. At first glance, Remeron may appear to offer the best profile of side effects because it protects against the three major problems caused by SSRIs. Serzone is another drug with the ability to reverse a number of side effects. However, both of these drugs are more likely to cause drowsiness than the other antidepressants. Also, Remeron is especially prone to cause weight gain. The pharmaceutical industry is working intensively to develop antidepressants with fewer side effects and better effectiveness in relieving depression. But, we still do not have a "perfect antidepressant."

The complexity of antidepressant pharmacology is one of the reasons you need to have a good working relationship with a doctor who is an expert in treatment with these medicines. Well-informed doctors know about the different actions of antidepressants on receptors and use their knowledge to select medications that they think will give you the best opportunity for recovery with the lowest risk of side effects. For example, if a person developed sexual side effects on an SSRI, one of the medications that can counter this difficulty (Wellbutrin, Serzone, or Remeron) could be substituted or added to the first antidepressant. We'll discuss how to use the information in Table 9.4 to manage side effects of SSRIs and other medications after we take a brief look at each of the other newer antidepressants.

EFFEXOR

This antidepressant comes in two forms, regular Effexor and a longer-acting form, Effexor XR (sustained release). The XR version was developed because Effexor is metabolized very rapidly. That means it leaves the system so quickly that it must be given twice a day unless the XR form is prescribed. The most common side effects of Effexor are nausea and indigestion. Some patients who take Effexor also have trouble sleeping. Problems with nausea usually go away if you stay on the medication for several days, but insomnia may persist. One unique difficulty with Effexor is a tendency to elevate blood pressure in a small percentage of patients. This side effect doesn't usually appear until higher doses are prescribed. Blood pressure monitoring is especially important if you already have a problem with hypertension, and it's a good idea to check blood pressure if you take Effexor at doses of 225 milligrams or more a day. Probably the best feature of Effexor is that it can stimulate all three of the neurotransmitters (serotonin, norepinephrine, and dopamine) involved in depression. Effexor XR is better tolerated than regular Effexor and is generally the preferred form of this drug.

WELLBUTRIN

If you want to avoid side effects, Wellbutrin is the antidepressant for you. This medication is the least likely to cause side effects of any of the antidepressants. Although Wellbutrin has appeared to be as effective as other antidepressants in research studies, many doctors don't consider it to be a first-choice medication for depression. The reasons for this aren't entirely clear to us or many of our colleagues. In our own practices we've seen excellent responses to Wellbutrin. But, we've found that most psychiatrists save this medication for those who don't respond to SSRIs or other antidepressants or who have side effects that don't go away.

Wellbutrin does slightly increase your risk of having seizures. Because this problem is usually confined to persons who have eating disorders or a history of seizures in the past, many doctors avoid using Wellbutrin for patients who have seizure disorders or eating problems such as bulimia or anorexia. Although side effects are not encountered very often, this antidepressant can cause anxiety, insomnia, restlessness, dry mouth, sweating, and tremor. When these problems do occur, they are usually mild. If insomnia is a problem, it sometimes helps to take the second dose no later than 5 P.M.

The dopamine-stimulating effect of Wellbutrin has some positive features in addition to working to relieve depression. One of these bonuses is that Wellbutrin can suppress craving. The drug Zyban, which is marketed for helping people to stop smoking, has exactly the same ingredient (buproprion) as Wellbutrin. A second bonus is that Wellbutrin can reverse the sexual side effects caused by other antidepressants. Wellbutrin is also known for its low risk for weight gain and its positive effects on energy and concentration.

SERZONE

This antidepressant works like the SSRIs to stimulate the three different types of serotonin receptors (S1, antidepressant action; S2 and S3, side effects), but it also has the reverse effect of blocking the S2 receptor. By blocking this receptor, Serzone has a reduced risk of causing a cluster of side effects including anxiety, insomnia, and decreased sexual functioning. Serzone also stimulates norepinephrine. This antidepressant is a good choice if sexual side effects are a concern. However, other side effects such as nausea, drowsiness, dizziness, dry mouth, weakness, blurred vision, and impaired concentration are sometimes a problem. Because Serzone is eliminated quickly from the bloodstream, it is usually given twice a day.

REMERON

The strong antihistamine effects of this antidepressant can help you get a good night's sleep. Unfortunately the antihistamine effect can be too strong for some people, causing excessive sedation and weight gain. Remeron exerts its antidepressant effect by stimulating both serotonin and norepinephrine. Thus, it might be helpful in situations where an antidepressant that doesn't activate one of these neurotransmitters has been tried previously. As we've mentioned previously, Remeron has the distinct advantage of reversing many of the side effects of SSRIs. The low risk for sexual side effects, anxiety, insomnia, and nausea has made this antidepressant a top choice of many doctors. Dosing with Remeron is usually uncomplicated. It can be given once a day at bedtime and is usually effective at a dose of fifteen or thirty milligrams a day. Interestingly, the problem with sedation often lessens if the dose of this medication is *increased.* You can check the doses and time schedules of Remeron and some of the other newer antidepressants in the next table.

Table 9.5
Other Newer Antidepressants: Dose Ranges and Timing

Antidepressant	Dose Range (mg/day)	Timing
Effexor (venlafaxine)*	75–375	Twice daily
Wellbutrin (buproprion)	150–300	Twice daily
Serzone (nefazadone)	100–600	Twice daily
Remeron (mirtazapine)	15–45	Once daily

*Sustained-release preparation available that allows once-a-day dosing.

Managing Side Effects of SSRIs and Other Newer Antidepressants

We'll give you some tips here on how to reduce or eliminate side effects, but remember to always discuss problems with your doctor before making any changes. Your doctor can give you advice on whether side effects are likely to disappear on their own or if you will need to have adjustments in your treatment to solve the difficulty.

The Five Basic Strategies for Managing Side Effects

1. Do nothing—wait it out.
2. Reduce the dose.
3. Change medications.
4. Add another medication that can counteract side effects.
5. Stop antidepressants altogether and focus on nondrug treatments for depression.

Most commonly people choose to wait it out because the majority of side effects don't cause much of a problem and fade away within a few weeks. Sometimes the second option, reducing the dose, is a good idea. But, you have to be careful not to lower the dose so much that the medication doesn't work. We've often seen individuals become more depressed after cutting their dose of antidepressants without consulting their doctors.

When side effects cause significant discomfort or they don't disappear after a few weeks, your doctor may recommend changing medication to resolve the problem. One way to do this is by "trial and error"—just trying anything else to see if it works better. However, doctors and patients who know about the different side-effect patterns of antidepressants can make choices that can beat guesswork. Managing the sexual side effects of antidepressants is a good example of how you can use knowledge of antidepressants to guide decisions.

SEXUAL SIDE EFFECTS

The SSRIs and Effexor can cause a lowering of sexual interest and decreased ability to experience orgasm. Some doctors will suggest lowering the dose or even taking "drug holidays" (going off the medication for one to three days) to revive sexual functioning. We haven't found these strategies to be of much use in helping with sexual side effects. Generally, we recommend against drug holidays because you can have symptoms such as headache and nausea if you stop antidepressants abruptly.

There are three ways to get around the problem of sexual side effects: (1) use an antidepressant that doesn't reduce sexual functioning, (2) add an antidepressant that can reverse the sexual difficulties, (3) add another medication that can act as an antidote. We generally prefer to handle sexual side effects by using one of the first two options if possible. You can check Table 9.4 for information on antidepressants like Wellbutrin, Serzone, and Remeron with a low risk for sexual side effects or actions that can restore sexual functioning.

Other medications that are sometimes used as antidotes include Periactin (an S2 blocker) and Ritalin and Dexedrine (dopamine stimulators). Several researchers, including Dr. George Nurnberg from the University of New Mexico and Dr. Maurizio Fava from Massachusetts General Hospital, have found that Viagra, the sexual stimulant, can improve sex drive and ability to achieve orgasm in men and women treated with antidepressants. Another possible antidote for sexual side effects is the natural remedy *Ginkgo biloba*. The exact reason why ginkgo may help sexual function is unknown. You can check out the references to scientific articles by Drs. Robert Segraves and Lawrence Labbate if you want to learn more about treatment of antidepressant-induced sexual side effects.

INSOMNIA, RESTLESSNESS, AND AGITATION

The double-barreled receptor actions of some of the antidepressants can be an advantage in handling other side effects such as insomnia, restlessness, and agitation. For example, if you develop these side effects on an SSRI such as Prozac, a change to a medication that can reverse these symptoms would be reasonable (see Table 9.4). One choice would be to switch to Remeron or Serzone, two antidepressants that have a low risk for these problems. A common strategy for coping with SSRI-induced insomnia is to add another antidepressant, Desyrel (trazadone)—a medication with strong sedating qualities. Desyrel is an FDA-approved antidepressant, but it isn't used as often as the other medications to treat depression because many doctors believe it is less effective than other drugs. However, it is not unusual for Desyrel to be given at bedtime along with an SSRI to help people sleep better.

Some of the best ways to cope with drug-related insomnia are to practice the good sleep habits described in Chapter 5 and to try to reduce your negative and worrisome thoughts by using the lessons taught in Chapters 3 and 4. You also might want to consider melatonin, which is a natural remedy available as an over-the-counter medication. Studies on melatonin have been inconclusive, but it sometimes can be a helpful medication for sleeplessness caused by SSRIs. Another herbal remedy, valerian, may also be able to help you get a good night's sleep.

Doctors will sometimes suggest that you take prescription sleeping pills to cope with insomnia. Sonata and Ambien give the most natural sleep, but they are more expensive than older prescription drugs like Dalmane (flurazepam) and Restoril (temazepam) that have generic forms. Use of prescription drugs for sleep is discussed in Chapter 7.

Tricyclic Antidepressants (TCAs) and Monoamine Oxidase Inhibitors (MAOIs): The Older Drugs Still Have a Place

The TCAs and the MAOIs were introduced in the 1950s and were the only drugs available for depression for many years. After Prozac and the other newer antidepressants came on the scene, the TCAs and MAOIs began to lose favor with doctors because these older medications aren't as safe and frequently cause side effects. Because MAOIs are particularly difficult to use, these medications are usually reserved for special situations and are hardly ever prescribed by doctors who are not specialists in antidepressant therapy. The TCAs are no longer drugs of first choice for depression, but at times they can provide valuable alternatives to the newer medications.

TRICYCLIC ANTIDEPRESSANTS (TCAs)

Although a number of TCAs are still marketed, only a few are used with any regularity in medical practice. Table 9.6 lists some of the more commonly prescribed TCAs. All of the TCAs: (1) help depression by stimulating norepinephrine and/or serotonin; (2) can cause side effects such as low blood pressure, dizziness, fainting spells, dry mouth, constipation, delayed urination, and blurred vision; (3) usually promote good sleep; (4) can be very dangerous or lethal in overdoses; (5) can cause disturbances in the rhythm of your heartbeat.

Some doctors still prescribe TCAs as first-choice treatments for depression. This is probably because they have grown comfortable with these medications over many years of practice. If your doctor suggests a TCA as the first treatment for depression, you might ask to discuss the pros and cons of using a newer drug. Most physicians will recommend an SSRI or another newer medication as an initial antidepressant.

TCAs may be useful for patients who fail to respond to full courses of the newer drugs. Generally, the starting dose of TCAs is at the lower end of the range in Table 9.6. The dose is then raised slowly until the depression is relieved or side effects become too uncomfortable to tolerate. The TCAs are typically given once a day at bedtime because their sedating properties enhance sleep.

Table 9.6
Tricyclic Antidepressants (TCAs)

TCA	Dose Range (mg/day)	Timing
Elavil (amitriptyline)	75–300	1–3 times a day
Norpramin (desipramine)	100–300	1–3 times a day
Pamelor (nortriptyline)	50–150	1–3 times a day
Sinequan (doxepin)	75–300	1–3 times a day
Tofranil (imipramine)	75–300	1–3 times a day

MONOAMINE OXIDASE INHIBITORS (MAOIs)

When people first hear about the risks of MAOIs they probably wonder why any doctor would prescribe these drugs. Yet, for a limited number of individuals, MAOIs may provide the best option for effective relief from depression. In particular, people with "atypical depression," characterized by sleeping too much, increased appetite and weight, a heavy weighted-down feeling, and intense fears of being rejected seem to respond well to MAOIs even when nothing else seems to work.

MAOIs act through a different mechanism than any of the other antidepressants. They suppress an enzyme that is involved in the breakdown of neurotransmitters. In doing so, they prevent the neurotransmitter from being dissolved or eliminated. The end result of this suppression is that more of the neurotransmitter is left around the cell to be used in sending messages or nerve impulses throughout the brain.

Unfortunately, MAOIs also slow the breakdown of other neurotransmitters that are involved with the control of blood pressure. If you eat foods that are high in a substance called tyramine while you are taking an MAOI, you can have sudden and dangerous elevations in blood pressure. Tyramine is a building block for the blood pressure neurotransmitters that are increased by MAOIs. In some cases, blood pressure has risen so high that strokes and even death have occurred. Later in the chapter we'll tell you about some of the foods with a high tyramine content.

Most psychiatrists only prescribe MAOIs when other safer approaches have failed and the patient is highly reliable and agrees to take all the necessary precautions. Several of our patients have had superb responses to MAOIs when other treatments haven't worked. Sarah is one of our success stories.

Sarah had been depressed "as long as I can remember." After having tried numerous other antidepressants including three of the SSRIs, most of the other newer antidepressants, and many of the TCAs, she was desperate and looking for some new ideas. Although her prior psychiatrist had tried some of the advanced strategies described later in the chapter of augmenting antidepressants with other medications such as lithium, none of these treatments had given her significant relief. Sarah thought that psychotherapy had been of some help, but she was still depressed.

Because Sarah reported the classic symptoms of atypical depression, including sleeping too much, overeating, and being exquisitely sensitive to criticism or rejection, a trial of one of the MAOIs was suggested. We started by going over the risks and benefits of MAOIs and discussing the special diet and medication restrictions that must be followed for these drugs to be taken safely. It was encouraging to see that Sarah asked for extra reading material on MAOIs. She wanted to learn as much as possible about how to take these medications in a responsible manner.

Four weeks after starting Parnate, an MAOI, Sarah was remarkably better. She had much more energy, was sleeping a normal amount of time, was eating less, and was starting to look for work. Over the last seven years, Sarah has continued to take Parnate without any significant side effects and has experienced only mild and very brief periods of depression. She has been able to work steadily, and most of the time she feels completely well.

Treatment with MAOIs doesn't always go as smoothly as it did with Sarah. The dietary restrictions are demanding, and you have to be on the lookout for drugs that can interact with MAOIs. If your doctor recommends one of these medications, you will have to get detailed instructions on what foods and drugs to avoid. A few of the foods that can be dangerous are aged cheeses, meat extracts, commercial soup stocks, fava beans, yeast extracts, caviar, and certain alcoholic beverages. Medicines that can interact with MAOIs to cause a high-blood-pressure crisis include: other antidepressants, cold and cough preparations, stimulants, and the pain killer Demerol. One special precaution is that SSRIs and other antidepressants *must* be completely out of your system before starting an MAOI.

Parnate and Nardil are the only two MAOIs available in the United States. The dose of Parnate is usually ten to forty milligrams a day, and Nardil is given in dose ranges of fifteen to sixty milligrams a day. Both drugs can cause side effects such as overstimulation, insomnia, low blood pressure, and dizziness. Sudden dramatic increases in blood pressure are uncommon and are almost always associated with a lapse in diet or use of another drug that interacts with the MAOI. We tell our patients to never take another prescription drug or an over-the-counter drug with an MAOI unless they first check it out with a doctor or a pharmacist.

What Can Be Done if the Medication Doesn't Seem to Work?

If you are certain that you have taken your medication as prescribed for several weeks and your symptoms have not improved, it may be time to try something new. There are several different strategies available to you. Here are the most common questions a doctor considers before making any changes to your treatment regimen. As you read about the options, you might start thinking whether any of these ideas could be part of your Personal Plan for Recovery.

If the Medicine Isn't Working

1. Should the dose be increased?
2. Should the antidepressant be switched?
3. Should two or more medications be used together?
4. Are there nondrug therapies that could help?

SHOULD THE DOSE BE INCREASED?

If you have been taking medications as prescribed, but still have a fair amount of depression after three or four weeks, the most frequently recommended next step is to increase the dose. Of course, you should always work together with your doctor in making decisions about the dose of medications. One example of a dose increase would be to try forty milligrams of Prozac daily if twenty milligrams doesn't do the job. Many times a dose increase will be enough to stimulate a full recovery. But, when this doesn't work, there are many other ideas to consider. The following strategies are based on the recommendations of two of the world's leading experts on biological treatments for depression, Dr. Michael Thase from the University of Pittsburgh and Dr. John Rush from the University of Texas, Southwestern Medical Center at Dallas.

SHOULD THE ANTIDEPRESSANT BE SWITCHED?

If an increased dose doesn't start to relieve the depression, the next step may be to try a different antidepressant. For example, if you were taking Zoloft (an SSRI), you might be switched to Effexor, which affects multiple neurotransmittters. Usually, an alternate SSRI or other newer antidepressant is selected before moving to a tricyclic antidepressant because of the increased rate of side effects of TCAs. Because MAOIs are so difficult to use and can't be combined with other antidepressants, they are usually saved as one of the strategies of last resort.

SHOULD TWO OR MORE MEDICATIONS
BE USED TOGETHER?

If switching to a different antidepressant doesn't give the desired results, the next option may be to add a second drug. A combination approach may be just what you need to break out of depression. Some frequently used combination treatments include adding lithium or thyroid hormone to an antidepressant or combining two or more antidepressants with different neurotransmitter effects. Less commonly used strategies are augmenting an antidepressant with Buspar (buspirone), pindolol, or new antipsychotic drugs like Zyprexa or Risperdal.

Researchers are not certain why adding lithium or thyroid hormone to an antidepressant can help some people recover from depression. However, many studies have shown that individuals who have not responded to antidepressant therapy often will have substantial symptom relief when lithium or thyroid hormones are used in combination with an antidepressant medication. If lithium helps to relieve your depression, it does not mean that you have manic-depressive illness. Likewise, when adding thyroid medication improves the effectiveness of your antidepressants, it does not indicate that you have a thyroid problem.

Using more than one antidepressant at one time can stimulate multiple neurotransmitter systems. Drs. Thase and Rush have noted that SSRIs combined with TCAs might offer a potent "one-two punch" on serotonin and norepinephrine. Buspar, pindolol, Zyprexa, and Risperdal are newly recommended augmentation strategies that haven't been studied extensively. These medications are thought to work by their actions on serotonin receptors.

Another method used by some doctors is to add a stimulant such as Ritalin (methylphenidate) or Dexedrine (dextroamphetamine). This aggressive form of medication therapy is usually reserved for patients who haven't responded to the treatments discussed previously. These drugs are typically used in the treatment of attention deficit disorder (ADD) and narcolepsy. Although stimulants are known to have an addictive potential, they can be used safely by patients with ADD or severe depression if monitored closely. Several of our patients with a diagnosis of both medication-resistant depression and ADD have had dramatic, positive responses to a combination of a stimulant, such as Ritalin, and a standard antidepressant.

ARE THERE NONDRUG THERAPIES THAT COULD HELP?

In Chapter 7 we discussed nondrug biological treatments for depression—light therapy and exercise—that can be used to augment antidepressants or help with medication-resistant depression. Light therapy can be useful if your depression gets worse in seasons of lowered daylight. Exercise is a good idea whether or not you are taking an antidepressant. If you haven't already done so, think about adding these options to your Personal Plan for Recovery.

Electroconvulsive therapy (ECT), sometimes known as shock therapy, is another nondrug biological therapy to consider. ECT is the most controversial treatment available for depression. This form of therapy got a bad reputation after it was used without modern safeguards many years ago and was depicted negatively in the movies. Do you remember *One Flew over the Cuckoo's Nest*? One glimpse of Jack Nicholson being treated with ECT has been enough to scare many people away from shock therapy. But, modern-day ECT is radically different from the shock therapy shown in movie scenes. Newer technology and the use of anesthesia have made ECT a safe and effective treatment for severe depression.

Generally, ECT is only used when other therapies have failed or the depression is so profound that immediate relief is needed. One type of depression that is especially responsive to ECT is major depression with psychotic features. We have seen individuals with very severe depression, complicated with delusions, who have responded to ECT after the first treatment. Usually, five to eight ECT treatments are given over a period of two to three weeks. Side effects of ECT can include headache, nausea, and temporary memory loss.

The newer methods of ECT have significantly reduced problems with confusion and memory impairment. Memory usually returns to normal in a few days to a few weeks after completing ECT. However, there may be some residual memory loss for things that happened in the time period when ECT was given. If ECT is administered to one side of the brain only (unilateral ECT), there is usually less memory loss. ECT is the most costly treatment for depression because it requires anesthesia, special equipment, and the services of specialists who are experts in the administration of this form of therapy. However, in some cases ECT can provide the best answer for severe, treatment-resistant depression.

One of the most valuable strategies may be to add a specific psychotherapy to the treatment plan if medications alone, or other biological treatments, haven't given full relief. In Chapter 7 we saw that adding CBT to antidepressants substantially increased the chances of responding to treatment for severe, chronic depression. We also learned that CBT was very useful in reducing symptoms that were still present after a full course of antidepressant medication.

Novel Biological Treatments for Depression

If you are being treated at a medical school or in a major research center, you may have access to therapies that have not entered the mainstream of medical practice because they are very new and are still in the early stages of investigation. Usually these therapies are reserved for research studies and may only be tried when more conventional treatments have failed to work. We'll give you a brief description of two of these promising novel treatments for depression.

TRANSCRANIAL MAGNETIC STIMULATION

In this form of therapy, the brain is stimulated with magnetic coils while you are awake. Transcranial magnetic stimulation (TMS) has been developed as a possible alternative to electroconvulsive therapy (ECT). The magnets used for TMS are much stronger than the magnets that are sold over-the-counter for stress relief. When the brain is stimulated with TMS the patient usually experiences only mild discomfort. Occasionally, TMS causes a mild headache. Because TMS does not require anesthesia like ECT, it would appear to offer certain advantages. However, a study by Dr. Leon Grunhaus in Israel found that TMS was somewhat less effective than ECT, especially for people who had the most severe type of depression with psychotic symptoms. Although some studies have found positive effects on depression, the efficacy of TMS and its role in the treatment of mood disorders are still unclear.

VAGUS NERVE STIMULATION

Researchers such as Dr. John Rush from the University of Texas, Southwestern Medical Center at Dallas, have begun to use a technique borrowed from the therapy of epilepsy to treat the most severe, treatment-resistant cases of depression. Vagus nerve stimulation (VNS) was originally developed to help patients with seizures who did not respond fully to treatment with anticonvulsant medication. The procedure involves implanting a small, battery-operated device, almost like a pacemaker, under the skin. Wires are attached to the vagus nerve, one of the major nerves in the body. The vagus nerve runs from the brain to several abdominal organs. The basic theory behind VNS is that stimulating the vagus nerve in areas outside the brain will lead to increased activity in brain regions that may be involved in depression. The exact mechanism of action of VNS remains unknown, but encouraging results of early studies have suggested that this dramatic new method might offer relief to persons with treatment-resistant depression.

Antidepressants for Bipolar Depression— A Note of Caution

Depression in a person with bipolar disorder can be somewhat more challenging to treat than in the more common unipolar form of depressive illness. There are two major risks in prescribing antidepressants for people who have both depression and mania. First, the antidepressant can work too well. You can climb right out of the depression and keep climbing into full-blown mania. The second problem with using antidepressants in bipolar disorder is that they can trigger rapid cycling between mania and depression. Thus, the medication of choice for someone who is depressed and who has bipolar disorder is a mood stabilizer—*not* an antidepressant. Currently most experts caution against using antidepressants as a routine therapy for depression in bipolar disorder. Nevertheless, there are some fortunate patients with bipolar disorder who can use antidepressants without aggravating their mood cycles. If you have bipolar depression, we recommend you carefully review with your doctor the risks and benefits of using antidepressants as part of your treatment program.

Mood Stabilizers

The mood stabilizers such as lithium, Depakote, and Tegretol (carbamazepine) are the mainstays of treatment of bipolar disorder. Because the focus of this book is on treatment of the unipolar, or nonmanic, form of depression, we won't describe the doses and side effects of mood stabilizers. Several excellent books have been written about the use of medication for bipolar or manic-depressive symptoms. We particularly recommend *Moodswing* by Ronald Fieve and *An Unquiet Mind* by Kay Jamison. *Cognitive Behavioral Therapy for Bipolar Disorder* by Monica Basco and John Rush describes psychological methods that can be used along with mood stabilizers to reduce mood swings.

St. John's Wort and Other Herbal Remedies for Depression

A number of plant extracts, such as ginseng, wild oats, lemon balm, wood betony, and basil, have been tried for depression. But, do any of these herbal remedies actually work? Drs. Wong, Smith, and Boon from the University of Toronto carefully reviewed the most frequently used herbal remedies for psychological distress (including black cohosh, chamomile, evening primrose, ginkgo, hops, kava root, lemon balm, passion flower, skullcap, St. John's Wort, and valerian) and concluded that St. John's Wort is the only herb that can be currently recommended for depression.

The Agency for Health Care Policy and Research, in their comprehensive assessment of treatments for depression, concluded that St. John's Wort appears to be more effective than a placebo for the relief of mild to moderate depressive symptoms. However, there are still many questions about how St. John's Wort works and whether it is as effective as standard antidepressants.

First used by the ancient Greeks, St. John's Wort is a garden plant that grows throughout much of the temperate zones of the world. Modern scientists who have been trying to uncover the reasons why this herb helps depression have found that it affects a wide variety of neurotransmitter receptors. St. John's Wort is usually taken in 300-milligram doses three times a day. A 450-milligram extended-release tablet is also available for twice-daily dosing. One of the myths about herbal preparations is that they have no side effects because they are "natural." Actually, herbal remedies can have many unpleasant effects. Some users encounter skin reactions from exposure to light, stomach upset, dizziness, dry mouth, drowsiness, restlessness, and constipation. There also may be drug interactions with other medications, so be sure to tell your doctor if you are taking St. John's Wort.

SAMe

In 1999, SAMe (S-adenosylmethionine) was heralded as a "breakthrough supplement that works as well as prescription drugs, in half the time, with no side effects." (See *Stop Depression Now* by Richard Brown, M.D., Theodoro Bottiglieri, Ph.D., and Carol Colman.) Several research studies, mostly done in Europe, have found that SAMe is more effective than placebo and is roughly equal in efficacy to the older tricyclic antidepressants. However, SAMe hasn't been subjected to the rigorous scientific investigations that are required for prescription drugs. It is still too early to tell if this drug can match up to the publicity it has received.

SAMe is contained in 200-milligram pills that are usually taken at doses of 400 to 800 milligrams per day. It is typically recommended that this medication be taken twice daily on an empty stomach about thirty minutes before meals to improve absorption. The drug is thought to relieve depression by releasing methyl groups—essential chemicals that stimulate a host of biochemical processes. Methyl groups play a role in activation of the DNA that controls manufacture of many of the chemicals in the brain. SAMe may also enhance the activity of neurotransmitters.

Preliminary studies performed in the United States at Massachusetts General Hospital by Dr. Jerrold Rosenbaum and his research group, and at UCLA School of Medicine by Dr. Bruce Kagan and associates, found SAMe to be well tolerated and helpful in relieving some cases of depression. Side effects such as nausea, diarrhea, and headache were mild and transient. Despite the generally favorable results, these studies used small numbers of patients and did not conclusively prove that SAMe is an effective antidepressant. Dr Kagen's study was stopped by the FDA after only eighteen patients were studied because of concerns about the stability of the tablets containing SAMe. Apparently SAMe pills can disintegrate rapidly if not properly processed.

SAMe has been available in Europe for some time, but has only recently been introduced in the United States. It is important to note that SAMe can be purchased only as a nutritional supplement in the United States. It has *not* been approved by the FDA as an antidepressant medication. This means that SAMe has not had to meet the same safety standards or testing requirements as prescription medications for depression. Another common concern about SAMe is its high cost.

Should You Choose an Herbal Remedy or SAMe as Part of Your Treatment for Depression?

We think the jury is still out on whether St John's Wort and SAMe are as useful as the more thoroughly researched prescription drugs for depression. Generally, our top recommendation for antidepressant therapy is to try an SSRI or another new antidepressant. For people who are not seeing a doctor or want to avoid prescription medications, St. John's Wort or SAMe may be alternatives worth considering. Just remember that if you decide to take St. John's Wort or SAMe you are actually taking an antidepressant drug that influences neurotransmitter receptors and has its own set of side effects.

The Biology Key in Your Personal Plan for Recovery

It's time now to pull together what you've learned about the Biology Key and to put your knowledge to work in designing your Personal Plan for Recovery. In Chapter 7, you were introduced to the biological theory of depression and how neurotransmitter and hormone imbalances may cause depressive symptoms. You also found out about biological influences, such as exercise, diet, sleep, and light exposure that you can control. In Chapter 8, you identified questions to ask your doctor about the physical side of depression and learned the inside story of using biological therapies. After reading Chapter 9, you should know the basics of treatment with antidepressants and over-the-counter drugs.

How does all this information fit into your Personal Plan for Recovery? Are biological factors an important part of your depression? What plans do you have to use the Biology Key? In Chapter 8, you heard about Alan, a man who became depressed after a heart bypass operation. Now you can look over Alan's plan for using biological treatments. After you read about Alan's ideas, we suggest that you write out your plans for using the Biology Key. You can use the worksheet that's provided in the Appendix for this portion of your recovery plan. Then you can move on to the next topic—how to fight depression with the Relationship Key.

Exercise 9.1
Personal Plan for Recovery Worksheet—Part VI
'My Plan for Using the Biology Key':

ALAN'S EXAMPLE

1. Do you have any physical symptoms or illnesses that could be playing a role in your depression? Could a medication be aggravating your symptoms? Write out a list of problems you would like to discuss with your doctor. Note any actions you can take.

Problems to discuss with my doctor:
   a. *Weakness after my bypass operation.*
   b. *Blood pressure is still too high.*
   c. *The Inderal for blood pressure could be making my depression worse.*

Things I can do:
   a. *Call cardiologist for an appointment this week.*
   b. *Discuss options for blood pressure medications with doctor.*
   c. *Ask if there could be any other physical reasons for my feeling so tired all the time. Did they ever test my thyroid?*
   d. *Work on reducing my stress—use Thinking Key to cut down on negative automatic thoughts and use meditation techniques (Spirituality Key) to calm myself down.*

2. Are you having trouble sleeping? If so, write out a plan for getting into a normal sleep pattern. You can use the tips for improving sleep described in Chapter 5 to get you started.

   a. *Reduce caffeine to only two cups of coffee in the morning—no caffeine after 12 noon.*
   b. *Try to stop caffeine entirely within a month.*
   c. *Use the thought stopping technique to stop worrying so much when I'm trying to go to sleep.*

    d. If these things don't work, use the Sonata that my doctor prescribed.

3. Are you getting enough physical exercise? In the Action Key (Exercise 6.5), we gave you suggestions for getting into a healthy exercise routine. Write down your plan here for using exercise to assist in your recovery from depression.

    a. Follow my doctor's recommendation to walk for at least twenty minutes, at least five times a week.
    b. Gradually increase my walking, if my doctor approves, till the point that I can walk at least three miles, five times a week.
    c. Each time I walk, log my progress in my notebook.

4. Is it possible that you have seasonal affective disorder (SAD)? If so, do you want to try light therapy?

    No, I don't think I have this type of depression.

5. Do you think any of your attitudes about antidepressant medication could interfere with your getting help from the Biology Key? Review your answers to the Medication Attitude Survey in Chapter 8, and write down any of your attitudes that could be improved. Then note your plans for changing them.

Attitudes I would like to change:
    a. I should be strong enough to not need antidepressants.
    b. Getting depressed after a bypass means I'm weak—I should have been able to tough it out.

Plan for change:
    a. Try to be logical about taking medications.
    b. Examine the evidence—realize that the medication is doing a lot of good, and that getting depressed wasn't my fault.
    c. Tell myself depression is an illness just like heart disease or high blood pressure.

6. If you are *not* taking an antidepressant, note your plans for what you would like to do about using medication for depression.

    I'm already on Zoloft.

7. If you are currently taking an antidepressant and still have symptoms of depression, use this worksheet to prepare for a discussion with your doctor. First write down the dose, length of therapy, how regularly you have been taking the medication, and your present level of depression. Before switching antidepressants, you and your doctor will want to know if you have given the present treatment an adequate trial. Next review the Biology Key to see if you have any ideas for changes that might help you do better. Write your ideas down here and discuss them with your doctor.

Current Medication and Dose: *Zoloft 100 milligrams a day*

How long have you been taking the medication? *Ten weeks.*

How regularly have you been taking the medication? *Only missed one dose in last month.*

Current level of depression: *I'm better, but I'm still feeling depressed. Five Keys Rating Scale = 29*

Ideas about medication to discuss with doctor:
   a. *Could increase dose, but I'm having side effects.*
   b. *I'd like to try another medication—maybe Wellbutrin or Serzone.*

8. If you are having side effects from antidepressants, check the information in Chapter 9 for possible solutions. Note possible answers to the problems on this worksheet. Then consult your physician to decide on a remedy.

Problems: *Sexual side effects*

Possible solutions to discuss with doctor:
   a. *Maybe he would be willing to add Wellbutrin or Serzone.*
   b. *I could go off Zoloft and try one of the other drugs.*
   c. *Ask if my blood pressure medicine could be part of the problem.*
   d. *Maybe gingko would be worth a try. I'll ask the doctor what he thinks about this idea.*
   e. *I want to make it clear he knows I want to get my sex life back.*

The Relationship Key

10

Can't Live with You, Can't Live without You

The women who attend the Depression Support Group can attest to the struggles of working to maintain healthy relationships while trying to overcome their symptoms of depression. Isabella's depression started when she found out her husband was having an affair. Julia's depression was now into its second year and was ruining her marriage. Geneva's husband reassured her that their marriage was fine. But, she still felt guilty for being too depressed to care for their home and their family the way she liked. Michelle's marriage ended in divorce. She was lonely for companionship, but afraid of taking a risk. In all of these cases relationship strain and depression seemed to go hand in hand. In fact, several researchers, such as Dr. George Brown at the University of London and Dr. Constance Hammen at UCLA, have found that relationship problems are commonly associated with the onset of depression. In particular, relationship losses through death or divorce seem to be the events that most often kick off a depression.

On the flip side, according to Dr. Paula Goering and colleagues, good relationships can make a big difference in recovery from depression. Support from family members and friends seems to help people get treatment, stick with it, and get better. Healthy relationships can fill in the gaps when you are feeling weak, burdened, and unable to function at your usual level. The important people in your life can give encouragement, reassurance, joy, and hope.

How to Use the Relationship Key

The goal of the Relationship Key is to help you learn to strengthen your existing relationships and to solve some common problems in relating to others that may be adding to your depression. The first thing we will do is to take stock of the positive aspects of your relationships and to help you use these assets as you work toward recovery. Then we'll explore how relationship problems and the symptoms of depression can form part of a vicious cycle that can pull you down. One of the ways to fight depression with the Five Keys is to reverse these vicious cycles. After helping you understand ways to manage some of the most frequently encountered relationship troubles, we'll end this chapter by describing methods for improving communication with the important people in your life. The next chapter will help you deal with changes that are set off by highly significant events such as death of a loved one, divorce, retirement, or breakups of relationships.

Identifying Positive Relationships

You can start using the Relationship Key by taking out your notebook and writing down your answers to some of the following questions. First, who are the positive people in your life? Positive people can be those who seem happy, cheerful, or pleasant. They may have an upbeat or positive attitude, give you encouragement, or think well of you. Positive people can be casual acquaintances, like the owner of the dry cleaners who always wishes you a pleasant day or a neighbor who waves when you pass her house each morning. Although you may not consider casual acquaintances to be the most important people in your life, they still count. When they are pleasant with you it can make you want to return the favor; and you may feel better, if only for a short while.

Positive people are not likely to be that way 100 percent of the time. But, when they are positive they can make you feel good about your relationship with them and about yourself. A spouse or partner can be one of the most important positive people in your life. And, children can be very positive too (even teenagers can be). They can be sweet, cute, funny, and lovable. (Yes, we know that they can also be demanding, annoying, and unpleasant some of the time.) Parents, siblings, grandparents, and distant relatives also can be included on the list if they have the ability to make you smile, laugh, and forget your troubles from time to time.

Now that you have your list, make a few notes about the strengths of these relationships. We've mentioned a few examples already, but there are many other aspects of relationships that can make them positive and healthy. When Michelle made a list of positive people in her life, she noted that the thing she found most important was an ability to feel comfortable with a person without having to talk about much. She valued being around people who thought and acted in a positive manner. Watching them and listening to their stories gave her ideas for how to work through her own difficulties. Although Tony's depression was triggered by his wife's success in her job and what he believed to be his lack of success in comparison, he also listed her as a positive person in his life. He admired her strength, her character, and her accomplishments. When he admitted it to himself, he knew that she could be an inspiration for how to succeed in life.

The next step is to think about how these people might help you cope with your problems. Perhaps friends or family members could help you see yourself in a more positive light if you shared with them your negative self-view, and then asked them if they see you the same way. Maybe a positive person in your life could help you accomplish a task that you have been putting off or have not had the energy to do on your own. Maybe a friend can distract you from your problems long enough to get some temporary relief from your sadness and to help you remember that life doesn't have to always be depressing. Positive people can help you break bad habits and build new ones. They can assist you with getting to doctor's appointments or getting your prescription filled, or talk you out of stopping the medication when you are having a bad day.

Although you probably would not tell people who are only casual acquaintances about your depression, they can help you in other ways. Positive people who don't know what you are going through will interact with you as if everything is fine. These more superficial contacts give you a chance to act and feel normal for a while. You don't have to explain yourself, tell your story, or cry on their shoulder. You can just smile and say, *"Have a nice day"* and let them be friendly in return. If you are

---

Exercise 10.1
Assessing Your Relationship Strengths

1. Who are the positive people in your life?
2. What are the strengths of your relationships with these individuals?
3. How could these people help you overcome your depression?

---

not making contact with these positive people in your life, maybe it is time to start.

How to Strengthen Good Relationships

If you are not having any difficulties with your current relationships, you might want to do a few things to keep them strong. All relationships require some attention and nurturance. When you are depressed it is easy to neglect them because your sadness and negative mindset turn your focus inward toward yourself rather than outward toward others. Let's use marriage as the most common example of a relationship that requires regular attention and maintenance. In a marriage, it is important to commit time to one another. It is not enough to just sit together on the couch watching television or attend events with the kids. You need to go out of your way to give one another your undivided attention. Sit alone from time to time without the kids, the TV, the bills, or the telephone. It doesn't always matter if you do not have much to say to one another. What is important is that you give each other the message that "you are important enough for me to take time to be with you." Whether it is a marriage, a friendship, or a relationship with a family member, to keep the relationship strong you have to make time to talk to one another and to do things together.

Some Nice Things to Do

Play with your children for thirty minutes each day or read them a bedtime story.

Prepare a meal with family members or friends.

Go out to lunch with a co-worker or friend.

Order pizza for your kids when they don't expect it, or bring your partner a cup of coffee.

Ask people how they are doing, then listen to what they have to say.

Tell your partner you love him or her.

Do a favor for a friend.

Make a dessert and share it with others.

Say, "Have a nice day" or "It's good to see you."

Send a friend a card, a note, or an e-mail message.

Help someone with a chore.

Play tennis, golf, basketball, or some other sport with a friend.

Go to church, a concert, or a community activity with someone you know.

Key Point

To strengthen good relationships make time to spend with others and return the favors they do for you.

If the positive people in your life are already doing nice things for you, you can help strengthen the relationships by returning the favors. If someone says nice things to you, then you can say nice things back. You do not have to match the type or size of the favor. Just take notice that someone was helpful and try to be helpful in return.

How to Prevent Relationship Problems

There are a number of things you can do to help prevent relationship problems from forming when you are depressed. First, tell the important people in your life about your depression and your treatment plans. Encourage them to ask questions. You may be reluctant to talk candidly with your kids. Keep in mind that if you don't, they will just make guesses on their own about why you are acting differently. You can go into as much or as little detail as you think they can understand, but at least tell them that you are not feeling well and that with time and treatment you will be back to your old self.

There are some educational videotapes as well as pamphlets and books your family members can read to help them understand depression. Your local library or bookstore should have several examples in the psychology or self-help sections. If you would like a free pamphlet on depression you can call the National Mental Health Association at (800) 969-6642 or the National Institute of Mental Health's Depression Awareness, Recognition, and Treatment Program (DART) at (800) 223-6427. Ask for some information on depression. Your community may have a Depressive and Manic Depressive Association group. It is a national self-help organization dedicated to helping people stay informed about the latest treatments for mood disorders. To find a chapter in your area you can call the National Depressive and Manic Depressive Association at (312) 642-0049. They usually have weekly meetings featuring expert speakers on depression and discussion groups for people who suffer from depression and for their family members.

Also, encourage key family members to go with you to see your doctor or to your therapy sessions. Involve them in your homework. Give them something to do. Typically, therapy goes better if your family gives you their support as you work on making changes in your life.

When you are depressed you will be naturally inclined to avoid other people. You might find them annoying, too happy to tolerate, or you might try to avoid disappointing them or showing them your weaknesses. While you are avoiding these things you are also missing out on all the positive interactions you can have with people that could help improve your mood and give you hope for the future.

If you waited until you had the energy to interact with people, it could be a long wait. Being with the people who care about you can raise your spirits and give you a boost of energy. Commit to shorter activities if you don't think you can make it through a longer day or event.

Another way to help relationship problems from starting when you are depressed is to avoid blaming others when you are the one who is showing anger or annoyance. Apologize when you know you have been wrong. If you have not taken care of your responsibilities, acknowledge this and ask others for help or for their patience.

Ways to Help Prevent Relationship Problems

1. Keep communication open about your depression.
2. Involve other people in your recovery.
3. Do not avoid or withdraw from others.
4. Make an effort even when you are tired.
5. Take responsibility for your actions and your mistakes.

Painful Relationships

Another way the Relationship Key can be used is to find answers to troubled or strained relationships. Throughout the remainder of the chapter we will talk about common relationship problems that people experience when they are depressed. We will try to help you get a clearer perspective on what is going wrong and on what you can do about it.

The first step is to identify relationships with others that need to be mended or healed in some way. You know who these people are and why you think there is a problem. Get out your notebook and make a list of people you are concerned about or are having a hard time communicating with at this time. For each of these people, jot down a few notes about what the strain in the relationship seems to be. At the end of this chapter and the next chapter you will have a chance to formulate a plan

Exercise 10.2
Relationship Challenges

1. Identify relationships with others that need to be mended or healed in some way.
2. What is the source of strain in the relationship?
3. Is it worth taking action at this time to try to improve the relationship?
4. Cross off your list any relationship problems that would not be worth addressing at this time or that might be too difficult to handle.

for improving your relationships. You can choose when to begin to use these ideas. As a rule of thumb, if a problem with another person is greatly stressing you and contributing to your depression, it is worth taking action sooner rather than later.

Which Came First—the Depression or the Relationship Problem?

Although it is difficult to say which came first, Dr. Alec Roy's research at the National Institute for Mental Health has shown that about half of the people who suffer from depression also have marital problems and about half of the people who have serious marital problems get depressed. Although they seem to be linked in some way, which came first is usually a matter of opinion. The good news is that studies like those of Drs. Steven Beach and Daniel O'Leary on the treatment of marriage and depression show that if you can repair relationship problems, the depression improves. Let's begin by trying to understand how depression and relationship problems interact. Later in the chapter we will talk about how you can try to fix these problems.

VICIOUS CYCLES

IRRITABILITY

When you get depressed you feel irritable in addition to feeling sad. You might act cranky, show irritability in the tone of your voice or your body language, or look like you are unhappy or angry with others, especially if you are not completely aware of how you are feeling. Irritability also can have an effect on your outlook and your way of interpreting events. It can seem like people are intentionally trying to be difficult, inconsiderate, loud, or unhelpful. Their small bad habits can seem monstrously annoying. You might even feel as if the world is out to get you.

In relationships, you can become more aggressive, more defensive, and more unreasonable when you are feeling irritable. Irritability can interfere with your ability to listen to your partner, keep an open mind, and see both sides of the story. You might tell yourself that if the other person were not so irritating you would not feel so irritable. In fact, the reverse is often the case. If you were less depressed, the other person would probably not seem so irritating.

You can learn to tell when irritability is a symptom of depression or when it is a fairly normal reaction to an annoying person. If it is due to depression, you will probably start the day feeling edgy, long before you've had a chance to interact with anyone. You will also find that many people get on your nerves. Co-workers, neighbors, family members, or even your pets can irritate you. If you are having a problem with irritability you might hear a harsher tone in your own voice and notice that you are snapping or arguing with others more easily than usual. In general, you will find it harder to let things slide off your back. Everything seems to matter.

The thinking errors we talked about in Chapter 3 often play a role in stimulating irritability. Jumping to conclusions about what is going on or about what others are thinking, or taking things personally, can lead to irritation. As you probably recall, thinking errors are distortions that keep you from seeing things accurately. If you react to others based on these errors, you can say the wrong things, make accusations, disagree with others, or fail to listen to their side of the story. Acting in these ways can fuel open arguments or produce silent tension. Then the increased conflict can make you feel hopeless about the future of your relationship, make you lose sleep, preoccupy you during the day, and worsen your depression. As your depression deepens, your irritability will probably become more of a problem.

LOW SEX DRIVE

One of the most common symptoms of depression is a decreased sex drive. You can lose interest in having sex, enjoy it less, have difficulty achieving or maintaining an erection, or be unable to reach orgasm. Because of these changes, sex can become something unpleasant and unwanted. Therefore, you might find yourself avoiding any affection or intimacy that you think might lead to sex. Our patients sometimes say that if they are not in the mood they do not want to give the wrong idea to their partner, so they avoid affection altogether. However, their non-depressed partners do not always understand what is going on. If they do not know that a low sex drive is a by-product of depression they may take it personally, feel rejected, or assume that you don't love them any-more.

If you are depressed, avoidance of all affection means missing out on pleasant interactions with your partner. Hugs, kisses, and tender touches are some of the things that can make you and your partner feel good about one another and reassure you that you can count on your re-lationship through tough times. Being affectionate is also a way of pro-viding emotional support. Affection can make you feel less alone in your depression.

The other downside of avoiding affection from your partner is that there is a good chance you will feel guilty for it later. You might notice the disappointment in your partner's face or perhaps hear complaints about not having enough sex. If you hear this enough you might begin to feel resentful and angry. The guilt and anger can intensify your depres-sion and add to your problems.

NOT PULLING YOUR OWN WEIGHT

One of the other symptoms of depression is low energy or fatigue. Changes in your energy level can keep you from being able to handle your usual responsibilities at home and in your relationships with others. Housework doesn't get performed in the usual way, meals may not get prepared as often, projects go undone, and tasks you would usually re-member to take care of are forgotten. You may want to do all the things you used to do, but the depression zaps your energy and holds you back.

If other people count on you to take care of a household or if you are the one who usually coordinates family activities, your partner or your children may become resentful if you are unable to keep up. For example, when mother forgets appointments or events, does not keep up with washing uniforms for the weekend games, does not have dinner waiting, or is unavailable to help children with their problems, everyone feels bad. The kids are angry, the mother is guilt-ridden and resentful, and the husband is not happy if the burden is passed to him.

The pressure from all of this weighs heavily on the working mother. She can feel like she is sinking in quicksand with no hope for survival. In this vicious cycle, the symptoms of the depression create new relation-ship problems, which in turn worsen the depression.

REVERSING VICIOUS CYCLES

Before you read further, take a moment to think about any vicious cycles you might be experiencing. You can spot a vicious cycle if you are having depressive symptoms that aggravate relationship problems, which in turn seem to make the depression get worse. There are two main ways you can reverse these cycles. The first is to use any of the Five Keys to help relieve the symptoms of depression. For example, if you are very irritable, you could try to use the Thinking Key to cut down on automatic thoughts that might be making you tense or cranky. If you are having problems with your sex drive and are on an antidepressant, you could get some ideas from the Biology Key on how to handle sexual side effects. And if you are suffering from low energy and motivation, you could use the Action Key to get going again.

The second major way to interrupt vicious cycles is to learn Relationship Key methods that you can use to resolve interpersonal problems, improve communication, or cope better with a difficult person or situation. If you would like to learn how to do this, there is reason to be optimistic. Dr. Neil Jacobson led a team of researchers who studied the usefulness of cognitive and behavioral interventions for people who suffered from depression and from relationship problems. They found conclusive evidence that these methods helped to stop marital conflict and improve communication in addition to relieving the symptoms of depression. In this chapter and the next, you'll find self-help exercises based on CBT that you can use to strengthen your relationships.

The Critical, Impatient, and Unforgiving Partner

It takes two people to make a relationship work and it usually takes two to create problems. How your partner handles you and your depression will have a great influence on how things work out. Partners who are supportive and patient with their depressed loved ones can facilitate recovery. They pick up the slack, stay hopeful when you are not, and they get involved in treatment.

Unfortunately, not all partners are compassionate and supportive. Sometimes no amount of information or explanations will help them comprehend the changes that are happening. Your partner might say, "I don't believe in psychiatry," and be unwilling to accept a psychological explanation for anything. This kind of problem can place a great deal of strain on the marriage and interfere with your recovery from depression.

When you are not depressed you may be able to cope with a disagreeable or difficult partner. He or she may not seem so bad, and you

Key Point

Depression affects relationship functioning, and, in turn, relationship problems worsen depression. It is not easy to tell which came first, but it probably doesn't matter. Both the relationship problems and the depression need to be fixed. Making improvements in either area often helps the other.

find it easier to overlook his or her weaknesses. You focus on the good points and remember the love you feel. However, when you are depressed you will probably be more sensitive to your partner's shortcomings and may not have the strength or patience to ignore them.

Critical partners can bring you down just as you are trying to pull yourself up. You can easily get into a stalemate where you think your partner is to blame for the relationship problems and your partner thinks it is all your fault. Then the focus is turned to who is right and who is wrong rather than on how to stop fighting.

Instead of trying to settle the argument about who is right and who is wrong, ask your partner to agree to put the conflict on hold long enough for you to get your bearings. Tell yourself and your partner that for the meantime it is OK if he or she does not understand what is happening to you. All you need is a break from the criticism and fighting while you work on helping yourself. You will try to take some steps toward fixing your problems. When that is done, the two of you can reevaluate the relationship.

Another strategy is to get your partner to see your doctor or therapist with you at least once to learn about the symptoms of depression. It may not seem fair, but people will often believe a health professional before they will believe their own family members.

"No One Understands Me"

Unless you have had firsthand experience with depression it is hard to fully comprehend what it's like. So if it seems that people just don't get it, you are probably right. Before having gone through it yourself, you might have had a hard time understanding it too. The way you are reacting to being depressed may be part of the problem. For example, if you try hard to keep up with your usual responsibilities or hide your problems from others, you may be successful in looking better than you feel.

Unfortunately, when this happens others may question whether you are really depressed.

One of the symptoms of depression that can mislead people is *reactive mood,* which means you brighten up when good things happen, even though you may be severely depressed. When the good event is over, your mood usually goes back down. People who see you during these pleasant moments may be confused; you may even be confused by it yourself. Other types of depression, like melancholic depression, in which your mood will not brighten no matter how pleasant an event is, are tough to get over without aggressive biological treatments. If your mood is reactive, this can really work in your favor to fight the depression.

When you feel as if you are misunderstood, do what you can to explain, but keep in mind that others may never really understand depression until they have experienced it themselves. Rather than get angry with them, consider the possibility that you may be expecting too much. Try to be as patient with them as you would want them to be with you.

Feeling Alone in a Crowd

No one likes feeling lonely or isolated. It is human nature to seek out connections with other people and to want to be accepted. When you are depressed, however, these kinds of interactions may seem too difficult, too energy consuming, or not worth the effort. For some, the anxiety about being around people is too strong to ignore. You worry that they will not understand you, will be critical of you, or will reject you. So you keep to yourself, do not return phone calls, and turn down invitations to visit, just to avoid any potential hurt. The people you turn away from may take it personally, assuming that you just don't want to be with them. In their withdrawal, you will have achieved both what you want, to be left alone, and what you don't want, to be isolated from others.

In Chapter 5 of the Action Key we introduced activity scheduling as a method for getting back into a normal routine. You can use this same technique for making improvements in your social life. You need people in your life. You need to laugh, play, and hear what is going on in the lives of those you love. Make a plan to have contact with people you like, schedule the time, and follow through with the plan.

With activity scheduling you use a daily calendar or planner to schedule time to answer phone calls or visit with people. Use your notebook or your personal planner to designate when you will try to see your family members or friends. You can block out time to play with the kids when you get home from work. You can plan ahead for a social activity

Key Point

Not feeling understood and feeling alone in a crowd can become self-fulfilling prophecies if you are not careful. Both of these ideas can make you pull away from others, give up on explaining what you are going through, and convince yourself that they don't really care. If you don't do your part to reach out to others they might not know what you need, or worse they might think that you want to be left alone.

on the weekend or invite someone to come to your home. If you have a close friend you can confide in, tell him or her about the trouble you are having making yourself go out. Ask your friend to help you, nag you, or not take no for an answer when he or she thinks you are avoiding social contact. Even though it may seem too difficult or not worth the trouble, once you get out you will benefit from having positive people around you. Try your best to avoid the "I'll wait and see how I feel" option. If you can make yourself schedule interactions with others on a regular basis you will probably find that it gets easier and more enjoyable as time goes on.

"It's Not Worth It"

Sometimes when you feel alone in a crowd it is because you have no close friends, or your family members live too far away or are too busy to make time for you. Even if you have had a history of tension with the important people in your life, you might still want support from them, although you might not want the free advice or criticism that goes along with it. Joanne used to say that it wasn't worth it. She didn't want to hear her mother's twenty questions about why she wasn't married yet, hadn't gotten a better job, or still lived in that small apartment. Joanne tried to tell herself that her mother meant well, but she still got annoyed. She dreamed of visiting her mother just once when she would get a hug and an open ear and nothing else, except for maybe her mother's famous cherry pie. When Joanne visited her mother, she dreaded the trip for a week before going because she anticipated how unpleasant it was going to be. And, she felt down for days afterward as she tried to shake off her mother's disapproving words.

Joanne never really told her mother how she felt. She convinced herself that confronting her mother would be disrespectful and would not do any good anyway. Joanne assumed that instead of relieving the problem, it would probably hurt her mother's feelings and then Mom would lay a guilt trip on her for "the rest of my life."

While there was no doubt that Joanne's mother was a challenge, there was probably more that Joanne could have done than just take it and feel miserable. To make things better, she needed to think about how she might be contributing to her problems with her mother. Maybe she could change the way she was acting so that their times together would be more pleasant. From Joanne's description it sounded like the misery she felt the week before she saw her mother was brought on, in part, by her own negative thinking. Because she anticipated things going badly and recalled bad experiences in the past, she felt more depressed and helpless. When her mood dropped, it was easy to view the situation as hopeless. When she felt hopeless, she would not try to think of a way out of the situation. She just told herself that she would have to bear it. In this case, her negative thoughts led to negative feelings and then to negative actions or a lack of action.

Joanne talked to her therapist about her mother, and together they came up with several ideas for dealing with the stress. First, they discussed how Joanne's thoughts, feelings, and actions were affecting each other. Joanne understood that she was helping to make herself miserable by anticipating the worst. When she really thought about it, she was able to recall times when her mother was hardly annoying at all, times when she was monumentally annoying, and times when she was only moderately annoying. Shorter visits always seemed better than longer ones.

Joanne admitted that her mother seemed to genuinely want her to visit. She did cook her favorite foods and, at times, bought her small gifts. By reviewing these things with her therapist, Joanne was correcting the thinking error called "ignoring the evidence." When you ignore the evidence you find it easy to remember or to notice things that fit with your negative view, but do not pay attention to the things that are contrary to this view. In Joanne's case, she could easily remember all the things her mother did wrong, but was not considering the things her mother did right. That's one of the reasons she felt worse as the visit approached. To begin to cope better she needed to make herself look at the big picture, to think through all the times when her mother was tolerable or even pleasant. When she did this she felt less hopeless.

The second step was a bigger one. Joanne needed to tell her mother what had been on her mind. This made Joanne very nervous because she quickly pictured the conversation in her mind's eye and saw it turn out all wrong. Everyone got angry, she ended up feeling terrible, and nothing really changed.

"That sounds like the worst case scenario," her therapist said. "I wonder if you could adjust anything to make it turn out better?"

"What do you mean?" Joanne inquired.

"Let's assume, for a moment," her therapist went on, "that your mother would never want to intentionally make you feel bad and that she thinks she is just showing concern and encouragement."

"That's not how it feels," Joanne replied.

"But could I be right?"

"Yeah, I guess you could be right. But, she sure has a strange way of showing concern."

Joanne's therapist inquired further. "Joanne, is it possible that your mother does not know how to express concern in a helpful way? Perhaps she never learned from her mother."

"You got that right. My grandmother is ten times worse than my mom. I avoid her at all costs and so does my mother. That woman could not say a kind thing if her life depended on it."

"Well there you have it," the therapist confidently replied. "If your grandmother is that bad, then there was no one to teach your mother to do it right. She sounds like she made some improvements over her mother's style, but she is still lacking what you need. Your job is to help your mother improve by telling her what you need. Give her some guidance about what is helpful and what is not. But, start with the assumption that her intentions are good."

"What am I supposed to say?" Joanne inquired with a skeptical tone.

"Here are some ideas for how to get started. The first thing to say to your mother is that you appreciate her concern and that you know she wants the best for you. Can you do that?"

"And sound sincere?"

"Yes, and sound sincere. I will practice this with you in therapy and we can work out the right words—your words. The next thing you have to do is tell her what you like that she does, what makes you feel worse, and how she can do it differently so that she accomplishes her goal of making you feel better."

"You make it sound so simple," Joanne said. "But, you don't know my mother."

"You're right. I don't know your mother, but I do know how to give people constructive criticism in a way that is helpful and not hurtful. I've had to do that with you in therapy haven't I?"

Joanne thought about it for a moment and then said, "Tell me what to say and I'll try."

Joanne and her therapist practiced the four steps for giving constructive criticism to others.

1. Acknowledge the other person's good intentions. "Mom, I know that in your heart you want the best for me and you want to help me have a happy life."
2. Say what parts of the interaction are helpful. "I like the fact that you are really interested in what's happening in my life, that you ask about how things are going."
3. Say what parts of the interaction are not helpful by sharing how they make you feel. "Sometimes the way you say things makes me feel worse rather than better. You probably don't mean to do it, but you criticize me when you give suggestions or you tell me that the way I am doing things is all wrong. It makes me feel like I'll never be able to get anywhere in life, and that I'll never be good enough to please you."
4. Tell the other person what they can say or do that would be helpful. "What would help is to just tell me that you are happy to see me. Ask me how I'm feeling and tell me that you have confidence in me to set things right. If you feel like giving me suggestions, ask me if I want advice before you give it. Sometimes I need the advice and am in a good place to hear your suggestions. But a lot of the time I know exactly what I need to do. I just have a hard time getting it done."

It is a good idea to prepare the person for this kind of conversation rather than catch him or her off guard. You can preface these four steps by expressing your concerns about having the conversation at all. You can say, "I really want to talk to you about something but I am afraid that I might make you mad or hurt your feelings. It is important to me. Would it be OK if we spent about five minutes talking about it?"

This type of conversation will usually go better if you are not angry or defensive. You need to feel strong enough to stay positive and nondefensive even if the person seems upset at first. Try to avoid using harsh or blaming words. Keep the tone in your voice neutral or soft. Avoid sarcasm, cursing, and loudness.

Remember that even with the best of intentions, most people do not change overnight. Be sure to acknowledge and praise any positive effort they make. "Thanks, Mom. That was nice. I appreciate you making the effort." Another approach is to say, "When you say it that way it makes me feel better. It's more helpful. Thanks."

When Joanne approached her mother, she was very tense. She told her mother so. As soon as she acknowledged her mother's positive intentions, the tension melted away. It also seemed to lessen any defensiveness her mother might have felt. Joanne's mother listened, thought about it, and gave it a try. She was not perfect, but then, Joanne thought, "Neither am I."

"They'll Be Better Off without Me"

When people try to convince themselves that they should commit suicide they sometimes have the fantasy that everyone will be better off when they are gone. This type of thinking *is* a fantasy because the person paints a mental picture where he or she disappears from the world in a painless way, and everyone else lives happily ever after. The remaining partner finds a better spouse who gives him or her attention when needed. The children have someone to care for them who is happy and wonderful and will not burden them with depression. Mother is rid of her disappointing child so she can turn her focus to her friends, whom she enjoys more anyway. It seems like a simple and perfect solution. In fact, this kind of fantasy can have a seductive quality. It is alluring and dangerous and completely out of touch with reality.

When you follow this line of reasoning you are seeing a rosy-colored picture and ignoring the facts. The first and most important fact is that when a friend or family member commits suicide it is devastating for everyone. No one's life is ever the same. Spouses do not go merrily on their way to find another partner. Children do not forget. In fact, research on suicide shows that children are at a greater risk of committing suicide themselves if one of their parents has committed suicide. It is as if they say to themselves, "It was OK for Mom, so it is OK for me." If you are a parent, that should stop you in your tracks.

When a child dies from suicide, parents never really recover from it no matter how old the child is at the time. The grief is tremendous and lasting. The same is true for losing a spouse. The "happily ever after" fantasy is what you would like to believe so that you don't have to feel guilty about the possibility of ruining people's lives.

When our patients have these fantasies we try to help them get a more realistic view by asking them how they would feel if their friend or spouse or child committed suicide. We also try to help them understand that sometimes when people think about suicide it is not because they want to die, but they can't think of any other way to stop the pain. We also encourage them to check out their fantasy with their spouses or their parents or friends. When you give people a chance to give their own opinion about how they would feel about losing you, they tell a very different story. No matter how much difficulty your depression might cause others, they always say that they would rather have the stress than lose you. Depression is temporary. It will pass and life will go back to normal. Death is permanent. There is no chance to make things better.

If you have suicidal fantasies, you may be hesitant to tell anyone about them. It would be better if you did. Tell your romantic partner, tell your best friend, or tell your mother or father. Confide in a brother or sister, or tell your minister at church. If you are a parent, it is probably not a good idea to choose a young child or teenager as your confidant. That burdens them with too much responsibility. If you have no one to talk to, get a therapist, a counselor, a crisis line worker, or your doctor. Reach out and let someone help you.

Last year, a thirty-four-year-old woman I (Monica) knew, developed postpartum depression and killed herself eight weeks after giving birth to her first child. I had not seen her in many years, but I remember that she had always looked forward to having a baby. She had been somewhat of a perfectionist and had reportedly been concerned that she might not be doing everything "right" for her new baby. As her depression worsened, she had convinced herself that she was never going to be able to be a good mother and that her baby and her husband would be better off without her. She apparently had the fantasy that her husband could find a more suitable mother for her child, and everyone, but her, would live happily ever after. She shot herself at home while her husband was upstairs holding the baby.

When she killed herself, the pain was felt by everyone who knew her. Her husband, parents, and friends were distraught. At her funeral people said, "If only she'd told me, I could have helped her. If only I had known I could have convinced her that everything would be OK." I had the same thoughts. We had been co-workers many years before. I did not even know that she was pregnant. I cried for her loss, and a year later still feel the pain knowing that she could have been helped and she could have recovered. Her depression kept her from being able to see how wonderful she was and how much everyone loved her and believed in her. The depression would have been temporary, and she would have been a terrific mother. Her daughter will know what happened to her mother and will carry that weight throughout her own life. Her husband will never forgive himself for not being able to save her.

We hear about suicide in the news all of the time. In my (Monica's) own city, a thirteen-year-old killed himself last week. My children had gone to school with him. He too had convinced himself that escaping through death would be the answer to his and his family's troubles. He was wrong, but no one was ever able to tell him so. When a child dies it is particularly tragic. From anyone else's perspective, it is easy to see how the fantasy that suicide is a reasonable solution could not possibly be true.

If you are depressed enough to have thoughts about death, give other people the opportunity to help you think it through. Do not let yourself be deluded into believing that others will be better off without you. Talk it over and let them help you see that there are better solutions to your problems.

Communication Errors

Throughout this chapter we have made the suggestion that you should communicate with others about your depression or your other concerns. While communication is essential, it is not always easy. When you are upset, you can lose your cool, say things you don't mean, or have things come out wrong. In this section we will help you learn about common errors people make in their communication with others and suggest some methods for improvement. If you follow this advice, you will have a better chance of getting your point across and hearing what others have to say.

Some of the more common errors that people make when they try to communicate with each other are listed in Table 10.1. Read over the list to see if any of these sound familiar.

KEEPING IT TO YOURSELF

There is something about asking for help that our patients seem to dislike. When we question them about it, they say that they would be willing to help any of their family members or friends if they asked, but they don't feel right asking for help themselves. Why not? Perhaps Tony put it best. "I should be able to handle this myself." So what does it mean to him to ask for help? Tony would say that it meant he was weak and a loser. When asked if he thought any of his friends who asked for help were weak or losers he would immediately defend them. "No. They're fine. They just need me to help with things I am good at. It's no big deal." Tony had a double standard about getting help. It was OK for others to ask, but not for him.

Do you have a double standard about asking for help? If you are like Tony perhaps it is not that asking for help means you are a loser, perhaps it is that you think others will see you as a loser. The reality is that most people like helping others. It makes them feel good about themselves, not bad about you.

Table 10.1 Communication Errors

Communication Error	Definition	Example
Keeping it to yourself	Do not confide in others about your problems	Don't tell partner that you are depressed When you are upset, you do not communicate this to others
Poor listening	Not giving your full attention to the speaker	Not making eye contact, planning your response while the other person is still talking, thinking about other things or doing a task while someone is speaking to you
Explosive anger	Displaying anger through words or deeds	Striking out at others instead of talking Cursing, yelling, making threats, hurling insults
Mind reading	Making guesses about what the other person is thinking or feeling; assuming you know more about what some people are feeling than they know about themselves	Jumping to conclusions without giving people a chance to tell their side of things; making guesses about someone's feelings without asking for verification
Defensiveness	Assuming that you are being attacked by another person and responding in a way to defend yourself, disagree with the other, or counterattack someone's actions	Disagreeing before thinking it through, making excuses for yourself, attempting to justify your position, lashing out at the attacker
Changing topics	Skipping from one topic to another during the course of a conversation	Starting a conversation about one topic and bringing in past events or difficulties before resolving the first
Invalidation	Any act that communicates to a person that his or her ideas are wrong, stupid, not valuable, or unacceptable	Disagreeing with someone who is just expressing a point of view; laughing at or making fun of someone's opinion or feelings

GETTING HELP FROM OTHERS

It is not unusual to hear from the family members of our patients that they just want to help, but they do not know what to do. They do not know whether to push you or back off and leave you alone, talk to you or give you your space. Give them a break and tell them how they can help. You will be doing yourself and them a favor.

POOR LISTENING SKILLS

It is pretty obvious when people are not listening to you. They do not look at you, answer only with "uh huh," or change the topic instead of responding to what you have said. Further indication that the other person is not listening to you is an abrupt, defensive response even before you have finished talking. This usually means that while you were talking, the other person was planning a response instead of hearing you out. You cannot fully listen to someone and plan your comeback line at the same time. Half of all good communication is listening. It is a skill that we sometimes take for granted because it seems to come so naturally. We only think about it when we believe someone is not listening to us. We are less likely to notice when we do it ourselves.

IMPROVING YOUR RECEPTION

If you want your communication with others to go more smoothly you can start with being a good listener. When you listen, it encourages others to listen as well. In this way you are teaching them by setting a good example rather than by giving them instructions. There are three parts to effective listening. The first is body language. A good listener's body language communicates that you are giving the other person your undivided attention. In his book *The Skilled Helper,* Richard Egan suggests that good listeners follow the SOLER rule. *S—squarely* face the person who is talking so that your body is facing toward them, *O*—have an *open* posture without crossed arms or legs, *L—lean* forward slightly to show interest, *E*—make *eye* contact, and *R*—keep your body *relaxed.*

The second part is listening with an open mind. While you are listening, do not interrupt, defend yourself, or debate. Just listen until the person has finished talking.

The third part of being a good listener is to let the other person know that you have heard what he or she had to say and you understand the message. You do not have to share the same opinion. At this point all you are trying to do is show that you have been listening and that you understand what the other person means. It may be very helpful to respond by summarizing what you think you heard. That way, if you have misunderstood or missed an important part, the other person can clarify or fill in the missing pieces. After you have taken a turn at listening, you can take your turn at speaking. Even if the other person does not do as good a job as you did at listening, by changing your own actions you have done a lot to improve the communication process.

EXPLOSIVE ANGER

One of the most common impulsive acts is to say angry words before you have taken the time to think through what you want to say. Anger colors your perceptions of events and of people. It will cause you to see only the facts that support your angry point of view and to ignore other information that might change your mind. Drs. Karen Schmaling and Neil Jacobson have shown that when you are depressed, your words are more likely to come out sounding aggressive. Angry and hateful words from you will often lead to an angry response from others and vice versa. Here are some suggestions for how to manage your anger when you are feeling like a volcano about to erupt.

LETTING OFF STEAM

There are times when it is perfectly reasonable to let off some steam as long as it is not directed at another person and does not hurt you. If you are angry, try out some of these ways to vent your emotions without hurting yourself or anyone else.

How to Vent Your Emotions

1. Yell to yourself in the privacy of your own car or home.
2. Call a friend and share your frustration.
3. Run around the block a few times until you wear yourself out.
4. Vigorously clean something, like a kitchen floor or your car.
5. Beat a rug or chop some wood.
6. Hit your mattress with a broom or tennis racket. Watch out for ceiling fans.
7. Go ahead and cry.
8. Write down your thoughts and feelings in a journal.
9. Attack a project in your home or yard.
10. Go to a batting cage or driving range and hit some balls.

Be smart about it. Make sure you are not scaring your children with an outburst. Do not get drunk first before you vent or you will have less self-control. After you have calmed down, find a way to deal with the problem that upset you in the first place. Make a vow to yourself never to hurt anyone or his or her property. The following things should be avoided when you want to blow off steam.

How NOT to Vent Your Emotions

1. Do not say things you know you will regret later. Think them as loudly as you want, but don't say them.
2. Never hurt or frighten a child or an animal with your anger.
3. Never drive off in your vehicle at high speed to vent your feelings.
4. Do not break things that belong to others, no matter how angry you are at them.
5. Don't vent on the job.
6. Never hurt yourself in any way.
7. Do not pack your things in haste and move out. Don't even threaten to do so.
8. Do not pick a fight with a stranger, especially someone who could hurt you or get you into trouble.
9. Don't argue with a cop or your mother-in-law.

MIND READING

Many people, especially married couples, seem to believe that they have the ability to read each other's minds. They think that since they have known one another for so long they can anticipate what the other is going to say, how she is feeling, or what he needs. They're so confident in this ability that they do not see any need to check out their assumptions. The trouble starts when their guesses are wrong.

It is not likely that you can read your partner's mind even if you have known that person for a long time. As we noted in the Thinking Key, people have many more private thoughts than the ones they speak out loud. Also, people change their minds or the circumstances change. In short, there are a myriad of reasons why it is extremely difficult to read somebody else's mind.

If you act based on the assumption that you know what your partner is thinking or feeling, there can be a big chance that you will be making a mistake. There is a simple solution to this problem. Ask questions rather than make assumptions. Try "What are you thinking?" "What can I do to help you?" or "Are you upset with me?".

DEFENSIVENESS

When you perceive that you are being attacked in some way, you can act in an overly defensive manner. Our basic instinct to protect ourselves from harm can make us go on the defensive before we have had a chance to determine whether the attack is real or intentional. Since the best defense is a good offense, we often defend by counterattacking. This usually gets the other person to go on the defensive, so he or she counterattacks, and the conflict continues.

If you are already feeling bad about yourself and you know you are not functioning as well as usual, you will be prone to go on the defensive when you think that others are being critical of you. Here is an example.

Julia was feeling more depressed than usual when she woke up one morning. Her husband, Tom, could tell from her body language that she was not at her best. He tried to be careful about what he said, but it didn't matter. She got her feelings hurt anyway, and he couldn't work his way out of it no matter what he said. The conversation went like this.

TOM: "Did you have trouble sleeping last night?"

JULIA: "Why do you ask? Do I really look that bad?"

TOM: "No. You look fine. I just thought maybe you were a little tired."

JULIA: "I'm sorry I can't be all perky and happy like you are in the morning. You just don't understand me."

TOM: "Look, I'm not trying to upset you. I was just making conversation. I'll shut up and leave you alone."

JULIA: "Sure, why not. No one wants to be around me. I can't help it. I'm going through a hard time."

TOM: "I know."

JULIA: "No you don't, or you wouldn't criticize me like that."

TOM: "Criticize you? Where did that come from?"

JULIA: "Just forget it. You never hear yourself. You think you're perfect."

TOM: "I give up. I'm going to work."

Tom left the room feeling exasperated. He did not intend to be critical. He knew that Julia was having a hard time, and she was at her worst the first thing in the morning. He tried to be patient with her, but it was difficult to do so on mornings like this. In the meantime, Julia was at home slowly getting ready, realizing at some level that she had overreacted. She felt guilty for sounding like such a jerk. This started a flow of negative automatic thoughts that brought her down further and made it hard for her to make herself go to work.

FIGHTING DEFENSIVENESS

A defensive response is usually triggered by the perception that you are being attacked. In the example above, Julia thought her husband was attacking her. While there may actually be times when you are attacked, depression can make you jump to this conclusion prematurely. Before you assume that you are right, use the Thinking Key exercises from Chapters 3 and 4 to evaluate the negative thought "I'm being attacked." If after you have had a chance to think about it you decide that you are not really being attacked, change your response so that you do not sound defensive.

Another option is to delay your response to a perceived attack and give the "attacker" a chance to explain. Say something like "From the tone in your voice it sounded like you were attacking me. Am I hearing you correctly?" or "Is it my imagination or are you angry with me right now?" Allowing others to clarify their statements before you respond defensively will keep you from misspeaking and creating conflict.

CHANGING TOPICS

Have you ever had one of those conversations that started off with talking about how your day went and ended with a heated discussion about bills? During the course of that discussion you might have also touched on the children, your mother, a friend, a vacation that never happened, a mistake that was made long ago, or perhaps a repeat of portions of a past argument. It is very easy to jump from one topic to another during a heated discussion because when you are upset you get flooded with negative automatic thoughts. Sometimes these thoughts include a long list of old arguments, hurtful events, and current complaints. It is hard to resist the temptation to bring these up during a conversation, especially if you are feeling defensive.

Unfortunately, you cannot solve multiple problems at one time and you certainly cannot undo bad events from the past. So when you are finished with one of these multitopic discussions, you usually feel tired and discouraged because you haven't solved anything.

ONE THING AT A TIME

When we treat couples, we listen to these multitopic discussions/arguments for a while to get a feel for the communication behaviors of each partner. As they jump from topic to topic we add it to a list of problems that we present to them when they are through. You can do this same exercise for yourself. If it is your tendency to bring up multiple issues all at the same time, keep a pen and paper handy while you are talking. When you find that you have shifted away from the original topic, say so and write the new topic on a list to be covered at another time. All you have to say is, "I think we are getting off the subject, let's finish this one first and talk about the next one at another time." It doesn't matter which person in the discussion takes responsibility for keeping things on track. It is just important that you stick to one topic at a time.

It also can be helpful to start a discussion by clearly stating what you want to talk about. For example, "I want to talk with you about my mother coming to visit us this summer." Another idea you can try is to set a time limit on discussions. If you cannot resolve an issue in twenty minutes, call time out, think about it individually, and come back to the issue at another time. When a discussion goes on too long, you can get tired, annoyed, and disgusted, all of which will keep you from using your best communication skills.

INVALIDATION

Statements such as "That's stupid," "I can't believe you think that way," or "You don't know what you are talking about " are clear examples of invalidation. Invalidation can also include being ridiculed, humiliated, mocked, or put down in more subtle ways. In fact, at times you may be aware of feeling invalidated, but be unable to put your finger on exactly what was said to make you feel so badly. Sometimes it is the words that are used. Other times it is a person's tone of voice or body language. In either case, you come away feeling as if you were not given due consideration.

Another type of invalidation is when someone makes your ideas seem absurd by exaggerating them or taking them to an extreme. For example, if you complain to your partner, an invalidating defensive statement might be to blow it out of proportion, like "Well I guess I'm just a total failure. Why don't you just leave me? It's clear I can't do anything right. " This kind of self-blame is usually said in an insincere and sarcastic tone. Your complaint is made to sound so huge that it is no longer believable. This kind of interaction puts you in the position of defending yourself by trying to convince your partner that he or she is not all that bad. This changes the focus from you pointing out his or her shortcoming to you pointing out his or her strengths. It is a fighting maneuver that usually leaves you feeling confused and invalidated.

SOLUTIONS

When someone invalidates you, bring it to his or her attention in a calm way. Say "When you say that to me, it makes me feel like you are not taking my feelings seriously. You don't have to agree with me, but I think it is important that we respect each other's feelings." If this method doesn't work, you can try a slightly different approach. Let the person know how you think the invalidation might be negatively affecting the relationship. Here is an example. "When you tell me that my opinion or my feelings are wrong, it makes it hard for me to take your feelings seriously. It also makes me not like you very much when you are doing that. I don't think this is good for our relationship."

Improving Your Relationships

Take out your notes from Exercise 10.2 where you identified your relationship challenges, and write down some ideas in your notebook on how you might change the way you handle these relationship problems. After writing in the name of the person you are having trouble with and the nature of the problem, add your proposed solution. Julia's list is given below as an example. You don't have to take action on all fronts at the same time, but you should begin to make a plan for the future. You will have an opportunity at the end of Chapter 11 to update your Personal Plan for Recovery. Consider setting a goal to address one of your relationship challenges. Remember that coping with stressful relationship problems might be a key to overcoming your depression.

Exercise 10.3
Julia's Relationship Challenges and Goals

Person	Problem	Plan
Tom (Husband)	I get angry with him when I think he's criticizing me.	I need to stop and think things through before I react. He's not trying to be critical.
Sammy (Stepson)	We don't communicate.	Ask him how he is doing and just listen to him when he is in the mood to talk.
Marjorie (Co-worker)	I think she is mad at me.	Ask her if she is mad at me and, if so, try to make it right.
Jimmie Sue (Neighbor)	Avoiding conversation with her because I don't want her to see me depressed and gossip about me to the other neighbors.	Just say hello. I don't have to tell her everything. Be friendly. Act normal.

11

How to Grow Stronger
When Relationships Change

Consuelo's depression began with the death of her husband Enrique six months ago. He was young, and his death was tragic and unexpected. Enrique suffered a heart attack when Consuelo was out of town on business. Though he was able to call the paramedics before he lost consciousness, they were unable to save him. Consuelo coped with the loss as best she could, staying busy, taking care of his financial affairs, and consoling the children while she suffered in silence. Her parents told her to be patient, that the pain would pass, that she would come to terms with the fact that sometimes in life tragic things happen. She had been patient, but the pain did not seem to get better. When she could no longer hide her tears from her children and her co-workers, Consuelo sought treatment.

As she told her story, it became clear that Consuelo had gotten into a pattern of negative thinking and poor coping habits that were keeping her from overcoming her grief. She blamed herself for her husband's death—"If only I had been there." Logically she knew that the paramedics had done all that they could. She knew that it was no one's fault. Yet, she found ways to make herself responsible.

She hadn't been able to sleep well since his death, so she would sit in her husband's favorite chair, rocking and crying for hours night after night. Consuelo told her therapist that she had always been a disappointment to her husband. As the therapist inquired further, a more complicated story unfolded.

Enrique had been a poor partner. He had a bad temper, often belittled her in front of the children. Consuelo was very careful to try to protect the memory of her husband by making excuses for his angry outbursts, his threats, and his unreasonable expectations. It was obvious to the therapist, however, that he had been physically and emotionally abusive throughout most of their marriage. Although she mourned his loss, she was secretly relieved to know that he could no longer hurt her or the children. This mix of emotions—sadness and relief—filled Consuelo with guilt. And, the guilt was feeding her depression. To overcome these feelings Consuelo had to accept the fact that while Enrique's death was tragic, it led to some positive changes in her life and the lives of her children. She had to purge herself of the guilt that came with this feeling of relief and acknowledge that it was reasonable for an abused wife to sometimes wish her husband would go away. Thinking such thoughts did not cause her husband's death.

Consuelo's therapist taught her about thinking errors and helped her to stop blaming herself for her husband's death. She knew that she had tried her best to be a good wife and that her husband had had problems of his own that had made him angry and intolerant. She could not have predicted that her husband would have a heart attack while she was out of town. If she had been there, she would have done her best to help. But, from what the doctors had told her, there was probably nothing she could have done that would have made a difference. The attack had been severe and sudden.

Keeping her problems to herself and then crying in solitude were two coping strategies that had been interfering with her recovery. Consuelo needed help to work through her negative thoughts about the loss of her marriage and about her own future rather than cry night after night with no real resolution of her grief. Within the first month of treatment Consuelo made considerable gains and was ready to chart a course for getting her life back.

Some of the most difficult transitions in life involve changes in relationships. Deaths, divorces, and separations are the most common stressful transitions, but according to research done on life events and depression, sometimes even positive life events, like moving into a new house and leaving old friends behind or watching your children grow up and move out on their own, can lead to feelings of sadness and depression. Events that change our lives, causing us to lose something we are familiar with or have gotten used to, are unsettling. It takes time to sort through the mix of feelings. In some cases, we get stuck in depression along the way. Take a moment to think about the life transitions that have changed your relationships with other people. A list of common life transitions can be found in Exercise 11.1. Put a checkmark next to those that might be contributing to your current distress. As you read the remainder of this chapter, think about how the exercises might apply to

Exercise 11.1
Life Transitions

Family Events
- ____ Death of a loved one
- ____ Divorce, separation, or abandonment
- ____ Family estrangement due to conflict
- ____ Separation from children
- ____ Moving away from family members
- ____ Moving back in with parents

Work events
- ____ Start of a new job
- ____ Going back to work after being a stay-at-home mom
- ____ Promotion, demotion, or being fired
- ____ Relocation to new workplace
- ____ Loss of employment
- ____ Disability or inability to work
- ____ Retirement

School Events
- ____ Graduation from high school
- ____ Graduation from college or other advanced education
- ____ Dropping out of school

Parenting Events
- ____ Birth of a child
- ____ Child starts school/end of infancy
- ____ No longer being needed or being needed less by your children
- ____ Child grows up and leaves home
- ____ Losing independence after becoming a parent

Friend Events
- ____ End of a friendship
- ____ Engagement called off
- ____ Friend becomes a spouse
- ____ Losing network of friends

you. At the end of the chapter, you will have another opportunity to update your Personal Plan for Recovery. Think about adding a plan to work through an important life transition.

Coping with Loss: The Stages of Grief

Elizabeth Kubler-Ross is famous for describing the stages many people go through when grieving. These stages, which will be described in more detail below, are denial, anger, bargaining, depression, and acceptance. Although this is the typical order, it is not unusual to go back and forth through these stages, repeating anger, for example, or beginning to accept a loss, but sliding back into sorrow and depression before finally recovering. Here is an example of how one woman went through each of the stages of grief in coping with the end of her marriage.

Isabella's depression started soon after her husband of twenty years announced that he was not in love with her anymore. Jim broke her heart when he told her that he was interested in someone new, and he wanted to be set free to reclaim the love and excitement their marriage no longer provided him. She was blindsided by his words. Jim hadn't really complained about their marriage. He had seemed content, but obviously he wasn't. "How could I have missed the signs? This can't be happening." Isabella felt devastated. She wanted to be angry with him, but she blamed herself instead. She told herself that she had become less attractive to him, had gained weight, and was less interested in going out with him. Because she believed she had failed him, Isabella was ready to give up and let him go. If this was what it would take for him to be happy, then so be it.

Isabella woke up the next day with a change of heart. In fact, she woke with a fire in her belly saying, "No. She can't have him. He's mine. I've invested twenty years in helping that man to be successful, and I will not just pass him on to some young bimbo to reap the reward of my hard work. Marriage to him hasn't been easy. I put in a lot of effort, a lot of hours, took his nonsense, kept my mouth shut. No way am I giving up that easily. I'm going to bring that man back to his senses." Her denial that her marriage was over had kicked in.

Jim wouldn't tell her who his love interest was, but she was able to figure it out fairly easily. When Isabella thought back she remembered the way his new assistant laughed at his "stupid" jokes and complimented him on his successes at work. But, when Jim talked about this "great new assistant" who was making his life a lot easier, Isabella had not thought anything of it. Furious now, she kicked herself for being so blind. She decided to go to Jim's workplace and confront them both and demand that he stop seeing her. Denial was giving way to anger.

Unfortunately, it was too late. Jim had made promises to his girl-friend. Plans had been made, and he had already been to his lawyer to file for divorce. Before she could get out the door, Isabella was met by a courier who served her with the divorce papers. Although this nearly knocked her off her feet, Isabella quickly regrouped, remembered the speech she was going to give her husband, and called him on the phone. Her denial that divorce was inevitable had reemerged.

The receptionist said that he had gone out of town and would not be back until the end of the week. His "assistant" was "out on sick leave." Shaken, but not dissuaded, Isabella figured out how to reach her husband and made contact with him before he got on the plane. She started out with a strong and forceful tone in her voice. It wasn't long before the tears flowed, and she found herself making promises to change and begging him to come home. The bargaining phase had begun. Isabella heard her own desperation to hold on to her husband and was disgusted with the pitiful sound. He promised to think about it and talk to her when he returned from his trip. She felt exhilarated and hopeful. The bargaining had been at least marginally successful. Rather than taking steps toward acceptance of her loss, she took a big step backward into denial.

Jim was scheduled to return on Friday afternoon, but extended his stay until late Sunday night. When he returned, he claimed to be too tired to talk and went straight to bed. Isabella was dying to confront him, but she didn't want to appear pushy, so she let him alone promising herself that tomorrow night they would reach an agreement. Isabella took a half-day off of work to prepare for the evening. She signed up for a workout program, bought some new walking shoes, had her hair done, and bought groceries to prepare his favorite meal. Everything was ready when he walked in the door. She tried to not make too much of the fact that he complimented her appearance, and she tried to ignore the fact that he did not kiss her hello. She waited and watched for any indication that he had changed his mind, but she was only fooling herself. When he finally sat down at the dinner table, he took one bite of food and pushed the plate away. He apologized for not having an appetite, blaming it on a flu bug going around the office. In a calm, but direct tone, Jim told her that their marriage was over. He said that he was sorry for hurting her, but he couldn't deny his feelings any longer. Isabella felt her insides melt-ing into tears. She couldn't speak, couldn't get angry. Jim got up, packed a few things in a suitcase, and left.

Isabella cried for the good part of a week. She called in sick at work and spoke to no one about what had really happened. She felt embarrassed and humiliated by it all. She knew that men had affairs and left their wives for younger women. Yet, she never dreamed that it could happen to her. She felt old, lonely, and hopeless about her future. She told herself that no one would want her, that she was unlovable, and that it made perfect sense that her husband would leave her for someone better. Isabella grieved over the loss of her marriage, over the loss of the future they had planned together, and over the loss of her youth.

Her initial sadness and despair had evolved into major depression as she began to experience physical symptoms such as sleeplessness and appetite changes, and started feeling more hopeless. These symptoms worsened over several months, but then began to slowly improve. By the six-month anniversary of her divorce, Isabella realized that, despite all that had happened, she was doing fine. She missed her husband, but otherwise her life-style had not changed dramatically. After all, her husband had always traveled a lot and Isabella was used to being alone. Since Jim had moved away, she had been going to the gym, losing weight, and feeling better about herself. Good friends had rallied around and encouraged her to spend time with them. A single's life was not as bad as she thought, and she was proud of herself for hanging in when she wanted to give up. Isabella had regained her self-respect and had discovered new talents and abilities that she never knew she had. She occasionally saw Jim around town and loved the fact that he admired her new look. Isabella had reached the final stage of grief by acceptance of the loss and by becoming the person she had always wanted to be.

We tell this story in the hopes that you will be able to recognize your experience of the stages of grief and realize that it is normal process. If you are reading this book, you may be stuck in the depression phase. If that is the case, there are some things you can do to complete the transition and work toward acceptance of the loss. We gave you some clues for how to get started in the Thinking Key chapters, the Action Key chapters, and the Biology Key chapters. If you skip ahead to the Spirituality Key you will find some ways to help you find new meaning in your life. Any

DABDA—The stages of grief

Denial
Anger
Bargaining
Depression
Acceptance

of these efforts will help you resolve your grief and move on to a happier life.

FEELING STUCK

There are some coping strategies that can slow the grieving process and prolong depression. Many people fall into the trap of trying not to think about the loss. Putting the problem out of your mind may work for a short while, but this truly is a case when "out of sight" never means "out of mind." If you have not resolved your grief, your memories of the loss may manifest themselves as nightmares or flashbacks of the loss event. In such cases, your brain is telling you that the loss is still a source of stress. The obvious solution is to spend time thinking and talking about the loss with a family member, a friend, a therapist, or other helper. Some people find that just writing down thoughts and feelings about the event, and reading them over, can bring them closer to acceptance of the loss. Others avoid thinking about a sad event because they believe they will come completely unglued or lose total control of their emotions. This type of avoidance can occur in people who are uncomfortable with big displays of emotion. If you are avoiding grief because of fear of strong emotions, you will probably find that your fears are unfounded. Let yourself feel the pain for short periods of time until you get used to it.

Another common consequence of trying to ignore your feelings is that you can develop physical symptoms of stress such as headaches or stomach problems. Although you may try to pretend that everything is OK, your body knows the truth. It feels the stress and reacts internally. You can help your body by allowing yourself to feel your emotions.

The bargaining phase is usually short, coming to an end when it becomes clear that negotiations have failed. In contrast, the anger phase can be prolonged if there is no movement toward resolution of the grief. It is easy to get mad and stay mad. Each time you rethink an upsetting event, review the details, or remind yourself of the words that were exchanged, you rekindle your emotions. Some people spend a lifetime

---

Key Point

When you are reacting to a loss you may show more feelings than usual, but that isn't necessarily a bad thing. Emotions cannot harm you. Only acting out your emotions in a troublesome way can hurt you.

---

holding a grudge. The anger consumes the energy they might have used to have fun, be successful, or enjoy other aspects of their lives. If this sounds like you, make a decision to let go of the anger. If it is not wearing off by itself, you will need to will it to stop.

Pick a self-statement from the list below or make up one of your own and rehearse it every time you feel angry. After a while you will probably find that you are angry less often. Getting past the anger does not necessarily mean that you will go through the depression stage of grief. Anger may have been part of your depression. If you can stop the angry thoughts, you can move on to accepting the loss and using your emotional energy for more positive things.

Self-Talk to Control Your Anger

1. I've been angry long enough. It is time to stop.
2. Let it go.
3. Staying angry is not helping me, it's only taking away from my life.
4. Whatever happened is in the past. You can't change the past. You can only try to have a better future.
5. I don't have enough energy to waste it on anger.
6. Thinking about it does not change the circumstances. It only brings me down.
7. When I'm angry, I'm the only one who suffers. It doesn't hurt those who made me angry in the first place.
8. Anger closes my heart and keeps me from experiencing the good things in life.
9. I don't want to be angry any more.
10. Today is the last day I will waste emotional energy on the past. Tomorrow I will start anew with a fresher outlook and a freer heart.

The Meaning of Life Transitions

The same life transition can have different meanings for different people. It is the meaning of events that determines our emotional reactions. If it means loss, you will feel sad. If it means opportunity, you will feel happy. One of the ways to cope with painful life transitions is to think about what those changes mean to you. Perhaps you are attaching an overly negative meaning to a potentially positive event. If so, you can use the skills you picked up in the Thinking Key to combat the negative thoughts that are fueling your depression. Like other stressful events, life transitions usually trigger thoughts about yourself, thoughts about others, including the world at large, and thoughts about your future. Exercise 11.2 includes some examples of negative automatic thoughts about life transitions. Review the list and write in your own negative thoughts

---

Exercise 11.2
Thoughts about Life Transitions

My life transition is _____

Circle any of the thoughts on the list that you have had about a life transition. Add any other negative thoughts you may have. Choose a few of the most important or troublesome thoughts. Use the Thought Change Record from Chapter 3 or other methods from the Thinking Key to develop alternative thoughts.

1. Thoughts about me   My Examples

   It's all my fault   _____
   I'm a failure   _____
   I don't like this change   _____
   I can't do it   _____
   I don't know what to do   _____

2. Thoughts about you

   You abandoned me   _____
   You rejected me   _____
   You don't appreciate me   _____
   You're controlling me   _____
   You did this to me   _____

3. Thoughts about the future

   I'll never find another you   _____
   I'll always be lonely   _____
   I'll never get over it   _____
   I'll never be able to stay here   _____
   It's going to be terrible   _____

about your life transition. Add these thoughts to your notebook and try to analyze them using the exercises you learned in Chapters 3 and 4.

If you are making predictions that things will turn out badly, ask yourself if there is any real evidence that this is true. If a bad outcome is possible, think of things you can do to prevent it from happening. If you cannot prevent it from happening, think about what you can do to cope with it when it happens. For example, if you think that divorce will leave you penniless, get some facts to determine if this is true. If it is not true, put your energy elsewhere. If it is possible, think about what you need to do now to keep it from happening. Get advice from others. Find out what can be done to prevent this. Have a backup plan for coping if it seems that a great financial loss is inevitable. Call upon others for help before it is too late.

If the thinking error you are making includes blaming yourself or others, try coming up with another way to look at the situation. What would someone else say about you? Could there be another explanation for what is happening? If a friend or family member had the same negative thought, what would you say to try to make him or her feel better?

"I'm Not Ready to Look at the Bright Side"

You might find that when you try to analyze and change your negative automatic thoughts about a life transition, you're not quite ready for it. Geneva recently lost her grandmother to Alzheimer's disease. Her grandmother was eighty-five years old when she died and had been ill and incoherent for many years. She could no longer recognize her family members or her surroundings. She was only able to lie in her bed and stare at the walls. Geneva knew that it was best that her grandmother no longer suffered. She knew that her grandmother had always believed in going to heaven when she died and was never afraid of that prospect. Although it had been clear for some time that the end was nearing, Geneva was not ready to let go of her grandmother. She did not want to be bothered with reassurances, bright sides, or any other rational comments from family members or friends about her grandmother's passing. Losing her was the most painful event in Geneva's life. No one was going to make her feel better about it. No one understood the significance of their bond. Her grandmother was the only stable force in her life and she was not about to let her go easily.

Geneva knew that there were rational or logical ways to look at things, but none of that mattered to her. She needed to grieve her loss. She needed to feel the pain before she could let it go. Feeling such intense sorrow was a reflection of how much she loved her grandmother. If she had just "looked at the bright side" and dealt with her grandmother's passing as others seemed to be doing, it would be doing their relationship a disservice. Geneva loved her dearly and felt an intense loss. If they had not been so close, her recovery would have started sooner.

It is normal to mourn over any life transition that leaves you with a feeling of loss. Death is the most obvious event, but divorce or other endings of a relationship can make you feel sad, even if it was your idea to call it quits. At least to some degree, you have to feel the loss before you can get over it. So it is OK to put off being rational and logical about your sorrow until you have had enough time to grieve.

How much is enough grief and how much is too much grief? It is not unusual for grief to persist for up to six months after a loss, with ups and downs in mood. It should be most severe in the beginning and slowly improve with time. There may be some difficulty in functioning at home or at work for several weeks, but this too should gradually improve. Grief that persists, continues to worsen, or interferes with everyday functioning is probably becoming more than just grief. It may be evolving into major depression. Other signs that grief is turning into a clinical depression are an excess of self-criticism, slowness in movement, speech, or thought, and suicidal ideation. If your symptoms are worsening, it is time to get some help for depression.

The Pros and Cons of Life Transitions

Change is not easy, even positive change like starting a family or moving to a new city to start a great job. You can try to make yourself look at the bright side, but still have doubts that things will turn out well. Most life transitions have positive and negative features. When it is a transition that catches us by surprise or a change we do not want to face, it is easy to see the downside. When the transition is something we have looked forward to for some time, it is much easier to see the pleasant side. If you have mixed feelings about a life transition, it might be helpful for you to figure out what bothers you most about the change and to try to minimize the stress in some way. The Life Transition Worksheet (Exercise 11.3) is a tool you can use to help you make a decision about a life transition or to help you cope with an event that has occurred or is about to occur. In your notebook draw a box like the Life Transition Worksheet. Notice that the four squares are numbered.

In box #1 list all the positive aspects of the transition. Think of all the ways in which your life will be better because of this change. This can in-

Exercise 11.3
Life Transition Worksheet

Type of Life Transition: _____

	Pros	Cons
Making the life transition	#1	#2
Not making the life transition	#3	#4

clude things you are looking forward to doing, welcomed changes in so-cial status, and ways in which the quality of your life will improve. In box #2 list the downside of making this life transition. In box #3 list the ad-vantages of not making this life transition (e.g., not getting a divorce, not moving, not having a new baby, not retiring). And, in box #4 list the dis-advantages of not making this life transition.

For example, since Bob and Brenda retired last summer, life hasn't been easy. They have had a lot of conflict and not a lot of fun. They both had imagined that retirement would be the best time of their lives. In-stead, it had been one of the worst. Bob started feeling extremely de-pressed. Although he described their conflict as emerging recently, it was clear to their marriage counselor that the transition into retirement was at the root of the problem. It did not make sense to them how something they had planned for and looked forward to for years was actually a source of misery. Their therapist explained the pros and cons of life tran-sitions and helped them take stock of the advantages and disadvantages of this new phase of life. They filled out the Life Transition Worksheet as they talked it over.

The next step after completing the worksheet is to try to pick the one or two items in each box that are the most important. Bob and

Bob and Brenda's Life Transition Worksheet

Type of Transition: <u>Retirement</u>

	Pros	Cons
Making the life transition	Not having to work. Less stress. Able to sleep late. No morning commutes in traffic. *Freedom to do as we please instead of having to work.	Slightly lower income. Not able to talk with old friends. *Less structure makes us lazy. Having to see each other all day. Taken less seriously by people who are employed.
<u>*Not*</u> *making the life transition*	Income would be higher. *We would have more to do each day. We would not have to spend so much time together. *We would feel a sense of purpose.	*We are tired of working. We would eventually be forced to retire. We would have to compete with younger staff. There is more to life than work.

Brenda put an asterisk next to the items that seemed most important to them. The major issues selected in boxes #1 and #4 are likely to be similar. In Brenda and Bob's case, it was the freedom to do what they pleased instead of work, which had become tiring over the last few years. This was the main advantage of making the life transition. The items from boxes #2 and #3 should also be similar. For Brenda and Bob, the items had something to do with productive use of their time. Work gave them structure and purpose. In retirement they were less active, less structured, and as a result, felt that they were wasting their time. This was the disadvantage of retirement.

The final step is to think of ways in which you can minimize the disadvantages of the life transition and maximize the advantages. The biggest disadvantage seemed to be that they were having difficulty structuring their day and using their time well. There were no deadlines, no appointments to keep, and no consequences for oversleeping, so they got lazy. They needed to find a way to make themselves take advantage of their free time and do the things they had always wanted to do. Together, Brenda and Bob did the Activity Scheduling exercise from Chapter 5 and made some plans for how they would spend their time. They decided that they would add activities to their schedule that were fun to do and would take on a few chores that would give them a sense of accomplishment.

Life Transition Worksheet Instructions

1. List the advantages of the life transition in box #1 and the disadvantages in box #2.
2. List the advantages of NOT making the life transition in box #3 and the disadvantages in box #4.
3. Pick out the most important item(s) from each box. Mark them with a check or an asterisk.
4. The items checked in boxes #1 and #4 tell you the main advantages of making the change.
5. The items checked in boxes #2 and #3 tell you the main disadvantages of making the change.
6. Think of ways that you can reduce, eliminate, or cope with the disadvantages of the change so that you can enjoy the advantages.

Making Peace with the Past

When you are forced to go through a painful life transition before you are prepared, you usually meet it with resistance and a lot of emotion. The intense emotions can stir inside you long after the event is over. As a result, you can continue to feel upset, overwhelmed, and stuck. Getting fired from a job is a good example of a life transition that is usually unexpected, unwelcomed, and hard to overcome. Getting "dumped" by a lover is another painful life transition that is hard to shake off. It is difficult to make peace with rejections. They shake our self-esteem, making us question our value as a person. Unfortunately, rejections are such common events in life that most of us will have to deal with one sooner or later. This section of the chapter is about ways to make peace with hurts from the past, to learn from them, and to go on to a better life. As you read through this section, think about how you might make use of some new methods for coping with painful life transitions. Add these ideas to your Personal Plan for Recovery at the end of the chapter.

GETTING PAST THE HURT

Ever since Lewis lost his job at Amtex Wood Products twelve months ago he has been unable to make any real progress toward finding a new one. He was sixty years old when his boss Carl, a friend for thirty years, called him into the office and laid him off. Amtex had been sold to a new firm. To keep his own job, Carl was forced to help with reorganization and downsizing. Lewis had helped Carl build Amtex back in the early 1970s. They had been through good times and tough times. Lewis had planned to stay on until retirement. The termination had left Lewis feeling betrayed and angry. He had lost a good job and a good friend. "How could he do this to me?" Lewis repeated to himself. Over the past year he had declined several offers of assistance from Carl in finding a new job. He was as angry now as he had been twelve months ago.

Stella, Lewis' wife, was eligible for retirement from teaching, but had to keep working until Lewis found a new job. She knew that he was so hung up on feeling betrayed that he could not muster the energy or the right attitude for job hunting. Although Lewis would deny it, Stella suspected that he would never go back to work. He had lost his drive and his pride in himself as a worker. Over these twelve months she had patiently allowed Lewis to take out his frustration on her, but she was getting sick of it. She decided to confront Lewis with his behavior, hoping to force him to stop complaining and take action toward doing something with his life.

Stella had been trained as a school counselor so she knew a little bit about how to manage hurt feelings. Stella had hoped that Lewis would pull out of this on his own. She did not want to have to get tough with him, given how painful this loss had been for him. But the time had come to lay it on the line. Stella knew that Lewis had always respected her opinion and would listen to what she had to say, even if it was painful for him.

Stella had a game plan. She wanted to get Lewis to let go of his anger so that he could feel free to go on with his life in a productive way. She had read that the first thing to do to get rid of anger in situations like these is to confront the person who upset you and say what needs to be said. After he got this off his chest he needed to stop talking about his anger and the betrayal by Carl. Every time he heard himself tell the story or bring up some detail about the event, Lewis would get angry all over again. This seemed to keep the fire of anger burning, and it needed to stop.

Stella also planned to help Lewis gain control over his emotions by getting him to think about how his anger was hurting him and his family and not doing a thing to Carl, the person who was the source of Lewis' hurt. If Lewis didn't buy this argument, Stella was prepared to ask him to guess how much energy he was using each week just to stay mad at Carl. She wanted him to compare that to the amount of energy he used each week to find a job. If nothing else made sense to Lewis, this would. Lewis hated wasting time, and he hated wasting energy. Stella just needed to appeal to the part of him that thought logically and rationally.

Stella and Lewis had been married for thirty-five years. They had a foundation of trust and honesty in their relationship. Lewis listened to Stella and knew that she was right. He cried for the first time since he was laid off. He cried for the loss of his job, for the loss of his friend, for the guilt he felt about hurting his family, and for allowing himself to become such an angry and pitiful man. He did not want to confront Carl with his anger, because he knew in his heart that Carl was not to blame; in fact Lewis knew he would have probably done the same thing if he had been in Carl's position.

Lewis had been so self-absorbed and so depressed in the last year that he had lost perspective altogether. He did not realize how offensive he had been to his wife. For that, he was truly sorry. He admitted that he was letting this loss keep him from taking control of his life. He needed to make himself stop hurting and make better use of the rest of his life. So, he made a plan for job hunting and got started the next day.

Key Points

1. Talk to the person you are upset with rather than taking out your emotions on family members or others.
2. When your thoughts become repetitive and do not help with resolution, make yourself stop thinking about the hurt.
3. Gain perspective by thinking about how your anger or other emotions are negatively affecting you and those you love.
4. Take stock of how much energy you are using to stay upset and to think about the stressful event. Ask yourself if you are spending more energy to stay upset than you are to try to get over the event and move on.

IS FORGIVENESS POSSIBLE?

Forgiving those who have hurt us is easier said than done. Some people may be difficult or almost impossible to forgive, or at least they may seem that way at first. For example, when people force us into an unwelcomed life transition, such as ending a relationship, it can be hard to find it in your heart to forgive them. Why is forgiveness necessary? It is not in your best interest to hold a grudge against someone. It hardens your heart and prevents you from experiencing warm and tender feelings toward others. It can feel like carrying a sack of rocks around all the time, weighing you down. You may be justified in your anger. It may be reasonable that you hurt. But after a while it is just a waste of energy.

Connie started feeling depressed after she and her best friend, Amelia, had a falling out that ended their lifelong friendship. It started with a misunderstanding over a piece of borrowed and broken jewelry and blossomed into a screaming match with each slinging insults and criticisms dating back to their childhood. The fight had been fueled by pent-up resentment, exhaustion, and tongues loosened by too much alcohol. The aftermath was a stalemate. Each refused to initiate contact with the other. For the first few months, Connie alternated between feeling angry and sad, hating Amelia, and missing her.

She tried to tell herself that she didn't need Amelia, didn't want to be friends with her, and would never forgive her for breaking her favorite bracelet and then lying about it. It wasn't really her nature to stay mad that long, and staying angry was exhausting for Connie. It was also wearing on the nerves of her other friends who understood Connie's complaints, but didn't want to take sides. Finally, Connie ran out of steam and had to decide what she was going to do to get over the hurt. Holding on to her hurt feelings meant that she was the only one suffering. The only reasonable alternative for Connie was to find a way to forgive Amelia and get on with her life. To pull this off, Connie wanted Amelia to know just how much their disagreement had hurt her feelings. She also wanted Amelia to know that she regretted the hurtful things she had said to Amelia during their argument.

Connie arranged a visit through a mutual friend and calmly told Amelia that she had hurt her feelings because she lied about the bracelet. Amelia did not believe that she had done anything wrong, but decided to apologize for the way she handled things and the mean things that she had said to Connie. Connie apologized as well. Although they forgave each other for the event, the hostility that emerged that night and the hurtful things that were said would not be soon forgotten. Amelia had no trouble resuming their friendship as it had been before the fight. Connie had always been the one whose feelings were most easily hurt. She tended to take things personally, especially when she was feeling depressed. She had more difficulty shaking off Amelia's criticisms.

The process of forgiveness involves releasing anger toward another person. When you have accomplished this you free yourself of the burden of holding on to those bad feelings. If you are not certain how to go about forgiving another person, you might find it helpful to talk with a forgiveness expert—a member of the clergy or a spiritual leader. The Spirituality Key also offers some new ideas for transcending hurt feelings and finding greater peace in your life.

Lessons Learned the Hard Way

It is human nature to look back on your life and your actions and have regrets. With perfect hindsight we can usually see what we should have done or said, what we wish we had done, and how we might have dealt with things better. When we realize that we handled a transition in life badly, hurting others, hurting ourselves, or just missing out on good times, we kick ourselves. It is OK to do this as long as you use your new insights to make positive changes in your life.

For example, there is almost always a lesson to learn in your experiences with your children. If you figure out a better way to handle things with them, do it next time. If your kids are grown, pass on the lesson to them or handle your grandchildren in a different way.

Relationships teach us a lot about ourselves. As you grow older you learn more about how you contribute in positive and negative ways to your marriage, your working relationships, and your friendships. Rather than beat yourself up when you realize you have made mistakes in the past, use the information to make improvements with the next person you meet, or at least try to avoid making the same mistakes again.

Adriana had been married three times, and all of the marriages ended in divorce. Each time she thought the relationship would be different, but each time she found that she had made the same mistake— choosing men who liked to drink. Adriana knew that she was making a mistake with husband #3, but she ignored that little voice of experience in her head and told herself it would be different this time. She was learning from her mistakes, but it was taking her a long time to get it right.

Joanie learned that she had been too overprotective with her first child, Liz. When Liz got out of high school and went to college she went berserk. Finally, out from under mother's control, Liz did everything her mother warned her against. Joanie knew why her daughter was acting this way and regretted being so controlling and restrictive. She did not want to swing completely the other way with her second daughter, but she clearly needed to loosen up. By the time her third daughter was in high school, Joanie had figured out when to say "yes" and when to say "no," when to make a big deal out of things and when to let it slide, when to insist on clothing choices and when to allow her daughter some freedom of expression. Joanie's younger two children did not have to try so hard to rebel when they went off to college, and Joanie was proud that she had finally gotten it right.

Shawn noticed that his father was much more patient with the grandchildren than he had been with him. Shawn complimented his father on this and inquired about why he had changed his philosophy of parenting.

> *I was so afraid of something happening to you and your sister that I always kept a close eye on you. I was afraid you would not learn to be a polite person, so I punished you when you got out of line even a little. I was afraid that harm might come to you, so I kept you from exploring in the woods or spending the nights at friends' houses. When I realized you and your sister turned out all right, that no harm befell you, I figured out that I had probably worried over nothing. If I could do it all again with what I know now, you probably would have had more fun growing up.*

Pat's graduate school professor was difficult to please, demanding, uncaring, and rude at times. Dr. Nelson was new to teaching at the time and Pat was his first real student. He was too young to have children of her age so he treated her the way he thought a professor should. He made a lot of mistakes, and Pat was right there to call him on it every time he messed up. Although he acted defensively at first, he respected Pat's assertiveness and learned how to be a supervisor during his time with her. He put his regrets to good use by learning to treat future students more fairly, by showing compassion for their struggle through school, and by relaxing more in the classroom.

Pat dealt with her "horrible" graduate school experience, by becoming "all that he was not." She enjoyed teaching and her students respected her. Her strategy was to "undo" all the stupid things that Dr. Nelson did to her by treating her students in a more respectful manner. After a while, both Pat and Dr. Nelson became excellent professors.

Romances Gone Sour

Most people, at some point in their lives, experience a painful ending to a romantic relationship. Usually we get over them with time, but

---

Key Point

Over time, you will learn how you contribute in positive and negative ways to your relationships with others. Rather than beat yourself up when you realize you have made a mistake, use the information to make improvements with the next person you meet or at least try to avoid making the same mistakes again.

---

until then we can react to the pain and humiliation of the loss in a way that can negatively affect new relationships. In the section below, we cover some common problems in the way that people respond to failed relationships. We offer some suggestions for alternative ways to cope that might give new relationships a better chance of flourishing.

"I'LL NEVER DO THAT AGAIN."

If you have been through a bad relationship, it is easy to say that you will never get involved again. In the aftermath, it might seem that relationships are not worth the trouble. When our patients say they'll never date again or never get married again, they are usually wrong. If you are a people person and you like being in relationships, you will very likely try to find love again. Your emotional wounds will eventually heal.

We have been saying throughout this book that the way you think about things will influence your choice of actions. If you think that you will get hurt again, you may avoid starting new relationships. Avoidance, however, leads to loneliness. Prolonged loneliness can set you up for depression. Believing that you will get hurt again may be jumping to conclusions. You cannot predict the future of new relationships before they start. The way to correct this thinking error is to test out your prediction.

Another reason that people swear off new relationships is because they view the past ones with tunnel vision. When you are feeling sad it is easy to remember only the bad times, forgetting the pleasant memories. Rather than thinking of past relationships as "bad" or "horrible" or "totally dysfunctional," make yourself think of both the good times and the bad times. This more realistic view will keep you from condemning the relationship altogether and will help you with your recovery.

"IT SEEMED SO RIGHT"

You've probably heard the old adage "You have to take the good with the bad." In relationships, good elements or good characteristics in a partner can have a flip side that is not so positive. For example, if you meet a man or woman who is involved in developing a career you may find this attractive. But, there may be a downside. Investing a great deal of time in building a career may mean that your partner has less time for you. You may feel left out, begin to question your priority in the relationship, and develop resentments. There are usually two sides to even the best characteristics. Knowing this will help you tolerate the bad aspects when you realize that they have a positive side as well. It will also help you not take a globally positive view of the other person and overlook potential pitfalls in the relationship.

Michelle was attracted to her husband's athletic skills and ability. He played ice hockey or refereed the sport several times each week. She enjoyed accompanying him to hockey games and cheering from the crowd, until their lives got so busy with children that she no longer had the time. Her husband, however, kept his hockey schedule, often missing family events or neglecting family responsibilities that conflicted with the games. The traits that Michelle first admired she eventually came to despise. His "priorities" became one of the points of contention that eventually ended the marriage.

Another common example of the flip side to positive qualities is when you meet someone who is currently in the process of ending an ongoing relationship. He or she may tell you about the problem in the current relationship and how you are so much more fun. Most people would not question this one-sided view of the relationship. Instead you are more likely to feel compassionate and understanding. You see the person's positive qualities, so it is easy to assume that the relationship problems are the fault of the other partner. While you are falling for this person, you may overlook one important detail. He or she is willing to start a new relationship with you before ending the previous one. It is very easy to fool yourself into believing that this is a unique occurrence and that it would never happen in a relationship with you. Many of our patients have kicked themselves for ignoring this fact when their partners eventually leave them for someone new. "I should have seen this coming. How could I be so stupid?"

ON THE REBOUND

When you are hurting from the traumatic ending of a romance you are vulnerable to falling too easily for someone new. Your emotions are usually mixed up and your perceptions of things are colored by your pain. You might see yourself as unlovable and pitiful. This mindset makes it easy to respond to someone who tells you otherwise. Getting attention from someone new and being complimented helps to dispel your negative beliefs about yourself. When you have a better self-view you start to feel better. It is easy to give all the credit for your recovery to the person who gave you the attention. When this happens it is easy to ignore the signs that this new relationship may not be a healthy alternative.

FINISH WHAT YOU START

The best way to assure that a new relationship is not colored by the loss of an old one is to give yourself time to recover from the loss before you launch into anything new. You can use the methods from any of the Five Keys to help you overcome your pain. Put the start of new relationships on hold until you feel like you are in pretty good shape. One way to know when you are ready is when you find yourself not needing a partner. When this happens, you can enter the new relationship because you want a partner, not because you need one.

Making New Plans

If you are faced with life transitions that you do not like there are four options that will help you resolve the discomfort. They are to: (1) learn to tolerate the change, (2) adapt to the change, (3) change your role, or (4) continue the role in a different form or with a different person. Much of this chapter has been dedicated to the first two options. By working through negative thinking about life transitions and making yourself look at both the pluses and minuses, you can learn to tolerate the transition or adapt to it.

If you do not like the role your life transition has left you with, there may be a way to change it. Obviously some roles can be relinquished while others cannot. If you have been made a supervisor on a job and you hate it, consider giving up that task or finding another job. If you are a stay-at-home mom and you find that it does not suit you well, go back to your usual activities and engage someone to help you with child care. If you do not like retirement, find another job or do a project on your own. If you do not like the role of spouse, work with your partner to change it in some way. Perhaps you could give up parts of the role you don't like (such as cooking dinner every night, giving your money over to someone else to manage).

There may be some circumstances in which you can continue a role in life rather than accept its loss. For example, if you are unhappy with an empty household after your children have left the nest and moved out on their own, you can find other people to care for in your home or in your community. If you are someone who is a caretaker by nature, put that talent to good use rather than settle for a life alone.

If you are used to being involved with people and it is time for you to retire, find new activities that allow you to interact with others. If you really liked caring for babies, try babysitting for other families. If you are someone who likes living alone and you are starting a new relationship, negotiate with your new partner for some alone time or solitary activities. Just make certain that you do not spend so much time by yourself that you neglect the relationship. These are all examples of keeping elements of your old role in life and applying them to new circumstances.

There are some roles that cannot change, may not be negotiable, and may not be very tolerable. Frances, for example, now takes care of her aging parents. They are ill, limited in their mobility, and completely dependent on her. Financially, it would be nearly impossible to hire someone else to do it. Frances is an only child so there is no one else to help, and her parents do not want to go to a nursing home. Frances doesn't want to feel stuck. She wants to have a positive and loving attitude about this new role as caretaker. To keep herself from getting depressed or becoming resentful of her parents, Frances needs to find ways to take a break from this role and take care of herself while she is caring for her parents. She decides that she will try to find someone to relieve her from her duties from time to time, make more contact with her friends, and find ways to enjoy her time with her parents.

The Relationship Key in Your Personal Plan for Recovery

It's time to update your recovery plan by selecting issues from the Relationship Key that need your attention. Here are a few questions to help you make a plan.

Exercise 11.4
Personal Plan for Recovery Worksheet—Part VII
'My Plan for Using the Relationship Key':

CONSUELO'S EXAMPLE

1. What are your biggest relationship challenges?
   Finish grieving the loss of my husband.
   Stop feeling guilty for feeling some relief that he is gone from my life.
   Develop new relationships.

2. Are you caught in a vicious cycle where your reactions to your symptoms are creating new problems? How would you describe the cycle?
   My crying jags are my way of letting out my pain, but are making me feel more sad and keeping me from getting on with my life.
   Trying not to burden others with my problems is creating distance between my friends and myself. They respect my need for privacy by keeping their distance. But without their support, I'm having a hard time making it on my own. My isolation is making me feel worse rather than better.

3. What are some things you can change about yourself that might help resolve your relationship problems?
   I can reach out to others.
   Rather than sit home alone and cry, I could call a friend, go out, and try to have a good time.

4. Which will you try first?
   I'll try accepting my friends' offers to go to dinner.

5. What are the life transitions that are causing you stress or distress?
   Being a single mother.
   Being a single woman who wants companionship someday.

6. In what ways are these problems for you?
   I worry about doing well by my sons.
   My husband had convinced me that I was ugly and unlovable. I'm not sure any man would want me.

7. What methods have you already used in trying to cope with these transitions?

I give my sons a lot of attention. I talk with them about losing their father. I give them a chance to share their feelings about their loss.

I haven't done anything about dating. I'm not ready to think about it yet.

8. What has worked?

    The boys seem to be responding to my efforts so far.

9. What new methods do you need to try?

    I need to try reaching out to others more, give my friends some attention, and have quality time with other adults.

    I need to ask my sons about their grief rather than assuming that they are in as much pain as I am.

10. Do you have any opportunities to change a role or elements of a role in a way that would make your life better?

    I have opportunities to socialize. I just haven't taken advantage of them.

11. Make a plan for how you are going to make these adjustments.

    I'm going to accept the next invitation to dinner that I get and make myself go even if I am tired.

    I will consider having a dinner party at my home. I might even invite a man from work.

The Spirituality Key

12

Finding Meaning

Spirituality is an especially important part of the Five Keys to recovery because it helps unite and give direction to all of the other approaches to depression. For most of us, spirituality is at the core of our being. It adds depth, meaning, and purpose to the other elements of daily life. And, a spiritual orientation gives a road map for the path ahead.

In our work with patients, we are continually impressed by the richness and diversity of spiritual beliefs, practices, and resources. Almost all of our patients describe themselves as spiritual persons, even if they do not have a traditional religious affiliation. Although everyone has his or her own unique spiritual life, some common elements are shared by many people from different cultures, backgrounds, religions, or other beliefs. The four elements of spirituality described below are adapted from the work of Dr. Fredrick Luskin from Stanford University and Dr. Roger Walsh, the author of *Essential Spirituality*.

Elements of Spirituality

1. Having meaning and purpose in life
2. Being connected to life and people, giving to others
3. Feeling that mind, body, and spirit are unified and whole
4. Having faith in a higher power and/or a greater good or purpose

Depression can have an impact on each of these four elements of spirituality. For example, if you are depressed, you may have trouble finding meaning in your life. When this happens you may be more likely to think about giving up and stop trying as hard to face your difficulties. The Viennese psychiatrist Viktor Frankl observed in his book *Man's Search for Meaning* that having a deep sense of purpose, and taking action to fulfill this purpose, can allow people to face the worst circumstances and to fight off hopelessness and depression. In making this point, Frankl often quoted the words of the philosopher Nietzsche: "He who has a 'why' to live for can bear almost any 'how'." A major part of using the Spirituality Key in the battle against depression is looking for the "why" in your life.

Most authorities on spirituality emphasize the importance of being committed to something that goes beyond your own personal needs and desires, so that you are connected to others and you give something to better the lives of other people. Depression can make you feel distant or disconnected from family or friends, work, or other involvements. Because depression often makes people turn inward, you can have a decreased ability to show concern for others. However, if you can resist the tendency to withdraw into yourself, and you can reconnect with the important people and commitments in your life, you will be taking a significant step forward in your recovery from depression.

Another possible spiritual problem in depression is losing a sense of feeling like a whole person. If you have ever attended a YMCA, you may remember seeing the slogan "Spirit, Mind, Body." There is a good purpose for using this slogan to convey the ideals of the YMCA. For many of us, spirituality is the glue that holds all of our pieces together—that gives us a sense of wholeness and integrity. Depression can make people go in the opposite direction to the point where they are fragmented, dispirited, and adrift. An advantage of paying attention to your spirituality as you work on recovery from depression is that you may feel more solid and whole again.

Depression can also affect basic beliefs such as faith in God or other fundamental philosophies of life. Some individuals become more involved with their churches or synagogues or have a deepening of their spiritual orientation. However, many others have a crisis of faith or drift away from their usual spiritual practices. Later in the Spirituality Key we will discuss methods of coping with the negative effects of depression on faith in a higher power or in a greater good or purpose.

According to Dr Fredrick Luskin and other experts on spirituality and wellness, having a positive spiritual orientation can have significant benefits in improving health. For example, many studies have shown that attendance at religious services increases the life span. Prayer has been shown to have a beneficial effect on treatment of patients with heart disease. And, putting spirituality into practice by doing volunteer work has been associated with dramatic declines in mortality rates. In a review of research on religion and depression, Dr. Dale Matthews and his associates from Georgetown University discovered that most studies found a decreased rate of depression and suicide in those who are involved in spiritual activities.

Key Point

A positive spiritual orientation can improve your physical health and mental well-being.

When we try to help our patients use the Spirituality Key, we use a broad definition of spirituality that includes all of the four elements: a sense of meaning; a connection to others and giving to others; a sense of wholeness in which spirit, mind, and body are united; and faith in a higher power and/or a greater good or purpose. This definition helps us reach the most people and allows us to give them the most assistance in using the spiritual dimension as a part of their Personal Plan for Recovery. The rest of this chapter will be devoted primarily to describing ways to develop a greater sense of meaning and purpose in life. The next chapter will help you work on building your spirituality as an antidote to depression.

Lessons from Logotherapy

Man's Search for Meaning by Viktor Frankl has been described as one of the *"ten most influential books in America"* by the Library of Congress and the Book-of-the-Month Club. In this book, Dr. Frankl tells how he developed a new form of psychotherapy, which he called "logotherapy," out of his experiences in World War II concentration camps. His wife, father, mother, and brother all died in a concentration camp. Only he and his sister survived. In the preface to *Man's Search for Meaning,* Dr. Gordon Allport wrote that "a psychiatrist who has personally faced such extremity is a psychiatrist worth listening to." We agree.

The central message of Dr. Frankl's work is that a sense of meaning can help humans cope with even the most horrific experiences while retaining a spiritual integrity and a positive life force. In describing his days in a concentration camp, he wrote, "One could make a victory of those experiences, turning life into an inner triumph, or one could ignore the challenge and simply vegetate." When prisoners in the camps would lose faith in the future and give up, they would often lie on the ground and do no more. Shortly thereafter, they would be dead. However, those who had a sense of meaning, who could still envision a purpose for their lives, who could focus on a future goal, were able to keep going and had a better chance of survival.

Of course it was exceedingly difficult to retain a sense of meaning in the face of the unbelievable brutality and deprivation of the concentration camps. But, Dr. Frankl and many others were able to do it. The fundamental belief that kept Dr. Frankl's spirit alive was that no one could take away the last of human freedoms—the ability "to choose one's attitude in any given set of circumstances—to choose one's own way."

Life in the concentration camps taught Dr. Frankl that there was no single answer for meaning. Every person needed to find a special reason to live. For some it was retaining dignity in bearing suffering, or in believing that life was still expecting something from you. For many it was love for the important people in their lives. Sometimes a sense of humor helped people to gain perspective and still believe that life had a purpose. Also, "little things" such as viewing a sunset or remembering seeing a work of art or hearing music were important ways to find meaning. After the war, Dr. Frankl became a Professor at the University of Vienna and spent a long career developing the methods of logotherapy, writing influential books, and inspiring people around the world to find purpose in their lives.

The term "logotherapy" is derived from the Greek word for meaning—*Logos*. There is no set path or specific technique used in logotherapy to discover what is meaningful. But, Dr. Frankl does offer some guidelines for what meaning is and how one might find it. He considers meaning a primary motivation for life and believes that it has these characteristics: (1) It includes striving for a worthwhile goal; (2) it can be completely *"down to earth"* and can include the little things—simple acts of experiencing life; (3) it includes acting responsibly in the world; (4) the more one moves from a self-centered existence to loving and doing for others, the more one is likely to find meaning; (5) a sense of meaning can change and evolve over a person's lifetime.

The message here seems to be that meaning can be found it many areas of our lives—it doesn't have to be a Mother Teresa type of dedication and commitment. For example, Dr. Frankl talks about finding meaning in an act of goodness or truth; in experiencing nature, beauty,

Key Point

To find meaning, you need to put your ideas into action.

or culture; in loving someone; or in creating a work or deed. Another way to find meaning is to accept an inevitable loss, such as a serious illness or a reversal of fortune, and make it a spiritual victory. Whatever you find to be meaningful, Dr. Frankl recommends that you take action to do something about it.

There are two parts to using the principles of logotherapy. First you need to find what is meaningful to you. Then you need to commit yourself to actively live in a way that expresses this meaning. In the next section of the chapter, we will give you examples of how some of the people we have known have done this.

Ways to Find Meaning

FACING AN ILLNESS, COPING WITH A LOSS

We have repeatedly seen examples of how the meaning one attaches to an illness or a loss can lead to a deepened sense of purpose and resolve. The story of a woman from one of our clinical practices illustrates the way that finding meaning in adversity can influence recovery from depression. Cecilia is a forty-two-year-old woman who had been depressed for over two years when she was referred for a consultation. After hearing about Cecilia's life, it was easy to see why she had been depressed. She had a host of problems that would have devastated many people. Her son, Alex, had a severe developmental disability and required intensive supervision. The demands of taking care of Alex had taken a toll on her marriage. John, her husband, had moved out three years ago, and now played only a minor role in helping out with Alex and her other two children. He occasionally sent child support, but Cecilia could never count on it. She was almost totally dependent on her salary as a teacher to make ends meet. And then to top things off, she had learned recently that she had rheumatoid arthritis—a form of bone and joint disease that can cause significant pain and deformities.

These problems could have defeated Cecilia. Yet, she was able to see a purpose in the challenges she faced.

THERAPIST: "You have so many problems to deal with everyday—what keeps you going? How do you keep fighting?"

CECILIA: "Sometimes I'm not sure. It's pretty tough to take care of Alex and somehow get off to work and take care of all of my other responsibilities. When it comes down to it, I guess what really keeps me going is believing that I can handle all this suffering—that if I can keep plugging away, I'll be a good Mom to my kids and I'll end up a stronger person."

THERAPIST: "How could having to cope with so many problems and going through a depression make you stronger?"

CECILIA: "I'm closer to the children than I ever was before, and I'm learning a lot about how to solve problems—or at least get them under control. You told me the story a couple of weeks ago about 'the things that don't break you can make you stronger.' I think the story is true. I know I have a hard road ahead of me, but I can learn to handle things better."

Cecilia found meaning in many other things in her life—her love for her children, close relationships with two of her old friends, and her work as a teacher. The depression had initially seemed to distance her from these important things. But, as she started paying more attention to what really counted for her, she found it easier to deal with her problems and work toward recovery from depression.

Could facing a significant illness or a loss be a way for you to find more meaning in your life? Anybody who becomes depressed has this opportunity. In his book *Care of the Soul,* Thomas Moore tells us that life doesn't always have to be cheerful. We can be "instructed by melancholy." Depression can be an "initiator, a rite of passage." We certainly wouldn't recommend that you become depressed in order to reexamine your life and find new meanings. After all, depression is a painful and sometimes disabling condition. But if you are depressed, why not view this problem as a potential learning experience—a way to grow and develop a newfound appreciation of life?

Instead of viewing depression as all negative, try to see how coping with this problem could make you stronger or add meaning to your existence. Our patients are often able to do this. Do you remember Vic, the architect from Chapter 3 who froze at his desk one night in a flood of depression and panic? Like Cecilia, he found a way to gain strength from his battle against depression. Vic was a perfectionist and a workaholic who couldn't accept himself the way he was or relax enough to enjoy life. After treatment for depression, Vic could see that even though his period of depression was very painful, it taught him to focus on the things that were truly important to him—his wife and children, doing good work for his clients, and making a difference in his community. Instead of being so self-absorbed and measuring himself all the time, he turned his energies outward and became a person with a more balanced and purposeful life.

Physical illnesses such as heart disease, stroke, and cancer or other significant stresses and losses can shake you up and make you think about what really counts in your life. A good friend, Jim Rives, had this happen to him after his heart stopped beating while he was in an airport in Chicago. Jim was one of the first people to be saved by defibrillators (heart-shocking devices that start the heart again) that have been installed in some airports and other public places. He had been coming home from a vacation with his wife when he suddenly felt faint. In a few moments he had stopped breathing and had turned blue. A young resident doctor, who had been trained in use of the defibrillator, just happened to be passing by and became Jim's *"savior."* A few days later, as I (Jesse) visited Jim in his hospital room, the air was thick with emotion. Here was a person who had been saved by what appeared to be a miraculous set of events. If he had been on the plane or at home, he wouldn't have been close to a defibrillator and probably would have died. What was to be made of all of this? Was there a reason that he was rescued? Where did he go from here?

These dramatic events had a profound effect on Jim. Even before his heart stopped and he was given a second chance, he was the kind of person who thought first about others, who went out of his way to learn about what they needed and what their problems were. And, he was a deeply spiritual person who continually lived his life with a clear sense of purpose. But after his recovery from the heart problem, he became even more attuned to the spiritual dimension of his life. He became a national spokesperson for installing defibrillators in public places to save lives. On a more personal level, he became exquisitely sensitive to and appreciative of the joys of living. Jim is an inspiration to many of us. He teaches us by his example to try to live our lives as fully and meaningfully as we can.

A final example of how illness or loss can play a role in the way you forge your direction in life comes from an experience that one of us had as a teenager. I (Jesse) was sledding one winter's evening many years ago with my two best friends when tragedy struck. Dall's sled crashed, and by the time we got to him he was unconscious. My other friend, Larry, and I had both been trained in first aid. Still we couldn't do anything to help Dall. He was taken to the hospital in an ambulance, but by the next morning he was dead.

I was devastated. What sense could you make of a really great kid dying when he was only sixteen? It was very hard to come to grips with this loss. And even today, thinking back over this incident still gives me a lot of pain. When I visit my old hometown and pass by the place where the accident happened, the images from that evening so many years ago still sear my heart and mind. Yet, Dall's death became part of my meaning in life. Because he wasn't able to grow up and do things with his life, I would have to make sure that, at least in a small way, I would live for him. And, I would need to do something to make things safer or better for others. As I reflect back on this tragedy and how it impacted me, I realize that my life's work as a doctor, and the love and concern I show for my children, is rooted in part to how I responded to the loss of my friend Dall.

The examples we have given here may not be exactly like the traumas that you have experienced. But almost everyone has had a loss or an illness that affects him or her deeply. One way to find meaning or purpose is to see how these problems can be converted into a positive life force, a direction for change, a way to learn new things, or a call to live your life differently in the future. There are many other ways to find meaning. As Victor Frankl has noted, you don't have to suffer to find a purpose for existing. For many people, a good part of the meaning of life comes from appreciating small things and savoring what life has to offer.

FINDING MEANING IN EVERYDAY THINGS

Roger Walsh, the author of *Essential Spirituality,* has observed that many of us act as if we are sleepwalking through life. We *"stumble mindlessly through our days"* and miss the beautiful and meaningful things that are right under our noses. Often these are everyday things such as the subtle aromas and tastes of food, the different rhythms and sounds of music, and the beauty of the world around us. William Styron, the Pulitzer Prize–winning author who suffered from depression, wrote about this in his book *Darkness Visible.* When Styron was in the deepest part of his depression, he was numb to the world. He had retreated into a cave of despair that shut him off from all of the things that used to mean so much to him. All he could think about was ending his misery. But, then by chance he heard an alto solo from a Brahms symphony that was being played in a movie he was watching. Suddenly he was struck with the great beauty of this music. As the music washed over him and he began to have feelings again, he thought of all the other things he would miss if he killed himself—seeing his family, working and loving, his pets, festivals, even "honestly earned slumber." Getting back in touch with how much music and some of the other everyday things meant to him was one of the turning points in his recovery from depression.

Jon Kabat-Zinn, the renowned psychiatrist and author of books such as *Full Catastrophe Living* and *Wherever You Go, There You Are,* recommends that we practice ways to be mindful of the joys of life and to seek out opportunities to experience what life has to offer. He urges all of us to fight the natural tendency to fall into a state of "mindlessness"— an ignorance of what is really going on around us. A spiritual goal for Jon Kabat-Zinn, Roger Walsh, and many other influential writers on spirituality and personal growth (see Recommended Readings in the Appendix) is to seek out a state of "mindfulness." Being mindful means that you pay attention, in a purposeful way, to the world around and within you so that you are fully in touch with life.

One of the techniques that Jon Kabat-Zinn suggests for accomplishing this task is "mindfulness meditation." We'll describe ways of meditating to expand spiritual awareness in the next chapter. Meditation can help people build awareness, become more mindful, and find meaning in everyday things. However, you don't have to meditate to become a mindful person.

Roger Walsh describes a number of different ways to increase your sense of awareness including: (1) eating mindfully—paying great attention to the textures, smells, taste, and appearance of your food; (2) becoming a good listener—to what people say, to music, to what you read; (3) finding beauty in the moment—appreciating what is happening now instead of putting off finding meaning until something great or momentous happens; and (4) developing a heightened awareness of your body.

The benefits of finding meaning in everyday things were illustrated vividly in the treatment of Anne Marie, the woman from Chapter 4 who was driven by the schema "If I choose to do something, I must succeed no matter what the cost." You may remember that she was having trouble both at work and in her marriage and wouldn't do anything unless she was striving for success. Her guiding philosophy was "I must succeed or else." Living with this kind of attitude left no room for appreciating everyday things. When she thought of joining a tennis league, it was only to prove she could be a good tennis player—not to meet new friends, to take pleasure in moving her body or striking the ball, or to laugh at her mistakes.

Part of Anne Marie's therapy was using methods to stimulate awareness, like the ones described in Exercise 12.1, to open herself up to the potential meaning of everyday things. Although it took some time, she eventually began to appreciate the world around her. This made her less self-centered and helped to enrich her life. She recounted one particularly striking example after she had accepted an invitation from a friend to go on a walk to see some wildflowers.

Her first inclination was to say no to the invitation. Ordinarily she would have thought that spending a Saturday having a leisurely lunch with her friend and then striking out to look at some flowers in the woods would have been a waste of time. It didn't fit well with her schemas about always pursuing success. But Anne Marie was trying to change, to open herself up to the "small things" that could give her life more balance and depth. So, she said yes and spent the Saturday with her friend.

Later she described what the day meant to her. "It was awesome! I hadn't felt that much pure joy in years. There were thousands, maybe millions of bluebells; and there were wood hyacinths everywhere. It was a sea of blue. I'd forgotten how much I love being out in nature. That section of the forest with all of those flowers has been there, virtually right in my backyard, without me even seeing it. Jane has been asking me to go there every spring for years and I always found an excuse not to go. I need to start doing more of this type of thing."

Here are some exercises you can try that could build your awareness of meaningful things around you.

Exercise 12.1
Building Awareness for Everyday Things

1. Try to open yourself up to the meaning of everyday things such as the food you eat, the work you do, a hobby, or other parts of your daily routine. Pick at least three of these things and savor them—try to get the most out of experiencing these things.
2. Set aside a day or a part of a day to appreciate the natural world. Go on a hike, work in a garden, or just sit and watch a sunset. Try to free your mind from worries and concerns so you can get in touch with the beauty around you.
3. Try something new that you ordinarily wouldn't do. For example, take a cooking class, go for a swim, or ride a bike if you aren't doing these things now. Take the opportunity to find out if things you have ignored or have been avoiding could be meaningful to you.
4. Make the effort to do something with a person you know. Try to increase your awareness of the other person. Step aside from your personal concerns and try to really listen to the other person so that you will know him or her better and will have a more meaningful relationship.
5. Try to open your senses fully so you can appreciate the music you hear, the words you read, the sports you play, or any of your other regular activities. Try to avoid "sleepwalking" through life. Pay attention to everyday activities that could have more meaning for you.

DISCOVERING YOUR LIFE PHILOSOPHY

We all have basic beliefs, attitudes, and guiding principles that give our life direction and meaning. In Chapter 4, we talked about the schemas that underlie self-esteem. If you completed the exercises in Chapter 4, you should have a list of some of these schemas in your notebook. In addition to these schemas, you probably have other, more fundamental beliefs that are part of your unique philosophy of life.

Roger Walsh urges his readers to try to capture their philosophy of life in three words. Gandhi's was "Renounce and Rejoice." This philosophy served Gandhi well as he led millions in the way of peaceful resistance. We think that Dr. Walsh's suggestion to articulate a philosophy of life in three words would be quite a challenge for most people. However, he has a good point. If you can think through your guiding principles and state them in a few short words or sentences, you may be able to get a better sense of what is truly meaningful to you.

For those with strong religious beliefs and values, a philosophy of life will probably contain a basic message about these important principles. A short statement of your personal philosophy might also contain your core beliefs about the meaning or purpose in your life and the key schemas or attitudes that you would like to emphasize in daily living.

As part of her recovery process from depression, Anne Marie worked on articulating a personal philosophy that was much broader than her old, narrowly focused drive for "success or else." As with many of us, her philosophy of life is still a "work in progress." At last account, Anne Marie listed these beliefs and attitudes as part of her core philosophy: (1) help others through my work; (2) try to do my best; let success come if it will, but stop pursuing it as a goal; (3) have faith in God and live a good life; (4) pay attention to little things; enjoy them.

Although it can be difficult to try to articulate your personal philosophy in a few words, the effort may be very worthwhile. Exercise 12.2 can help you focus your attention on the things that count most for you in life.

LOVING AND GIVING

All of the world's great religions extol the virtues of loving others and giving as a way of finding meaning and purpose in life. In the Introduction to *Essential Spirituality,* the Dalai Lama notes that all people, even those without a religious affiliation, can share compassion. Viktor Frankl also believes that love for others should have a central position in everyone's personal philosophy. In *Man's Search for Meaning* he writes

Exercise 12.2
Writing Down Your Personal Philosophy

1. Spend some time thinking about your philosophy of life. Try to capture this philosophy in a few words or sentences.
2. Think of your religious beliefs or your beliefs in a greater good or purpose. Include a statement about these guiding principles in your philosophical statement.
3. Other common things to include in a philosophical statement are your core attitudes about relationships with others, work, or life goals.
4. Try to include in your philosophical statement something about what is meaningful to you and what you plan to do about it.
5. Don't write your philosophical statement *"in stone."* Be willing to revise or expand the statement as you go through life and have new experiences.

that "love is the ultimate and highest goal to which man can aspire. . . . The salvation of man is through love and in love."

Some of the most touching parts of Frankl's writings concern his love for his wife—a love that transcended the brutality of the concentration camp, a forced separation from his wife, and the ultimate realization that she was dead. "My mind still clung to the image of my wife. A thought crossed my mind: I didn't even know if she were still alive. I knew one thing—which I have learned well by now: Love goes very far beyond the physical person of the beloved. It finds its deepest meaning in his spiritual being, his inner self . . . nothing could touch the strength of my love, my thoughts, and the image of my beloved."

Depression often mutes or disguises feelings of love. Because depression makes you turn inward, you may inadvertently pull away from your loved ones or have difficulty in showing compassion for others. You also may find that it is difficult to love God or yourself. Tony, the man described in Chapters 2 and 3 who was having trouble with his wife's promotion, is a typical case of the negative effects of depression on loving relationships with others. He had become jealous of his wife's success, and at the same time was putting himself down for not matching her achievements in life. As he became more depressed, he withdrew affection from his wife, treated himself like a loser, and became more isolated and self-absorbed. Part of his recovery from depression was based on using the Thinking Key to change his negative automatic thoughts and the Action Key to reduce his self-defeating behavior. But, he also needed to work on getting back to some of the things that had meant the most to him, particularly his feelings of love for his wife. Ultimately he was able to care for her deeply again, to share in her successes, and to give her his loving attention.

In her book, *Love Is a Verb,* Mary Ellen Edmunds underscores the need to put love into action in order to fulfill one of the central purposes of life. She tells us that love is not an "armchair philosophy." Just thinking in a loving way is usually not enough for people to have love give them deep personal meaning. You need to do something to share your love. Putting love into action can include big things such as making a major sacrifice for someone you love, devoting a large part of your life to service to others, or putting someone you love before yourself. It also can include day-to-day things like washing the dishes when you don't want to do it, showing a small kindness to a person, or going out of your way to do a favor for someone. Depression can make it hard to do these things. But if you can work on building this meaningful part of your life, it may help you get back to your old self.

CREATING SOMETHING OR DOING A DEED

Another way to find meaning is to create something or to do a deed that can make a difference, if even in a small way. During his three years in the concentration camp, one of the things that kept Victor Frankl going was creating the book that was to come from his experiences there. Even though he had no paper and pencil, he kept thinking of the ideas. After he was released, *Man's Search for Meaning* poured out of him in only nine days. Few people have the genius to create a work like Frankl's. Yet, most people are capable of creating something that can make a difference to them or others and give their life added dimension.

Michelle, the woman from Chapter 1 who became depressed after a divorce, had reached the point where she felt she was useless. She had dropped out of most of her activities and was avoiding contact with her friends. As part of her recovery plan, Michelle tried to think of things that would make her feel alive again—that would start to fill her life with some purpose. After she started back attending church, an opportunity fell right in her lap. The choirs of all of the churches in her part of town were planning a joint concert. They really needed someone to head up the publicity efforts for the concert—to get the word out so that people would know about the event.

Michelle had done some publicity work before for a community theater group, so she knew what needed to be done. Although she was still feeling somewhat depressed, she decided to take on this project. It would give her something to take her mind off her divorce, and it would be a good thing to do for others. She wasn't creating any grand piece of art, writing a book, or designing a beautiful sculpture. But, she was doing something that was meaningful to her and to other people.

Earlier in this chapter we outlined the two basic tenets of logotherapy: finding things that are meaningful and then taking action to do something about it. Michelle did both in this example. She found a project that meant something to her, an activity in which she could use her energies, her intelligence, and her creative skills; and then she set to work.

If you can find a way to create something that connects to other people, in which your actions could possibly have an effect on them, then you are likely to have a deeper sense of purpose in the activity. You can do this in your work, your hobbies, your creative outlets, or in your relationships with the people in your life. Here are some examples.

As Vic was recovering from depression, he began to realize that he had been ignoring how much the creative side of his work as an architect meant to him. He had become so focused on measuring his performance and worrying about project deadlines that he had forgotten why he chose to be an architect in the first place—to use his creative abilities to design buildings that made life better for people and that made them feel good about the places where they lived or worked. The same kind of positive changes occurred when Anne Marie began to get better. Anne Marie found a renewed meaning in her everyday work as a doctor after she started to pay attention again to things like the excitement and challenge of making a difficult diagnosis and the good feelings she got when she was able to use her knowledge to make people better. Tony had stopped doing work on an old car he was restoring. It just seemed like too much effort when he was depressed. But, he got going again when he began to think about how much fun his two brothers would have with him if he could get the car ready and they could all go to the car shows next year.

Many people have creative outlets such as music, art work, or gardening—or interests such as collecting things, playing bridge or chess, or refinishing antiques—that are very meaningful to them. For some, the creative process and the things they produce are part of their life's work and are central to their sense of purpose. For others, their creative side is only a small portion of what makes their life worthwhile. The negative filter of depression can sometimes make it difficult to see how you are taking action to create things in your life now or what you might be able to do in the future. Exercise 12.3 may help you get some ideas for creating things, large and small, that could give you a deeper or broader sense of meaning.

Exercise 12.3
Create a Work or Do a Deed

1. Think back to the time before you were depressed, when you felt better about yourself. What were you creating then or what deeds were you doing that seemed to give your life purpose? Consider both the big and little things.
2. What creative or constructive activities are you doing now that add to the meaningfulness of your life?
3. What ideas do you have for the future? What are the ways you might be able to increase your sense of meaning through creative or constructive outlets?
4. As you reflect over your activities in the past, present, and future, try to develop a plan for capturing a deepened sense of purpose by creating a work or doing a deed. Write this down in your notebook.

STUDY AND CONTEMPLATION

One of the time-tested methods of searching for meaning is to study the works of great teachers such as religious leaders, philosophers, and others who can give wise guidance and who have demonstrated deep purpose in their own lives. Roger Walsh calls this "learning from the wise." Some of the obvious examples he gives are religious founders such as Jesus, Buddha, Confucius, and Mohammad; or more contemporary persons such as Gandhi or the Dalai Lama. But as Dr. Walsh notes, history has produced a multitude of other wise and influential people who have much to teach us.

In 1999, the magazine *Common Boundary* published a list of the 100 most influential psychospiritual books of the twentieth century. The list contained books that the editors and the readers of the magazine considered to be the best books to read about spirituality and psychological health. We won't have room here to repeat the entire list, but we have added several of these influential books to our *"Recommended Readings"* found in the Appendix. Some of the books highlighted by *Common Boundary* magazine were *Man's Search for Meaning* by Viktor Frankl, *The Prophet* by Kahlil Gibran, and *The Seven Storey Mountain* by Thomas Merton.

Dr. Roger Walsh also recommends that we cultivate experiences and relationships with people who may have something to teach us—to look for role models in the world around us. He quotes Confucius: "To make friends with the straight, the trustworthy in word, and the well-informed is to benefit." If you are fortunate, you will have many of these kinds of people in your life—teachers and mentors, pastors, rabbis, or other spiritual leaders; friends who are wise and thoughtful; and family members who inspire you with their sense of purpose.

If you don't seem to have these types of influences in your life, there could be two types of problems. First, it may be that the negative thinking of depression is making it hard for you to spot opportunities for learning from others. You may be so pessimistic that you are missing out on learning from positive people with positive messages who are in your lives everyday; or you may be so preoccupied with worries that you have forgotten about people who have been a positive influence in the past. Another possibility is that you actually may not have teachers, religious leaders, friends, or family who can serve as models or inspire you to live a meaningful life. In this case, you may need to develop a plan to actively seek out these opportunities. For example, you could take a class, go to church more regularly, or try to make new friends with the kind of values and life-style that might help you with your sense of direction and purpose.

The process of studying the works of the wise and learning from the wise people in our midst commonly leads to self-contemplation—thinking in depth about what counts most for us in life. Helen had been a championship athlete in college and had gone on to a successful professional career in her sport. But, now she was thirty-five years old and had been retired from her career for over a year. She was the envy of many of her old friends because she had done so well as a professional athlete. However, Helen was depressed and lonely. Her sport had seemed to mean everything to her. And now that she was too old to compete any longer, Helen was drifting aimlessly. Her life had lost its purpose.

As part of her therapy, Helen read several books, including *Man's Search for Meaning* and *Full Catastrophe Living*. And, she agreed to arrange some conferences with the chaplain for her old team. The chaplain was a person she had looked up to and trusted. Helen believed the chaplain might be able to give her some advice that would break her out of her rut. After several weeks, Helen began to talk about how she was considering changing the direction of her life.

> *The books you suggested really got me to thinking. I've been acting like a robot—just moving through life without really appreciating the things around me, without being committed to anything. And*

you know, my problems are really nothing compared to what others have had to face.

I've been talking with the chaplain and getting some ideas about how I could get back in touch with life. One thing I've been missing is getting really close to other people. When I was in the thick of my career, the travel and the effort to keep in shape all the time consumed me. I didn't have time, or didn't take the time, to know my friends well or to stick with relationships.

I've been thinking about what I could do with the rest of my life. And, I'm pretty sure now that I want to do something different—to get out of sports entirely. I might go back to school for another degree so I can do research. Whatever I decide to do, I want to be able to look back over my life and feel like it's made a difference to someone. I'm not going to vegetate and just sit around crying about the past.

Helen was starting to use introspection or self-contemplation to re-examine her direction for life. In our therapy with patients, we know that we are beginning to make progress when they are getting excited about finding new meanings or changing directions, and they are stimulated to think about their options and opportunities. If you feel that your life lacks the level of meaning or purpose that you desire, try reading some inspirational books, look to your teachers and friends, and spend time in self-contemplation. However, one word of caution—if you are depressed you need to be careful to avoid spending too much time pondering life issues or life meanings. Because depression makes people turn inward, there is some risk that you will become too self-absorbed or will end up just mulling things over and over without taking the actions you need to pull out of depression. Remember to use the other Keys to recovery and to develop a balanced and comprehensive plan for getting well.

Breaking through the Veil of Depression to Find Meaning

Many of the symptoms of depression, including guilt, low self-esteem, hopelessness, low energy, and problems with concentration, can make it difficult to feel that your life is worthwhile or to find ways to use spiritual resources to change things for the better. If you are having trouble searching for meaning or find yourself blocked in using your spirituality to attack depression, you may need to consider some other approaches that will reduce your symptoms and allow you to see your life more clearly.

Treatment with antidepressants is one option that can bring people back to the point where they regain a sense of purpose or commitment. We have seen many patients who were feeling disconnected from life, were alienated from the things that used to count for them, and were questioning some of their basic beliefs who have had dramatic reversals of these problems after starting on antidepressant medication. In these situations, it appeared that chemical imbalances in the brain were interfering with their ability to effectively use the spiritual dimension of their being.

Methods from the Thinking, Action, and Relationship Keys also can help you make the most of your spiritual resources. You can use the Thinking Key to reduce negativism and to change self-schemas that may be holding you back. If you are getting stuck on finding a sense of purpose for your life, you could review the list of schemas you wrote out in Chapter 4 and try to make changes in the ones that are interfering with your progress. For example, when Michelle revised her maladaptive schema "without a man, I'm nothing," it allowed her spiritual dimension to grow ("God loves me whether I'm married or single . . . I can have value and make contributions without a relationship with a man . . . In some ways I could do more without spending so much time worrying about men or being with men.")

As Viktor Frankl has noted, finding your true self involves not only having a sense of meaning, but doing something to put your ideals or your life purpose into action. Although the Action Key is designed primarily to reverse the behavioral symptoms of depression, you can also use these methods to unlock your potential for using the Spirituality Key. Here is an example. Michelle knew that she had been pulling away from her friends and that she had become much less involved in church activities after her divorce. She also had been doing less with her children. As she began to think about how her life could have some meaning again, she realized that a commitment to her religious beliefs and her family and friends was extremely important to her. Some of the Action Key methods she used were: Activity Scheduling (see Chapter 5) to break through the inertia of her depression (scheduling specific times for church activities and doing things with her friends and her children); and Graded Task Assignments (Chapter 5) to gradually increase the amount of time she spent going out with friends and to step up the social demands of the outings (starting with short visits with one or two friends and building up to the point where she could go to parties and entertain others).

This example also illustrates use of the Relationship Key in getting back a sense of meaning. As Michelle spent more time with her single friends, she began to learn about the things that seemed to give them purpose and direction. They talked about their careers and families, classes they were taking, books they were reading, and the things that kept them going every day. These discussions helped Michelle straighten out her priorities and build more meaningful relationships with the important people in her life.

Your Search for Meaning

During a single day in our offices we usually have the opportunity to learn about many different directions and purposes for life. In one hour, we might talk with a religious agnostic who has devoted his life to the rescue and care of stray animals. Although he professes no religious faith, he is deeply committed to doing something to make the world a better place and to act in a loving way to others. In the next hour, we might be trying to help a devout Christian who doubts her faith after the death of a loved one. This person is feeling abandoned and alone. Yet, we think that she will find a way to get back to the beliefs that are so important to her and to find a renewed sense of purpose. Later that day, we might meet with a businessman who is considering a radical career change. He has been hugely successful in business, but in his heart he always wanted to be an artist. Each of these people is searching for meaning in his or her own way.

We hope you have been thinking about your own personal sense of meaning as you have been reading this chapter. Finding meaning is one of life's great challenges—and one of its greatest satisfactions. For most of us, the search for meaning is a continuing process throughout life. There may be anchor points that are stable and unwavering for all of our years. But, our sense of meaning can evolve as we grow and develop—as we face the demands of life and experience its joys.

When you are in the depths of depression, it may be hard to see any good in having to suffer through this illness. However, depression does sometimes force you to reexamine your life. In the process, you may be able to find a revitalized or deeper sense of meaning that will lead to many positive changes. We have seen this happen many times with our patients. The next chapter focuses on ways to build your spiritual resources and to surmount the obstacles you may have to using the Spirituality Key. These methods may give you some additional ideas on ways to find meaning.

Before you go on to the next chapter, take some time to think about these questions. What gives your life meaning and purpose today? As you review your past, what meaningful things could you have strayed away from or forgotten? Are any of these things worth bringing back into your life? Do you want to make any changes that will give your life a new direction? What might give you a greater sense of meaning or purpose in the future?

13

Making the Spiritual Connection

In making plans to write about depression and spirituality we struggled with the fact that there are many views on spirituality and a seemingly infinite number of beliefs, practices, and experiences. We wanted to convey the message that tapping into your spiritual resources can be a way to gain the strength needed to fight off depression and to stay well. The dilemma was to provide guidance that many people could find helpful without suggesting that any one religion, philosophy, or practice was best. We decided to try to cover aspects of spiritual development that seemed common across cultures and religions. We have also included a discussion of common spiritual dilemmas presented to us by our patients.

Another challenge in including a Spirituality Key is that while we clearly advocate the use of logic in the other four Keys, spirituality is not necessarily achieved through logical or intellectual activity. It is an experience of the heart or of emotion more than an experience of reason. We generally accept our spiritual beliefs without proof. They are the ideas we were taught as children by our families or through our own study as adults. We hold these beliefs because they fit with our view of the world and our experiences, and because they give us comfort.

Spirituality is more than just a set of beliefs or practices. It includes touching the lives of others or sharing intense emotions such as joy or love. Feeling a sense of peace as you marvel at the wonders of a brilliant sunset, a mountain lake, lilacs blooming, or a starry night connects you to nature through that feeling of awe and to one another if those moments are shared. Spirituality includes a search for what is sacred and holy in life and for a relationship with a higher power such as God, a universal energy, or a greater good or purpose in life. When we feel that spiritual connection we know that we are not alone. Instead, we feel that we are a part of something great and beautiful.

When we practice religious faiths, we have opportunities to participate as a community of believers. We speak in one voice expressing faith and gratitude or seeking direction and assistance in our lives. In the companionship of other believers, our burdens can be lessened and we receive comfort. Feeling a spiritual bond to others, to nature, to God, or to the world in general can give the strength needed to get your life back when you are depressed.

Spirituality and Cognitive-Behavior Therapy

When we are troubled, our minds and hearts are full of negative thoughts and negative feelings. Our bodies react to the stress and our actions are often impulsive and hurtful to ourselves or to others. We feel disconnected or out of control. When we are not troubled, we are calm in our mind and in our spirit. We do not feel that inner turmoil. Our bodies and our hearts do not ache. And we act in more positive and healthy ways. This book has been about how your thoughts, actions, and bodies work as one. Your spirit connects them all. When any one is out of balance, the others are affected. We have taught you ways to control your negative thinking and your negative actions. We have told you how to work toward balance in your body through developing a healthier lifestyle and through medications to mend any chemical imbalances. In this chapter, we offer ways to help you tap into your spiritual life, and reawaken beliefs that might have brought you comfort and strength in the past.

Your Spiritual Strengths

With each of the other four keys, we have asked you to begin by taking stock of your strengths in that area. Exercise 13.1 is a checklist of common spiritual beliefs and actions. Next to each item mark the strengths you possess or you would like to develop. Think about how each might help you in your efforts to reduce your symptoms of depression.

Exercise 13.1
The Spirituality Key: Personal Strengths Checklist

Instructions:
Although you may feel weakened by depression, you probably have strengths that can help you solve problems and feel better. Use this rating system to identify possible strengths for using the Spirituality Key.

++ = A current strength.
+ = A strength I would like to develop.

___ I have a sense of meaning in life.
___ I have faith in a higher power.
___ I believe in a greater good or purpose in life that goes beyond my own personal existence.
___ My spirituality helps make me a whole person.
___ I pray.
___ I meditate or take time to become more aware of the world around me.
___ I am connected to others and want to do things for them.
___ I attend church, synagogue, or other religious services.
___ I take time to nurture my spiritual life.
___ I can find meaning in everyday things such as music, nature, or my daily work.
___ I read spiritual books or other kinds of literature that make me think about my purpose in life.
___ I consider myself a spiritual person.
___ I have the capacity for forgiveness of myself and others.

Obstacles to Spirituality

Some people with severe depression feel downhearted, lonely, and hopeless. Sometimes they don't feel the presence of God in their lives, have little interest in organized religion, or don't feel as if their lives have any great meaning. Their spiritual lives may be close to nonexistent. Some are secretly angry for being subjected to depression, for the occurrence of tragedy in their lives, or for being let down. Some blame God for their misfortunes. Others blame the unfair world we live in. Their anger eventually turns inward where it festers and causes pain.

As they tell their life stories, they compare depression to times in the past before their troubles began, when they had faith, felt blessed, or knew peace in their hearts. To rekindle their spirituality, they must figure out how depression interfered with their spiritual beliefs and practices. In the next section we will discuss some common factors in depression that cause people to lose their spiritual direction. If you can identify the roadblock in your spiritual life, you can remove it and get back on the track toward greater fulfillment.

A DARKENED HEART

In Chapters 10 and 11 we talked about how anger can interfere with your relationships with others because it perpetuates tension rather than leading you to resolution. Because it's a barrier over your heart that holds in the hurt and blocks out positive feelings, anger can keep you from tapping into your spirituality.

Janie was so furious with her family that she could no longer talk to her parents or her sisters without losing her temper. Civil conversation hardly had a chance because she would take issue with just about anything they said. Janie couldn't remember how it all started, she could only recall feeling angry with her family since about age sixteen. Her mom was the biggest problem. She'd always been quick to criticize Janie, but could never bring herself to show love or affection. Everyone else interfered by trying to patch things up between them. It became so irritating that Janie decided to stop contact with her family altogether. She tried to close off her heart so that she would not need them or miss them. This strategy seemed to work for a while. The only problem was that by closing off her heart to her family, she had inadvertently closed off her heart to everyone else as well. Consequently, she had no close friends and no lasting romances. She found a job that allowed her to work independently so she "didn't have to deal with other people."

Janie's satisfaction with this "peaceful" life-style changed when she met David. He was kind, not pushy, and had an easygoing manner that made conversation easy. After a few months of dating, David invited Janie to attend synagogue with him and his family to celebrate the Sabbath. She had always been curious about Judaism, so she agreed to go. She attended the service, taking in the people and the activities around her. She had been a little nervous about meeting David's family, but they turned out to be a warm and friendly group who were happy to have her among them. When she returned to her empty apartment later that night, a wave of loneliness overwhelmed her. She looked around her neat little apartment that she had decorated in her image—simple, tasteful, uncluttered by the belongings of others or by family memorabilia. She saw the kinship of David's family members and friends and wanted to feel that same kind of connection. She wanted to be part of something bigger than herself, but she was not certain that she could let down her emotional guard. Janie's anger had protected her well all these years, but it had left her spiritually barren

Spiritual experiences across cultures begin with an open heart, one that allows positive feelings to be received and expressed. A heart darkened by anger, hurt, or resentment is closed to these feelings. We touched on coping with anger in Chapter 11 of the Relationship Key. In the sections that follow, we will discuss other ways of removing this and other obstacles to your spiritual life.

RIGHTEOUS INDIGNATION

"It isn't fair. It isn't right. It shouldn't be like this." When things happen in your world that are wrong or unjust, it is your sense of justice that makes you feel angry. It is your logical and practical side that gets furious when people make stupid mistakes or when decisions are made that benefit some, but hurt others. And it is your sense of fairness that makes you feel indignant about unwelcomed changes that are beyond your control. These are all normal human responses that stem from positive feelings and intentions. However, righteous indignation can interfere with your spirituality if it is too intense or occurs too frequently. Some people blame God when unjust things happen, either for allowing them to occur or for not fixing the problem. When this happens, disappointment or disillusionment with the notion of a higher being can be the beginning of losing faith altogether. Their expectations of a God-like power were not met; therefore, they conclude that such a power must not really exist. This can be an example of all-or-none thinking.

SELF-PITY

There is a difference between acknowledging that you feel depressed and having self-pity. When people get stuck in self-pity, they feel bad for themselves, helpless to control their situation, and resigned to suffer. Self-pity can make you reject the help of others, preferring only to share your pain rather than take action to eliminate it. It makes you turn inward, putting up a wall to the healing efforts or positive intercessions of others. Because spirituality, in its various forms, requires an openness of heart, self-pity is an obstacle that limits expression and experience of the spirit.

Negative thoughts and feelings about yourself or others can block your path to spiritual experiences and expressions. Work toward purging yourself of anger, resentments, and hurts, and give your spirit a chance to grow.

SHAME

Like self-pity, shame is a one-way street that often ends in a blind alley. It gets you nowhere. You blame yourself, feel guilty and embarrassed, and carry these feelings around like a heavy weight around your neck. To find your way down a spiritual path, it is just as necessary to forgive yourself as it is to forgive others. If you are stuck at "it's all my fault and I'm a bad person," use the exercises we described in the Thinking Key to help yourself make peace with the past. Work through your guilt and shame so that you can open your heart to better and more healing spiritual experiences.

Cognitive Aspects of Spirituality

When you are depressed, it can be difficult to hold on to spiritual beliefs that at one time may have led to good feelings such as hope and serenity. You might even conclude that depression is evidence that you have been spiritually let down, rejected, or ignored. Or even worse, that the spiritual beliefs you once clung to were false. These kinds of ideas fit with the negative mindset of depression and might be examples of thinking errors like the ones you learned about in Chapter 3.

If you have a pessimistic view of spirituality, your reactions might be to emotionally pull back from your old belief system, stop attending worship services, give up on prayer, or cultivate a spiritless view of the world. Lewis, whom we talked about in Chapter 11 as getting depressed when he lost his job after nearly thirty years of dedicated service to his company, gave up on some of his values as well as on his best friend who was forced to lay him off when the company reorganized. Lewis thought that if he did not believe in God or in a spiritual life beyond his day-to-day experiences, then he would not feel so let down. He stopped believing in the importance of loyalty to others, deciding instead that giving to others was a waste of time. He even rejected his old belief that things always work out for the best. Lewis was trying to make sense out of being laid off by his best friend and business partner. His analysis was that he had been naïve in the past to expect that if he was good to others, the favor would be returned. So he hardened his heart to his friends and family and to his more generous life principles. This was easier for Lewis than feeling sad about his losing his job and thinking that he had been let down by God. Unfortunately, this switch in his spiritual outlook did not make matters any better.

You can see from this example that the distortions in thinking we discussed in Chapters 3 and 4 can affect your spiritual outlook as well. Fortunately, some of the tools we suggested for combating negative thinking can also help you in sorting out your spiritual beliefs.

COMBATING MENTAL FILTERS BY GIVING THANKS

As we noted in Chapter 3 on thinking errors, depression can cause you to look at the world with tunnel vision where you focus only on the things that are going wrong in your life and overlook the things that might be going right. Many spiritual philosophies advocate a broader view of life in which you take time to consider the positives in life and not only the negatives. Some faiths suggest that you attribute your good fortune to God and that you give appropriate thanks. That is sometimes difficult to do if you believe that God has overlooked you in your time of depression. If what you have to be thankful for comes from your own efforts, acknowledging pleasure or gratitude for having such abilities or strengths is one way to gain a more balanced and less negative view of yourself, thus fighting off the tunnel vision.

When you are feeling low it can be difficult to think of anything that is going right in your life, let alone be thankful. You might be prone to the "yes, but…" error. For example, "Yes I do have a home, but the mortgage is killing me." "Yes I do have healthy children, but they don't help out around the house and they never listen." "Yes I do have a supportive family, but I don't deserve them." "Yes, I am lucky to have a good job, but it doesn't really matter to me." When you say, "yes, but…" you are invalidating or disqualifying the positives in your life instead of taking credit for them.

Sometimes we take for granted the smaller things in life, failing to acknowledge their existence or importance. For example, we may not even notice the constancy of people we encounter or experiences that lie in the background of our lives. Some examples might include the day care worker who makes your child comfortable, the smiling clerk at your favorite breakfast shop, your good health, a car that works well, a pet that is happy to see you, or a friend who is always there when you need him or her. If you do not make an effort to take stock of the smaller things in life, you may miss them altogether.

A way around this is to make a list of daily experiences that you are thankful for. What went right today? Who was kind to you today? Who stopped being a problem or solved a problem? What gifts or talents do you have that others might lack? What blessings do you have that others wish they had? What are some things that are going right in your life that you can see going wrong in the lives of others? Are there aspects of your life that you have successfully accomplished, fixed, or overcome? Make a list of these things in your notebook. Then, make it a habit at the end of each day to take stock of who you are and what you have. Force yourself to see the positive and be thankful for the good things in your life.

INCREASING AWARENESS AND MINDFULNESS

Spirituality usually requires a heightened awareness of experiences within yourself and the world around you. As we mentioned in the last chapter, mindfulness means attending to all aspects of existence including thoughts, sensations, sounds, people, and nature. Depression can cause you to pull inward making you intimately aware of your misery, but blocking out most everything else. Because your view of reality is created by your awareness of what is going on around you, if you are only aware of discomfort, your overall view of life will be negative. To be mindful, you need to allow yourself to pay attention to the positive elements in your surroundings. In Exercise 12.1 in the last chapter, we suggested several ways in which you could increase your mindfulness. Make it your goal to notice something new in your world each day. A Pawnee Indian song summed up this sentiment as follows:

> *Remember, remember the sacredness of things,*
> *Running streams and dwellings,*
> *The young within the nest,*
> *A hearth for sacred fire,*
> *The holy flame of fire*

COMBATING NEGATIVE BELIEFS
ABOUT GOD AND PUNISHMENT

People can sometimes become disillusioned with God and with organized religion when bad things happened to them that they felt were undeserved. For example, Sally got depressed after she lost her mother to cancer, somehow blaming herself for her mother's misfortune. "This must have happened because I cheated on my husband. It is my punishment from God." Not only was Sally depressed about the loss of her mother, she was worsening her pain by beating herself up with guilt. Sally, like many of us, often uses simple cause-and-effect explanations for life's events. Event A caused event B. "I didn't check the oil in my car when I should have. That's why the engine overheated and the block cracked." When there is no direct evidence of a connection between events we may stretch to form an explanation that fits with our beliefs about how life is supposed to work. Sally had always held the belief that what goes around comes around and that if you make mistakes in life, you will eventually be punished. So she concluded that her mother's cancer was a direct result of her extramarital affair. But her belief did not explain why bad things also seemed to occur in the lives of people she knew who always played by the rules.

In his best-selling book *When Bad Things Happen to Good People*, Rabbi Harold Kushner offered a helpful explanation for how bad things can happen to people who have led decent lives. He says, "Maybe God does not cause our suffering. Maybe it happens for some reason other than the will of God." Kushner went on to suggest that while God can provide love and comfort, He may not be able to protect us from the forces of nature, from the bad choices we make, or from the hurtful actions of others. He proposed this view of God after considerable study of the Bible, his observations of good people struggling with trauma, and his experience of the loss of his young child to a rare and deadly disease. From this perspective, it made more sense why sometimes bad things happened to good people and why bad things didn't always happen to bad people. According to Kushner, if we accept this view, we can stop blaming God for our misfortunes, and we can also stop blaming ourselves. And, if we have more realistic expectations of God, we can call for comfort and assistance in the areas where He can help.

Sally didn't really believe that God caused her mother's lung cancer, but she wanted her mother to recover. So she got angry with God when she prayed that the cancer would go away, and it didn't. After reading Kushner's book, Sally came up with a less self-blaming view of her mother's cancer. Although she thought it was appropriate to feel guilt for her infidelity, she thought it had little to do with her mother's sickness. Her mother had been a heavy smoker, and her doctors had warned her for years to give up her habit. Sally accepted the possibility that it was beyond God's control to stop the disease from spreading. While she liked holding a straightforward cause-and-effect view that good behavior leads to good outcomes and bad behavior gets punished, she realized that it is not always that simple.

Key Point

Sometimes bad things happen for no particularly good reason. It is easy to point the finger of blame, but sometimes it is no one's fault.

Actions that Improve Spirituality

MAKING TIME FOR SPIRITUAL WORK

Like the learning of any other set of skills, it takes time and practice to develop your spirituality. Although you may have heard people talk about eye-opening experiences in which their hearts and minds were suddenly awakened to the spiritual realm, most of the time your spiritual development occurs in small steps over a long period of time. There is a great deal to learn, experiential exercises to try, and ideas to contemplate. Directions, answers, and insights do not always come overnight. Therefore, think of your spirituality as a journey of growth accomplished through slow and steady effort.

In the Action Key chapters we talked about Activity Scheduling and Graded Task Assignment as methods for helping yourself get started on new tasks and for accomplishing your goals. Consider using those strategies for working on your spirituality. Set small goals at first, for example spending one hour each week reading about spirituality, attending a religious service, or talking with a spiritual advisor. If you wanted to learn to meditate, you might start with a small goal of working at it for ten minutes each day, then increasing that time and the complexity of your exercise. Remember the warning we gave you about taking action. Don't try to do too much all at one time or set unreasonable goals for yourself. If you are unable to achieve those goals it will only give you more fuel for self-doubt and self-criticism.

MEND RELATIONSHIP RIFTS

Anger, hurt, or resentment toward others can weigh heavily on your mind and heart. Even if you are justified in your feelings, holding on to them prevents you from having an accepting and loving spirit. To free yourself from this burden you have to find a way to make peace with the past. We discussed forgiveness in Chapter 11 of the Relationship Key, but there are a few other strategies you might use to free your spirit of hurt feelings.

If you have ever been hurt, you probably know that while you may be able to forgive someone for his or her wrongdoing, you may not be able to forget about it. "I'm not angry about the divorce anymore," Isabella told her best friend. "But, I will never forget what I went through. It was horrible. Every time I think of it I can feel the sadness wash over me. What bothers me the most is that I still don't understand why it happened the way it did. What went wrong? How did it all fall apart so quickly after all those years together?"

Isabella was a logical person. She wanted to understand how her husband could have taken up with another woman and left her. It made no real sense to her. She had already been through blaming herself, blaming the other woman, and blaming her husband, but was never completely satisfied with the conclusion. Isabella assumed that if only she could understand how and why this happened to her marriage, she could finally let it go. She could stop questioning herself and perhaps she could even stop missing her husband. The problem is that when people hurt one another, it is not usually for logical reasons. You can search your mind, think and rethink it, or get a therapist to help you analyze yourself and the circumstances, but you may never reach a satisfactory conclusion. And while you search for answers, you continue to carry around the hurt until you find a place to lay it to rest.

A good question to ask when you are searching for explanations for hurtful events might be: "Is there any possible explanation that would make me feel any better about what happened?" Given some time to consider the options, you might conclude that there are no explanations for the experience that would suddenly make you feel OK about it. If this is the case, you probably need to stop analyzing and accept the fact that what happened to hurt you was not necessarily logical or rational. Sometimes people do stupid things. Even really smart people who know better do stupid things. They hurt each other because they do not consider all the implications of their actions before they act. Trying to find a logical explanation for their actions will only frustrate you further.

Acceptance, like forgiveness, is an act that requires an effort of both the mind and the heart. Acceptance that a bad event happened for no good reason means that you stop telling yourself that there must be an explanation, and you let the hatred, anger, resentment, or hurt leave your heart. It actually takes a great deal of effort to hold on to bad feelings. You have to stoke the fires to keep them burning by replaying the hurtful experience in your mind, by wishing harm to those who hurt you, or by looking for opportunities for revenge. If you stop holding on to the hurt, you might find that it will diminish in time and you will have more energy to focus on the more positive things in your life.

Another strategy is to ask yourself if unrealistically high expectations may have played a role in creating the hurt. Janie had not forgiven her mother for how she had been treated as a child. She believed that her mother made a number of mistakes along the way, leaving Janie with low self-esteem. As a kid, Janie thought it was her own fault when her mother had acted in rejecting ways. Later she came to blame it on her mother.

Janie's therapist asked her about her expectations for her mother as a way of helping Janie find a way to let go of her ill feelings.

THERAPIST: It sounds like your mother let you down on a number of occasions. She was not the kind of mother you wanted.

JANIE: No, she wasn't. I envied my friends because their mothers seemed so nice. It seemed like my mother was either angry at me for some mistake I had made or too busy to deal with me.

THERAPIST: Do you think you will ever forgive her for that?

JANIE: I don't think it's forgivable. She has caused me a lot of grief. And the worst part is that now she acts like she hasn't done anything wrong. She wants us to be close. But I don't trust her.

THERAPIST: Is there a down side of staying angry with her and not letting her get close.

JANIE: Yes. I've always wanted to be close to her, to be accepted. I just don't think she is capable of real love.

THERAPIST: Why is that?

JANIE: She never learned how from her mother. Her mother got depressed after my mother was born and, from what I've heard, never fully recovered. Her older sisters and her dad took care of her. My grandmother died when my mom was only ten years old.

THERAPIST: You sound like you understand where she is coming from.

JANIE: I understand her, but she still makes me mad.

THERAPIST: Janie, it sounds to me like you had a picture in your mind of what a mother ought to be like. It's not an unreasonable picture, but it is something your mother just couldn't be. When we are kids we assume our parents know what they're doing, that they're right, or that they're perfect. But in reality, our parents are people just like us. They make mistakes, don't always have the answers, and sometimes let their emotions get the best of them. I'm wondering if what you need to do is accept the fact that your mother didn't have the skills to do a good job with you. She was ill equipped and did not have the natural talent to figure out what you needed from her.

JANIE: So you want me to forgive her because she just wasn't capable of doing the job, and I was the unlucky one who got to be her first child.

THERAPIST: You are the oldest. Was she any better with your little sisters?

JANIE: By the time my youngest sister was in high school, my mother had loosened up a lot.

THERAPIST: So your mother developed better skills with experience. You were the unlucky one who was born first. You were on-the-job training.

JANIE: I guess I was.

THERAPIST: When you think about it that way, does it seem more likely that you would be able to forgive her some day?

JANIE: Well, it certainly makes it harder to stay angry with her. I'm not sure we'll ever be able to be close the way I wanted, but maybe it's time for me to let it go. I'm tired of being angry with her anyway. I just want to get on with my life.

Janie's therapist was trying to make the point that your expectations about people can set you up for disappointment if those individuals are not capable of fulfilling your expectations. Is it their fault that they could not act as you desired or is it your fault for expecting too much? Perhaps it is a little of both. Maybe what blocks your capacity for forgiveness is your unwillingness to accept the weaknesses of others. This brings us to the next strategy for developing a forgiving heart.

If you are like most people, you have probably made mistakes from time to time. Perhaps there are things you've done for which you are remorseful. If they involve other people you might even wish you could turn back the hands of time and change your course of action. It is hard to live with yourself when you have done something to hurt someone you love. If this has happened, you probably hope that whoever you hurt will forgive you for your transgressions, accept your apology, or allow you to make amends. Forgiveness is something we all hope to receive, even when we find it difficult to offer.

If you are having trouble letting go of hurt feelings, perhaps you can think about the times you made mistakes or hurt others, even if only accidentally. If you can acknowledge your own faults, and your own desire to make good on them, you can start by doing the same for others. If you are successful, you will free your heart so that it is more open to cultivate the spirituality you desire.

SEEKING AND ACCEPTING HELP

"I used to feel close to God. I attended church regularly, found it easy to give thanks for a good life. That seems like a long time ago. Now I feel alone and abandoned. It seems like my depression will never end." This is what Consuelo wrote in her Personal Story before she began to work through the Five Keys. She went on to describe herself as emotionally disconnected from everyone and everything since the loss of her husband, like she was "adrift in a sea of misery." When she really thought about it, she had to admit that this feeling started long before her husband had died. "When our marriage was good, I felt good about life. When it started getting ugly, I lost my connection to anything outside the marriage and the kids."

Consuelo is not unique in that she felt spiritually healthy when times were good and spiritually disconnected when times were bad. Like many people, she became preoccupied with the stresses and difficulties in her life until these elements consumed her mind and spirit. She neglected her positive relationships with friends and her parents, and she forgot that she did not have to be alone in her suffering.

Consuelo tried to deal with her abusive husband through the years and even as she attempted to work through her mourning after his death, she believed that she had to handle things on her own. Consuelo didn't consider asking for assistance from her friends let alone from God. She made herself an island and there she sat feeling alone. On the six-month anniversary of her husband's death she went to his favorite church and lit a candle in his memory. Father Joe stopped to greet her and asked how she was faring, although it was clear from the dark circles under her eyes and her weight loss that she was not doing well. Consuelo didn't want him to feel sorry for her, so she did her best to put on a happy face and say that things were getting better. Father Joe looked at her with his gentle smile and warm, loving eyes and said, "Consuelo, don't forget that you don't have to do it all by yourself." As she said goodbye and walked out of the church, Consuelo smiled to herself. He's right, she thought. She had been so caught up struggling with her problems that she had forgotten that she was not alone in the world. Her therapist's words popped into her head as she climbed into her car: "There's no prize for handling it all on your own. Don't be afraid to ask for help."

Regardless of their concept of God, when people are desperate they often look to the heavens and ask for assistance. In these humbling moments, usually after trying unsuccessfully to cope alone, they realize that they need help. This type of humility is one of the avenues to spiritual growth. To be humble is to see oneself as a single element in a greater entity whether it is the universe, a community of humans, or a part of the life force. It means giving up the notion that you stand alone in the center of your world—that you alone can and must solve problems and overcome adversity. When you accept the existence of a power greater than your own, it becomes easier to acknowledge that you do not have all the answers and that you are fallible because you know that help is within your reach. Asking for help is a positive action that can set you on the road to recovery. Consuelo realized this after talking with Father Joe. She made it her mission to ask God and her family for help and consolation and to give up the idea that she was supposed to manage all on her own.

MEDITATION AND SELF-AWARENESS

Although it has not been well tested as an intervention specifically for depression, there has been new research on the usefulness of meditation in combating chronic pain, cancer, and severe anxiety. Perhaps the most prominent investigator in this field is Jon Kabat-Zinn from the University of Massachusetts Medical School. Meditation, which originated from Buddhism and Hinduism where it is a practice embedded in the philosophy of those religions, has been adapted in Western cultures as an exercise aimed at relaxation, increasing self-awareness, and facilitating spiritual growth. There are two general types of meditation, concentrative meditation and mindfulness meditation. Concentrative meditation is used to calm the mind and body through focus of attention on specific objects, such as staring at a flame, sensations such as breathing, or words said in repetition. Mindfulness meditation, which is often taught after the individual has mastered the concentrative processes, focuses on becoming increasingly aware of one's thoughts, feelings, and physical sensations, particularly as they change over time. With both types of meditation, the goal is to become acutely aware of your perceptions of yourself and of the world, particularly how they can change as your feelings change. Secondarily, meditation teaches you to examine your thoughts and experiences in a detached manner, as if you are standing on the outside looking in at yourself. Consistent with the Eastern religions from which it was born, the ultimate goal of meditation is to develop self-acceptance and self-love through mindfulness. Mindfulness allows you to strip away distorted perceptions of reality, seeing things for what they are without influence from others, from your emotions, or from your past experiences.

Meditation, like the cognitive interventions in the Thinking Key, helps people to achieve an objective perspective on their lives so that they will be better able to separate emotionally laden and unreliable thoughts from reality. Alan Marlatt from the University of Washington believes that the outcome of increasing self-awareness for those who suffer from psychological stress is that they can come to see their negative thinking patterns in an objective way. That is, they can notice how their thinking becomes more negative when they are depressed rather than believing each negative thought as it pops into their heads. In this way, mindfulness meditation can help you gain the objective point of view you need to control negative thinking.

It is beyond the scope of this book to teach you how to meditate effectively. But, we can pass on the advice of Alan Marlatt and Jean Kristeller from their work on mindfulness and meditation. These researchers suggest ten to twenty minutes of meditative practice twice each day in a quiet place, free from distractions. Early-morning and late-afternoon or evening sessions are recommended. Sitting comfortably and upright to discourage falling asleep during practice, close your eyes and focus on your breathing patterns. If you become distracted by sounds or your own internal thoughts, simply acknowledge that you are becoming distracted and turn your focus once again to your breathing. To enhance your concentration you can repeat a word or phrase to yourself as you focus on your breathing. They suggest words such as "calm," "peace," or any other words or sounds that are comforting to you and easy to repeat in your mind.

When this exercise is mastered, you can move toward more of an insight-oriented meditation by allowing your mind to wander and exploring the thoughts and feelings that might have distracted you during your initial practice sessions. Rather than be self-critical or judgmental of your ideas or experiences, the goal of mindfulness meditation is to accept these thoughts and feelings as merely existing in your consciousness. They are neither bad thoughts nor good thoughts. They are merely thoughts. If you can see events without the filter of self-evaluation, you may uncover insights that help lead to resolution of the issues.

Such methods have helped people to overcome destructive urges such as alcoholism and binge eating by focusing mindfully on the feeling of the urge, recognizing its existence through meditation, rather than being led by it. Like other methods we have discussed in the Spirituality Key, meditation can open your mind and your heart to positive experiences and emotions and allow you to connect to a greater life force as well as to other people.

PRAYER

If you believe in a force or power greater than yourself, such as God, prayer is a way to experience a connection between yourself and that entity. There are many forms of prayer, but according to researchers on the effects of prayer on personal well-being, such as Dr. Douglas Richards of Atlantic University, the most common types are prayers asking for guidance for oneself, for healing for others, prayers of thanksgiving, and those that ask for protection of others. Prayer and meditation can go hand in hand. Meditation calms your mind so that you can experience that connection without worldly distraction. Prayer is the sending and receiving of messages while in a mindful state.

There is a great deal of clinical research to suggest that prayer can be helpful in coping with and preventing the harmful effects of stress. There are many ways and times that people pray, and no single method or pattern seems best, perhaps because prayer is a highly personal and individualized experience. Larry King recently wrote a book called *Powerful Prayers*, which includes his interviews with famous and powerful people about their belief in and practices of prayer. King was challenged by his daughter to learn about this mysterious activity which King himself did not practice or accept. He talked with sports legends, international and business leaders, actors, and clergy and found that they engage in a variety of prayer methods from reading and contemplation of the writings of holy books to informal conversations with God.

There is no right or wrong way to pray. You just have to make the time to do it. You can begin with methods you might have been taught in your religious education or make up your own style along the way. All that is required is belief in the power of prayer, a few moments of quiet to collect your thoughts, and a sincere declaration of your beliefs. According to Drs. Margaret Poloma and Brian Pendleton, there seem to be four main categories, colloquial prayer, petitionary prayer, ritualistic prayer, and meditative prayer. There is some overlap among these categories depending on the specific beliefs and practices.

Shannon believed in the power of prayer, but also knew that not all prayers are answered in the way she might expect. Rather than asking for specific things, such as a winning lottery ticket, she usually asked for a boost in her personal fortitude so that she could make it through difficult times. When Vic prayed, he asked for guidance in decision making. He believed that if he quieted his mind and listened closely, answers would present themselves. These are both examples of what Poloma and Pendleton called colloquial prayers. Marlene, Tony's wife, prayed that her husband would listen to her and take advice from his doctors. Michelle prayed for a good night's sleep. These are petitionary prayers. They are more specific in their requests. Consuelo prayed the rosary, a traditional catholic ritual prayer, while Lewis was comforted when he recited the *Shm'a,* a Jewish ritual prayer. Each would tell you that his or her prayer was answered in some way. Andrea practiced meditative prayer in which she tried to clear her mind of worries and focus on connecting with a higher being. None questioned the source of the answer or whether or not it was wishful thinking or just chance happenings. They believed that their prayers would be answered and that was enough.

If you believe in the power of prayer, worshiping with a community of similar believers can help give you the strength you need to work through your depression especially at times when you are feeling weak and overwhelmed. Although it may seem more awkward to be the one asking for help than providing it to others, asking others to pray for you and with you can be a moving and enriching experience.

Prayer is difficult for people to accept if it is not part of their system of faith. Larry King talked with dozens of people and got personal advice from a rabbi who befriended him, and still the concept of prayer made no sense to him. Many people told him to try it out, but he had trouble bringing himself to buy into the whole idea. If you are like King, you may not be able to be convinced to pray just because someone tells you to do so. And you will probably not find proof of its effectiveness anywhere either. Prayer is one of those leaps of faith that assumes that there is a listener.

JOIN A FAITH COMMUNITY

Organized religion is not for everybody. But for those who seek a spiritual communion with others as well as with God, joining a faith community, such as a church, temple, synagogue, or mosque, can fulfill these needs. If you were raised in a religious community you might feel the comforts of your childhood when you worship with others. That sense of belonging can reassure you in times of trouble. If you make an effort to get to know those with whom you attend services, you can become a type of family, giving and taking support from the larger group.

The constancy of practices and traditions of your worship group can be reassuring in a world where things change all the time. The rituals you may have complained about as a child can give you a sense of belonging as an adult. When the choir sings a traditional hymn, when prayers are chanted, or when you see the icons of your religion displayed as they have been for centuries, you may feel reassured that God and your community of fellow-believers are still at your side.

In religious services that are structured and repetitious it is easy to turn on your automatic pilot and follow along in a mindless way. While this may be pleasant for some, others find it unappealing. To get the most out of your religious service try to listen closely to the words, remember why each phrase is spoken, and mean what you say.

In most congregations, religious leaders and laypersons are trained to provide you with guidance and support through difficult times. Some faith communities meet in small groups in people's homes for study, discussion, prayer, and social events. These are the people who can come to your aid when you are depressed and feeling lonely. Let them offer you their strength and hope when you have run out of your own.

ACTS OF KINDNESS

Sometimes we feel most spiritually fulfilled when we are responding to the needs of others. In those moments, we are at our best. We give of ourselves, we receive gratitude and self-satisfaction, both of which can help break the negative cycle of depression. Naomi had suffered from severe and chronic depression for a good part of the last five years. She had lost her job, her husband, and her passion for life. In her darkest moments, she had lost hope and considered suicide. As each week passed, it was harder and harder for her to find reasons to keep going. She had tried all the medications, been to therapy, and had prayed for relief from her pain. Despite the fact that her children, her grandchildren, and her brothers and sisters loved her and tried each day to give her hope, Naomi had ceased to find meaning in life.

Then an unfortunate event occurred that helped Naomi regain her strength to fight off her depression. Her older sister had a stroke that left her unable to care for herself. Naomi loved her sister dearly and felt tremendous compassion for her as she lay in her bed partially paralyzed. When her sister was released from the hospital, Naomi made it her mission to care for her each day. After tending to her own family and her home each morning, Naomi drove across town to help her sister out of bed, feed her, and dress her. Although her sister had trouble speaking clearly, Naomi could see the gratitude in her sister's eyes. Being helpful made Naomi feel good about herself, like she had resumed her place in the living world. With this newly found purpose, Naomi's desire to work on her depression was revitalized. She had found a reason to live.

Try doing a kind and helpful act for others in your family or in your community and see what it does to your mood. Perhaps you will be like Naomi and benefit from a boost in self-esteem and from the positive feedback you receive from others. When you are kind to others your focus is turned away from your personal misery long enough to give you a break from feeling bad and to see yourself in a new light. It proves that others need you, that you have a place in the world, and that you are capable of making positive changes.

Key Point

Rather than sit and wait for divine intervention, take some positive actions toward improving your spiritual life.

Emotions and Spirituality

Across cultures and creeds, spirituality involves a commitment from the heart, for example having faith, keeping hope alive, and expressing love for others. In depression, these emotions are often lacking. Sadness and emptiness replace more positive feelings, just as sleeplessness, fatigue, and loss of appetite replace normal physical functioning. When people struggle with depression, they can lose faith that their prayers will be answered. They lose hope that they will ever return to normal, and they lose the capacity to experience joy or love. Fortunately, as their depression lifts, their positive feelings reemerge.

Rather than wait for those emotions to return on their own, you can work to regain the capacity for love, your hope for the future, and your faith. You might remember from our introduction to CBT in the early chapters of this book that your thoughts, feelings, and actions affect one another. A change in any one will cause a change in the others. It is difficult to change your feelings from sad to happy or from hopeless to hopeful unless you change either your thoughts or your actions. In the next section we will suggest actions you can take that may increase your capacity for hope, faith, and love as you work to overcome your depression and regain your spiritual life.

THE POWER OF HOPE

According to research on depression by Aaron Beck and his colleagues at the University of Pennsylvania, hopelessness can lead to suicidal thoughts and actions. Without hope for change, people can give up, assuming that any effort is futile. If the pain is too great to tolerate, they sometimes convince themselves that death is the only alternative. At the end of Chapter 1, we asked you to try to list reasons that you should have hope. When you are feeling hopeless or thinking about death you need a reason to keep going. Thinking about all the reasons you have to live, no matter how small, is a way to generate hope. Read though your reasons for hope from time to time and add items if you can.

Your spiritual faith can also give you hope if it is something you have relied on in the past for comfort or for direction. Although times might be tough, Adriana always found comfort in her belief that she was not alone in her suffering. She believed in God and thought that ultimately her faith would lead her in the direction of recovery. This was all she needed to fight off ideas of giving up. Shannon felt the same way. When she was feeling her darkest, she would pray for direction or assistance in making it through another day. At times, she wondered if God was really answering her prayers or if her desire to believe was making her motivate herself. It didn't really matter to her. She liked believing that there was a force greater than hers that could give her strength when she couldn't muster it on her own. The point in these examples is that your spiritual beliefs can be the key to sustaining your hope. And your hope that things can be better will motivate you to take the necessary actions to recover from your depression.

REGAINING FAITH

Faith is another element of spirituality that is fueled more by emotion than logic or reasoning. It is based on trust in certain spiritual principles or doctrines. If things happen in your life that seem contrary to your beliefs, you might start to question whether or not your beliefs are true. For example, Lewis always believed that if you lived a good life, treated others well, and respected God's rules, everything would turn out all right. When he lost his job after years of unselfish dedication, he started to question whether or not he had followed the right principles. "Maybe I shouldn't have been such a sap. I've always been such a do-gooder and look where that got me. Maybe I should have been selfish. Maybe I should have done what was best for me rather than what was best for the company. If I had known that I'd be treated like this in the end, maybe I wouldn't have been so uptight about always being honest in business, always putting the needs of the team above my own. I've been a good guy all my life and look where I am now. Maybe only the rotten ones get ahead." Lewis' work principles and his religious principles had always been similar. When his work failed him, he questioned his other principles. He lost faith in the notion that things would turn out well if only he followed the rules.

Michelle lost faith for a while when she was going through her divorce. She prayed that her husband would come back to her, but he never did. She felt abandoned by him and by God. She had always believed that if you ask God for help, you will get it. She had never really asked for anything before this, and when she finally did, the answer was something like "Sorry, I can't help you." Michelle's first instinct was to say that God doesn't really exist. At that time, she figured that if God did exist, she would never have lost her husband. She talked this over with her sister, Melanie. Melanie didn't agree or disagree, because she knew that arguing with Michelle was usually unhelpful when she was in a bad mood. Instead, Melanie asked her, "Are you willing to tell your children that God does not exist and that they should stop saying their prayers?"

"No way!" Michelle quickly replied.

"If you won't say this to your kids then maybe its because you don't really believe it," Melanie gently suggested.

Giving up your beliefs after a bad event in your life is an example of all-or-none thinking. Either your beliefs hold true in all situations you encounter or you throw them out as false. It's easy to have faith in good times, when your ideas are not challenged by misfortune. Lewis' actions on the job were driven by his personal philosophy. They had not always led him to make the most profit, but he felt good about being true to his values. Lewis and Michelle were angry when things did not turn out the way they had always hoped. They looked for a place to lay their blame. When their prayers were not answered as they had hoped, it was easy to lay their blame on God. Fortunately for both, when they were able to overcome their hardships and get their lives back on track, their faith returned. They took time to reevaluate their faith and decided to keep it.

You might hear people say, "You've got to have faith." The question for you is, faith about what? Should you have faith in yourself, in other people, in a higher entity, in the balance of nature, in science, in God? The answer will be different for each person. There are organized doctrines of faith and there are informal personal philosophies. Regardless of which is the case for you, strengthening your faith will give you something to hold on to in times of crisis. It can guide your decisions and practices, and it can be the leaning post that keeps you standing when you are ready to fold.

If you have gotten out of the habit of practicing your faith, perhaps now is the time to consider beginning anew. What did you like about your prior faith? What were the positive aspects? Can you think of times in your life that you relied on your faith, and it served you well? If you could change anything about your practices of faith, what would you do differently? Is it worth it to you to try to regain your faith? If so, make a plan to get started.

The easiest way to get back on track with your system of faith is to return to your old practices. That might mean attending a service, carving out time for meditation and prayer, or other actions that demonstrate your profession of faith. Another avenue is to talk with someone who shares your system of faith. Get them to advise you, help you, or work with you on your faith journey. Spiritual leaders in your community are

Key Point

Faith in a higher power or a greater good or purpose is one of the center-pieces of spirituality. Building or strengthening your faith can help safeguard you in times of trouble.

good resources to help you talk through your reservations and to find a way of spiritual self-expression. There are many books on building your faith as well as classes you can attend that might help to get you started. Use the resources around you to explore how strengthening your faith might help you to recover from depression.

SOFTENING YOUR HEART

You cannot force yourself to have love for another person, but you can try to remove the obstacles from your heart that might be preventing you from feeling the love that is already there. It is not unusual to hear romantic partners say, "I don't think I love him" or "I'm not in love with her anymore." Sometimes parents and their children have had so much stress in their relationships that they are unable to feel any genuine love for one another. Having hardships in their lives can make people so bit-ter that they no longer feel any love for mankind. In these scenarios a great deal of love can remain, but it is masked by the hurt and angry feel-ings.

Making attempts to reconcile the conflicts would be a good start. Another strategy is to imagine what you would feel like if you did not have those people in your life any more, that you lost them permanently through death or estrangement. If you are completely honest with your-self and you recognize a sense of sadness or loss with their departure, then you probably still have the remnants of love for them in your heart.

If you wish to tap into your spiritual strengths, one way is to allow yourself to experience loving feelings. If this comes naturally to you, you will only need to make time each day to be with those people or things that you love. Don't make excuses that you have too much to do. Don't tell yourself that they are too busy for you. Schedule the time to talk to your parents over the phone, to play with your children, to write your best friend a letter, to take your dog for a walk, or e-mail your favorite aunt. Make the effort to express the love you have in your heart. It is not enough to know that you love someone. You have to show it occasionally. The easiest way to do that is to say the words. If it's not comfortable to say them directly, write them in a note or send them in a card. You can show your feelings through acts of kindness or through physical displays of affection. Every time you make an effort, you open your heart.

Medicine versus Prayer

There are many people whose strong faith in prayer has led them to refuse medical interventions for their illness. They have gotten better and have professed that it was a direct result of their prayers being answered. There are also some who believe that relying on medication is contrary to having faith in God. That is, if they truly believe then they will be cured. So if they take medication, it must mean that they do not really believe. This presents a dilemma if your doctor tells you that you need medication for depression. Viewing medications or prayers as two opposing choices makes it hard to reconcile the fact that both seem to work for some people.

The research on CBT for depression shows that it is an effective alternative to medication. If you are not comfortable with the idea of taking antidepressant drugs, use the other Keys or natural biological remedies to help you recover. If you do not get the relief you need, talk over your concerns about the morality of medical treatment with your faith leaders and your physician.

Armando suffered from chronic depression for which he took medication and prayed to God daily for help. He believed that all good things, even medical breakthroughs, had divine inspiration, so relying on medical treatments didn't mean that he had less faith. Armando didn't think that God created his depression so he didn't think that he had to rely on only God for a cure. But sometimes, Armando didn't get the results he needed from prayer or from medication.

He had read a great deal about mood disorders and had been in therapy for many years. His symptoms would wax and wane, but there were some days when he felt so devastated by his depression he could hardly make it through the day. In those times, he didn't know what to do, so he prayed for guidance. He didn't always get a straight answer and that depressed him further.

One day in therapy, he discussed his religious faith and how he prayed in times of trouble. He described how he would get so muddled in misery that he didn't know what to do. So he prayed.

THERAPIST: What do you pray for?
ARMANDO: I ask God for guidance. I ask what I should do next.

THERAPIST: And sometimes you don't get an answer and that makes you feel worse?

ARMANDO: Yes.

THERAPIST: I'm not sure how these things work, but could it be possible that God already gave you the answer for what to do during those times.

ARMANDO: I don't know what you mean.

THERAPIST: Maybe you are supposed to use the answers you have found in therapy and in all the books you have read. Maybe the answers are all around you. Maybe God doesn't give you a new answer each time because you already have the answer.

ARMANDO: When I am that depressed, it's so hard to use those techniques. My mind goes blank. All I can think to do is pray.

THERAPIST: If it happens again, maybe in addition to prayer, you could pull out the notes you have kept and try some of the skills you have developed for combating the negative thinking and for gaining new hope.

ARMANDO: So maybe instead of praying for more guidance, I should just be praying to remember what I'm supposed to do to feel better. That makes sense.

The Spirituality Key in Your Personal Plan for Recovery

It is time to make a plan for improving your spiritual life as a way of helping you recover from your depression. If your spiritual life is already a source of strength, try to continue your practices or increase the amount of time you commit to it. If the thought of working on your spirituality makes you feel even more depressed, skip it for now. Work through the other Keys and when you feel up to it, try some of the exercises in Chapters 12 and 13. If you are somewhere in the middle, it is time to add to your Personal Plan for Recovery. We have given you an example of Janie's personal plan for improving her spirituality. You will find a blank form in the Appendix to create your own plan.

Exercise 13.2
Personal Plan for Recovery Worksheet—Part VIII
'My Plan for Using the Spirituality Key':

JANIE'S EXAMPLE

1. What types of things give my life meaning and purpose?
    Doing a good job at work. Having good friends. Making my home look nice.

2. Are there things I want to do to build my sense of meaning and purpose? What is my plan for doing this?
    I feel alone much of the time. I want to belong to something, like a community or a family. I want other people to know me and to count on me. I'm going to start by taking people up on their offers to join their families for special events and by getting to know my own neighbors.

3. How will I make time to work on my spirituality? When will I fit it in?
    Instead of watching television every night, I will set aside one evening to read about spirituality. I've always wanted to join a Bible study group. I'll try to join a class one evening each week.

4. Who could help me with my spiritual journey? Will I join a faith community?
    I will join David and his family at the synagogue more often to see if I fit in. Maybe I'll go back to my parents' church some time and see how that feels. I need to talk it over with someone. I'll ask David what he thinks.

5. What are some ways in which I can connect better to people in my life? What opportunities do I have to be more loving and giving with others?
    I would like to make peace with my mother. I'd like to do nice things for her. I will have an opportunity over the holiday season to do something nice. I'll take the first step toward breaking the ice with her. I will also try to connect better with my little sisters and their children. I may not be able to be a good daughter, but I can be a good aunt and a good sister.

6. What will I do to become more mindful of my experiences and my environment?

When I take my morning jogs, I will try to use that time to tune into things around me. I'll write down my observations in my notebook.

7. Are there any obstacles that are keeping me from having a full spiritual life? What are they? What do I need to do to remove them from my path?

   My mother is a big obstacle. I need to make peace with her so that my heart is not so blocked by all those bad feelings. I will have to find a way to let the past go and to give her another chance. Also, getting caught up with day-to-day worries is a problem. I have to remind myself to get the big picture. The things that happen each day are not really that important. I need to make a commitment to add spirituality to my life. I'm going to get that book about not sweating the small stuff.

8. Do I have any negative thoughts about my spirituality? What methods can I use to evaluate those thoughts?

   I don't have any negative thoughts about it.

9. What opportunities do I have to practice forgiveness of myself and of others? How will I go about these tasks?

   I have a great opportunity with my mother. I'm not sure I can do it, but I'll try to remind myself that she probably didn't have a good role model for parenting and so she did not always know how to handle me. I'll try to accept the fact that not all mothers are perfect. I will have to show her that I forgive her by making contact with her. I'll start by sending her a birthday card. I can forgive myself. I just need to make a conscious effort and tell myself that I can't be perfect.

10. How can meditation and/or prayer help me to develop my spirituality? What is my plan for getting started?

    I used to meditate when I was in college. I'll start that up again. Maybe I'll take time to meditate on the mornings that I don't jog. I have a book on meditation. I'll read it through again. I know how to pray. I just need to remind myself to do it. Maybe I'll put a sticky note by my nightstand to remind myself to pray at bedtime.

14

Making Your Plan Work

Michelle was talking with members of her Depression Support Group about her experiences with the illness. She used the Five Keys to work her way out of depression and was feeling better about herself and about life in general.

"I've been working so hard to get out of this slump, I almost didn't notice that I was pretty much back to normal. The funniest thing happened the other day. I heard myself laughing with the children. I realized that it had been a long time since I had heard that sound. I was happy about it, but it also made me feel a little sad. I wondered what else I had been missing out on."

Isabella spoke up next and agreed with Michelle. "I know what you mean. Now that I'm better I'm acting like I used to when I was younger, like getting silly, and enjoying the dumbest things. I really feel like I've finally gotten my life back. That must sound really sappy."

"No, not at all," Consuelo chimed in. "I've been noticing lots of things I missed while I was depressed. I used to think that it was absurd that people got tickled over little things, like TV commercials or bumper stickers. Now, I laugh over the same goofy things. My only regret is that I was so self-absorbed with depression that I missed out on a lot."

"I try not to think about that," said Adriana. "I just want to go forward. I want the past to be left behind, regrets and all. It's like a bad chapter in my life story. I don't need to reread it. I know what happened."

When you come out of a depressive episode, it can feel like a whole segment of your life passed by in a blur. You might have trouble remembering with any detail what happened during those weeks, months, or even years. Although you may want to forget your experiences and just focus on the future, there is something to be gained from reviewing how you pulled out of depression. You can find clues to help you stay well and prevent your symptoms from returning.

No one wants to think about this, but depression is a recurrent illness. According to research on the course of depression, there is a 50 percent chance of experiencing a recurrence of depression after you have had one episode. After you have had a second episode, the risk of the symptoms coming back goes up to 70 percent. After your third episode, you are at an even higher risk of continuing to have bouts of depression. Relapses are not inevitable, however.

In this chapter we'll help you learn ways to reduce the chances of depression returning or, at least, to stop the symptoms early in their development. But you may not be quite at the point yet to work out a relapse prevention plan. Maybe you are still feeling down or are having trouble with making your recovery plan work. So first we'll offer some tips for troubleshooting your Personal Plan for Recovery. You can try these ideas for making your depression a thing of the past.

Breaking through Roadblocks to Recovery— A Troubleshooting Guide

HITTING A PLATEAU

When people recover from depression, they often do not experience steady day-to-day progress. Instead there can be plateaus where they may seem to get stuck for a while. These plateaus can be a normal part of getting better. However, if plateaus extend for two or more weeks, you should probably start working on ways to get moving again toward recovery.

Dr. Steven Stahl wrote a scientific article with a great title: "Why Settle for Silver, when You Can Go for Gold?" This paper focuses on the problem of having only a partial recovery from depression. The therapy works, but stops somewhere short of full wellness. Dr. Stahl points out that the goal of treatment should be to "go for the gold"—a full recovery. Otherwise, you can be left at a plateau with symptoms that interfere with daily living and limit the potential for growth. We have had many patients referred to us for second opinions who have been at one of these plateaus for months or years. When we encounter this type of problem, we try to look at all areas of the Five Keys for possible answers.

If you seem to be stuck and are not sure what to do, go back over the earlier parts of this book and your notebook for ideas. There may be parts of your recovery plan that you haven't implemented yet or you haven't given a fair chance. Also, there may be methods that have helped you, but you have stopped using them for some reason. For example, many of the people whom we treat with CBT get a great deal of benefit from identifying and changing their automatic thoughts early in treatment. Yet, some of them seem to drift away from using these effective methods after the worst of their depression is over. Getting back to some of the basics of these self-help techniques is often enough for them to break out of plateaus in their recovery process.

If you think you have hit a plateau and are not continuing to make progress toward full recovery, there are many biological approaches worth considering. Perhaps you haven't tried an antidepressant yet. If this is the case, you could consult a doctor about taking medication. If you are currently using an antidepressant, but haven't gotten full relief, the strategies in Chapter 9 for increasing the chances of treatment response may give you the answer. Some of these include raising the dose of an antidepressant, switching to a new medication, taking more than one antidepressant, or adding other medications such as lithium or thyroid pills. If your family doctor is prescribing your antidepressant and is not familiar with some of the more advanced or complicated pharmacological treatments, you can ask for a referral to a specialist to help you reach the goal of complete recovery.

STRESSFUL EVENTS DERAIL YOU

Unfortunately, life does not slow down while you are working your way out of a depression. You may be doing your best to keep a positive attitude and resolve your problems. However, other people can discourage you, lay new challenges in your path, or make your life chaotic. We have had many patients who come in with a new crisis each session—child problems, in-law problems, money problems, housing problems. They say that they do not have time to work on themselves because they are too busy trying to cope with all of these problems. They have trouble seeing a light at the end of the tunnel. So they become discouraged and hopeless, and their depression worsens.

Instead of jumping from crisis to crisis, we suggest that they change their strategy to do these things: (1) narrow the focus of their recovery plan, for the time being, to just a few manageable problems, and (2) expend most of their efforts on mending themselves.

The reason to work on solving a small number of problems is that you can become distracted and overwhelmed by shifting from one crisis to another, and, you may end up getting nothing accomplished. However, if you put just a few of these things on your plate at a time, you may have a better chance of solving some of these difficulties. The reason to devote most of your effort toward mending yourself is that if you are stronger you will be better equipped to cope with stress. You can be a better mother, father, spouse, or friend if you take care of yourself first. Then you will be able to manage your life problems with greater success.

ARE YOU TRYING TO DO TOO MUCH?

If you are someone who commonly takes on complicated or challenging problems, it can feel frustrating to start again at square one or to take small steps at a time. Even if you are a high achiever, depression can zap your energy, lower your ability to concentrate, and take away your motivation. To get back to normal, you have to fight against these symptoms. So, be careful that you don't take on too much, too soon in trying to control your depression. The most important thing is that your depression goes away and stays away. We suggest that you work slowly, but steadily. Choose interventions that you can do at this time and seem to help. Methods that seem too complex or hard to use at present can be put off for a later day.

PROCRASTINATION

"I'll do it tomorrow." Have you heard yourself utter that promise? Despite your good intentions, you still may be holding yourself back from taking the steps you need to recover from depression. Maybe you have forgotten to monitor your negative thoughts. Perhaps you have a tendency to get caught up in the emotion of the moment and fall back into unhealthy coping strategies rather than try out a new coping plan. It could be that you are waiting for the "right moment" to begin to make changes. A treatment plan cannot work unless you use it. If you are procrastinating in beginning your Personal Plan for Recovery, go back to Chapter 6 and read the suggestions for overcoming procrastination. Do not wait for the motivation to act. Act now, and your motivation will build as you see yourself successfully combat the symptoms of depression.

TROUBLE MANAGING YOUR MEDICATIONS

For many people, taking a medicine every day is no easy task. They can be bothered by side effects, get complacent after feeling well for weeks or months, or simply have trouble remembering to take the medication. We have seen innumerable patients who have had less than optimal treatment responses, or relapses, because they didn't take an anti-depressant regularly or they stopped a medication prematurely.

You can do several things to help increase the chances that you will take your antidepressant and allow it to work for you. The first is to set up a reminder system such as putting notes on your daily calendar or on the mirror above your bathroom sink. Or, you can buy a seven-day pill container at your pharmacy and use it to keep track of your medication. Another strategy that often works is to take your antidepressant at the same time every day along with something else that you do routinely, like brushing your teeth.

If side effects are getting in the way of taking medication, call your doctor and work out a plan to handle the problem. Perhaps you still have negative attitudes about using antidepressants. If this is the case, you can check your answers to the Medication Attitude Survey in Chapter 9 and use Thinking Key methods to develop healthier attitudes.

LACK OF POSITIVE REINFORCEMENT

One of the reasons why people can have trouble in making their re-covery plan work is that they are not getting enough positive reinforce-ment for their accomplishments. Many research studies have shown that if people get positive rewards for their efforts they are more likely to con-tinue them. If you have joined a health club or have participated in pro-grams like Weight Watchers, you will probably be familiar with some of the positive reinforcers that are built into their programs. The YMCA that one of us (Jesse) attends has a computerized system of monitoring work on exercise machines. Since this system was installed, the number of people who use the exercise equipment has more than doubled. The computer system gives feedback on calories expended and "fitness points" earned. Users can get lots of positive reinforcement in seeing that they are making progress.

You don't need an elaborate computer system to record or log your progress. Just make an effort to routinely write out a record of what you are doing to change. You can do this in your notebook. For example, you might keep a log of your exercise, your daily activity schedule, or at-tempts you are making to try out new schemas.

It might also help to think of other things that could give you posi-tive reinforcement for sticking with a plan for recovery. Could you build in rewards for carrying out some of your plans or meeting some of your goals? Shannon, the woman from Chapter 5 who was having trouble with daily chores, decided that she would allow herself a leisurely Saturday af-ternoon bubble bath if she kept the kitchen clean all week. Michelle promised herself a needlepoint kit she had been wanting if she followed her plan to resume a social life after her divorce. She knew it would be hard to face her anxiety about getting out with people again. So, she thought of something that would give her extra motivation to change. One of Vic's favorite activities was fly-fishing. He and his wife agreed to take a short vacation to do some fishing if he could demonstrate lasting changes in his habit of being critical of himself and others.

Staying Well

Once you get your symptoms under control, it is a good idea to start thinking about ways to keep depression from returning. In this last section of *Getting Your Life Back,* we'll help you work out a plan for staying well. If you are receiving psychotherapy or are taking a medication, you will want to know how long to keep going with treatment. Although continuation on a medication has received the most scientific testing of all relapse prevention methods, there is evidence that people who are treated with CBT also have a reduced rate of relapse. In our experiences with patients, we've found that people who learn the basics of CBT have good tools that they can use to fight the return of depression. So, we'll offer some ideas from CBT that you can use to spot symptoms early and keep them away.

Keys to Staying Well

Don't stop treatment too soon.

When to Stop Treatment

HOW LONG IS LONG ENOUGH ON MEDICATIONS?

The American Psychiatric Association *Practice Guideline for the Treatment of Depressive Disorders* recommends that medication be continued for sixteen to twenty weeks after remission of a single episode of depression. Experts such as Dr. Martin Keller and Dr. Michael Thase have reviewed a great number of research studies and have concluded that staying on medications substantially reduces the risk for relapse. If you have recurrent depression (typically defined as two or more episodes), it is usually recommended that you stay on medications for longer periods of time—perhaps indefinitely. Long-term therapy with antidepressants has helped a great number of people avoid the pain and suffering of recurrent depression.

We have many patients in our practices who have been taking antidepressants for long periods of time and are completely well. In the past they were buffeted with multiple episodes of depression, but now their lives are going very smoothly. Ed, a sixty-one-year-old man who owns a farm implement store, is a good example. Nine years ago when Ed was fifty-two, he consulted with one of us (Jesse) for treatment of depression. By that time in his life, he had already had four periods of deep depression and had been in and out of treatment with counseling and medication. We began a treatment plan that included an antidepressant and CBT.

Fortunately, Ed responded nicely to the therapy and pulled completely out of depression. Ed had learned some important skills from CBT that could help him keep depression away. But, with Ed's history of frequent relapses, a strong recommendation was made that Ed continue on his antidepressant indefinitely. He had no significant side effects, and the antidepressant had great potential for keeping him well.

Ed has had lots of stress over the past nine years. He had a heart bypass operation five years ago and subsequently had to cut back on his hours at work. There have been some financial worries, and he lost both of his parents. But, Ed has been able to weather these storms with no return of depression. In fact, he feels happier now and more satisfied with his life than at any time he can remember. He takes his medication faithfully and comes in for a brief appointment twice a year. Here is what Ed has to say about taking antidepressants. "I never want to stop. Why would I want to risk it? The medication works great. And, who would ever want to get depressed again?"

HOW MUCH IS ENOUGH THERAPY?

Most of the research on the treatment of depression shows that people can get over depression in nine to twenty visits if the treatment follows a standard protocol or method such as with CBT. However, some persons with depression may need more time to deal with their problems, particularly if they are suffering from additional difficulties such as substance abuse, anxiety, posttraumatic stress disorder, or family problems. In these cases we recommend longer-term treatment lasting a year or more.

You should stick with therapy if it is helpful to you. When you feel that you have achieved your goals or have learned enough to cope with additional problems on your own, it is usually a good idea to stop. We like it when our patients taper off their visits slowly so that we can help monitor their progress and watch for any return of symptoms. For example, after weekly therapy for four to ten weeks we might switch to having sessions every two weeks for a few months, then once a month for about two to three months, with a follow-up visit six months later. We give our patients the option to be seen sooner if they feel there is too much space between visits or to call and cancel visits if they feel they are doing fine. When therapy has ended, we love it when our patients drop us a note or call to let us know that they are doing well or to share good news about their accomplishments.

SHOULD I STAY IN THERAPY AFTER I FEEL BETTER?

In general, we do not believe that people should have more therapy than is necessary to achieve their treatment goals. Unfortunately, some patients can become too dependent upon their therapists and have difficulty discontinuing treatment. They lack confidence and are afraid to be on their own. In these cases, the patient may attribute too much of his or her success in treatment to the therapist rather than taking credit for making the changes that helped get his or her life back. Remember that a therapist is only with you for just a short time each week. The rest of the time, you are doing the work to feel better.

A therapist can be a helpful person, but he or she is not a substitute for family and friends. You need support from other people in your life. Your goals for treatment should include building a support network and completing therapy. We think it's great when our patients say they don't need us anymore. For us, this is a therapy success.

Keys to Staying Well

Keep a healthy life-style:

Exercise regularly.
Keep good sleep habits.
Maintain a healthy diet.
Keep relationships strong.
Keep stress under control.

Life-Style Management

SELF-CARE THROUGH EXERCISE, SLEEP, AND DIET

One way to work on staying well is to develop a healthy life-style. You have probably heard enough from the media and your doctor about the importance of a healthy diet and exercise. If you have started to use some of the self-help exercises from Chapters 5 and 6 to improve your habits, keep the effort going even after your symptoms go away. Continue your exercise program so that you can stay strong and fit. Remember that research studies have shown many positive benefits of exercise on depression. A normal sleep pattern can also give you an edge on keeping depression away. You can find suggestions for improving your sleep in the Action and Biology Keys.

KEEP RELATIONSHIPS STRONG

In Chapters 10 and 11, we discussed how positive relationships can not only help you recover from depression, but also contribute to the overall quality of your life. It is easy to take good relationships for granted. When they are going well, we can assume they do not need attention. Use the suggestions in Chapter 10 to be certain that your positive relationships stay strong.

If you do not have enough positive people in your life, try to find some. Make yourself talk to others such as neighbors or co-workers. Other people can be sources of information, support, and pleasure. If you are shy or tend only to spend time with family members, make yourself reach out and expand your social network. When our patients want to make friends, but have trouble finding them, we suggest they look for opportunities to be with others. For example, join a support group, a volunteer organization, or a club. You can find out about these in your local newspaper. Start attending a Sunday school class at church. Take dance lessons at the local community center or college. Find a singles group or sign up for tennis lessons. Visit your family members more often, invite them to your home, or have a party. Use the thought-recording exercises from Chapter 3 to work out your negative automatic thoughts about socializing and make time to be with others.

STRESS MANAGEMENT

Methods from all five Keys to recovery can help you reduce the impact of stress on your life. For example, from the Thinking Key we usually suggest that people learn how to cut down their negative automatic thoughts and thinking errors, and that they continue their work on replacing maladaptive schemas with healthy attitudes. If you have balanced, logical thinking and healthy attitudes you will be much more likely to avoid overreacting to stressful situations. Some of the stress management techniques that we recommend most highly are listed below. Check over this list to see if you are doing some of these things to reduce the stress in your life.

How to Manage Stress
A List of Our Favorite Methods and Techniques

1. Develop a logical style of thinking and healthy attitudes so that you don't overreact to stress. (Chapters 3 and 4)
2. Use activity scheduling to keep organized and to accomplish tasks when stressed. (Chapter 5)
3. Develop a physical exercise program to relieve stress. (Chapters 4 and 7)
4. Use relaxation exercises to reduce muscle tension. (Chapter 6)
5. Learn more effective communication skills. (Chapters 10 and 11)
6. Use meditation, prayer, or other spiritual exercises that calm you and keep you centered on things that count instead of stressful distractions. (Chapters 12 and 13)

Some additional things you can do to help manage stress are: (1) Pick your battles carefully so that you are not taking issue with every annoying thing that comes your way. Or, as Richard Carlson advises in his best-selling books, "Don't sweat the small stuff, and it's all small stuff." (2) Make time to relax regularly, not just on vacations. And, (3) try to have fun so that your life feels more balanced. The pleasant experiences in your life will make the unpleasant ones seem more tolerable.

Keys to Staying Well

Know your symptoms.

Develop an Early-Warning System

If you can identify the early signs that depression may be returning, you will have an opportunity to stop the symptoms before they become severe. In addition to the symptoms in the Five Keys Depression Rating Scale and those described in Chapter 2, you may have your own unique signs. Make a list of symptoms, sensations, and signs to watch for in your notebook. When you are not feeling well, review your list. If you have more than a few symptoms and they seem to last more than a week, it is probably time to take any actions necessary to keep them from worsening. Another way to monitor your symptoms is to fill out the Five Keys Depression Rating Scale once each month or so. If the score is higher than usual, monitor your symptoms closely and use what you have learned from the Five Keys.

Symptoms of depression can sneak up on you or can be mistaken for physical problems, such as the flu or PMS. If you are uncertain about the nature of your symptoms, talk them over with your doctor or therapist. Our former patients call us periodically to ask our opinions on whether or not their depression is returning. We can often tell from their descriptions if they are having symptoms of depression or just a reaction to stress. When we are uncertain, we suggest that they watch their symptoms closely and call us back if they worsen or if more symptoms appear. And, if there are symptoms that suggest a possible physical illness (see Chapter 7 for information on medical problems associated with depression), we recommend a medical consultation.

Keys to Staying Well

Be prepared for the future:

Identify triggers for depression.
Prepare for stressful events.
Use cognitive rehearsal methods.

Manage Your Vulnerabilities

IDENTIFY TRIGGERS FOR DEPRESSION

For many people who suffer from depression there are patterns of stressors, or times of the year, that can predictably trigger a return of depression. If you have seasonal affective disorder (see Chapter 7 for a reminder of the symptoms) your trigger may be the winter months. Dr. Zindel Siegel at the University of Toronto found that if you are vulnerable to a specific kind of stress, and that particular stress occurs, you are more likely to get depressed. He described two types of vulnerability patterns. People who were sensitive to achievement-oriented stressors got depressed if they had a failure experience, like losing a job. Those who were sensitive to interpersonal stressors got depressed when they had relationship problems. If you know what is going to make you depressed, you have a better chance of preparing for the event and fighting off the symptoms. Some stressors come by surprise, giving you little time to prepare. However, if you are aware of what kinds of events are likely to stress you, you can make a plan for coping with them the next time they occur.

Adriana had always been vulnerable to relationship problems. She invested a great deal of energy into new romances. When they went sour, she would crash into despair. Adriana didn't want to keep repeating this cycle so she made a plan to cope better with the next relationship. She knew from prior experiences that she had a tendency to use tunnel vision in sizing up new partners, seeing only their good side and ignoring any negative characteristics. Also, she tended to devote so much attention to new romances that she neglected the rest of her life. When this happened, Adriana would temporarily ignore her close friends, her parents, her job, her hobbies, and even her health. She wouldn't exercise if it conflicted with her new friend's schedule and would change her diet to match his. In other words, she would lose herself in the relationship.

To keep this from happening again, Adriana vowed that she would start new relationships slowly and get to know the man well before emotionally diving off the deep end. She made a commitment to stick with her exercise schedule and good eating habits. If he was the man for her, he could adapt to her healthy habits rather than expect her to change to his habits. Fighting against tunnel vision was her biggest challenge. She was an open-minded and optimistic person by nature. She tended to see the good in people, despite their faults. This tendency, while positive in some circumstances, set her up for heartbreak when it kept her from seeing the warning signs that the relationship was not good for her. By knowing her vulnerabilities, Adriana was able to plan ahead and stop the cycle of depression.

PREPARE FOR STRESSFUL EVENTS

Sometimes the onset of depression can be tied to specific recurring events, like the holidays or the anniversary of a sad event, such as the death of a loved one. If you know the event is coming, you can use the Five Keys to help prepare for and cope with these events so that they do not lead to depression.

Geneva was most vulnerable during the holidays, especially since she lost her grandmother. She wasn't certain if it was seasonal affective disorder or just the pressure she felt preparing for Thanksgiving, Christmas, and New Year's Day. Since her grandmother had become too ill to handle the preparation, Geneva had been the one everyone counted on to make holidays special. She was thoughtful in giving gifts, organized for parties, and always on time with Christmas cards. Her holiday table was beautifully set. The meals were delicious. And, she always looked happy.

What few people knew was that Geneva dreaded the holidays. She forced herself to put on a happy face in front of others even when she got little satisfaction from her work. Geneva decided to prepare for the next holiday season differently so that she would not be so exhausted and depressed. Part of her plan was to stay on antidepressants and to begin using light therapy in October before giving her symptoms a chance to return. She also decided to let someone else take the lead in planning the holiday festivities. She knew that the other women in the family wanted an opportunity to have the parties in their homes. So Geneva planned to take a year off to see how it felt. Because she really did like Christmas shopping, she decided to keep that activity but lighten up on the wrapping and allow her kids to help out. It would not be the end of the world if the ribbons did not match the paper. The last part of Geneva's plan was to not allow herself to get so exhausted. She would go to bed at a reasonable hour whenever possible and pace herself during the day.

Geneva's plan was a success. She continued to take her antidepressant, and she began to use light therapy in late October. No one minded helping with the festivities. The celebrations turned out differently than she would have liked, but she thought that was a fair price to pay for avoiding a full episode of depression.

USE COGNITIVE REHEARSAL TECHNIQUES

In CBT, patients are often taught rehearsal techniques for helping to prevent relapse. We described this method in Chapter 3 as part of the Thinking Key. First think of a specific event or trigger that could throw you off course. Then imagine that this event actually happened. Write down the automatic thoughts, emotions, and behavior that you would likely have in this situation. Now stand back from the situation and try to think it through logically. How could you approach the situation in a rational and sensible manner? What kind of actions could you take to have a successful resolution of the situation? Now practice thinking and acting in this logical, problem-solving mode.

It might also help to write down your thoughts for how to best handle the situation on a coping card (see Chapter 4 for details of how to use this method). You can use coping cards as reminders of action plans that you have thought out in advance.

Michelle used cognitive rehearsal after she had recovered from depression, but was still trying to get back to a full social life in the aftermath of her divorce. One of her vulnerabilities was feeling like she shouldn't be out socializing without a man—that somehow people would look down on her as a divorced woman who was out with a few of her female friends. Her anxiety about getting back into a social life had led her to refuse many invitations and to spend lots of lonely nights at home by herself.

When she imagined herself out at a party with a few of her friends, she was able to recognize some automatic thoughts and behavior that would make the situation worse.

Automatic Thoughts: "Everybody knows that I just got a divorce. They must be wondering what I did wrong. I'd be better off at home where I wouldn't have to face anyone. I'll never feel comfortable going out like this. Who would want to do anything with me?"

Emotions: Anxiety, shame

Behavior: "I'd want to get out of there as fast as I could—to retreat to the safety of my own bedroom where nobody could see me or criticize me."

Michelle recognized that this kind of response could drag her back into depression and would interfere with her getting back into a full life after her divorce. So, she rehearsed a more logical way of handling social events and wrote down her strategy on a coping card.

Michelle's Coping Card
"My plan for going out with my friends"

1. Tell myself that I deserve to be out socializing as much as anyone else.
2. Realize that everybody has their own problems and concerns—they aren't spending all their time thinking about me or judging me.
3. Ask other people about what is going on in their lives instead of worrying about what they are thinking about me.
4. See myself as who I really am—a good friend, a nice person, someone who is intelligent and has something to say—instead of putting myself down as someone who has been rejected.
5. Make a plan to go out at least once a week and stick with it. After a while it will get much easier.
6. Choose things I really want to do so that I'll have a good time and enjoy myself.

The general principle in all of these strategies for managing your vulnerabilities is using methods from the Five Keys to plan in advance for coping with challenges that may lie ahead. By doing this, you can improve your problem-solving skills and decrease your risk for negative, depressive reactions to these situations. Can you think of one or more events or situations that could set you back—that might make you upset or depressed again? Try to use the strategies we have described here to work out a plan for coping in a healthy way and growing stronger in the process.

Keys to Staying Well

Mend troubled relationships.

Coping with Relationship Stress

As we mentioned in the Relationship Key chapters, you can change the way you handle relationships, but you may not be able to solve problems without the cooperation of the other person. Even then, smoothing out the bumps in relationships takes time, effort, and patience. Marriage counselors can be very helpful because they do not take sides and they make sure that each person gets a chance to be heard.

Another possible solution to interpersonal problems is to negotiate a truce. If each person can agree to let go of the past, you may have a chance to create a new beginning. This is tough to do if it is your nature to hold a grudge, bring up the past during arguments, or want revenge. You would have to give up all of these strategies and keep your focus on improvement. As Tony was getting over his depression he realized that he had said a number of negative things to his wife, had not been supportive of her career, and had not communicated well with her. He felt bad about this and wanted a chance to start over again. Marlene was able to forgive Tony for his criticisms, his sexist remarks, and his anger because she knew that he had not been acting like the real Tony. The ugly words came out of a depressed Tony. Marlene agreed to try to leave the past behind and give Tony another chance.

If you have a relationship that is fraught with disagreements, tension, or a lack of intimacy, it may be easier to add positive experiences to relationships rather than try to decrease negative experiences. When you can enjoy one another's company, share leisure activities, or laugh together, the negative times may seem less stressful and more tolerable. Pleasant events can balance out the occurrence of negative events, making the emotional tone of the relationship seem more positive and hopeful. Use the Action Key exercises from Chapter 5 to add pleasure to your relationships with others.

Keys to Staying Well

Don't hesitate to ask for help when you need it.

Reaching Out to Others

People who know you well will notice the subtle changes in your mood or attitude that might signal the return of depression. Ask them to tell you when they notice these changes. Sometimes they will be wrong. But, your job is to take their concerns seriously and evaluate yourself. Could your symptoms be returning? If so, take action.

If you believe that your symptoms of depression are returning or seem to be worsening, call your doctor or therapist and ask for advice. Don't call if you've just had a bad day. Wait until you see a daily pattern of symptoms. On the other hand, don't wait until you are completely miserable before calling for help. It is frustrating for us when patients wait until they have been depressed long enough to have hit rock bottom before they call for help. They don't want to bother us, so they wait until they are in crisis or cannot function well at home or work. We want to hear from them before they ever get to that point. Usually it is easier for people to recover when symptoms are mild.

Keys to Staying Well

Focus on Personal Growth:

Tap into your spiritual strengths and cultivate your inner resources.
Learn new skills.
Build a support system.
Develop healthy attitudes that open doors to the future.

Becoming a Better Person

DEVELOP SPIRITUAL RESOURCES

Do you remember Amelia and Connie from Chapter 11? After they reconciled their friendship, Amelia invited Connie to go with her to her church group on Thursday evening. Connie had never been much of a church-goer. And she was a little uncomfortable with people who seemed well grounded in their religious faiths. Amelia convinced her to come by promising Connie that she would not have to speak up in the group if she didn't want to talk. Connie went and listened to what others had to say. She didn't really understand their discussion about faith, but she did like being around the other people. They seemed content with their lives and supportive of one another. She planned to visit the group a few more times. Maybe the peacefulness they felt would rub off on her.

Many people find a greater sense of satisfaction with life when they strengthen their spiritual orientation. For some, this happens through meditation and reading. For others, it comes from attending a church or synagogue. In addition to reading the works of prominent spiritual leaders, we prepared for writing the Spirituality Key by talking about spiritual matters with friends, colleagues, patients, and family members. What was most striking was that people were eager to talk about their philosophies and spiritual beliefs. We learned a lot about the many ways that people find meaning, pray, and worship. If you are uncertain about how to strengthen your spiritual life, perhaps you can do as we did and ask other people for their opinions and guidance. They may not give you all of the answers you need, but the ideas of others may help you begin your journey.

LEARN NEW SKILLS

This book is full of suggestions for developing new ways to cope with depression. Once you have mastered them, you may want to develop other skills or strengthen old ones. Frances had always been a good musician, but had long ago given it up when she got busy with work and family responsibilities. She had been looking for a hobby or diversion that would give her a break from the stress of caring for her aged parents. She decided to commit thirty minutes each week to taking piano lessons. Because Frances had played the piano as a child, she didn't have to start at the beginning. In fact, her parents still had her old piano in their home. Her mom and dad thought this was a great idea. They had always enjoyed listening to her play. Frances found someone to stay with her parents while she went across town to meet her teacher. Practicing the piano brought happy childhood memories back to Frances and her parents. So, everyone's spirits were lifted.

BUILD A SUPPORT SYSTEM

If you have learned that you are too isolated from others, it's time to make some changes. Consuelo had become isolated from her friends and family members during her marriage. Her husband had always been very controlling and made it difficult for Consuelo and their sons to spend time with others outside the family. After her husband died, many people rallied around Consuelo. But, she had been so used to being on her own, she was uncomfortable allowing other people into her life. One of the goals Consuelo set for herself was to reunite with her family, cultivate relationships with friends, and encourage her sons to do the same.

Many people are not as lucky as Consuelo. They do not have a support system already in place. They have to build one from scratch. The easiest way to gain support from others is to provide support to others. Do something helpful for someone in need. Ask people how they are doing and offer assistance if you see an opportunity. You become part of their support network by reaching out. When it is your turn, they are likely to return the favor.

Many cities have depression support groups or therapy groups. It can be comforting to talk with people who are struggling with problems similar to yours. If you are interested, ask your doctor or call one of the national mental health organizations listed in the Appendix. They may be able to tell you where to call for groups in your area.

DEVELOP HEALTHY ATTITUDES AND BELIEFS

In the Thinking Key, we talked about developing rules of wellness that can help you solve problems and promote personal growth. And, in the Spirituality Key we suggested that finding meaning in life not only serves as an antidote to despair, but also leads to a sense of greater fulfillment and purpose. When we do CBT with our patients, we try to bring these two Keys to recovery together to help people get beyond depression to a fuller and richer life.

Anne Marie, the doctor who had the schema "If I choose to do something, I must succeed no matter what the cost," and who was at the brink of suicide before treatment, transformed her life by working with the Thinking and Spirituality Keys. You may remember that she modified the driven quality of her success-oriented schemas and learned how to get involved in relaxing activities. Even after her therapy ended, she continued to work on developing healthier attitudes. At a follow-up session six months after stopping active treatment, Anne Marie told an inspiring story.

> It's hard to describe how much I've changed since I first came for treatment. I used to be such a workaholic. I spent all day and most of the night worrying about what I was or wasn't getting done—and measuring my success. No matter what I did, I always seemed to come up short. Nothing satisfied me. I couldn't enjoy anything. I was totally preoccupied with my own misery and couldn't appreciate what was going on in anybody else's life. But, now my attitude is totally different. The funny thing is that I'm actually getting more accomplished since I stopped worrying so much and driving myself into the ground.
>
> I went back and reread my personal story that I wrote when I started treatment for depression. When I read it now it sounds like another person talking. I can't believe how hopeless I was. I felt sorry for myself and could only see the dark side of life. I'm not like that anymore. In fact, I didn't just get my life back; in some ways my life is actually better than it was before the whole nightmare began.

Anne Marie went on to describe how her attitudes had changed and how she was making commitments that gave her life a deeper sense of meaning. Some of her newer, more adaptive schemas were: "Focus on what really counts in life—the people you love, the work you can do to help others, learning new things, appreciating the beauty in the world—instead of measuring your success. Work hard and try to do well in life, but spend time doing things where success doesn't matter. Use my sense of humor everyday to lighten the load and make me less driven. Don't waste all my energy plodding along in life striving for the trappings of 'success'—take some chances, do things that make a difference."

These healthy attitudes led to changes in the way she was living her life. Her marriage was much better now that she was trying to appreciate her husband's good points and to nurture the positive parts of their relationship. She was appreciating the joys of her medical practice and the help she could give to others instead of worrying all the time about the business side of medicine, managed care, and the hassles of her daily work.

Another big change was that she was much more mindful of the meaningful things that she could find "in the moment." In the past, she couldn't appreciate good things that were right under her nose, because she was always thinking about some future major project or goal that would tell her that she was succeeding. She never had been really happy before because as soon as she would accomplish one task, another would take its place. Her life had been an unending struggle to accomplish more and more in order to feel OK. Now Anne Marie was able to savor and appreciate the meaning of everyday things, like the smile of a person she was treating, a trip to the bookstore, or a visit with her friends. She was no longer sleepwalking through life.

Anne Marie also had changed how she was viewing the contributions she could make to her community. Previously, her model for success had been rather narrow—build a thriving medical practice, have a good marriage, be a fine doctor. As she was recovering from depression, she began to think more broadly. What could she do that would give her a sense of fulfillment? When she looked back over her life, what would make her feel like the time had been well spent? Although Anne Marie was still working on the answers to these questions, she had already decided that she would try to get involved in improving educational opportunities for children with medical problems and learning disabilities. She had done some research on these problems when she was a medical student and knew enough to make a contribution.

We have seen many people who are able to make depression a learning experience and to keep growing stronger after their symptoms are under control. If you want to work on building healthy attitudes that will foster personal growth, we recommend that you check over the self-help exercises on developing *"rules of wellness"* from Chapter 4 and the exercises on finding meaning from Chapter 12. Choose some healthy attitudes you want to promote and design a plan to put them into action. Identify some ways of finding meaning that will help you grow beyond recovery from depression. Think of how you want to live your life differently in the future.

Your Plan for Staying Well

The last part of your Personal Plan for Recovery is an outline of the methods you will use to try to reduce the risk for return of depression. As you read over this chapter, you may have found some ideas that you will want to be sure to use and others to keep in mind if you start to notice any symptoms coming back. Before you finish your work with this book, be sure to make some notes on the plan you have designed to keep depression away. We can't overemphasize the importance of developing a strategy to stay well. Whether it is taking a medication regularly, continuing to practice ways of combating negative thinking, working on personal growth, or combining several different methods, your efforts can pay off in giving you the chance to have a full life.

Winning the Fight against Depression

You've met people from many different backgrounds in this book. All have had their own unique story to tell, but each one had to face the challenge of recovering from depression. Vic worked on changing the perfectionistic schemas that drove him into depression and made him an overly demanding parent. Consuelo learned how to accept the support of her family and to build a new life for herself after the death of her husband. Tony and his wife, Marlene, worked together to build his self-esteem, make good choices about his career, adjust to Marlene's promotion, and grow stronger as a couple. Michelle needed practice with cognitive rehearsal, among other things, to overcome her tendency to stay in a shell after her divorce. Anne Marie completed her recovery by using the Spirituality Key to rekindle a sense of purpose for her life and to open her heart to others.

Each of their stories turned out well. These people were able to find ways to beat depression and get their lives back. But, the fight wasn't always easy. Often a good dose of perseverance was needed to meet treatment goals. The world's greatest golf player, Tiger Woods, has had more success in reaching goals than most of us could ever imagine. One of the techniques that he uses was reported by the columnist Pat Forde during Tiger's march to his second straight PGA championship (*Louisville Courier Journal,* May 19, 2000). To keep his mind focused on the task at hand he repeats a very simple mantra: "Keep playing steady, keep plodding along, hit your fairways, hit your greens, make a few putts."

What sayings could you repeat in your mind that would help you win the fight against depression? Perhaps you could pick out the most useful ideas or the most encouraging messages that you have learned in reading this book. If you are using all five Keys, a general message to keep you focused might be: "Control negative thinking, take action today to make things better, take medication, build up relationships, find meaning." As you finish your work with this book, you might think of a basic message to yourself that will capture the essence of your recovery plan and will remind you to continue to use methods that will help.

During our years of practicing psychiatry and psychology, we have seen dramatic breakthroughs in the treatment of depression. A whole new generation of antidepressants has been developed. Specific psychotherapies have been described, tested, and found to work. Novel approaches such as light therapy, augmentation strategies for antidepressants, and transcranial magnetic stimulation have been introduced. Computer-assisted methods have been shown to have potential for helping people learn depression management skills. Herbal remedies and diet supplements have been used by many people to control mood, and lifestyle changes, such as getting physical exercise, are gaining acceptance as methods of combating symptoms.

The outpouring of new research has made us even more hopeful that each person can find a way to end the suffering of depression. Our plan in writing this book was to bring the advances in the treatment of depression together into a practical guide for using self-help and working together with doctors and therapists. We hope that you will use the Five Keys, will get professional help if you need it, and will look for solutions until you can put depression behind you. Our wish is that you will have every success in getting your life back and having a future that is full of promise.

Appendix I

PERSONAL PLAN
FOR RECOVERY WORKSHEETS

Part I. My *Symptoms* Are:

Please refer to the chart on the following page.

Part I. My Symptoms on the Five Keys Rating Scale Are:

RATING	WEEK 1	WEEK 2	WEEK 3	WEEK 4	WEEK 5	WEEK 6	WEEK 7	WEEK 8
THINKING KEY								
ACTION KEY								
BIOLOGY KEY								
RELATIONSHIP KEY								
SPIRITUALITY KEY								
TOTAL SCORE								

Part II. My *Strengths* Are:

- Things I have going for me now

- Strengths that others would see

- Strong points from the past that I may be forgetting

- Strengths that could be developed further in the future

Part III. My *Goals* for My Recovery Plan Are:

- Short-term goals (Identify 3–6):
    1.   2.
    3.   4.
    5.   6.

- Long-term goals (Identify 1–3):
    1.   2.
    3.

Part IV. My Plan for Using the Thinking Key

1. What are some common automatic thoughts that can make me depressed?

2. Which kinds of cognitive distortions cause me the most trouble?

3. What do I plan to do to reduce my negative automatic thoughts and cognitive distortions?

4. Which maladaptive schemas are causing me the most trouble?

5. What do I plan to do to modify my negative schemas?

6. What are my most useful adaptive schemas or rules of wellness?

7. What do I plan to do to build up these positive schemas?

8. What ideas do I have for finding new rules of wellness?

Part V. My Plan for Using the Action Key

1. What are my strengths that can help me to take action in solving problems?

2. Is there anything that I am doing in response to stress that is either not really helpful or is causing new problems for me?

3. Am I using avoidance as a way to cope? If so, what do I want to do about it?

4. Are there any self-defeating actions that I need to change? What other coping strategies do I want to use instead of those that can be self-defeating?

5. Are there times when I am impulsive in my words or in my actions? Which ones do I want to start learning to control?

6. Am I going in circles instead of solving problems? Which strategy do I want to try to overcome this cycle?

7. Do I give up too easily? What encouragement can I give myself to keep trying?

8. Goals for the future. After I start to feel better, what goals would I like to achieve over the next year? The next five years?

   One-year goals:

   Five-year goals:

Part VI. My Plan for Using the Biology Key

1. Do you have any physical symptoms or illnesses that could be playing a role in your depression? Could a medication be aggravating your

symptoms? Write out a list of problems you would like to discuss with your doctor. Note any actions you can take.

Problems to discuss with my doctor:

Things I can do:

2. Are you having trouble sleeping? If so, write out a plan for getting back to a normal sleep pattern. You can use the tips for improving sleep described in Chapter 5 to get you started.

3. Are you getting enough physical exercise? In the Action Key (Exercise 6.5), we gave you suggestions for getting into a healthy exercise routine. Write down your plan here for using exercise to assist in your recovery from depression.

4. Is it possible that you have Seasonal Affective Disorder (SAD)? If so, do you want to try light therapy?

5. Do you think any of your attitudes about antidepressant medication could interfere with your getting help from the Biology Key? Review your answers to the Medication Attitude Survey in Chapter 8, and write down any of your attitudes that could be improved. Then note your plans for changing them.

Attitudes I would like to change:

Plan for change:

6. If you are *not* taking an antidepressant, note your plans for what you would like to do about using medication for depression.

7. If you are currently taking an antidepressant and still have symptoms of depression, use this worksheet to prepare for a discussion with your doctor. First write down the dose, length of therapy, how regularly you have been taking the medication, and your present level of depression. Before switching antidepressants, you and your doctor will want to know if you have given the present treatment an adequate trial. Next review the Biology Key to see if you have any ideas for changes that might help you do better. Write your ideas down here and discuss them with your doctor.

Details of medication use:

Ideas about medication to discuss with doctor:

8. If you are having side effects from antidepressants, check the information in Chapter 9 for possible solutions. Note possible answers to the problems on this worksheet. Then consult your physician to decide on a remedy.

   Problems:

   Possible solutions to discuss with doctor:

Part VII. My Plan for Using the Relationship Key

1. What are your biggest relationship challenges?

2. Are you caught in a vicious cycle where your reactions to your symptoms are creating new problems? How would you describe the cycle?

3. What are some things you can change about yourself that might help resolve your relationship problems?

4. Which will you try first?

5. What are the life transitions that are causing you stress or distress?

6. In what ways are these problems for you?

7. What methods have you already used in trying to cope with these transitions?

8. What has worked?

9. What new method do you need to try?

10. Do you have any opportunities to change a role or elements of a role in a way that would make your life better?

11. Make a plan for how you are going to make these adjustments.

Part VIII. My Plan for Using the Spirituality Key

1. What are my spiritual strengths?

2. What types of things give my life meaning and purpose?

3. How will I make time to work on my spirituality? When will I fit it in?

4. Who could help me with my spiritual journey? Will I join a faith community?

5. What are some ways in which I can connect better to people in my life? What opportunities do I have to be more loving and giving with others?

6. What will I do to become more mindful of my experiences and my environment?

7. Are there any obstacles that are keeping me from having a full spiritual life? What are they? What do I need to do to remove them from my path?

8. Do I have any negative thoughts about my spirituality? What methods can I use to evaluate those thoughts?

9. What opportunities do I have to practice forgiveness of myself and of others? How will I go about these tasks?

10. How can meditation and/or prayer help me to develop my spirituality? What is my plan for getting started?

Appendix II

RECOMMENDED READINGS

The Art of Happiness: A Handbook for Living by H. H. D. Lama and H. C. Cutler, Riverhead Books, 1998. Putnam Pub group: East Rutherford. N.J.

"Canadian Consensus Guidelines for the Treatment of Seasonal Affective Disorder" by R. W. Lam and A. J. Levitt, *Canadian Journal of Diagnosis,* 1999. www.fhs.mcmaster.ca/direct/depress/sad2.html

Cognitive-Behavioral Therapy for Bipolar Disorder by M. R. Basco and A. J. Rush, Guilford Press, New York, 1996.

Couple Skills: Making Your Relationship Work by M. McKay, P. Fanning, and K. Paleg, New Harbinger Publications, New York, 1994.

A Couple's Guide to Communication by J. M. Gottman, Research Press, Oregon, 1979.

Essential Spirituality: The 7 Central Practices to Awaken Heart and Mind by R. Walsh, John Wiley & Sons, New York, 1999.

Feeling Good by D. D. Burns, William Morrow, New York, 1980.

Full Catastrophe Living: Using the Wisdom of Your Body and Mind to Face Stress, Pain, and Illness by J. Kabat-Zinn, Hyperion, New York, 1990.

The Highly Sensitive Person: How to Thrive When the World Overwhelms You by E. Aron, Broadway Books, New York, 1997.

I Don't Want to Talk About It: Overcoming the Secret Legacy of Male Depression by T. Real, Fireside, New York, 1998.

Listening to Prozac by D. D. Kramer, Penguin, New York, 1997.

Living the Mindful Life by C. T. Tart, Shambhala, Boston, 1994.

Love, Medicine and Miracles: Lessons Learned about Self-Healing from a Surgeon's Experience with Exceptional Patients by B. S. Siegel, Harper & Row, New York, 1990.

Man's Search for Meaning by V. E. Frankl, Boston, Beacon Press, 1992.

Mind over Mood: Change How You Feel by Changing the Way You Think by D. Greenberger and C. A. Padesky, Guilford Press, New York, 1996.

Never Good Enough: How to Use Perfectionism to Your Advantage without Letting It Ruin Your Life by M. R. Basco, Touchstone, New York, 2000.

A Path with Heart: A Guide through the Perils and Promises of Spiritual Life by J. Kornfield, Bantam Books, New York, 1993.

Prozac and the New Antidepressants: What You Need to Know about Prozac, Zoloft, Paxil, Luvox, Wellbutrin, Effexor, Serzone, and More by W. S. Appleton, Plume Books, New York, 1997.

Psychiatric Side Effects of Prescription and Over-the-Counter Medications: Recognition and Management by T. M. Brown and A. Stoudemire, American Psychiatric Press, Washington, D.C., 1998.

Psychopharmacology of Antidepressants by S. M. Stahl, Martin Dunitz, Ltd., London, 1997.

The 7 Principles for Making Marriage Work by J. M. Gottman and N. Silver, Three Rivers Press, New York, 2000.

Ten Days to Self-Esteem by D. D. Burns, Quill, 1999.

An Unquiet Mind by K. R. Jamison, Vintage Books, New York, 1996.

When Bad Things Happen to Good People by H. S. Kushner, Avon Books, New York, 1994.

Wherever You Go, There You Are by J. Kabat-Zinn, Hyperion, New York, 1994.

Winter Blues: Seasonal Affective Disorder: What It Is and How to Overcome It by N. Rosenthal, Guilford Press, New York, 1998.

Appendix III

WEB RESOURCES

You can go to the *Getting Your Life Back* web site (gettingyourlifeback.com) to find out more about this book and to download copies of the Five Keys Rating Scale and Personal Plan for Recovery worksheets. Some other web sites that could give you information on depression are:

Antidepressants

www.ahcpr.gov (Agency for Health Care Policy and Research report on newer pharmacotherapies for depression)

Computer-assisted Therapy

copewithlife.com (Interactive Voice Response program that uses telephone to assist people with depression)

mindstreet.com (Multimedia computer program for CBT developed by Jesse Wright, Andrew Wright, Aaron Beck, and Paul Salmon)

www.maiw.com (Computer program with lessons about depression and interactive exercises; text only, no video or audio)

Depression—General Web Sites

depression.com (Commercial web site that discusses therapies and medications)

depression-screening.org (National Mental Health Association web site that offers screening for depression and links with other mental health associations) www.nimh.nih.gov/publicat/depressionmenu.cfm (Brochure and other information on depression provided by the National Institute of Mental Health)

Light Therapy

http://www.fhs.mcmaster.ca/direct/depress/sad.html *(Canadian Consensus Guidelines for the Treatment of Seasonal Affective Disorder)*

Medical Web Sites—Information Sources for Patients and Clinicians

Medem.com (Sponsored by American Medical Association and American Psychiatric Association)
WebMD.com
onhealth.com
Lifescape.com
MyNetMD.com
Medscape.com

Appendix IV

MENTAL HEALTH ASSOCIATIONS AND PROFESSIONAL ORGANIZATIONS

ACADEMY OF COGNITIVE THERAPY
1 Belmont Avenue
Suite 700
Bala Cynwyd, PA 19004-1610
(610) 664-1273
info@academyofct.org

AMERICAN PSYCHOLOGICAL
  ASSOCIATION
750 First Street, N.E.
Washington, DC 20002-4242
(202) 336-5500
www.apa.org

AMERICAN PSYCHIATRIC ASSOCIATION
1400 K Street, N.W.
Washington, DC 20005
(202) 682-6237
www.psych.org

ASSOCIATION FOR THE ADVANCEMENT
  OF BEHAVIOR THERAPY
305 Seventh Avenue, 16th Floor
New York, NY 10001-60008
(212) 647-1890
www.aabt.org

FREEDOM FROM FEAR
306 Seaview Ave.
Staten Island, NY 10305
(718) 351-1717
http://freedomfromfear.com

NATIONAL ALLIANCE FOR THE
  MENTALLY ILL
Colonial Place Three
2107 Wilson Blvd., Suite 200
Arlington, VA 22201-2042
(703) 524-7600
www.nami.org

NATIONAL DEPRESSIVE AND MANIC-
  DEPRESSIVE ASSOCIATION
730 N. Franklin Street, Suite 501
Chicago, IL 60610-3526
(800) 826-3632
(312) 642-0049
www.ndmda.org

References

Chapter 2

American Psychiatric Association: *Diagnostic and Statistical Manual of Mental Disorders, Fourth Edition*. Washington, American Psychiatric Press, 1994.

Judd, L. L., Akiskal, H. S., and Paulus, M. P.: "The role and clinical significance of subsyndromal depressive symptoms (SSD) in unipolar major depressive disorders." *Journal of Affective Disorders* 45 (1–2):5–17; discussion 17–8, 1997.

Kessler, R. C., McGonagle, K. A., Zhao, S., et al.: "Lifetime and 12-month prevalence of DSM-III-R psychiatric disorders in the United States." *Archives of General Psychiatry* 51:8–19, 1997.

Kick, S. D.: "An educational intervention using the Agency for Health Care Policy and Research Depression Guidelines among internal medicine residents." *International Journal of Psychiatry in Medicine* 29 (1):47–61, 1999.

Wright, J. H., Bell, R. A., Kuhn, C. C., et al.: "Depression in family practice patients." *Southern Medical Journal* 73:1031–1034, 1980.

Chapter 3

American Psychiatric Association: "Practice Guideline for the Treatment of Patients with Major Depressive Disorder." Supplement to *American Journal of Psychiatry* 157 (4):1–45, 2000.

Robinson, L. A., Berman, J. S., and Neimeyer, R. A.: "Psychotherapy for the treatment of depression: a comprehensive review of controlled outcome research." *Psychological Bulletin* 108 (1):30–49, 1990.

Webster, D.: "Walking a wildlife highway from Yellowstone to the Yukon." *Smithsonian Magazine,* November 1999, pp 58–72.

Wright, J. H., and Beck, A. T.: "Cognitive therapy," in *American Psychiatric Press Textbook of Psychiatry,* Third Edition. Edited by Hales, R. E., Yudofsky, S. C., and Talbott, J. A. Washington, DC, American Psychiatric Press, 1999, pp. 1205–1241.

Chapter 4

American Psychiatric Association: "Practice Guideline for the Treatment of Patients with Major Depressive Disorder." Supplement to *American Journal of Psychiatry* 157 (4):1–45, 2000.

Robinson, L. A., Berman, J. S., and Neimeyer, R. A.: "Psychotherapy for the treatment of depression: a comprehensive review of controlled outcome research." *Psychological Bulletin* 108 (1):30–49, 1990.

Wright, J. H., and Wright, A. S.: "Computer-assisted psychotherapy." *Journal of Psychotherapy Practice and Research* 6:315–329, 1997.

Wright, J. H., Wright, A. S., Albano, A. M., et al.: "Computer-Assisted Cognitive Therapy for Depression." Presented at the 2000 Annual Meeting of the American Psychiatric Association, Chicago.

Chapter 5

Kryger, M. H., Roth, T., and Dement, W. C.: *Principles and Practice of Sleep Medicine.* Philadelphia, Saunders, 1989.

Chapter 7

Bell, I. R., Edman, J. S., Morrow, F. D., et al.: "B complex vitamin patterns in geriatric and young adult inpatients with major depression." *Journal of the American Geriatric Society* 39:252–257, 1991.

Benton, D., and Donohoe, R. T.: "The effects of nutrients on mood." *Public Health Nutrition* 2:403–409, 1999.

Berritini, W.: "Psychiatric Genetics of Mood Disorders." Presented at 2000 Annual Meeting of the American College of Psychiatrists, Naples, FL.

Blumenthal, J. A., Babyak, M. A., Moore, K. A., et al.: "Effects of exercise training on older patients with major depression." *Archives of Internal Medicine* 159:2349–2356, 1999.

Brown, T. M., and Stoudemire, A.: *Psychiatric Side Effects of Prescription and Over-the-Counter Medications: Recognition and Management.* Washington, DC, American Psychiatric Press, 1998.

Craft, L. L., and Landers, D. M.: "The effect of exercise on clinical depression and depression resulting from mental illness: a meta-analysis." *Journal of Sport and Exercise Psychology* 20:339–357, 1998.

Fava, M., Borus, J. S., Alpert, J. E., et al.: "Folate, vitamin B_{12}, and homocysteine in major depressive disorder." *American Journal of Psychiatry* 154:426–428, 1997.

Gelenberg, A. J.: "Omega 3 fatty acids and psychiatric disorders." *Biological Therapies in Psychiatry* 23:15–16, 2000.

Hendrick, V., Altshuler, L., and Whybrow, P.: "Psychoneuroendocrinology of mood disorders: the hypothalamic-pituitary-thyroid axis." *Psychiatric Clinics of North America* 21:277–292, 1998.

Hibbeln, J. R.: "Fish consumption and major depression." *Lancet* 351:1213, 1998.

Lam, R. W., and Levitt, A. J. (editors): *Canadian Consensus Guidelines for the Treatment of Seasonal Affective Disorder: A Summary of the Report of the Canadian Consensus Group on SAD.* Vancouver BC, Clinical & Academic Publishing, 1999.

Moore, K. A., and Blumenthal, J. A.: "Exercise training as an alternative treatment for depression among older adults." *Alternative Therapies in Health and Medicine* 4:48–56, 1998.

Musselman, D. L., Evans, D. L., and Nemeroff, C. B.: "The relationship of depression to cardiovascular disease: epidemiology, biology, and treatment." *Archives of General Psychiatry* 55:580–592, 1998.

Plotsky, P. M., Owens, M. J., and Nemeroff, C. B.: "Psychoneuroendocrinology of depression: hypothalamic-pituitary-adrenal axis." *Psychiatric Clinics of North America* 21:293–307, 1998.

Somer, E.: *Food and Mood: The Complete Guide to Eating Well and Feeling Your Best,* Second Edition. New York, Henry Holt & Company, 1999.

Stahl, S. M.: *Psychopharmacology of Antidepressants.* London, Martin Dunitz Ltd., 1997.

Stahl, S. M.: "Basic psychopharmacology of antidepressants, part 2: Estrogen as an adjunct to antidepressant treatment." *Journal of Clinical Psychiatry* 59 (suppl 4): 15–24, 1998.

Thase, M. E., Reynolds, C. F., III, Frank, E., et al.: "Polysomnographic studies of unmedicated depressed men before and after cognitive behavioral therapy." *American Journal of Psychiatry* 151:1615–1622, 1994.

Thase, M. E., Simons, A. D., Reynolds, C. F., III: "Abnormal electroencephalographic sleep profiles in major depression." *Archives of General Psychiatry* 53:99–108, 1996.

Thase, M. E., Dube, S., Bowler, K., et al.: "Hypothalamic-pituitary-adrenocortical activity and response to cognitive behavior therapy in unmedicated, hospitalized depressed patients." *American Journal of Psychiatry* 153:886–891, 1996.

Wright, J. H., Bell, R. A., Kuhn, C. C., et al.: "Depression in family practice patients." *Southern Medical Journal* 73:1031–1034, 1980.

Young, E., and Korszun, A.: "Psychoneuroendocrinology of depression: hypothalamic-pituitary-gonadal axis." *Psychiatric Clinics of North America* 21:309–323, 1998.

Chapter 8

Fava, G. A., Grandi, S., Zielezny, M., et al.: "Cognitive behavioral treatment of residual symptoms in primary major depressive disorder." *American Journal of Psychiatry* 151:1295–1299, 1994.

Fava, G. A., Rafanelli, C., Grandi, S., et al.: "Prevention of recurrent depression with cognitive behavioral therapy." *Archives of General Psychiatry* 55:816–820, 1998.

Keller, M. B., McCullough, J. P., Klein, D. N., et al.: "A comparison of nefazodone, the cognitive behavioral-analysis system of psychotherapy, and their combination for the treatment of chronic depression." *New England Journal of Medicine* 342:1462–1470, 2000.

Kramer, P. D.: *Listening to Prozac.* New York, Viking, 1993.

Chapter 9

Agency for Healthcare Policy & Research. "Treatment of Depression—Newer Pharmacotherapies." Evidence Report/Technology Assessment: Number 7, March, 1999. Available Free by calling 1-800-358-9295 or on Internet (http://www.ahcbr.gov/clinic/deprsumm.htm).

Basco, M. R., and Rush, A. J.: *Cognitive-Behavioral Therapy for Bipolar Disorder.* New York, Guilford Press, 1996.

Brown, R., Bottiglieri, T., and Colman, C.: *Stop Depression Now: SAM-E, the Breakthrough Supplement that Works as Well as Prescription Drugs, in Half the Time . . . with No Side Effects.* New York, G.P. Putnam's Sons, 1999.

Fava, G. A., Grandi, S., Zielezny, M., et al.: "Cognitive behavioral treatment of residual symptoms in primary major depressive disorder." *American Journal of Psychiatry* 151:1295–1299, 1994.

Fava, G. A., Rafanelli, C., Grandi, S., et al.: "Prevention of recurrent depression with cognitive behavioral therapy." *Archives of General Psychiatry* 55:816–820, 1998.

Fava, M., Rankin, M. A., Alpert, J. E., et al.: "An open trial of oral sildenafil for antidepressant-induced sexual dysfunction." *Psychotherapy and Psychosomatics* 67 (6):328–331, 1998.

Fieve, R. R.: *Moodswing: Dr. Fieve on Depression.* New York, Bantam Books, 1997.

Grunhaus, L., Dannon, P. N., Schreiber, S., et al.: "Repetitive transcranial magnetic stimulation is as effective as electroconvulsive therapy in the treatment of nondelusional major depressive disorder: an open study." *Biological Psychiatry* 47:314–324, 2000.

Jamison, K. R.: *An Unquiet Mind: A Memoir of Moods and Madness.* New York, Vintage Books, 1996.

Kagan, B. L., Sultzer, D. L., Rosenlicht, N., et al.: "Oral S-adenosylmethionine in depression: a randomized, double-blind, placebo-controlled trial." *American Journal of Psychiatry* 147:591–595, 1990.

Keller, M. B., McCullough, J. P., Klein, D. N., et al.: "A comparison of nefazodone, the cognitive behavioral-analysis system of psychotherapy, and their combination for the treatment of chronic depression." *New England Journal of Medicine* 342:1462–1470, 2000.

Labbate, L. A.: "Sex and serotonin reuptake inhibitor antidepressants." *Psychiatric Annals* 29:571–579, 1999.

Nurnberg, H. G., Lauriello, J., Hensley, P. L., et al.: "Sildenafil for iatrogenic serotonergic antidepressant medication-induced sexual dysfunction in 4 patients." *Journal of Clinical Psychiatry* 60:33–35, 1999.

Ostroff, R. B., and Nelson, J. C.: "Risperidone augmentation of selective serotonin reuptake inhibitors in major depression." *Journal of Clinical Psychiatry* 60:256–259, 1999.

Rosenbaum, J. F., Fava, M., Falk, W. E., et al.: "The antidepressant potential of oral S-adenosyl-1-methionine." *Acta Psychiatrica Scandinavica* 81:432–436, 1990.

Rush, A. J., George, M. S., Sackeim, H. A., et al.: "Vagus nerve stimulation (VNS) for treatment-resistant depressions: a multicenter study." *Biological Psychiatry* 47:273–275, 2000.

Segraves, R. T.: "Antidepressant-induced sexual dysfunction." *Journal of Clinical Psychiatry* 59 (suppl 4): 48–54, 1998.

Stahl, S. M.: *Psychopharmacology of Antidepressants*. London, Martin Dunitz Ltd., 1997.

Thase, M. E., and Rush, A. J.: "When at first you don't succeed: sequential strategies for antidepressant nonresponders." *Journal of Clinical Psychiatry* 58 (suppl 3):23–29, 1997.

Thase, M. E., Howland, R. H., and Friedman, E. S.: "Treating antidepressant nonresponders with augmentation strategies: an overview." *Journal of Clinical Psychiatry* 59 (suppl 5):5–12, 1998.

Wong, A. H. C., Smith, M., and Boon, H. S.: "Herbal remedies in psychiatric practice." *Archives of General Psychiatry* 55:1033–1044, 1998.

Chapter 10

Beach, S. R., and O'Leary, K. D.: "Treating depression in the context of marital discord: outcome and predictors of response for marital therapy vs. cognitive therapy." *Behavior Therapy* 23:507–528, 1992.

Brown, G. W., and Harris, T. O.: *Life Events and Illness*. New York, Guilford Press, 1989.

Goering, P. N., Lancee, W. J., and Freeman, S. J.: "Marital support and recovery from depression." *British Journal of Psychiatry* 160:76–82, 1992.

Hammen, C.: "Generation of stress in the course of unipolar depression." *Journal of Abnormal Psychology* 100 (4):555–561, 1991.

Jacobson, N. S., Dobson, K., Fruzzetti, A. E., et al.: "Marital therapy as a treatment for depression." *Journal of Consulting and Clinical Psychology* 59 (4):547–557, 1991.

O'Leary, K. D., and Beach, S. R.: "Marital therapy: a viable treatment for depression and marital discord." *American Journal of Psychiatry* 147 (2):183–186, 1990.

Roy, A.: "Five risk factors for depression." *British Journal of Psychiatry* 150:536–541, 1987.

Schmaling, K. B., and Jacobson, N. S.: "Marital interaction and depression." *Journal of Abnormal Psychology* 99 (3):229–236, 1990.

Chapter 11

Brown, G. W., and Harris, T. O. *Life Events and Illness.* New York, Guilford Press, 1989.

Kubler-Ross, E.: *On Death and Dying.* New York, Collier Books, 1997.

Chapter 12

Edmunds, M. E.: *Love Is a Verb.* Salt Lake City, Deseret Book Company, 1995.

Frankl, V. E.: *Man's Search for Meaning.* Boston, Beacon Press, 1992.

Hafen, B. Q., Karren, K. J., Frandsen, K. H., et al.: "The healing power of spirituality," in *Mind/Body Health: The Effects of Attitudes, Emotions and Relationships.* Boston, Allyn & Bacon, 1996.

Kabat-Zinn, J.: *Full Catastrophe Living: Using the Wisdom of Your Body and Mind to Face Stress, Pain, and Illness.* New York, Hyperion, 1990.

Kabat-Zinn, J.: *Wherever You Go, There You Are.* New York, Hyperion, 1994.

Luskin, F.: "Review of the effect of spiritual and religious factors on mortality and morbidity with a focus on cardiovascular and pulmonary disease." *Cardiopulmonary Rehabilitation* 20:8–15, 2000.

Matthews, D. A., McCullough, M. E., Larson, D. B., et al.: "Religious commitment and health status: a review of the research and implications for family medicine." *Archives of Family Medicine* 7 (2):118–124, 1998.

Moore, T.: *Care of the Soul.* New York, HarperCollins, 1992.

Simply the Best II, *Common Boundaries Magazine.* November/December, 1999.

Styron, W.: *Darkness Visible: A Memoir of Madness.* New York, Random House, 1990.

Walsh, R.: *Essential Spirituality: The 7 Central Practices to Awaken Heart and Mind.* New York, John Wiley & Sons, 1999.

Chapter 13

Kabat-Zinn, J., Lipworth, L., and Burney, R.: "The clinical use of mindfulness meditation for the self-regulation of chronic pain." *Journal of Behavioral Medicine* 8: 163–190, 1986.

Kabat-Zinn, J., Massion, A., Kristeller, J., et al.: "Effectiveness of a meditation-based stress reduction intervention in the treatment of anxiety disorders." *American Journal of Psychiatry* 149:936–943, 1992.

King, L.: *Powerful Prayers.* New York, Renaissance Books, 1998.

Kushner, H. S.: *When Bad Things Happen to Good People.* New York, Avon Books, 1981.

Marlatt, G. A., and Kristeller, J. L.: *Mindfulness and Meditation, Integrating Spirituality into Treatment: Resources for Practitioners.* Edited by Miller, W. R. Washington, DC, American Psychological Association, 1999.

Martin, J., and Booth, J.: "Behavioral approaches to enhance spirituality," in *Integrating Spirituality into Treatment: Resources for Practitioners.* Edited by Miller, W. R. Washington, DC, American Psychological Association, 1999.

Miller, W. R., and Thoresen, C. E.: "Spirituality and health," in *Integrating Spirituality into Treatment: Resources for Practitioners.* Edited by Miller, W. R. Washington, DC, American Psychological Association, 1999.

Poloma, M. M., and Galuo, G. H.: *Varieties of Prayer.* Philadelphia, Trinity Press International, 1991.

Poloma, M. M., and Pendelton, B. F.: "The effects of prayer and prayer experiences on measures of general well-being." *Journal of Psychology and Theology* 19:71–83, 1991.

Richards, D. G.: "The phenomenology and psychological correlates of verbal prayer." *Journal of Psychology and Theology* 19:354–363, 1991.

Stone, J.: *Every Part of Earth Is Sacred: Native American Voices in Praise of Nature.* Stonework Editions, 1994.

Walsh, R.: *Essential Spirituality: The 7 Central Practices to Awaken Heart and Mind.* New York, John Wiley & Sons, 1999.

Chapter 14

American Psychiatric Association: "Practice Guideline for the Treatment of Patients with Major Depressive Disorder." Supplement to *American Journal of Psychiatry* 157 (4):1–45, 2000.

Keller, M. B.: "The long-term treatment of depression." *Journal of Clinical Psychiatry* 60 (Supplement 17):41–45, 1999.

Segal, Z. V., Shaw, B. F., Vella, D. D., et al.: "Cognitive and life stress predictors of relapse in remitted unipolar depressed patients: test of the congruency hypothesis." *Journal of Abnormal Psychology* 101(1):26–36, 1992.

Stahl, S. M.: "Why settle for silver, when you can go for gold? Response versus recovery as the goal of antidepressant therapy." *Journal of Clinical Psychiatry* 60 (4):213–214, 1999.

Thase, M. E.: "Redefining antidepressant efficacy toward long-term recovery." *Journal of Clinical Psychiatry* 60 (Supplement 6):15–19, 1999.

Index